Family Entrepreneurship

Matt R. Allen • William B. Gartner
Editors

Family Entrepreneurship

Insights from Leading Experts
on Successful Multi-Generational
Entrepreneurial Families

Editors
Matt R. Allen
Babson College
Babson Park, MA, USA

William B. Gartner
Babson College
Babson Park, MA, USA

ISBN 978-3-030-66845-7   ISBN 978-3-030-66846-4   (eBook)
https://doi.org/10.1007/978-3-030-66846-4

This Palgrave Macmillan imprint is published by the registered company Springer Nature Switzerland AG.
The registered company address is: Gewerbestrasse 11, 6330 Cham, Switzerland

For my wife Heather and my three beautiful children. I believe there is at least a little entrepreneurship in every family. It explains, in part, how a family is always much more than the sum of its members. Mine is most certainly the best excuse that I can offer for anything useful I have ever done.

Matt R. Allen

For all of the prior generations who sought a better future, my family of diverse talents and dreams, and to my wife, Saunie, for her wisdom and courage in our adventure together.

William B. Gartner

Contents

Notes on Contributors

Matt R. Allen is an Associate Professor in the Entrepreneurship Division and family fellow in the Institute for Family Entrepreneurship at Babson College. His expertise is in the effective management of human capital within entrepreneurial environments, especially family enterprises. His current research is focused on the role of the family in the entrepreneurial process and how entrepreneurial capability across generations should be built. His research has appeared in publications such as *Personnel Psychology* and *Entrepreneurship Theory & Practice and Strategic Organization*. Allen designed and is leading the Family Entrepreneurship Amplifier program, a one of a kind education program for business families that engages students and their families in the learning process in order to build entrepreneurial capability. In addition, Allen teaches other entrepreneurship and family business courses at the undergraduate, graduate, and executive level and has been involved in executive education programs across the world with a special interest in Latin America.

In addition to working with his father as an accountant and consultant to family businesses and other privately held organizations, he has held positions in corporate finance at IBM and Hewlett Packard. He earned his BA from the University of Utah, MBA from the University of Notre Dame and PhD from Cornell University.

Dalal Alrubaishi is an Assistant Professor in Entrepreneurship and Family Businesses at the College of Business Administration in Princess Nourah bint Abdulrahman University, Saudi Arabia. She holds an MBA from Prince Sultan University in Riyadh and a PhD from Royal Holloway, University of London, UK. Coming from a family business herself, Alrubaishi research focuses on the entrepreneurial behavior of Saudi family businesses. Her research interests include family business, entrepreneurship, succession, the noneconomic aspects of family businesses, and family business innovation. Dalal published several research articles and book chapters in scientific outlets on the topic of family business.

Jia Bao is a PhD student at the National University of Singapore. Her research focuses on serial entrepreneurship and corporate governance. In the field of serial entrepreneurship, she is currently looking at the role of an entrepreneur's experience in corporate strategic choices. In the field of corporate governance, she is studying the influence of board diversity on corporate behavior.

Sam Bruehl has extensive experience working with family businesses in North America, Southeast Asia, and the Middle East. The focus of his work is family and owner governance and next generation development. Bruehl also has experience working with family businesses to create family entrepreneur programs and to support coaching of members of the next generation on their business ventures.

Jess Chua is Faculty Professor of Finance and Family Business Governance at the Haskayne School of Business of the University of Calgary. He is also Distinguished Professor of Family Business at the Lancaster University Management School and a visiting professor at the School of Management of Zhejiang University. His research has received numerous awards and he has been listed by Web of Science among the top 1% of the most cited scholars in the world in the combined field of economics and business.

Allan R. Cohen is Distinguished Professor of Global Leadership (emeritus) at Babson College, where he also served as VP Academic Affairs and Dean of Faculty, and interim graduate Dean. He is co-author of *Entrepreneurs in Every Generation*; *Influence Without Authority*; *Power Up*; and *Managing for Excellence*. His Doctoral dissertation *Tradition, Change and Conflict in Indian Family Business*, was published by Mouton. He conducts management consulting and training for clients large and small.

Eliana Crosina is an Assistant Professor of Entrepreneurship at Babson College. She holds a Bachelor of Science in Business Administration and a Master in Business Administration from Babson College, as well as a Master of Science and a PhD in Organization Studies from Boston College. Crosina's current research interests lie at the intersection of identity and organizing in entrepreneurial contexts. Her work has appeared in publications including the *Academy of Management Journal*, the *Annual Review of Organizational Psychology and Organizational Behavior*, and *Harvard Business Review*.

James H. Davis is the Buehler Endowed Professor of Management, Executive Director of the Stephen R. Covey Leadership Center, Executive Director of Executive Education and the Marketing and Strategy Department Head in the Huntsman School of Business at Utah State University. Prior to that, he was the John F. O'Shaughnessy Professor of Family Enterprises and associate professor of strategic management in the Mendoza College of Business at the University of Notre Dame. While there, he launched and directed the nationally ranked Gigot Center for Entrepreneurial studies. He researches trust and stewardship in family business.

Nick Di Loreto has guided leading families in North America, Asia, Europe, and the Middle East to design their enterprise governance, to evaluate their business portfolios and organizational capabilities, and to plan for generational transition for the past decade. Di Loreto has also been a facilitator at the Families in Business Program at Harvard Business School, has written for many leading publications including *Family Business Magazine* and *Harvard Business Review*, and speaks regularly on family business transition topics.

Luis Díaz-Matajira is Assistant Professor at the School of Management Universidad de los Andes, Bogota, Colombia, where he is Director of Management Academic Area. He has also served as Director of the Undergraduate and Specializations Programs. His research interests are in the fields of family business strategy, public management, and corporate social responsibility. He holds a BA in Economics, an MSc in Development Studies and a PhD in Management. He did his postdoctoral research at Audencia Business School. He serves on STEP's Latin-American Council and Global Board. He has been part of FERC Academic Board 2018–2021.

W. Gibb Dyer (PhD MIT) is the O. Leslie and Dorothy Stone Professor of Entrepreneurship and the Academic Director of the Ballard Center for Social Impact in the Marriott School of Business at Brigham Young University. Professor Dyer is a recognized authority on family business and entrepreneurship and has been quoted in publications such as *Fortune, The Wall Street Journal, and The New York Times*. In 2008, he received the outstanding faculty award from the Marriott School. His research focuses on family business and entrepreneurship and he has been recognized as one of the most cited family business scholars with over 14,000 citations (Google Scholar).

Alain Fayolle is Professor of Entrepreneurship at Center for Innovation and Entrepreneurship Activities (CREA), University of Cagliari, Italy. He has been Distinguished Professor and the Director of the Entrepreneurship Research Centre at Emlyon Business School, France. Fayolle has forty books and over two hundred articles to her credit. In 2013, Fayolle received the 2013 European Entrepreneurship Education Award and has been elected Chair of the AOM Entrepreneurship Division for the 2016–2017 academic year. In 2015, he has been awarded Wilford L. White Fellow by ICSB.

William B. Gartner is the Bertarelli Foundation Distinguished Professor of Family Entrepreneurship at Babson College. He is recognized as a leading scholar in the field of entrepreneurship by such awards as the 2005 Swedish Entrepreneurship Foundation International Award for outstanding contributions to entrepreneurship and small business research; the 2013 Academy of Management Entrepreneurship Division Foundational Paper Award; and the 2016 Academy of Management Entrepreneurship Division Dedication to Entrepreneurship Award. His scholarship spans a wide array of topics in the entrepreneurship field such as entrepreneurship as practice, the social construction of the future, varieties of value creation and appropriation, translating entrepreneurship across cultures and countries, the poetics of exchange, the demographics of entrepreneurial families, and, the nature of legacy in family entrepreneurship.

Nathan T. Hayes is a PhD Candidate in Entrepreneurship and Strategic Management at the Jerry S. Rawls College of Business at Texas Tech University. His research interests include social capital, strategic entrepreneurship, family business, initial public offerings, and psychological aspects of entrepreneurs. His work has been published in *Family Business Review*.

Fernanda Jaramillo is a partner at Lansberg, Gersick & Associates working primarily in Latin America, supporting multigenerational family enterprises in their continuity efforts across generations, including in the development and implementation of complex corporate and family governance structures. Jaramillo is also a frequent speaker at institutions that support the education of business families and serves on several boards of family businesses as independent director. She holds a BS in Industrial Engineering, an MBA from the Haas School of Business, University of California at Berkeley and a Master's degree in Family Advisory from the Javeriana University in Cali, Colombia.

Peter Klein is Professor of Family Business at the HSBA Hamburg School of Business Administration and is responsible for IMF Institute for Mittelstand

and Family Firms in Hamburg. He has extensive management experience in family businesses and is board member of the Nissen Foundation.

Philipp Köhn is a PhD student at Siegen University joining the Chair for Entrepreneurship and Family Business and the Chair for Service Development in SMEs and Crafts. His research considers the impact of the business family on entrepreneurial activities within family firms.

Ivan Lansberg is an organizational psychologist based in New York City. He is the faculty of the Kellogg School of Management where he is Co-director of Family Enterprise Programs. He is also a founding partner of Lansberg, Gersick & Associates LLC, a research and consulting firm specializing in family enterprise. Lansberg has written extensively on family enterprise. His book *Succeeding Generations*, published by the Harvard Business School (HBS) Press, is on succession and continuity in family enterprises. He is also one of the authors of *Generation to Generation*, also published by HBS Press and was founding Editor-in-Chief of the *Family Business Review*. Lansberg earned his PhD, MA and BA degrees from Columbia University.

Vincent Lefebvre is an associate professor of entrepreneurship at Audencia Business School, France where he coordinates entrepreneurial education. After working for ten years as an entrepreneurship consultant in public and private business support organizations in France and Spain, he did a PhD in entrepreneurship and engaged in an academic career while continuing to support start-up and take-over entrepreneurs. His research examines entrepreneurial networks and social capital, entrepreneurial processes and practices, business support mechanisms and management transfer in family business succession. Lefebvre has written papers in journals such as *Entrepreneurship & Regional Development, Technovation and Futures*, among others.

Miriam Lehmann-Hiepler is a research fellow at the chair for Entrepreneurship and Family Business at Siegen University. Her research interests focus on business succession processes, social capital, and network structures of family businesses.

Maura McAdam is Professor of Management at Dublin City University. She is a nationally and internationally recognized scholar in the area of entrepreneurship, having a particular expertise in gender, entrepreneurial leadership, technology entrepreneurship and family business. Accordingly, her research has been published in top rated North American and UK journals including *Entrepreneurship Theory and Practice, Journal of Business Research, Small Business Economics and Journal of Economic Geography*. In addition, she has authored the book *Female Entrepreneurship* and co-authored the book *Entrepreneurial Behaviour*. McAdam is currently leading a European Commission-funded one million Euro project that investigates gender inequalities in the entrepreneurial ecosystem.

Petra Moog holds the Chair for Entrepreneurship and Family Business. Her research covers family business and entrepreneurship issues based on economic or behavior theories as well as democratic issues.

Mattias Nordqvist is Professor of Entrepreneurship at the House of Innovation, Stockholm School of Economics, and affiliated Professor at the Center for Family Entrepreneurship and Ownership, Jönköping International Business School, Jönköping University, Sweden. He is a former Co-Director of the Global STEP Project founded by Babson College and a former Director of the Center for Family Entrepreneurship and Ownership. He was recently ranked among the 25 most cited and impactful researchers in all areas of social sciences in Sweden.

G. Tyge Payne is the Kent R. Hance Regents Endowed Chair in Entrepreneurship and Professor of Strategic Management at the Rawls College of Business, Texas Tech University. His work has been published in top journals including *Entrepreneurship Theory & Practice, Family Business Review (FBR), Journal of Management, Journal of Management Studies, Organizational Science, Strategic Entrepreneurship Journal*, among others. He is currently the Editor-in-Chief of *FBR*, which is the leading journal dedicated to the study of family businesses.

Jennifer Pendergast is the John L. Ward Clinical Professor of Family Enterprises and Executive Director of the Center for Family Enterprises at the Kellogg School of Management at Northwestern University. The Center is a leader in executive education and supports Kellogg's MBA and EMBA programs as well as research, case writing, and community engagement. Previously she was a consultant with Egon Zehnder, Family Business Consulting Group and McKinsey & Company. She holds a PhD from The Wharton School and a BS from the McIntire School of Commerce at the University of Virginia.

Stefan Prigge is Professor of Finance and Accounting at HSBA Hamburg School of Business Administration and a member of the IMF Institute for Mittelstand and Family Firms in Hamburg. His major fields of interest are governance and finance that he has applied to family firms (since 2011) and professional sport (since 2014).

Miruna Radu-Lefebvre is a Professor of Entrepreneurship at Audencia Business School, France. She is Head of the Chair Family Entrepreneurship & Society and Pilot of STEP France (Successful Transgenerational Entrepreneurship Practices), she explores and theorizes the interplay of emotion, identity, and gender in start-up and family business contexts, with a micro-level social psychological approach. Her articles have appeared in *Organization Studies, International Small Business Journal, Journal of Small Business Management, Entrepreneurship and Regional Development and International Journal of Entrepreneurial Behavior and Research*, among others.

Marcela Ramírez-Pasillas is an Assistant Professor on Entrepreneurship and Sustainability at Jönköping International Business School (JIBS) in Jönköping University, Sweden. She is affiliated to the Center of Family Entrepreneurship and Ownership (CeFEO) and served as the first Programme Director of the Bachelor in Sustainable Enterprise Development. She was twice holder of international awards on sustainability (2015 CEEMAN Responsible Management Education Champion and 2017 Excellence in Advanced Sharing Practices on Sustainability Progress Reporting by the Global UN PRME). She has served as Chairman of the STEP European Leadership Council of the Global STEP Project for Family Enterprising founded by Babson College.

Kathleen Randerson is Associate Professor of Entrepreneurship at Audencia Business School, France. Her research interests include corporate entrepreneurship, family entrepreneurship, and international contexts. Randerson's research has been published in *Entrepreneurship and Regional Development*, the *Journal of Small Business Management*, and the *International Small Business Journal*, among others. She has held leadership roles in the Entrepreneurship Division of the AOM, and in the STEP project.

Wendy Sage-Hayward is a family business owner, educator, author, and consultant. As a fifth-generation director of her family's 135-year-old firm for 20+ years and an owner operator of an agricultural tourism family business, she brings real world experience to her writing about the complexities that family enterprises face. Wendy has consulted with business leaders, family firms and their boards around the world. She is an adjunct professor at the University of British Columbia's Sauder School of Business and the Academic Director of the Family Enterprise Exchange. Sage-Hayward is also co-author of the book *Human Resources in Family Business: Maximizing the Power of Your People*.

Fernando Sandoval-Arzaga is Associate Director of the Institute of Enterprising Families for Mexico and Latin America at Tecnologico de

Monterrey. He holds a PhD in Administrative Sciences from ESADE Business School and did a Postdoctoral Fellowship at London Business School. He is a professor and consultant on family businesses and strategy for more than 15 years. He is a pioneer in teaching and has designed massive online courses (MOOCS) both in Coursera and in edX on Family Businesses, with more than 15,000 students from 20 countries. His research focuses on intergenerational dynamics, sharing knowledge in family groups and governance mechanisms in Latin American countries.

Pramodita Sharma is a Professor and the Schlesinger-Grossman Chair of Family Business at the Grossman School of Business (GSB), University of Vermont and is a visiting professor at the Kellogg School of Management and the Indian School of Business. Having studied *Entrepreneurial Family Firms* and *Entrepreneurs in Every Generation*, she has turned her attention to *Patient Capital: The Role of Family Firms in Sustainable Business*. Her next book: *Patient Capital Strategies of Pioneering Family Firms in Sustainability* will be released in April 2021.

Geraldina Silveyra is Director of the academic efforts at Instituto de Emprendimiento Eugenio Garza Lagüera. She earned her PhD in Business and Management applied to entrepreneurship, small businesses, and family firms from the Universidad de Cantabria in Spain. She has developed expertise in entrepreneurship education with a specialty in Lego Serious Play, development of methodologies for startups and new venture creation. She has been a consultant and a mentor mainly on business models, business, and team development. Her research focuses on entrepreneurship education, entrepreneurship competencies and intention models, entrepreneurial ecosystems and the startup process.

Scott N. Taylor, PhD is the Arthur M. Blank Endowed Chair for Values-Based Leadership and an Associate Professor of organizational behavior at Babson College. The primary focus of his research is leader assessment and development. His research has focused on competency development (especially emotional and social competence), leader self-awareness, 360-degree feedback assessment, executive coaching, gender, and sustainable individual change. The *Harvard Business Review* Idea Watch, *MSNBC*, *Business Week*, *The Wall Street Journal* blog, *Nature*, the *Society for Human Resource Managers*, the *Academy of Management*, *The Globe and Mail*, and several other such publications have featured Scott's research.

Peter Vogel is Professor of Family Business and Entrepreneurship, holder of the Debiopharm Chair for Family Philanthropy and the Director of the

Global Family Business Center at IMD. Vogel works with families, owners, boards, and executives of family enterprises and family offices around the world. He has written academic articles and books, is frequently referenced by leading media outlets around the world and he is a sought-after keynote speaker. Vogel is the founder and Chairman of Delta Venture Partners, an Associate Partner of the Cambridge Family Enterprise Group and features among the "Top 100 Family Influencers" by Family Capital.

Sachin Waikar is a business writer who works with the Kellogg School of Management, Stanford University, and multiple other organizations and individuals. His co-written works have been published in *Harvard Business Review*, *The Washington Post*, *Forbes*, and many other outlets. Previously he was a consultant with McKinsey & Company and a clinical psychologist in private practice. He holds a PhD in clinical psychology from UCLA and a BA from Stanford University.

Judy Lin Walsh advises owners of the world's largest family businesses and family offices on generational transition. Her specialty is working in complex family ownership systems to align the goals of the senior and next generations and to build sustainable governance. Judy has written extensively for *Harvard Business Review, Trusts & Estates Magazine*, and *Family Business Magazine* on "Should You Join the Family Business?", "The Inheritance Effect", and "Is Your Next Generation Entrepreneurial Enough?" She has been quoted in *The Financial Times*. Walsh holds a BS in Economics from MIT and an MBA from the Tuck School at Dartmouth.

Marta Widz is a research fellow at IMD Business School, Lausanne and embraces the worlds of research, advisory, and practice in the family business field. She serves as a Co-Chair of the Program Committee of the 2020 Family Firm Institute (FFI) Global Conference, "Learning & Exchange" Track Chair at 2020 International Family Enterprise Research Academy (IFERA) Conference. She is a frequent presenter for the Family Business Network (FBN), the Hénokiens, and the Institute for Family Business (IBR).

Saisai Wu is a PhD candidate at the School of Management of Zhejiang University, China. She was a visiting PhD student at the Haskayne School of Business of the University of Calgary. Her research interests are long-term orientation and ambidextrous innovation in family businesses.

David S. Xotlanihua-González is full time faculty of the Entrepreneurship Academic Department at Tecnologico de Monterrey and is a PhD student in Law and Management Sciences, with a major in Entrepreneurship and Family

Business at Universidad de Cantabria, Spain. As a consultant, he was enrolled with the business incubator and family business centre. His areas of interest are entrepreneurship learning, education, intrapreneurship from the family business, entrepreneurial intentions, and entrepreneurial behavior gap.

Ramona Kay Zachary is the Jonas S. Jonas Distinguished Professor of Entrepreneurship in the Narendra Paul Loomba Department of Management, Zicklin School of Business, Baruch College of The City University of New York. Her research centers on entrepreneurial and family firms relative to family dynamics, business dynamics, and sustainability: the Sustainable Family Business Theory (SFBT) and the Entrepreneurial Value Creation Theory (EVCT). Zachary has published in *Journal of Business Venturing, Entrepreneurship Theory and Practice* and *Family Business Review;* is Co-Editor of *Entrepreneurship Research Journal;* and co-authored a book titled, *The Theory of Entrepreneurship: Creating and Sustaining Entrepreneurial Value.*

List of Figures

List of Exhibits

List of Tables

1

The Secrets of Successful Entrepreneurial Families: Insights from the World's Experts on Multi-Generational Entrepreneurial Families

Matt R. Allen and William B. Gartner

Introduction

This book focuses on family entrepreneurship and the role that families play in starting, growing, changing and transforming businesses. If you are interested in knowing more about how families act entrepreneurially across generations in terms of gaining insights into practical knowledge that can be applied, as well as learning about the ideas and the reasons behind this practical knowledge, then you will find this book to be of great value. We have assembled leading experts on multi-generational entrepreneurial families to address this issue.[1] These experts, as consultants, educators and researchers on family entrepreneurship, represent the collected wisdom of hundreds of years of experience working with and studying successful entrepreneurial families.

---

[1] Please note that due to page limitations not all of the recognized experts in family entrepreneurship are included in this book. So, for many of our colleagues who were not included, please accept our apologies that you were not included in this edition. More is to come, so, we look forward to your involvement in future collaborative work on this topic.

M. R. Allen • W. B. Gartner (✉)
Babson College, Babson Park, MA, USA
e-mail: mallen4@babson.edu; wgartner@babson.edu

© The Author(s), under exclusive license to Springer Nature Switzerland AG 2021
M. R. Allen, W. B. Gartner (eds.), *Family Entrepreneurship*,
https://doi.org/10.1007/978-3-030-66846-4_1

All the authors who contributed to this effort were asked to respond to this question:

How does the family, as a system, establish, develop, promote, support and teach entrepreneurship as a behavior, belief or value across generations?

You will find a variety of approaches and perspectives on what families can do to enable entrepreneurship to flourish, and, the book offers many different theories and ideas as to why these approaches work in practice. As one of the primary goals of this book is to provide useful knowledge and wisdom that families can apply, each chapter offers examples of how the ideas and perspectives of these authors have been used in the everyday activities of successful entrepreneurial families. Also, we requested that the authors keep the chapters to a short, manageable length so you can get the gist of each approach without laboring through a long academic treatise on these perspectives and practices. Finally, each chapter addresses the expected outcomes and consequences that following these insights and recommendations would generate for families.

While this book was written primarily for families interested in pursuing entrepreneurship, we know that there is value to be found for practitioners, researchers and teachers as well. For business families, you will find multiple methodologies for understanding, building, shaping and continuing an entrepreneurial approach within your own family. For practitioners, especially those providing much needed advice and expertise to business families, the book provides a multitude of new ideas and approaches to consider. For the researcher, the book is a celebration of the beautiful complexity involved in mixing family and entrepreneurship and demonstrates the many different theoretical approaches that are available to describe and understand this phenomenon. For the teacher/professor tasked with educating members of business families, especially those that represent the next generation of leaders, the book provides theory coupled with real-world examples to help students understand and apply different methodologies and approaches for themselves and their families. While no book can be all things to all people, we hope that the effort proves useful to all those who study, consult with, teach or belong to entrepreneurial-minded families everywhere.

While we organized the book around seven topics that emerged from our reading of these contributions, each of these chapters captures a broad array of topics and issues about family entrepreneurship, so, please, don't assume that a chapter under a particular heading is only about that issue. In fact, while you might read the book from cover to cover, we think you will find each chapter could serve as either the start or end of your odyssey into family entrepreneurship. We hope you will dive into this with the knowledge that you will be getting a wide variety of ideas, theories, insights and practices to enable families to achieve their entrepreneurial goals.

As faculty members at Babson College, we are obsessed with furthering entrepreneurship in all of its forms. Indeed, one of the mottos of Babson College is "Entrepreneurship of All Kinds." What is not commonly known is that the most important way that "Entrepreneurship of All Kinds" occurs around the world is through families. Recently, we completed a study of entrepreneurial activities across 48 countries (Kelly, Gartner, & Allen, 2020) and found that 75% of the entrepreneurs who were actively engaged in starting and growing new businesses were either co-owned and/or co-managed with family members and that 81% of all business owners in these countries, had some family involvement.[2] In other words, most entrepreneurship across the world is family entrepreneurship. Therefore, we believe this book is a timely contribution that focuses on the family, itself, as the primary enabler of entrepreneurial activity, rather than on the business(es) that families own or manage, or on individual members of the family.

Finally, we acknowledge the intellectual and practical insights that we have received from our colleagues at Babson College who are constantly pushing the boundaries of knowledge and practice in entrepreneurship, as well as Babson College's Institute for Family Entrepreneurship where we are pioneering new ways to enable families to meet the challenges of the future through entrepreneurship.

Reference

Kelley, D., Gartner, W. B., & Allen, M. (2020). *Global Entrepreneurship Monitor Family Business Report*. Babson Park, MA: Babson College Press.

---

[2] Note that these findings are based on un-weighted data from respondents in 48 countries, and, that the survey, in total, is comprised of responses from over 150,000 adults, with minimum of 2000 responses from each participating country.

Part I

Characteristics of the Entrepreneurial Family

2

Family Capital: The Key to Entrepreneurial and Family Success

W. Gibb Dyer

Over my 36-year academic and consulting career, I've spent most of my time studying and helping family-owned businesses. From my experience, one thing is abundantly clear: families often provide the key resources that entrepreneurs need to launch a successful business. I call these resources "family capital": *the human, social, financial, and other resources that are available to individuals or groups as a result of family affiliation.* "Family human capital" consists of the skills, knowledge, and labor of family members; "family social capital" refers to the social connections and reputation shared by family members, and "family financial capital" encompasses a family's financial and other tangible assets.

In many instances a business couldn't be founded or succeed without family capital. For example, one of my early family business clients was General Growth Properties (today, Brookfield Properties), founded by Martin and Matthew Bucksbaum. These two brothers were joined at the hip as they started their real estate empire in the 1950s. Martin had great vision regarding various commercial real estate projects while Matthew was more adept at running the day-to-day operations of the business. Together, they made a formidable team as they turned their shopping malls into a multi-billion-dollar business. In the case of Bill Gates, he likely wouldn't have been able to

W. G. Dyer (✉)
Marriott School of Business, Brigham Young University, Provo, UT, USA
e-mail: W_dyer@byu.edu

© The Author(s), under exclusive license to Springer Nature Switzerland AG 2021
M. R. Allen, W. B. Gartner (eds.), *Family Entrepreneurship*,
https://doi.org/10.1007/978-3-030-66846-4_2

get his Microsoft software into IBM computers were it not for his mother's social capital—a close social connection with IBM Chairman John Opel (they served on a nonprofit board together). Bill's mother Mary introduced the two, and, as they say, the rest is history. Family financial capital played a significant role in the founding of Wal-Mart. Sam Walton's wealthy father-in-law provided him with significant seed money to launch Wal-Mart, which has grown to sales of over $500 billion and over 2.2 million employees worldwide. One might argue that these three companies wouldn't have been as successful if it weren't for the family capital provided to these firms' founders.

In this chapter I will present a model of family capital which I've found useful to understanding how family capital affects families and business performance.[1] The model helps us understand why family capital is so important and why, in the United States and many other countries, it is declining at an alarming rate—the result being less entrepreneurial activity since potential entrepreneurs have fewer familial resources to draw upon.

The two factors that have a tremendous impact on the formation of family capital are (1) the stability of family relationships and (2) the size of the family kinship network. Stable relationships allow trust and norms of reciprocity to develop in a family which encourages the sharing of family resources. Larger families also provide more opportunities to reach out to family members with resources. Today, family structures are more varied than they have been in the past. In general, families are smaller and less stable. Some families have a structure that's labeled the "nuclear" or "traditional" family: a married father and mother with children. Just under 50% of all families in the United States are nuclear families but this familial pattern has declined in recent years (Blackwell, 2010). Today, we see more "blended" families (8.7%) as a result of divorce and remarriage, families led by cohabiting partners (3.1%), families led by a single parent (generally a woman) (16.3%), multi-generational families (19%), and families headed by same-sex couples (1%). Moreover, this pattern of family formation, with families becoming smaller and less stable, is becoming more common throughout the world.

---

[1] For more details and the citations for the various statistics, see: Dyer, W. G. *The Family Edge: How your biggest competitive advantage in business isn't what you've been taught—It's your family* (Sanger, CA: Familius, 2019).

Model of Family Capital

In Fig. 2.1 is the model showing the factors that influence family capital as well as its outcomes. At the bottom of the model are those societal and individual attitudes toward marriage, child-bearing, divorce, cohabitation, and out-of-wedlock births that have a direct impact on family structure. Family structure provides the scaffolding upon which family capital is built and has the most significant impact on family capital. However, other factors in the model such as "family culture," "family activities," "family trust," and

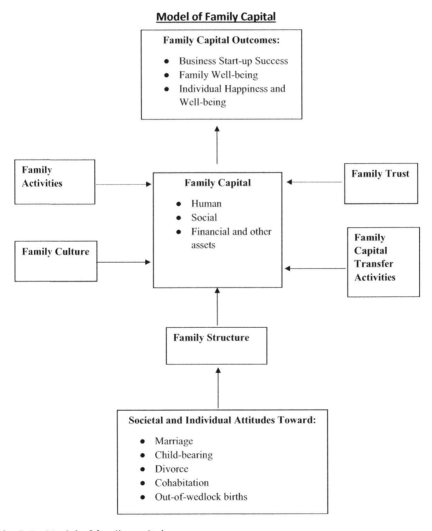

Fig. 2.1 Model of family capital

"family capital transfer activities" also are important to develop family resources. Finally, the major outcomes of family capital are (1) business start-up success, (2) family well-being, and (3) individual happiness and well-being. I'll discuss each of these factors in turn.

Family Structure

Family structure has a significant impact on family size and stability. In general, marriage supports stable family relationships and birth rates increase family size. Divorce, cohabitation, and single-parenthood tend to have a negative impact on family stability and often family size. Some of the trends in the United States along these five dimensions are as follows:

- Marriage rates are at historic lows in the United States. In previous generations, marriage was deemed by almost everyone to be a primary goal in life. Now, one in seven adult Americans says they never want to get married.
- Birth rates are nearing all-time lows (1.7 per woman)—not even high enough to replace the population.
- Slightly less than one-half of all marriages in the United States end in divorce. The divorce rate in the 1960s was about half that, around 25%.
- There has been a significant increase in cohabitation in the United States since 1960. Cohabiting relationships tend to be more unstable than marriage relationships which can have a negative impact on both partners and children.
- Forty-one percent of American children are born out-of-wedlock today (versus about 5% in 1960).

The net effects of these trends are as follows: (1) fewer people are willing to marry and create a family unit; (2) families are smaller; and (3) families are less stable, with many children growing up in a home with only one parent (thus often having access to only one parent's resources). In other countries, I found similar trends. For example:

- There are approximately 100 million fewer women than men in Asia—primarily due to selective abortions and female infanticide. Thus, many Asian men will find it difficult, if not impossible, to find mates, get married, and have children.

- At its current birth rate, the Japanese will disappear from the earth by the year 2500. This is true in many other countries as well (e.g., Korea and Singapore).
- Some countries, such as Columbia (84%) and Iceland (66%), have extremely high out-of-wedlock birth rates.
- The prevalence of HIV/AIDS in Africa has left many African children orphans who will grow up without parental guidance and support. In Swaziland, about one-fifth of all children are orphaned, primarily due to HIV/AIDS which afflicts 31% of Swazis.
- Some countries, such as Russia, have divorce rates over 50%.

These data suggest that families will be smaller and less stable in the future, likely leading to less family capital available to family members. We may be already seeing some of the effects of these trends in the United States. If family capital is in decline, then we should be seeing fewer start-ups. Data from the United States show this to be true. Start-ups in the United States have declined about 20% over the past decade or so. There were a little over 500,000 start-ups per year 15 years ago, but only 414,000 in 2015 (Samuelson, 2017). Moreover, millennials (those between the ages of 20 and 34) are much less likely to start new businesses than previous generations (Harrison, 2015). This trend is certainly troublesome for the American economy.

Family Culture

I have found that the culture of one's family also has an impact on family capital since it defines the rules for how family members relate to one another and their environment. In general, "family culture" can be defined as *socially acquired and share rules of conduct that are manifested in a family's artifacts, perspectives, values, and assumptions* (Dyer, 1986). Let's break this definition down into its various components.

Artifacts are the overt manifestations of family rules. There are physical artifacts—one's dress, the state of the rooms in home, implements used for work or school, and so on; verbal artifacts—the language and stories shared by a family; and behavioral artifacts—the rituals and common behavior patterns used by a family. Artifacts are the tangible aspects of culture—things that we can hear, see, or touch and are manifestations of a family's rules of conduct.

Cultural *perspectives* are situation-specific rules of conduct followed by family members. For example, in a specific situation like greeting someone in

Japan the appropriate behavior is to bow. In the United States and most of the Western world we shake hands. In the context of a family, perspectives are the situation-specific rules for dealing with things like greeting family members, deciding rules like curfews, or showing physical affection in public. In my home, my father used to kiss his children (even the boys) on the lips before leaving on a trip—that was deemed appropriate behavior in the Dyer household in that situation. We assumed this tradition came from my grandfather who was born in Wales.

Cultural *values* are more general, trans-situational rules that are reflected in cultural perspectives and artifacts. For example, some homes have numerous rules about doing chores and helping family members with various tasks to keep the home clean and repaired. These rules in a family could be summarized in a value that might be labeled "we are obligated to help maintain our home." Other values that I've seen in families that I've consulted with include, "respect for one's elders," "honesty in all one's dealings," and "hard work is expected." These values are often articulated by members of the family and the family attempts to have these values serve as guides to their actions.

The most fundamental aspects of culture are what we call *basic assumptions*. These are the basic beliefs that underlie the artifacts, perspectives, and values of the family. These assumptions are the basic premises, often unspoken and generally invisible, that "account for" the more overt aspects of culture.

Previous studies of cultural assumptions have suggested several categories that are common to many groups; I've found the following categories of assumptions particularly applicable to families and their ability to develop and transfer family capital (Dyer, 1986). These categories include:

Assumptions About Human Nature: Are family members basically good, basically evil, or neither? In other words, can they be trusted?

Assumptions About Relationships: Are family relationships assumed to be hierarchical (someone is always above someone else in the pecking order), are relationships "collateral" (more or less equal in nature), or are relationships individualistic in nature (it's everyone for themselves—self-interest is dominant)?

Assumptions About the Environment: Do we assume that the environment—the physical and social world we live in—can be tamed and shaped by us, do we assume that we are victims of a world that we can't change, or are we supposed to "harmonize"—be one—with our environment?

Assumptions About Truth: Do we learn "truth" from external authority figures (typically father or mother) or do we gain knowledge and truth through personal investigation and testing?

Assumptions About the Nature of Human Activity: Do we assume that family
    members are valuable for what they can do for us or do we see them as
    individuals with unlimited potential that need to be developed in their
    own right?
Assumptions About Time: Should we be primarily focused on following the
    past, living in the present, or preparing for the future?

From my review of the literature and my own consulting practice with family
firms I find that families that develop family capital have a culture based on
the following assumptions: (1) we trust one another; (2) children should
move from a dependent relationship with parents to an interdependent one
over time; (3) the family should be proactive in trying to adapt to and change
its environment for the betterment of family members; (4) children initially
learn from parents, but over time it's assumed that they'll come up with their
own answers to important questions; (5) the role of the family is to help
family members reach their full potential; and (6) our family values our
heritage but recognizes when it needs to change to adapt to future needs. On
the other hand, I have found that families with assumptions that reflect
distrust, exploitation, or abuse of family members, authoritarian leadership,
and an unwillingness to change or explore new avenues to improve family
functioning have great difficulty developing and sustaining family capital.

Family Activities

Families can also strengthen family capital through the following activities:
(1) family identity activities; (2) family rituals and traditions; (3) demonstrating
commitment to family; (4) coping with crises; and (5) "spiritual wellness."
These characteristics create stability within families that allow family capital
to grow.

   Families that have significant family capital tend to have their individual
and family identities inextricably connected. This may play out by a family
creating a family mission or values statement. One such family is Stephen
Covey's family. Steve Covey, author of *The Seven Habits of Highly Effective
People*, was a member of the organizational behavior department at Brigham
Young University when I was a student there, and I had the opportunity to
serve as his teaching assistant for one semester. He also attended one of my
family business workshops since he had family members working in his
consulting firm. One of the things that Steve did to strengthen his family

identity was to create a family mission statement. Steve wrote the following about family mission statements:

> Write a family mission statement—identify what kind of family you want to be. For instance, what qualities define your family, what kinds of feeling do you want in your home, how do you want to build relationships? Get everyone involved in these questions and write something that describes your family and how you want to be. (www.stephencovey.com/blog/?tag=family-mission-statement)

Mission statements or other actions that demonstrate "who we are" as a family tend to create stronger bonds where family capital can be shared and developed.

Family rituals and traditions also play a significant role in creating familial bonds that strengthen family capital and contribute to developing a distinct family identity. In my own family there are the rituals and traditions that we have developed over time. Here are a few of them:

1. Vacations to the beach in Oregon to go crabbing and clamming.
2. Vacations to Cedar City, Utah to see Shakespeare's plays and go fishing.
3. Having a special Christmas day breakfast of finnan haddie (smoked cod) and "Robbs" (scones named after the Robb family).
4. Visiting our ancestors' graves on Memorial Day.
5. Taking a family picture on Dyer Street in Lake Oswego, Oregon under the street sign. (This is the street where my grandfather supposedly lived while growing up.)

These traditions represent a mix of traditions from both my family and my wife's family. These traditions are highly anticipated by family members and are fondly remembered in stories often told within the family.

As I have reviewed the patterns of the families that I've consulted with who have been able to develop family capital, they tend to emphasize the importance of spending time with family members and demonstrating commitment to the family. Since most of my clients are entrepreneurs, this isn't easy given the pressures they feel to achieve in business as well as meet the needs of their families. For many years, surveys of entrepreneurs have noted their hectic work schedules. For example, one early study by Boyd and Gumpert (1983) found that 70% of those entrepreneurs who had been in business between six and ten years worked evenings while 58% of those in business for ten or more years were frequently gone at night. A seminal study of 3000 families conducted by Stinnett and DeFrain noted that "commitment to family" was the first "secret" of a strong family (Stinnett & DeFrain, 1985). They tell the story of one man who was saved as a child when his mother dove in front of an automobile and pushed him out of the way. Such an act clearly reflected the mother's love and commitment to her child and left an indelible impression on the son. While such heroic acts are compelling, simpler acts such as taking time for family vacations, going to the park, attending children's sporting or cultural activities, and having regular family dinners demonstrate the commitment that family members have for each other.

"Strong families" also have the ability to help one another during a crisis. In my own family we had a major crisis after my daughter Emily and her husband Burke adopted a baby girl who they named Evelyn. Three months after her birth she was rushed by ambulance to Primary Children's Hospital in Salt Lake City with what was thought to be a serious infection. After a series of tests it was determined that Evelyn had a condition called Hemophagocytic Lymphohistiocytosis (HLH). HLH is a very rare condition caused by one's immune system running wild, generating lymphocytes and macrophages that produce high amounts of inflammatory cytokines, which then damage vital organs. Without treatment, it is invariably fatal. The only cure for Evelyn would be chemotherapy followed by a bone marrow transplant. For the next year, from February 2009 until the spring of 2010, Evelyn was in and out of the hospital (mostly in) and one of her parents stayed with her the entire time. Family members, particularly my wife Theresa, would periodically go to the hospital to tend Evelyn and give Emily or Burke a well-deserved break. After enduring chemotherapy and finding a matching bone marrow donor in Germany, Evelyn experienced a successful transplant. Without the expertise of those doctors and nurses, Evelyn would not have survived, but the social support given by the family to Evelyn and her parents was as important, if not more important, in helping the family cope with this crisis. Evelyn is now a healthy and happy 12-year-old.

One final characteristic of families that develop and share family capital is what Stinnett and DeFrain call "spiritual wellness," which means the family is engaged in achieving a purpose that transcends the fact that family members are merely living together as a biological or economic unit. They write: "[spiritual wellness is] a unifying force, a caring center within each person that promotes sharing, love, and a compassion for others. It is a force that helps a person transcend self and become part of something larger" (Stinnett and DeFrain, p. 101). In some families this means the family is committed to following the values espoused by their religion. It means living a life consistent with one's religious values and typically involves some sort of service to others—particularly those in need. However, families that are not religiously inclined can also achieve spiritual wellness. I have seen families with little or no religious affiliation sponsor relief activities for the poor in developing countries or service projects in their local community. It's an interesting paradox that I see in families with strong identities: they strengthen their own family by going outside the family to help and support others. The key to developing this higher purpose is for the family to clearly identify how its members, as representatives of the family, can contribute to society in a meaningful way. This might be done through discussions within the family at a "family council" or developing a family mission statement that articulates the family's beliefs and values as they relate to service and achieving a higher purpose in life. Again, the notion that a family has a higher purpose in life generates commitment on the part of family members to each other and encourages them to cooperate and help each other to achieve the family's goals. This serves as a powerful force in generating family capital.

Family Trust

To build and share family capital requires family members to have a certain amount of trust. We can define trust as "a psychological state comprising the intention to accept vulnerability based on positive expectations of the intentions or behavior of another" (Kim, Dirks, & Cooper, 2009, p. 401). In other words, we agree to be vulnerable in some way based on our belief that we will benefit by our relationship to a person, a group, or an institution. Furthermore, there are primarily three "types" of trust that are part of trust dynamics in families. These are:

- *Interpersonal Trust:* Interpersonal trust is based on one's relationship with another person and is primarily based on one's history with that person. To the extent that another person has proven to be predictable and behaves reliably in certain situations, they are deemed to be trustworthy.
- *Competence Trust:* Competence trust is based on the skills, abilities, and experience of the other party. If we believe the other person has the necessary expertise to help us with a particular concern or problem, we "trust" his or her judgment and advice. One's status in the family, academic degrees, certifications, reputation, and so on are often the way we "know" that someone can be trusted. We trust that our credentialed doctors know what they are doing when they treat us.
- *Institutional Trust:* Institutional trust is based on whether we see "the family," "the system," "the rules," or "the processes" as being fair and

trustworthy. Family members want to know if they will have a place to stay, food to eat, and receive social support. They also want to know if they can air their grievances when not treated fairly in the family and receive a fair hearing in order to solve their problems.

My role as a consultant to families who want to strengthen family capital often involves the repairing of these three types of trust. To do so, I typically encourage my clients to take the following approaches:

Repairing Interpersonal Trust

The steps to repairing interpersonal trust are as follows:

1. Confession. Does the person admit his or her mistake and ask for forgiveness?
2. Remorse. Is the offender truly sorry for what happened?
3. Restitution. Can the person "make up" for what was lost due to the violation of trust?
4. Avoid repeating the offense. To the extent that there are repeated violations of trust, it will be more difficult for trust to be restored.
5. Willingness on the part of the person offended to extend forgiveness.

Repairing Competence Trust

Repairing competence trust in a family may involve one or more of the following activities:

- Support schooling or other types of training to improve a family member's skills and abilities.
- Encourage honest, open, and supportive feedback within the family to help family members recognize their weaknesses and develop plans to improve.
- Develop fair and consistent disciplinary procedures to deal with family members who violate expectations in the family and provide support for family members to repair the trust that was lost.
- Require credentials certifying competence.

Repairing Institutional Trust

Repairing institutional trust—trust in "the family"—generally requires creating systems and processes that allow for transparency in the family. The following are just some of the activities that can help to repair institutional trust:

- Clarify and share the details regarding what will happen when one or both parents die. Sharing one's will with children (when they reach an appropriate age) can build feelings of trust and confidence between the parent and child.
- Share pertinent financial information regarding family assets with family members on a regular basis. In my case, my wife Theresa and I periodically meet with our children and their spouses to review our will and to discuss our financial condition. We do this to make sure there will be no significant surprises for them when we pass away.
- Ensure that the processes for making important decisions are transparent (e.g., activities such as vacations or important purchases that would affect the family).

Family Capital Transfer Activities

The final variable in the family capital model concerns family capital transfer activities. If families don't create processes to transfer family capital to the next generation, it may be lost or severely compromised. The steps to making this transfer begin by having the family answer the following questions:

1. What kinds of family capital (human, social, financial) will be helpful to future generations of family members?
2. What family capital do we currently have that needs to be transferred to the next generation or other family members?
3. Who has access to this family capital, or if we don't have the family capital that is needed, how do we develop it so it can benefit future generations?

Hopefully family leaders are aware enough to think about these questions as they begin the process of transferring family capital. However, my own experience as a consultant and my review of the literature on succession planning suggest that most company founders (and their families) are ill-prepared for succession. Thus, to facilitate the process of transferring all three types of family capital, I have found it useful for families to do the following:

1. Initially, create a genogram of one's nuclear and extended family, and
2. Create a "family capital genogram" that identifies who in the family needs family capital,
3. Develop a plan to improve relationships between those who have family capital and those who need it, and
4. Develop specific plans to transfer family capital from one person to another typically by using a "learning by doing" approach. The "learning by doing" approach involves giving potential heirs experiences and holding them accountable to help them prepare for future responsibilities and to develop the skills, knowledge, and relationships needed to carry on the family legacy.

The Outcomes of Family Capital

At the top of the model in Fig. 2.1 are listed the outcomes of family capital. Many studies have indicated that those individuals who have access to family capital start more businesses and those businesses are more successful than those who don't have family capital to draw upon. In a recent study I conducted with my research team, we used data from over 8000 teenagers to examine their access to family capital and whether that access influenced them to start businesses later in life (Dyer, 2019). The data showed that those youths who had access to family capital: (1) started more businesses, (2) their businesses had greater longevity, and (3) their businesses had significantly higher profits than those youths who had less family capital. Moreover, I have found, as have other family scholars, that families and their members who have family capital experience the following benefits:

- More resilience in dealing with life's challenges.
- A greater sense of well-being, security, and happiness.
- More likely to be in healthy and stable family relationships.
- Better school performance and fewer behavioral problems in their children.

Thus the benefits of family capital cannot be overstated. It benefits society from an economic standpoint as new businesses are created and it promotes the psychological, social, and economic welfare of families and their members.

Conclusion

As mentioned in previous sections on family structure, families today are smaller and face more instability than almost any time in history. This does not bode well for the future of family entrepreneurship as well as the other benefits received by society and families as the result of family capital. Divorce rates are still 40–50% in most Western countries. Cohabitation has grown rapidly as have out-of-wedlock birth rates. Moreover, fewer people feel the need to be married and have children. Thus, the future of family capital from a societal standpoint is rather bleak in my opinion. However, I have seen individual families make a conscious effort to develop, maintain, and transfer family capital and have experienced its benefits. Thus, I'm optimistic that we can strengthen our own families so we can see the favorable impact of family capital in our families and in the lives of family members.

In summary, the keys to building family capital are as follows:

1. Create a strong and stable partnership between spouses or significant others. Marriages typically last three to four times longer than cohabiting relationships, so marriage should be encouraged. Children who grow up in a stable family environment have the best outcomes and are more likely to develop family capital. Those couples with relationship problems should seek counseling.
2. Encourage a culture in the family that is based on trust, facilitates the growth of each family member, and supports positive change within the family.
3. Encourage family activities that create norms of reciprocity and support within a family. Thus, family mission statements, family traditions, and spending time together as a family are important. Creating a higher purpose for the family is also a way to strengthen family relationships.
4. Build trust within the family by repairing interpersonal trust when it is broken. Develop competence trust by encouraging family members to develop skills and abilities and create institutional trust within the family by sharing information and being transparent.
5. Transfer family capital by identifying where human, social, and financial capital and other assets reside within the family. Then create a succession plan to ensure that these forms of family capital are transferred to the next generation. Without such a plan, family capital can be lost forever.

While having a "strong family" that develops, maintains, and effectively transfers human, social, and financial capital is likely to be more difficult in the future, I have seen those families who have been able to do it reap significant rewards.

References

Blackwell, D. L. (2010). Family Structure and Children's Health in the United States: Findings from the National Health Interview Survey 2001–2007. *National Center for Health Statistics*, 10, no. 246, p. 2.

Boyd, D. P., & Gumpert, D. E. (1983). The Effects of Stress on Early Age Entrepreneurs. In J. A. Hornaday, J. A. Timmons, & K. H. Vesper (Eds.), *Frontiers of Entrepreneurship Research* (pp. 180–191). Babson Park, MA: Babson College.

Dyer, W. G. (1986). *Cultural Change in Family Firms: Anticipating and Managing Business and Family Transitions*. San Francisco: Jossey-Bass.

Dyer, W. G. (2019). *The Family Edge: How Your Biggest Competitive Advantage in Business Isn't What You've Been Taught—it's Your Family*. Sanger, CA: Familius.

Harrison, J. D. (2015, February 12). The Decline in American Entrepreneurship— In Five Charts. Retrieved from https://www.washingtonpost.com/news/ on-small-business/wp/2015/02/12/the-decline-of-american-entrepreneurship-in-five-charts/?utm_term=.76471c72591e

Kim, P. H., Dirks, K. T., & Cooper, C. D. (2009). The Repair of Trust: A Dynamic Bilateral Perspective and Multilevel Conceptualization. *Academy of Management Review, 34*(3), 401–422.

Samuelson, R. J. (2017, October 8). *Washington Post*.

Stinnett, N., & DeFrain, J. (1985). *The Secrets of Strong Families*. Boston: Little, Brown.

3

The Essential Role of Trust in Family Business Entrepreneurship

James H. Davis

Risk is at the heart of entrepreneurship. Entrepreneurs take risk by starting a business, putting personal reputation and wealth in jeopardy. Risk taking in a family business is walking away from security and entering the world of stress and uncertainty. Those investing land, capital, labor and status in a new venture risk losing their wealth and position. The failure rate of new ventures is incredibly high. About 75% of venture-backed start-ups fail (Gage, 2012). Over 50% of US companies fail after five years and 70% after ten (Henry, 2017). About 70% of family-owned businesses fail or are sold before the second generation (Stalk & Foley, 2012). Given these failure rates, why would anyone willingly take risks in entrepreneurial relationships? Where do these risk takers come from? The answers might surprise you.

A recent Huffington Post article reported that 48% of all entrepreneurs grew up in family businesses (O'Keefe, 2017). A PricewaterhouseCoopers family business survey found that 80% of "next-generation" family members wanted to introduce new products, invest in new technology or introduce new operational strategies (PWC, April, 2016). Family business is *the* fertile soil for creating entrepreneurs! Entrepreneurial characteristics and drive may be the legacy handed down to future generations.

J. H. Davis (✉)
Utah State University, Logan, UT, USA
e-mail: J.Davis@usu.edu

Not only are family businesses the source of most entrepreneurs, entrepreneurial orientation is critical to the success of family business. A recent Harvard Business Publication argued that families that want to stay in business need to encourage entrepreneurship in and out of their family business (Roberts & Davis, 2014). Most of the initial investment in the family business produces entrepreneurs who come from their family. Yet, Roberts and Davis warned that investment in family entrepreneurs must be done objectively based upon the potential of the deal and kept within the family. In short, they seem to argue that for entrepreneurial ventures to be successful, relationships within the family must be objectified.

A recent study by Castoro and Krawchuk (2020) stated that the lack of trust and communication in family businesses accounts for 60% of the failure rate. Thus, while a large percentage of entrepreneurs come from family business, family relationships, specifically the lack of trust in the family venture, may be the primary determinant of the success or failure of the venture. This suggests that while new venture judgment must be "objectified" as suggested by Roberts and Davis, trust must be present for a deal to succeed. I believe that the foundation of successful entrepreneurship within a family business is trust.

Trust: What Is It?

Most articles refer to trust without really explaining what it is. Trust is trust, just like salt is salt. Understanding trust is fundamental to managing it. After years of research we have determined that trust is a willingness to be vulnerable to and take risk in someone else, person or organization (Mayer, Davis, & Schoorman, 1995). Trusting behavior is defined as actually taking risk in a relationship. If a parent in a family business invests in a new idea of another family member, they are taking risk in the relationship; they become vulnerable. They are trusting the family member. Thus, in an entrepreneurial venture or investment, the trusting family or individuals make themselves vulnerable by taking risk in the venture or in the relationship with the family member entrepreneur. The risk one takes or the vulnerability one assumes depends upon the nature of the deal and the characteristics of the entrepreneur(s) in charge. How can a family member who wants to start a new venture build trust with family members? What should family members examine in the person(s) starting a new venture within the family to determine the risk/vulnerability they should assume? In short, should they trust and if so how much? I will now explore the drivers of trust in a family entrepreneurial venture and what to do if trust is broken.

Building Entrepreneurial Trust

Trust has been an area of research for a very long time resulting in a wide variety of definitions and prescriptions. A number of approaches to building trust have been suggested in the literature without really understanding what trust is (Mayer et al., 1995). Knowing that trust is the *willingness* to take risk in another person and then actually *taking* that risk in the relationship helps us know what a person must do to build trust and manage the trustor's risk/ vulnerability. To build trust one must find ways to reduce or manage the vulnerability and risks to the trusting party. If the family has to decide whether to take a risk in an entrepreneurial venture, then the family member(s) desirous of launching that venture will stand a much greater chance of support if they can build trust by managing the risk and vulnerability that they bring to the family.

Extensive research and statistical validation over the past 25 years have resulted in three characteristics that the entrepreneur must possess to be trusted. Those three characteristics include the entrepreneur's ability, benevolence and integrity (Fig. 3.1). Statistically speaking, those three characteristics have been found to explain the willingness to be vulnerable and assume risk in multiple studies in a range of industries throughout the world. Simply put, they drive trust.

In most cases these characteristics may only be perceived by the trusting party; however, it is different in a family business where relationships and knowledge of family members have been built over years of association. In family business the characteristics underlying trust are more "known" and less "perceived" by the family members than in other settings. The family makes

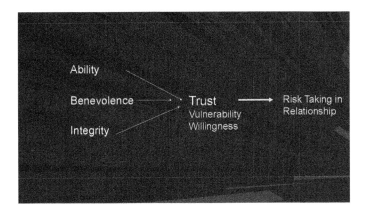

Fig. 3.1   Trust model (Mayer et al., 1995)

decisions on entrepreneurial ventures introduced by family members based upon their *knowledge* of three characteristics of the entrepreneur(s) that determine the trust or vulnerability they are willing to allow and the risks they are willing to take in the relationship. This knowledge is both an advantage because judgments are better informed and a disadvantage because judgments may be more rigid and not allow for change. Family members may affix labels to each other, "you are this way" and not allow for learning, growth and change. When labels are attached to a person it also fixes the trust that person is allowed, the level of vulnerability and risk a person is willing to take with that family member. Having a clear understanding of the drivers of trust (ability, benevolence and integrity) may help family members make a more informed decision about trust and the level of the risk to take. It may also help family members needing to be trusted know how to build trust with family members.

I now turn to an explanation of ability, benevolence and integrity in family entrepreneurial relationships.

Ability: The Skill to Succeed and Risk of an Assassin

The first aspect of a business model that most investors think about in a new venture after examining the deal's value proposition and market potential is the management team that will launch and manage the business. An opportunity can have the best, most revolutionary potential in the world, but if the entrepreneur/team lacks the ability to execute, the venture will struggle and likely fail. Investors quickly reject great ideas with weak teams. The same is true in a family business. A family member can have a phenomenal idea, but if other family members don't believe they have the ability to do the deal, they will reject the idea. They are not willing to take the risk; they will not trust. Family decision makers must believe the family entrepreneur who wishes to launch a new venture has the skills and experience to do the deal or the family cannot and should not take the risk in the deal.

Ability is defined in the entrepreneurial context as the competencies, experience and skills to do what needs to be done to successfully launch and grow the new business. Ability is domain or context specific. For example, a member of the family may have fantastic people skills but may not have the technological ability to launch a new venture.

I once worked with a family member who had only worked in operations area of his family's transportation business. He grew tired of both his job and the industry and decided he wanted to launch a pizza restaurant. He had never worked in the food industry but liked the idea and felt he could make a go of it. He wanted his family to trust him by taking the risk to invest in the pizza restaurant. The family decision makers weren't willing to trust and be vulnerable to that family entrepreneur because they didn't believe he had the ability to do the deal. The entrepreneur simply lacked the knowledge, experience and ability to launch a pizza restaurant. While they might trust him to do a deal related to operations in the transportation industry, they could not trust him to launch a venture outside that domain. There must be a good match between the entrepreneur's abilities and the skills needed in the new venture for trust to exist, for risk taking in the relationship to occur and for the venture to be seriously considered by the family.

If the new venture is unrelated or a big extension to the family's current business, the skills of family members within the business may not be those needed for the new venture. In short, a great idea with the wrong family member entrepreneur. A number of family business studies and consultants have encouraged family businesses to expand the next generations' abilities through education and working outside the family business. Next-generation family members can gain critical abilities by working for suppliers, competitors, customers or related and unrelated industries. In this way family members can gain valuable abilities, experience and knowledge, as well as new venture ideas, that can increase family perception and appreciation for entrepreneurial ability needed for trust. This type of informed venturing is grounded solidly upon increased ability and keeps family business vibrant and relevant. Eric Shinseki, Chief of Staff of the US Army, said, "If you dislike change, you're going to dislike irrelevance even more." Family business must bring new abilities and experience into the organization and be entrepreneurial with them, or they risk becoming irrelevant in their industries.

To build trust the family entrepreneur must demonstrate or signal that they have the ability and experience to successfully launch and manage the new venture. They can signal ability and experience through outside the family business work and/or education. The family must at least perceive that the entrepreneur has the ability to do the deal if they are to gain the trust necessary for the family to support the venture.

The good news is that if trust is broken because of ability it is repairable. Gaining and demonstrating that the entrepreneur now has the ability they lacked, overcoming the shortcomings to the family, trust is restored.

Is ability enough? If a person only has ability and lacks the other characteristics necessary for trust, benevolence and integrity, they may become an assassin. They have skills, but little regard for the family and may not have a code of principles to guide their self-serving behavior. From a management theory perspective, such a person is a self-serving, opportunistic agent who does not owe allegiance to the family business or the family. Such a person cannot be trusted, and the expense of monitoring and control of the entrepreneur are necessary to protect the wealth and reputation of the family and the family business. Ability is a necessary driver of trust, but ability alone is not enough to manage vulnerability and take risk in an entrepreneurial relationship.

In summary, the perception or knowledge of the entrepreneur's ability to launch and manage the new venture is a necessary component of trust. Trust is grown by demonstrating and gaining ability through education and experience. Broken trust can be restored by demonstrating that the ability shortcoming causing the problem has been overcome and the entrepreneur now has the ability and the problem will not happen again. While ability is an important driver of trust, benevolence and integrity are needed. Without them, the family risks putting an assassin in charge, putting family wealth, legacy and reputation in jeopardy.

Benevolence: The Care and Concern for the Family and the Risk of the Schlemiel

Benevolence is the perception and/or knowledge that the family member being trusted would never knowingly harm the family or trusting party in the relationship. If the family entrepreneur has the best interests of their family at heart, they are perceived to genuinely care about the trusting party's welfare, economic or otherwise.

If the trusting individual believes that another party has benevolence toward them, they are more likely to take risk in their relationship and trust them. It would be irrational to trust someone who is believed to be unconcerned about your welfare. To do so would be to put you at risk. The assassin described above is a good example of an unconcerned individual who seeks gain at the trusting party's expense. The assassin is unconcerned with your risk or loss as long as they are protected and rewarded.

The founder of the family business is often a "benevolent dictator" and that may be the leadership style in first and some second-generation family businesses. The benevolent dictator who cares about others in the family and in the business is more trustworthy than the non-benevolent dictator/autocrat who may be the assassin described above. As family businesses age and grow, more family and non-family members become involved. As this happens the perceptions/knowledge of the benevolence by decision makers in the family business of family member entrepreneurs becomes a critical determinant of their willingness to take risks in the relationship by investing in the venture.

How to build benevolence? Perceptions of benevolence can be increased by spending time on relationships and focusing on the other party's interests, being less "me-centered." You must demonstrate the other person's importance to you as a person, not simply viewing them as a position or an asset in the relationship. You must show that you really care about them as a person. Benevolence is not egocentric. It cannot be grown if you are simply trying to develop a relationship for your own well-being and self-interest. The other party will see it and it will actually hurt their perceptions of your benevolence toward them.

Would benevolence alone be enough to trust the family member entrepreneur? After all, they would never do anything to purposefully hurt the trusting party. If the entrepreneur is benevolent and lacks ability and integrity, he/she is a schlemiel! Schlemiel is a Yiddish word used to describe an incompetent person who is constantly falling into unfortunate situations and is seen as unlucky. This person will constantly make mistakes, often the same ones over and over again, but will always apologize and work hard to show how sorry they are and how much they care. The trusting party is put in a very awkward position. They have been hurt, but have a hard time being mad at the entrepreneur because they didn't do anything to purposefully hurt them, they aren't an assassin. Still, they can't be trusted because they did hurt the trusting party even if they didn't mean to hurt them. They might have violated a deeply held family value; however, "they didn't mean to, it was only an accident." Clearly, more than just benevolence toward the trusting party is needed. It is an essential part of trust, but ability and integrity are also needed.

Integrity: Principle-Driven Leader or the Risk of the Zealous Martyr

The perception about the integrity of the family member being trusted is the third critical element that drives trust. Integrity in a trusting relationship is defined as the trusted, family member entrepreneur's adherence to values and beliefs that the trustor (the family decision maker) also finds important and acceptable. For example, one value most people view as important is honesty. One would likely never trust or take risk in a dishonest family member. They would never make themselves vulnerable to such a person. If they had no choice but to do business with a dishonest family member, they would not engage in a relationship of trust. They would implement oversight, monitoring and control to ensure that the other party stays in line with agreements and takes advantage of them.

There are a number of fundamental values that most people would agree as important to trust. In addition to honesty, described above, they might include thriftiness, loyalty, courteousness, openness, dependability, transparency and accountability. The key to integrity is that those trusting perceive that the family member entrepreneur actually lives those values. Hypocritical people and organizations espouse values, but do not actually live those values. They cannot be trusted.

The trusting party must also accept the values adopted by the entrepreneur as appropriate. It doesn't necessarily mean that a value in and of itself is right or wrong. For example, an entrepreneur who values revenue above family harmony and unity may not be trusted by family that may not agree. There is a plethora of family business research that shows that family business often values family socio-economic wealth over simply financial gain. It does not mean that the value of financial gain is wrong. It may simply be inconsistent with other values. The family business entrepreneur motivated by financial gain over family socio-economic wealth may have a value in conflict with family decision makers. Their integrity will be perceived to be low and they will not be trusted. Stephen M.R. Covey once said that it is possible to have integrity without trust; however, it is impossible to have trust without integrity.

If the family entrepreneur is perceived to have integrity and no ability and benevolence will they be trusted? An entrepreneur with values and no ability or benevolence could be considered a zealous martyr. This is a person that is absolutely letter of the law/value and puts that above the family or anyone else. There is no "gray area" in decision making for the integrity only entrepreneur. Unfortunately, they also have no skills and as a result they will go down with the ship! They are the martyrs who will die for the cause or value that no one in the family agrees with. If the integrity only entrepreneur at least had ability they might succeed, but without family support. If they had benevolence along with integrity they would likely fail, but they would at least be loved and appreciated by the family. Integrity alone is not enough for the family to take risk and be vulnerable to the family member entrepreneur.

Broken Trust

Perceptions of ability, benevolence and integrity are all needed for the family to trust the family member desirous of family support in an entrepreneurial venture. Think of trust as a three-legged stool. If a leg is missing the trust stool cannot stand. A one or two-legged stool may be possible, but trust is weak, and support is uncertain.

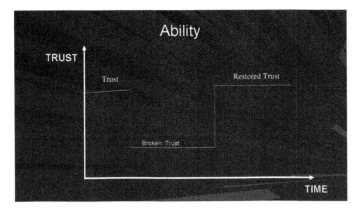

Fig. 3.2   Trust restoration resulting from ability violation

What happens if trust is broken? When describing ability above I argued that when ability is questionable or lacking, it can easily be repaired by gaining the ability through education and/or experience. Once the entrepreneurial family member demonstrates ability has been gained or restored broken trust resulting from this dimension of trust is repaired. This is demonstrated in Fig. 3.2.

If trust is broken as a result of violation of benevolence and/or integrity, restoring trust is very difficult. If the trusting family thought the entrepreneur family member had benevolence toward them or integrity and the entrepreneur did something that showed their perceptions were wrong, trust is broken and declines. The family is no longer willing to be vulnerable and take risks with that family member. Over a very long period of time the entrepreneur family member may work hard to demonstrate benevolence and integrity and trust may improve, but it never returns to the original level. When benevolence and/or integrity is violated, the trusting party is hurt in a more personal way and any efforts on the entrepreneur's part are very difficult to believe or perceive. See Fig. 3.3 for the restoration of trust when benevolence and/or integrity is violated.

In short, the entrepreneur may have a chance of restoring trust if the trusting family sees the break as a result of ability. If the trusting family sees the break as a result of benevolence toward them or the family or a violation in deeply held family values, trust will be difficult to repair and may never come back to what it once was. It may be the reason that people who violate trust because of benevolence or integrity claim that it is an addiction or habit and they can overcome with counseling or therapy. They try to make it an ability

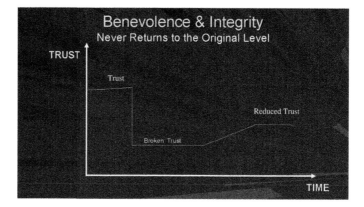

Fig. 3.3 Trust restoration resulting from benevolence &/or integrity violation

issue! Unfortunately, it is much deeper than an ability issue and the behavior will likely be repeated in the future, guaranteeing that broken trust will likely never be restored.

Ability, benevolence and integrity are all necessary to engender trust for the entrepreneur in the family business. Risk is at the heart of entrepreneurship. The Austrian economist Joseph Schumpeter called entrepreneurship creative destruction. The family business will not become vulnerable to creative destruction and engage in risk taking in a relationship with a family member entrepreneur if they do not believe that the entrepreneur possesses the ability, has benevolence toward them and has acceptable values that they live, integrity.

References

Castoro, A., & Krawchuk, F. (2020, May 20). 4 Tensions in Family Business—And How to Work Through Them. *Harvard Business Review.*

Gage, D. (2012, September 20). The Venture Capital Secret: 3 Out of 4 Start-Ups Fail. *The Wall Street Journal.* Retrieved from https://www.wsj.com/articles/SB10000872396390443720204578004980476429190.

Henry, P. (2017, February 18). Why Some Startups Succeed (and Why Most Fail). *Entrepreneur.* Retrieved from https://www.entrepreneur.com/article/288769.

Mayer, R. C., Davis, J. H., & Schoorman, F. D. (1995). An Integrative Model of Organizational Trust. *Academy of Management Review, 20*(3), 709–734.

O'Keefe, J. (2017, October 27). 48% of Entrepreneurs Grew Up in a Family Business. *HuffPost.* Retrieved from https://www.huffpost.com/entry/48-of-entrepre-neurs-grew-_b_12663536.

Price Waterhouse Cooper. (2016, April). *Next Generation Survey of Family Business Leaders*. Retrieved from https://www.pwc.com/gx/en/family-business-services/publications/assets/next-gen-report.pdf.

Roberts, M. J., & Davis, J. A. (2014, August 13). Family Businesses Need Entrepreneurs for Long-Run Success. Forbes: HBS Working Knowledge. Retrieved from https://www.forbes.com/sites/hbsworkingknowledge/2014/08/13/family-businesses-need-entrepreneurs-for-long-run-success/#d5c3d6762254.

Stalk, G., & Foley, H. (2012, January–February). Avoid the Traps that Destroy Family Business. *Harvard Business Review*.

4

Managing Legacy, Achievement and Identity in Entrepreneurial Families

Eliana Crosina and William B. Gartner

In discussions with entrepreneurial families about their futures, we often suggest that each family member should consider four aspects of their lives—achievement, happiness, significance and legacy—as a broad framework to explore their goals and values and to reflect on "who they are" and ultimately "who they want to be." This framework comes from *Just Enough*, a book written by Laura Nash and Howard Stevenson that focuses on the meaning of "success" for highly accomplished individuals and families. In this chapter, just as in our conversations with the members of entrepreneurial families, we first describe and contextualize the framework. We then focus on two specific elements of the framework—legacy and achievement—because they tend to be a primary source of conflict and misunderstanding among the members of entrepreneurial families. Finally, building on insights from our own ethnographic research with entrepreneurial families, and from scholarship on identity, we reflect on what it might take to create an environment in which certain family members' aspirations for legacy and others' need for achievement coexist in unison. We believe that by fostering this alignment, the family's entrepreneurial activities might have a greater chance at lasting success.

E. Crosina • W. B. Gartner (✉)
Babson College, Babson Park, MA, USA
e-mail: ecrosina@babson.edu; wgartner@babson.edu

© The Author(s), under exclusive license to Springer Nature Switzerland AG 2021
M. R. Allen, W. B. Gartner (eds.), *Family Entrepreneurship*,
https://doi.org/10.1007/978-3-030-66846-4_4

35

A Framework for Success in Family Firms

"Success" for both individuals and families is composed of a multitude of goals and values, which, following Nash and Stevenson (2004), may be broadly categorized in terms of **achievement, happiness, significance** and **legacy**. Consider **achievement** to be goals that one desires to accomplish. Each person may have various goals that are more or less important to them: for instance, one family member might want to be an artist exhibiting paintings at Art Basel in Miami Beach, while another might want to develop a new product line as part of the family business. **Happiness** encompasses various positive emotions, but at its core are contentment and satisfaction. Contentment and satisfaction span several aspects of our lives—ranging from our relationships to community, as well as our own selves. **Significance** is about having a positive impact on others: we all want to be of value, whether by raising our children, providing a product or service that others use or solving issues in our communities. Finally, **legacy** is enabling one's accomplishments and values to benefit others in the future.

Achievement, happiness, significance and legacy are all dynamic: the priorities of each might change over time, as well as how they might relate to each other. In other words, what brings us happiness, achievement, significance or legacy today is likely to vary as circumstances in our lives evolve. Conflict arises when we fail to recognize that our own success criteria change. However, given how quickly our environments evolve, it is especially challenging to stop and *pay* attention to ourselves and to our situation. We emphasize the *pay* in "pay attention" because there is a cost associated to taking the time to be present, and reflect. The framework (achievement, happiness, significance and legacy), then, provides a way to focus on ourselves, consider where we are now, where we might want to be in the future, and perhaps most importantly, why.

Although all aspects of the framework invite critical self-reflection, when focusing on family entrepreneurship we zero in on issues related to legacy and achievement. These issues tend to be closely coupled, and are both consequential and problematic in family firms. Indeed, evidence from research and practice suggests that the legacy that senior family members may want to pass on to their offspring often does not align with what the next generation desires, leading to a mismatch between senior generation's legacy ambitions and next generation's achievement goals (Barbera, Stamm, & DeWitt, 2018; Jaskiewicz, Combs, & Rau, 2015). For example, our conversations with the senior members of a family that owns and operates a successful multi-generation business in oil well services suggest that the junior generation is not interested in joining a firm that deals with oil. Rather, junior members have ambitions to pursue more "environmentally friendly" endeavors, despite the success and resiliency that the family oil business has demonstrated over the years. Put differently, the senior generation sees the business as the legacy to be transferred, while the junior generation holds different achievement goals.

Faced with such discrepancies, how might entrepreneurial families go about fostering environments that would enable greater alignment between legacy and achievement? The answer is not simple, as it requires effort from both seniors and juniors. To start, seniors need to become aware of what they can transfer, take stock of what they *must* and *could* transfer and become actively involved in a purposeful transferring process. In our prior example of the oil business, beyond a focus on oil per se, seniors might start by recognizing that the business thrived over the years because of *how* it addressed client problems in harsh and unpredictable environments. In other words, the business fostered unique ways of operating in a volatile industry that may be applicable to other sectors or raw materials, well beyond oil. This type of knowledge/understanding is generally tacit—not codified or made explicit in "how to" manuals of any sorts (Von Krogh, Ichijo, & Nonaka, 2000). In addition, with the passing of time, tacit knowledge tends to become "taken for granted," or implied in how one/an organization acts and relates to others (Wenger, 1998). As such, tacit knowledge is not easily surfaced or transferred. However, because tacit knowledge informs behaviors and relationships, it is critically important for the very functioning of the business. As we will elaborate, tacit knowledge is often the most vital legacy that seniors can provide to the next generation.

Lessons from Field Research

Sociologists and anthropologists have long noted that in any given social setting the most important insights tend to be the ones that people take for granted (e.g., Whyte, 1984), and that deep immersion in the field may be a gateway toward a better understanding for how things work in practice (Geertz, 2008). So, how might this notion translate for seniors looking to transfer their entrepreneurial legacy to the next generation? We suggest that seniors and the next generation must first become aware of how much of the family's entrepreneurial capabilities, as well as the practice of managing and owning the family's business(es), is taken for granted knowledge. For the family in oil services, this might involve the senior generation helping the junior generation learn the business as more than a generator of wealth from oil; while for the junior generation remaining open to what the senior generation so enthusiastically loves about oil services.

Cognizant of this, seniors must then help the next generation gain "access," not only by being open to, but also by facilitating the next generation's inquiry. This way, rather than just "giving" something to the next generation, seniors should first welcome the next generation as active inquirers, allowing them to observe and question what they do. In this vein, the next generation becomes "ethnographers," researchers who enter the field with the primary goal of understanding. Just as mapmakers who set foot on unchartered territory, ethnographers need to embrace the notion that "they cannot set out to locate deposits of iron ore" (Spradley, 1980, p. 81). Ethnographers must be aware of and open to the experience of mundaneness and boredom, as well as to the possibility of surprises, in their journeys (Barley, 1990). As ethnographers doing field work, the first few days, sometime even weeks or months in the field, might not yield anything of value because it takes time to "fit into the scene, adjust to people, gain acceptance, and begin to understand what is going on" (Whyte, 1984, p. 27).

Here comes an important lesson: there is a critical difference between entering the field and gaining access. Gaining access implies achieving openness, transparency and trust from one's informants. Access is not "given," but it is earned through a combination of demonstrating interest, deferring judgment, as well as by being present. This way, despite their ostensibly "insider" status as members of the family, the next generation must realize that they are often effectively "outsiders" to the business (and often to the inner workings of the family as well) and that they must work together with their seniors to gain access. Seniors can play a critical role in this process by welcoming the next generation into their networks, helping them break through any barriers they might encounter, and ultimately by sharing the motives that underpin how tasks are accomplished and business and family decisions made. Keeping with our ethnography metaphor, seniors can play the role of key informants—serving as the primary links between researchers (the next generation) and the context under study (the family and the businesses) (Tremblay, 1957).

In particular, for the oil-services family, this process of gaining access involved inviting the junior generation to explore all facets of the oil-service business, as well as pairing them with senior members of the family to observe and participate in the multiple roles and responsibilities that day-to-day operations require. The invitation was initially articulated as follows, "you may not like the oil business, but, we would like you to see and experience the kinds of problems and challenges we face which might provide valuable insights for what you may want to do in the future." With involvement comes surprises (more on this later).

Our discussion so far highlights layers of knowledge and access in furthering family entrepreneurship toward the next generation. The process—how entrepreneurial skills and capabilities are passed down—is as critical as, and not independent from, the content—or what is transferred. Related to this, the act of "receiving" the legacy of family entrepreneurship is not nearly as passive as the verb suggests. Rather, it involves active engagement, interest and ultimately careful inquiry on the part of the next generation. Therefore, even when seniors and juniors share ambitions, the outcomes of this process are far from simple. Matters become even more complicated in the face of conflicting aspirations—when the hopes of one generation do not align with those of the other. How might entrepreneurial families, then, go about fostering such alignment, and in doing so, set themselves up for a chance at lasting success?

Identity Questions and Tensions

Underpinning questions of legacy and achievement (as well as of happiness and significance) are fundamental questions of identity—who we are and who we want to be— both as individuals and more collectively as a family (Shepherd & Haynie, 2009). Identity provides a lens through which individuals make sense of ambiguous and complex situations and offers powerful explanations as to why people might act as they do (Weick, 1995). Put differently, identity motivates and sustains behavior. In entrepreneurial contexts, in particular, founder identity plays a pivotal role in how entrepreneurs evaluate opportunities (Fauchart & Gruber, 2011); respond to adversity (Powell & Baker, 2014); secure resources (Navis & Glynn, 2011); as well as how they frame and address conflict (Shepherd & Haynie, 2009).

Besides recognizing the centrality of identity throughout the entrepreneurial process (see Crosina, 2018, for a review), it is important to understand that individuals may define who they are (or who they want to be) in relation to either the roles they occupy (identity theory) or the social groups to which they belong (social identity theory). Specifically, identity theory suggests that people's actions are influenced by how committed they are to a given role, and by how salient such a role is compared to others. Roles that are higher in the hierarchy of salience tend to be more self-defining. Salience, in turn, is determined by degree of commitment—expressed as the number and strength of relationships that one has associated to a given role (Stryker, 1980; Stryker &

Serpe, 1982). For example, one's role as "sister" may be more self-defining than one's role as "friend" or "daughter" if one has established more valued connections with others through that role.

Social identity theory, instead, suggests that people draw selectively upon their membership in different groups to define themselves, and ultimately to achieve identities that are self-enhancing (Tajfel & Turner, 1979). This way, when a given social group becomes "unsatisfactory" or "undesirable" people may seek to leave that group, or to deemphasize their membership to it, in efforts to maintain their positive identity. For example, if one's affiliation with one's family becomes problematic or threatening, one might privilege other self-categorizations, such as "member of a given profession" or religious group.

Taken together, one's identity is hardly static or fixed. Rather, it is a constant "work in progress," subject to active work on the part of individuals (see Lepisto, Crosina, & Pratt, 2015 for a review). Such "work" occurs in relation to the roles and social groups one occupies, and often happens around moments of transition or change, when individuals are primed by the circumstances in their respective contexts to (re)think who they are—such as the case may be when seniors are getting ready to "pass the baton."

Issues of identity are especially relevant, and unique in some ways, in family firms. Unlike other types of organizations, family enterprises encompass multiple, intersecting, personal and work-related identities. Perhaps even more uniquely, these identities are chronologically ordered and interdependent: one's membership and role(s) in the family precede and often imprint one's membership and role(s) in the business. On the one hand, such identities might bolster the process of "passing down," the organization by providing family members psychological, social and material resources. On the other, they might undermine it and create conflict—especially when seniors and juniors' respective aspirations do not align (c.f., Shepherd & Haynie, 2009).

In family businesses, *family* takes center stage, informing what members do, and more profoundly, why they act as they do in the day-to-day. Perhaps even more consequentially, during the process of business transfer, the family generally weighs on the self-defining roles seniors and juniors might (or not) adopt. Primary criteria for role acquisition include trust—developed within the family domain; and relatives' understanding of one another's ambitions, skills and expertise—all influenced by family interactions. As one might imagine, the potential for both role depletion/incongruence and role enrichment is paradoxically high. This potential is magnified when seniors are looking to pass their entrepreneurial legacy to juniors because the "transfer" process itself concerns multiple concurrent role transitions that involve *both* seniors and juniors. For example, not only might a senior be both "mother" and "boss" in the business, but also as seniors work with juniors these two roles might be combined into "partner." As juniors grow into new roles—such as from son or daughter to employee, partner and eventually boss—relationships evolve. Yet, it is difficult for many parents to imagine taking orders from their children (even when their "kids" are in their 40s and 50s!).

With respect to role depletion/incongruence, for example, there might be disagreement in the very claiming and granting dynamics that underpin the acquisition of a new role—how a business role is pursued, and/or how such role is ascribed (DeRue & Ashford, 2010). In addition, one's behavior as a family member might be at odds with how one might be expected to act in one's business role—leading to discrepancies between how one has traditionally acted, and how one is expected to act now. On the brighter side, role enrichment is also a possibility. For instance, by surpassing others' expectations in and around the execution of tasks, juniors and seniors might build renewed trust, respect and create the psychological space to deepen their pre-existing relationship. When individuals are able to create such safe space, they are more likely to be receptive to feedback, remain creative and even become more willing to experiment (Kisfalvi & Oliver, 2015). In this way, relational deepening might lead to greater openness to learning and exploration on the part of both juniors and seniors.

Taken together, family constitutes a critical "pre-existing structure," or a unique basis for the construction of individual members', and more broadly for their family business', identity (Cardador & Pratt, 2006). Family can be as much a foundational asset as a liability, needing ongoing upkeep. When mismanaged, it might even become an identity threat—an impediment for members to be or become who they want to be (Petriglieri, 2011). What can family members do to accommodate the potentially differing ambitions of various generations so that family *does not* become an identity threat, but an *identity workspace*—an environment that promotes and supports individuals' respective goals rather than limiting them (Petriglieri & Petriglieri, 2010)?

Making Family an Identity Workspace

Research suggests that people are likely to invest in an institution (e.g., organization, family and business) when the institution "provides a coherent set of reliable social defenses, sentient communities, and vital rites of passage" (Petriglieri & Petriglieri, 2010, p. 51). Social defenses are collective arrangements—such as a given organizational structure—upon which individuals may rely to cope with uncertainty, anxiety or stress (Jaques, 1955). Sentient communities provide references for "social comparison" and serve as "emotional anchors" in the process of personal learning (Higgins & Kram, 2001, p. 278). Finally, rites of passage are "established ceremonial events that manage major role transitions within a social system." As such, they facilitate self-exploration and experimentation, particularly during transition phases (Trice & Morand, 1989, p. 398).

We propose specific practices around these three dimensions—social defenses, sentient communities and rites of passage—that would likely enable a family to become a laboratory for the dynamic self-definition and fulfillment of its members. Our suggestions center around the recognition that although family members' identity aspirations or "who they want to be" may be held individually, due to the interdependence and close coupling of family and business roles, for such aspirations to be fulfilled, they must fit with the aspirations of others, like the pieces of a puzzle. At a basic level, then, such aspirations need to become clear for individuals themselves, and then shared with other family members. Much of the discussion that follows is about how to create space for sharing, deepening personal and professional relationships within the family, and as a byproduct, make room to explore entrepreneurial opportunities.

Social defenses. To start, for members to rely on the family as a vehicle to appease their uncertainties and placate their stress, it is critical to create structured opportunities for open discussion around one's ambitions, goals and struggles. One of the implicit goals here, then, is to shift the conversation from the well-being of the business to the well-being of individual members—making everyone feel safe in expressing their respective ambitions and issues, as well as heard by others. What might this mean in practice?

To make sharing more comfortable and effective, consistent, frequent and focused interaction is paramount. Drawing from our earlier field research examples, it takes time to develop rapport and build relational closeness to learn what is actually occurring. In family firms, such rapport and relational closeness should not be taken for granted just because of pre-existing blood relationships. To *actually* surface and pay attention to what on the face of it may appear as non-business matters, structured opportunities for sharing need to be institutionalized.

These could take a number of formats, including periodic face-to-face meetings or retreats in which members take turns to share how they feel about what they are doing, what they might want to do, why, as well as any possible impediments they face. We suggest that three basic ground rules should guide these gatherings: make no judgment, take no offense and provide no solutions. Make no judgment and take no offense so that even far afield ideas and feelings may be shared, and relationships may not be compromised in the process. Provide no solutions so that the focus may remain on surfacing issues, rather than on trying to fix them. Following these meetings, participants may (and we advise that they should) follow up individually with others as needed to brainstorm concrete action steps. This way, the information learned about others during these meetings will serve as the backbone of business conversations and decisions, rather than a byproduct of them or only an afterthought.

Sentient communities foster perceptions of belonging among their members, and anchor their learning. Specifically, a sentient community provides the psychological, social and relational resources to ground one's development. In family firms, although both seniors and juniors comprise the "community," seniors are in a critical structural position to help jump start this type of community. One promising way to do so is by making space for juniors, offering them access to the business long before passing it on to them. How might this be accomplished? Back to our field-research example: through *participant* observation.

As the adjective suggests, participant observation implies the active involvement of the observer in the research process. Here, we might imagine juniors not only immersed in shadowing, but also *doing* things—ranging from mundane to sophisticated tasks. The "doing" part of this is critical. By engaging in activities (rather than just watching work being executed) juniors may gain trust, and continue to build rapport with seniors, as well as with others involved in the business. Importantly, juniors will also develop greater understanding for what it takes to accomplish certain jobs, as well as broaden their networks within the family firm. Together, new understandings and relationships will likely promote humility, a critical asset to becoming insiders.

Rites of passage make visible to others decisions and/or developments that might otherwise go unnoticed but to the people who are directly involved, thus symbolizing the importance and value of such events within a given social system. Van Gennep (1960) described three central rites of passage in organizations: rites of separation, transition and incorporation. As Ashforth (2000) noted, rites of separation facilitate role exit; rites of transition help with the journey "in between" roles; and rites of incorporation ease role entry. Here too seniors can play a critical function. In the context of succession, specifically, they can help decide what to, and what not to, make public, as well as how.

Albeit often discounted as "formalities," we encourage members of family firms to consider what they may want to give visibility to through the institution of rites of passage, as these rites are likely to impact the extent to which those involved might (or not) feel validated, especially as they undergo role transitions. For example, "retirement dinners"—whereby seniors may be lauded for their accomplishments and for their legacy—formalize and heighten the importance of the transition to the next generation. In addition, such events signal to members of the family changes in the roles that they will occupy, as well as to non-family members with whom to interact following these new role arrangements.

In this context, the value of "how and what" entrepreneurial families say about their past is critical. An important ritual for some entrepreneurial families has been participation in generating a history of accomplishments, challenges, and the evolution of the family's entrepreneurial successes and failures. Recounting these stories, either through an official written history of the entrepreneurial family or through the telling and re-telling of these stories at family gatherings and/or in public venues, all serve as important touchstones for articulating the family's values and ways of doing things.

Conclusion: Achieving an Entrepreneurial Legacy

In closing, to create an environment in which family members' aspirations for legacy and their need for achievement are both nurtured such that the business, along with the family, might have greater chances of success, *the family needs to become an identity workspace for its members*. Easier said than done. With this chapter, our hope is to have offered family firms fruitful guidance through the articulation of specific practices, grounded in conducting ethnographic research. As this chapter is but a brief introduction to some of the issues our involvement and research with entrepreneurial families has surfaced, we end with highlighting some of the practical insights that one might take away from this reading:

1. The legacy that seniors might want to "give" to the next generation may not be what the next generation wants to "get" to achieve their own goals and aspirations. Constant conversation about values and goals between and among generations is critical for entrepreneurial families.
2. The importance of the tacit knowledge that seniors have accumulated over time should not be under-estimated. The next generation needs to be posi-

tioned to learn this knowledge through participant observation and continual engagement in the family, and in the family's business(es). Much of this knowledge is the real legacy that seniors can gift to the next generation.

3. Entrepreneurial families need to create "space" for supporting the development of an "entrepreneurial family" identity that will be actualized in different ways among various family members. Such a safe space requires a conscious effort to develop "social defenses," "sentient communities" and "rites of passage." Facilitating an "entrepreneurial family" identity takes work.

We end this chapter with one last insight that we would like entrepreneurial families to dwell on as they progress in their journey: families are not their businesses! It is critical for families to realize that the businesses they own and manage, as well as any other resources that are attached to these efforts, are but means to an end, rather than an end in themselves. As we have implied earlier, the primary legacy that seniors can provide to the next generation are their entrepreneurial capabilities and insights. While these entrepreneurial attributes may, in the present, be manifest in specific businesses and activities, they need to be considered as broader resources for future use by the next generation—especially to develop and enhance the next generation's own entrepreneurial achievements. Success that lasts across generations is a matter of identity and skill rather than material endowments.

Coda

And, what happened to the family in the oil-services business? As seniors engaged many of the juniors to observe and participate in all of the facets of their endeavors, as might be expected, some juniors found nothing to like in what their seniors were involved in and left to pursue other opportunities that the family supported and invested in (e.g., a crisis management firm utilizing similar skill sets and capabilities applied in the oil-service business, and a wind turbine maintenance company). And, some juniors saw new opportunities in oil services to generate new businesses (e.g., methane capture) that provided important environmental benefits. While some of the juniors hoped to, at some point, get out of the oil-services business, altogether, they also saw they could achieve some of their goals to better the environment by innovating in the business the family had held for generations.

References

Ashforth, B. E. (2000). *Role Transitions in Organizational Life: An Identity-based Perspective.* Mahwah, NJ: Routledge.

Barbera, F., Stamm, I., & DeWitt, R. L. (2018). The Development of an Entrepreneurial Legacy: Exploring the Role of Anticipated Futures in Transgenerational Entrepreneurship. *Family Business Review, 31*(3), 352–378.

Barley, S. R. (1990). Images of Imaging: Notes on Doing Longitudinal Field Work. *Organization Science, 1*(3), 220–247.

Cardador, M. T., & Pratt, M. G. (2006). Identification Management and Its Bases: Bridging Management and Marketing Perspectives through a Focus on Affiliation Dimensions. *Journal of the Academy of Marketing Science, 34*(2), 174–184.

Crosina, E. (2018). On Becoming an Entrepreneur: Unpacking Entrepreneurial Identity. In P. Greene & C. Brush (Eds.), *Elgar Research Agenda for Women and Entrepreneurship. The Construction of Social Identity: The Case of Women Entrepreneurs* (pp. 93–113). Northampton, MA: Edward Elgar Publishing.

DeRue, D. S., & Ashford, S. J. (2010). Who will Lead and Who will Follow? A Social Process of Leadership Identity Construction in Organizations. *Academy of Management Review, 35*(4), 627–647.

Fauchart, E., & Gruber, M. (2011). Darwinians, Communitarians, and Missionaries: The Role of Founder Identity in Entrepreneurship. *Academy of Management Journal, 54*(5), 935–957.

Geertz, C. (2008). *Local Knowledge: Further Essays in Interpretive Anthropology* (3rd ed.). Basic Books.

Higgins, M. C., & Kram, K. E. (2001). Reconceptualizing Mentoring at Work: A Developmental Network Perspective. *Academy of Management Review, 26*(2), 264–288.

Jaques, E. (1955). Social Systems as a Defence Against Persecutory and Depressive Anxiety. In M. Klein (Ed.), *New Directions in Psychoanalysis* (pp. 478–498). London, UK: Tavistock.

Jaskiewicz, P., Combs, J. G., & Rau, S. B. (2015). Entrepreneurial Legacy: Toward a Theory of How Some Family Firms Nurture Transgenerational Entrepreneurship. *Journal of Business Venturing, 30*(1), 29–49.

Kisfalvi, V., & Oliver, D. (2015). Creating and Maintaining a Safe Space in Experiential Learning. *Journal of Management Education, 39*(6), 713–740.

Lepisto, D. A., Crosina, E., & Pratt, M. G. (2015). Identity Work within and beyond the Professions: Toward a Theoretical Integration and Extension. In A. Desilva & M. Aparicio (Eds.), *International Handbook about Professional Identities* (pp. 11–37). Rosemead, CA: Scientific and Academic Publishing.

Nash, L., & Stevenson, H. (2004). *Just Enough: Tools for Creating Success in Your Work and Life.* John Wiley & Sons.

Navis, C., & Glynn, M. A. (2011). Legitimate Distinctiveness and the Entrepreneurial Identity: Influence on Investor Judgments of New Venture Plausibility. *Academy of Management Review, 36*(3), 479–499.

Petriglieri, J. L. (2011). Under threat: Responses to and the consequences of threats to individuals' identities. *Academy of Management Review, 36*(4), 641–662.

Petriglieri, G., & Petriglieri, J. L. (2010). Identity Workspaces: The Case of Business Schools. *Academy of Management Learning & Education, 9*(1), 44–60.

Powell, E. E., & Baker, T. (2014). It's What You Make of It: Founder Identity and Enacting Strategic Responses to Adversity. *Academy of Management Journal, 57*(5), 1406–1433.

Shepherd, D., & Haynie, J. M. (2009). Family Business, Identity Conflict, and an Expedited Entrepreneurial Process: A Process of Resolving Identity Conflict. *Entrepreneurship Theory and Practice, 33*(6), 1245–1264.

Spradley, J. (1980). *Participant Observation*. Belmont, CA: Wadsworth Cengage Learning.

Stryker, S. (1980). *Symbolic Interactionism: A Social Structural Version*. Menlo Park, CA: Benjamin/Cummings Publishing Company.

Stryker, S., & Serpe, R. T. (1982). Commitment, Identity Salience, and Role Behavior: Theory and Research Example. In W. Ickes & E. S. Knowles (Eds.), *Personality, Roles, and Social Behavior* (pp. 199–218). New York, NY: Springer-Verlag.

Tajfel, H., & Turner, J. C. (1979). An Integrative Theory of Intergroup Conflict. In W. G. Austin & S. Worchel (Eds.), *The Social Psychology of Group Relations* (pp. 33–47). Monterey, CA: Brooks-Cole.

Tremblay, M. A. (1957). The Key Informant Technique: A Nonethnographic Application. *American Anthropologist, 59*(4), 688–701.

Trice, H. M., & Morand, D. A. (1989). Rites of Passage in Work Careers. In M. B. Arthur, D. T. Hall, & B. S. Lawrence (Eds.), *Handbook of Career Theory* (pp. 397–416). Cambridge, UK: Cambridge University Press.

Van Gennep, A. (1960). *The Rites of Passage*. Chicago, IL: The University of Chicago Press. (Originally published 1905).

Von Krogh, G., Ichijo, K., & Nonaka, I. (2000). *Enabling Knowledge Creation: How to Unlock the Mystery of Tacit Knowledge and Release the Power of Innovation*. Oxford University Press.

Weick, K. E. (1995). *Sensemaking in Organizations*. Thousand Oaks, CA: Sage.

Wenger, E. (1998). *Communities of Practice: Learning, Meaning, and Identity*. Cambridge University Press.

Whyte, W. F. (1984). *Learning from the Field*. Beverly Hills, CA: Sage.

5

Discerning the Importance and Nature of the Family System in Relation to the Family Firm: A Paradigm Shift

Ramona Kay Zachary

Introduction

Pervasively throughout history and our world, the family has been recognized as a social unit that serves as the building block of societies (Ponzetti, 2003). Families emerged from dyads of individuals that form organically for reasons of procreation, protection, and production, among other purposes (Ponzetti, 2003). Multiple or groups of families logically progress to organized communities of families, leading in turn, to commerce and trade within and among various communities and families, near and far (Hareven, 1982). Thus, families sequentially preceded communities and communities fostered commerce. Ponzetti (2003) notes that families in concert with their local communities often sustain themselves by self-sufficient means. Given inherent entrepreneurial behaviors and activities, scholars recognize such an enterprise as the family firm!

This chapter builds upon earlier work in Zachary, R. (2011). "The Importance of the Family System in Family Business." *Journal of Family Business Management*, 1(1), 26–36.
This book chapter is dedicated to my brother Melvin Archie Zachary.

R. K. Zachary (✉)
The City University of New York, Baruch College, New York, NY, USA
e-mail: Ramona.Zachary@baruch.cuny.edu

Today, family firms, including both publicly and privately held, are the most prevalent firm/business formation throughout the world (Morck & Yeung, 2004). Family firms make up a majority in the economies of most countries. Most importantly, family firms in less-developed countries often provide a vital role by assuming risk of emerging markets and economies (Aguilera & Crespi-Cladera, 2012; Goel, Mazzol, Phan, Pieper, & Zachary, 2012).

Defining the Family Firm

To date, family firm definitions (e.g., Pearson, Carr, & Shaw, 2008) make limited use of the notion of family entrepreneurship. However, some definitions encompass both family businesses and business families. Gartner (1985, 1990, 2001) has repeatedly challenged entrepreneurship and family firm scholars to establish clear definitional boundaries and modeling assumptions as well as offer sufficient detail to ensure clarity of the research purpose.

Most family firm definitions include considerations of (1) family ownership, (2) family control and/or management, (3) family involvement, and/or (4) the intention to transfer the family firm to the next generation (Eddleston, Kerrermanns, Barnett, & Pearson, 2008; Heck & Trent, 1999; Rutherford, Kuratko, & Holt, 2008). Definitions range from very narrow and limited, such as limiting family firms to those with at least two generations involved in the business, while others are inclusive of any business owned by one or more family members (Winter, Fitzgerald, Heck, Haynes, & Danes, 1998). Litz (1995) identified family businesses conceptually based on ownership, management, and intention to transfer. In comparison, Handler (1992) identified four ways in which scholars usually define family business: (1) degree of ownership and/or management by family members, (2) degree of family involvement, (3) potential for generational transfer, or (4) multiple criteria.

Simply put, the family's presence—meaning the family system-juxtaposed to the business—meaning the business system—is often the manifestation of the internal dynamics of the family system, in and of itself. Some scholars have recognized the notion of "familiness" of a family firm (Eddleston et al., 2008). Habbershon and Williams (1999) and others that followed have attempted to identify the influence of the family on and in the business by delineating ways in which the family's factors were present within the business. Pearson et al. (2008) and Rutherford et al. (2008) have explored this concept of "familiness" further. Nonetheless, scholars generally still only recognize the presence of family members in the business. *These same scholars, among others, have not fully recognized or explored the importance, nature, and dynamics of the family system itself relative to the business or entrepreneurial activity.*

Winter et al. (1998) defined a "family business" as a business owned and managed by one or more family members. These same researchers used the concept of a *family household* which was defined as a group of people related by blood, marriage, or adoption, who shared a common dwelling unit and participated in the ownership of a business. For the nationally representative 1997/2000/2007 National Family Business Panels (NFBPs), a minimum of a one-year work intensity requirement for the owner-manager was also imposed. Specifically, the owner needed to work at least 6 hours per week, year-round or a minimum of 312 hours annually in the business (Heck & Trent, 1999). Family firms can include startups or any stage of maturity and with ownership by any generation and any combination of family members. Further, family firms can be publicly or privately owned of any size or scale.

Although the business enterprise is vital to the long-run sustainability of the family firm, the *family is of equal importance to the same* (Danes, Lee, Stafford, & Heck, 2008; Stafford, Duncan, Danes, & Winter, 1999; Zachary, 2011). The family can facilitate and create the forces enabling both emerging and sustained entrepreneurial behavior. Beyond entrepreneurial aspects, the family firm also encompasses a myriad of inimitable behaviors and activities, such as (1) family spirit, (2) shared values, (3) trusting and cooperative relationships and work contributions among family members, (4) conjoint visions and strategic planning, and (5) succession planning. In addition to these unique traits, there may be hidden and embedded *family firm secrets* that may enable both positive and negative outcomes (Jaffe, 2014).

Purpose and Objectives

This chapter details the conceptual nature and dynamics of the *family system* by recognizing its importance to the family firm. Overviews of Sustainable Family Business Theory (SFBT) (Danes et al., 2008; Danes & Brewton, 2012) and the Entrepreneurial Value Creation Theory (EVCT) (Mishra & Zachary, 2014) are also presented. Further, the conceptual nexuses between family and entrepreneurial firms are explored. This chapter presents the conceptual premise and empirical research that the long-run sustainability of the family firm depends upon the equal importance of both the family system and the business system. Both systems are vital to the family firm and must be recognized, examined, analyzed, and developed with equal vigor. To do otherwise is a myopic and bias approach or paradigm.

From this conceptual base and known research to date, the *family firm's secrets* are explored by delineating and examining the prevailing myths of the family firm along with the apparent and counter dilemmas of such misconceptions. By identifying the nexuses between family firms and entrepreneurship, 13 exemplars of secrets or hidden truths are identified for consideration.

Finally, this chapter explores the *challenge of a paradigm shift* and its implications for researchers, educators, and practitioners as well as family business owners and their families. Family business owners/leaders must recognize that two equal systems are involved in the family firm and each system must be nurtured and supported to achieve long-run sustainability. The recognition and development of both the family system and the business system yield functional, effective, and sustainable family firms as well as the same for the owning families. All researchers, educators, practitioners, owners, and family members are offered the challenge to make a paradigm shift to highlight and enhance both the family system and business system as well as their dynamic interactions.

The Importance of the Family System in Relation to the Family Firm

Many scholars have mistakenly assumed that the study of *only* the family business as an entity is sufficient to understand the influence and effect of the family and the understanding of the family system itself. However, the family firm is most often the manifestation of the associated family system. To fully understand the family business, one must examine the family system separately and in conjunction with the business system. *The role of the family system in relation to the family business and entrepreneurial activities is paramount and closely related to outcomes such as business success and quality of family life* (Heck, 1998a, 1998b; Heck, Hoy, Poutziouris, & Steier, 2008; Zachary, 2011).

The family system operates with its own dynamics and is an important and fundamental entity for creating and sustaining behaviors that scholars generally describe as entrepreneurial behaviors or experiences (Cramton, 1993; Danes et al., 2008; Danes, Matzek, & Werbel, 2010; Rogoff & Heck, 2003; Stafford et al., 1999; Zachary, 2011). For example, family capital, the total resources of owning family members, enables and fosters short-term family business success and long-term sustainability (Danes, Stafford, Haynes, & Amarapurkar, 2009).

Relative to history and nations, businesses and families have existed, to a large extent, in conjunction with each other (Heck, Owen, & Rowe, 1995; Kepner, 1983; Morck & Yeung, 2004; Rogoff & Heck, 2003). Among other motivators, lifestyle and wealth accumulation goals play an important role in whether a particular family member or members choose to start a business. The economic necessity of earning a living and supporting a family is often the underlying motivation for starting and growing a business (Winter et al., 1998). Simultaneously, the business supplies income to the family and the family may supply paid and unpaid labor, as well as contribute additional resources such as money, space, equipment, and other factors of production to the business (Danes et al., 2009). Other scholars (such as Rogoff & Heck, 2003) noted that "the growing body of research points to the fundamental guiding principle that the combustion of entrepreneurship cannot ignite and grow without the mobilization of family forces" (p. 560).

Olson et al. (2003) provided the first conceptual and empirical evidence of the separate but interdependent natures of the family system and the business system. These scholars empirically showed that both business outcomes and family outcomes are determined simultaneously by factors from and within *both* the family and business systems. Later in a separate study (Danes et al., 2009), the contribution of family capital to family firms in the short term, all types of family capital explained 13.5% of variance in gross revenue and 4% of variance in owner's perception of success. Over time, all types of family capital explained 26.7% of variance in gross revenue and 11.6% of variance in owner's perception of success. In a longitudinal study of spousal capital as a resource for couples starting a business, Matzek, Gudmunson, and Danes (2010) and Danes et al. (2010) found that spousal capital affects both the business sustainability of a new venture and the couple's relationship quality. Cardon, Wincent, Singh, and Drnovsek (2009); Cardon, Gregoire, Stevens, and Patel (2013) have linked passion and entrepreneurial sustainability.

Conceptual Frameworks of the Family Firm

Through evolving development, the family system has become the *crux* of family firm as well as vital to the current state of conceptualization and theory building. Understanding the role of the family system is critical to the understanding of how entrepreneurial or family firms emerge and sustain themselves via interactions with environmental contexts both near and far.

Conceptually, after years of studies centered on the entrepreneur as an individual, scholars have begun reexamining the entrepreneur through a wider lens. Scholars have conceded that focusing only on the entrepreneur provides an incomplete picture of the entrepreneurial phenomenon (Zachary & Mishra, 2010, 2011; Mishra & Zachary, 2014). Researchers can no longer ignore a broader and more comprehensive view of entrepreneurial activity, namely, the role played by the family system (Bowen, 1985; Cramton, 1993; Danes et al., 2008; Danes et al., 2009; Rosenblatt, Mik, Anderson, & Johnson, 1985).

Several conceptualizations and theories are applicable to the notion of the *family firm or family entrepreneurship*, as follows.

(a) Sustainable Family Business Theory Model (SFBT Model) (Danes et al., 2008; Danes & Brewton, 2012; Heck et al., 2006; Stafford et al., 1999);
(b) Family Embeddedness Perspective (FEP) (Aldrich & Cliff, 2003);
(c) Bullseye model of an open-system approach (Pieper & Klein, 2007);
(d) Family Influence, F-PEC Scale (Klein, Astrachan, & Smyrnios, 2002; Rutherford et al., 2008);
(e) Resource-Based Framework (Habbershon & Williams, 1999); and
(f) The Unified Systems Perspective of Family Firm Performance (USP) (Habbershon, Williams, & MacMillan, 2003); and
(g) Theory of Agency and Altruism in Family Firms (TAA) (Schulze, Lubatkin, & Dino, 2003).

Only two of these recent frameworks have integrated a multi-perspective with internal system detail. These include the SFBT (Danes et al., 2008; Danes & Brewton, 2012; Heck et al., 2006; Stafford et al., 1999) and the FEP (Aldrich & Cliff, 2003). Only these two frameworks have specified the family system in relation to the business system, although each has conceptualized these systems and their relationship to each other differently.

The Bullseye model of an open-system approach (Pieper & Klein, 2007), the F-PEC scale (Klein et al., 2002), and the notion of familiness (Habbershon et al., 2003; Habbershon & Williams, 1999; Rutherford et al., 2008) only model family firm level concepts and associated measures. As a result, these frameworks do not identify or recognize that the family system in and of itself, is separate from, yet inextricably intertwined with the business system. These models examine family constructs as manifested within the business only, and do not address the family system as a separate, whole, and unique system relative to the business. Finally, discipline-based frameworks such as TAA attracted significant attention because of their ability to allow a specific representation of economic concepts and theories. At the same time, they also are less comprehensive in scope (Schulze et al., 2003) and Greenwood (2003) has argued that economics as a singular framework may not be sufficient.

The increasing number of frameworks allows researchers varied approaches based on the scope and depth of the research questions and foci under study. At the same time, researchers must acknowledge the advantages and disadvantages of the framework choice. Research that recognizes both the family system and the business system will offer the most comprehensive examination and are the most likely to increase our future understandings of the family firm and family entrepreneurship (Danes et al., 2008; Dimov 2007; Jennings & McDougald, 2007; Heck et al., 2006; Rogoff & Heck, 2003).

The Sustainable Family Business Theory

The Sustainable Family Business Theory (SFBT) posits that the owning family (i.e., business families) combines and generates the resources and conditions that enable entrepreneurial behavior that emerges and is sustained over time. Yet the family system reveals its own unique dynamics as well as nurtures behaviors and experiences that are entrepreneurial in nature (Danes et al., 2008; Danes & Brewton, 2012; Stafford et al., 1999; Zachary, 2011; Zachary, Danes, & Stafford, 2013).

The SFBT represents "...a dynamic, behaviorally based, multidimensional family theory of the firm that accommodates the detail and complexities [sic, within each system as well as their overlap] and provides a useful framework for the analysis of key concepts related to family firm" (Danes et al., 2008). Both conceptual and operational considerations of the SFBT (Danes et al., 2008; Stafford et al., 1999) allow examination of vital contributions made by the family system in relation to a family business. A comprehensive and flexible theory such as the SFBT enhances our understanding of the dynamic role of the family in the family firm as well as demonstrates the integration of family, business, and community. Astrachan (2003) has commented that the SFBT both conceptually and empirically "...exemplifies what is at the heart of the family business field: the study of the reciprocal impact of family on business" (p. 570).

The Sustainable Family Business Theory Constructs

Families and businesses contribute _resources_ to the entrepreneurial endeavors of family members in the form of social capital, human capital, and assets including both financial and physical capital. Social capital includes the inter-relations between and among family members. For example, trust is a specific aspect that is crucial to entrepreneurial activity. Family firms have an advantage over non-family firms due to the enhanced possibility of trust among family members. Human capital includes the human attributes of the individuals in the family such as personal time and energy, as well as emotional support. The concepts of financial and physical capital include money, credit, and financial investments of all kinds, as well as land, real estate, and equipment (Danes et al., 2008; Danes & Brewton, 2012; Zachary, 2011).

Numerous _constraints_ impose limits on entrepreneurial activity for the families and the businesses. An array of social, cultural, legal, economic, and technical constraints may exist for both the family system and the business system. Socio-cultural constraints relate to the norms and mores of the community and the social sanctions related to the violation of these norms. Legal constraints are derived from laws and regulations levied by political entities. Economic constraints are limitations resulting from finite resources. Technical constraints are enforced by the natural laws of biology, chemistry, and physics that affect processes (Danes et al., 2008; Danes & Brewton, 2012).

The resources and constraints created by the family and the business are facilitated by _family structure_ as well as _business structure_. Family structure includes the roles and rules of the family system. Owning families may need additional family structure, for example, a family council may handle or manage family matters relative to the family firm. Such family structures help to reveal perspective roles of various family members as well as the management family resources and any adjustments of constraints. Ownership and governance are generally regarded as the major business structures to be considered (Danes et al., 2008; Danes & Brewton, 2012; Zachary, 2011).

Both families and businesses experience _disruptions_. Normative disruptions are those, for example, that may occur when major family events occur such as birth or death. Non-normative disruptions are those that are unpredictable and unusual. For example, a natural disaster cause closures of family firms (Danes et al., 2008; Danes & Brewton, 2012).

Both families and businesses engage in _processes_, processes within the family system and the family firm that represent forms of social capital and operate during times of stability. Such processes are identified routines, or standard operating procedures. Processes in settings of change occur in the overlap of the family system and the business system and reconciliations are manifested (Danes et al., 2008; Danes & Brewton, 2012).

In sum, _resources_ and _constraints_ along with _disruptions_ are facilitated by _processes_ and result in families and businesses _achievements_ which are evaluated in multidimensional ways, where subjective indicators such as family and business trust, satisfaction in the family and in the business, and the achievements of goals in both systems are as important as financial success (Stafford et al., 1999). In addition, the family firm connects with its community and the community affects both the family system and business system. Both short-term family business viability and long-term family business sustainability continue over time as modeled by the SFBT and its inherent dynamic nature (Danes et al., 2008; Danes & Brewton, 2012; Zachary, 2011).

The SFBT Sustainable Family Business Theory Assumptions

Uniquely, the SFBT is derived from *eight assumptions* about the relationship between the family system and the business system. First, the two systems stand on their own merit and are distinct from each other. Research documents studies of families and business having equal merit. However, these disciplines have developed, for the most part, distinct from each other. Family firm scholars are challenged to look beyond their usual singular disciplines and work in tandem with scholars in other disciplines (Heck et al., 2008; Litz, 1995; Zachary, 2011).

Second, each system may exist and operate independent of each other. In other words, families exist without business ownership and businesses can start and operate independently of families. However, in case of the family firm, these same two systems overlap. The SFBT is unique in its assumption that the family system is *equal* to the business system in importance and vice versa. A family that dissolves is not less important than a business that shutters its doors. Within the SFBT, each system is represented in detail; namely, the family system has internal dynamics and details, as does the business system and the interface between the family system and the business system.

Third, both the family system and the business system are social systems driven with purposefulness and rationality. Neither system has a monopoly on any specific purpose. The family system deals with emotions of family members while the business system faces the emotional state of its employees. Both systems are capable of reason and rational thoughts and processes in dealing with their respective concerns. For example, the family system and its members can balance their household expenditures as well as the business system can manage its own financial functioning via a CFO leader.

Fourth, both equal systems utilize an array of available resources and each system faces specific constraints. Fifth, in a family firm both systems operate simultaneously. Both the family system and business system are dynamic in nature by transforming available resources and conforming to their respective constraints. Their respective interpersonal and resource transactions result in achievements, such as happy family members within the family system as well as higher net profits within the business system.

Sixth, both systems strive for achievements representing objective and subjective outcomes. Objectively, families achieve financial wealth as well as non-financial wealth in the form of real estate and land. Subjectively, families succeed in creating family harmony and other forms of family social capital such as satisfying family relationships relative to spousal support, nurturing parental relationships, and/or supportive sibling relationships (Danes et al., 2009). Likewise, businesses produce objective outcomes such as goods and services, healthy net profits, or other forms of growth such as well-trained and engaged employees. Examples of subjective achievements of the business system include satisfied employees and functioning and cooperative work teams.

Seventh, both the family system and the business systems are impacted by environmental changes ranging from healthy or declining communities, to the availability of financial services, to the effects of climate change in the form of natural disasters.

Eighth, the SFBT delineates the interface or overlap between the family system and the business system. Events in either or both systems must be reconciled in relationship to each respective system. For example, family events such as marriages, births, or deaths may occur within the family system but also affect the business system relative to the availability of family workers or leaders. Likewise, business events such as bankruptcy or continued growth will impact the owning family. The SFBT interface or overlap represents the interactions and reconciliations between the two systems.

In sum, the SFBT is unique among the family firm theories that have emerged to date and its assumptions are as follows:

1. Two dimensions: family system and business system.
2. Family is _equal_ to business in detail and importance.
3. Both family and business are social systems which are purposeful and rational.
4. Both family and business take available resources and constraints.
5. Both family and business transform available resources and constraints via interpersonal and resource transactions into achievements.
6. Achievements are both objective and subjective.
7. Both family and business are affected by environmental change, structural change, or both.
8. Overlap varies as well as divergence of goals and achievements.

The SFBT provides clarity in the study of the family firm and assures a comprehensive view of such a business setting. To do otherwise is to fall short in our understanding of the family firm with theoretical and empirical models that are under- or mis-specified, resulting in biased results that lead to misconceptions of the realities of the family firm.

Entrepreneurial Value Creation Theory in Relation to the Family Firms

The Entrepreneurial Value Creation Theory (EVCT) is a unification of existing, disparate segments of the entrepreneurial process into a broad, comprehensive theory with sufficient detail to research the interiors of the entrepreneurial process. Such an approach requires a broad and comprehensive view with a multidisciplinary complexity. Myopic thinking or single-disciplinary views are no longer acceptable and multiple and functional disciplines must be employed, such as economics, finance, decision sciences, sociology, psychology, management, among others (Mishra & Zachary, 2014).

The EVCT delineates a two-stage value creation and appropriation framework consisting of venture formulation and venture monetization, accordingly. External forces of either entrepreneurial intention or opportunity set in motion Stage 1—Formulation. Starting with either instigating force, the entrepreneur internalizes an opportunity with their available resources to create the critical element of entrepreneurial competence. Internally, within this nascent stage, the entrepreneur iterates this formulation process via the feasibility comparator and the effectuation multiplier. Few entrepreneurs survive this stage and others take years to achieve their entrepreneurial competence needed to move forward to venture monetization (Mishra & Zachary, 2014).

The entrepreneurial competence that is developed in Stage 1—Formulation—propels the entrepreneur into Stage 2—Monetization. During monetization, investors face an adverse selection when the entrepreneurial ability is uncertain and the venture quality is difficult to assess. Entrepreneurs signal their high ability and the quality of the venture by using incentive signals such as the entrepreneurial competence and the amount of personal financial investment (Mishra & Zachary, 2014).

This second stage reconfigures entrepreneurial competence to generate entrepreneurial reward and sustainable value. Entrepreneurial competence is reconfigured and appropriated using a business model design that embeds isolating mechanisms and dynamic capabilities. The Business Model Theory captures the interior processes of Stage 2—Monetization (Mishra & Zachary, 2014).

The challenge for researchers is to expand and recast their theoretical approaches and to reexamine their empirical tools to encompass the overall entrepreneurship process and interior sub-processes by using the unified and integrative EVCT (Mishra & Zachary, 2014).

The Unique Nature and Dynamics of the Family Firm

With the best of intentions, early family firm research was dominated with field observations of consultants working with corporate firms with family members in tow at board meetings and other official company events (Donnelley, 1964). Other scholars agreed that something had been overlooked and understudied: the internal dynamics of the family firm and often involving family members in and out of the family firm participating (Cramton, 1993; Dyer & Handler, 1994). Cramton (1993) suggested that there was a "public" presentation of the family firm devoid of any emphasis on family members. However, the "private" dimensions of this same firm revealed, in sharp contrast, a business with family members involved at many levels and in some cases, unpaid supportive workers (Heck & Trent, 1999; Heck & Walker, 1993; Winter et al., 1998). Today, family firm research is still often plagued with insufficient data and inferior empirical rigor which results in noncomprehensive views of the family and business systems.

After the 1997 National Family Business Survey (1997 NFBS) (Stafford et al., 1999; Winter et al., 1998; Winter, Danes, Koh, Fredericks, & Paul, 2004) and the conceptualization and use of the SFBT, scholars finally were able to properly specify the internal dynamics of the family firm in detail (Olson et al., 2003). This allowed researchers to study simultaneously families and businesses (Olson et al., 2003; Trent & Astrachan, 1999).

Prevailing Family Firm Myths

Unfounded myths have emerged and still persist among family firm scholars. These myths stem from the lack of understanding about the existence of the two distinct systems within the family firm. In turn, this misrepresentation about the importance of the family system causes some researchers to ignore the existence of the family system entirely.

Some of the common myths unsubstantiated by prior research findings are as follows:

1. The family system and the business system are two "naturally separate" entities.
2. The "best" recommended strategy for successful coexistence of these two systems suggested by both business management consultants and family therapists is to maintain separate and definitive boundaries between the two systems.
3. The business is *only* results-oriented, basing decisions on output and profits.
4. The family is *only* emotion-oriented and irrational while motivated by biological demands and social norms.
5. One extreme view chosen by some researchers suggests that it is only one system; namely the family firm.

Rigorous research has debunked these myths by providing the correct specification of the two major systems with a family firm; namely, the family system and the business system. With the advent of correct model specifications and detailed and high-quality data, the fundamental approach to family firm research must involve theoretical constructs and empirical measures in both systems. For example, Haynes, Walker, Rowe, and Hong (1999) have shown that the family firm is riddled with intermingling of financial and nonfinancial resources. The nonsensical notion that families and business are segregated relative to their respective functions of emotional intelligence or rationality also does not reflect the realities of the family firm (Danes et al., 2009). Researchers have found families rich in family capital of all kinds ranging from decision-making and strategic management to vital social and human capital resources. The family contributions have a powerful effect on the sustainability of both the family itself and the business over time (Danes et al., 2009; Olson et al., 2003). Businesses often necessitate emotional intelligence, particularly in the family firm setting where family members are needed in the business and work together within and among generations. Finally, mounting empirical evidence shows that a one-system family firm unfounded (Danes et al., 2008; Rogoff & Heck, 2003; Stafford et al., 1999; Zachary, 2011).

The Dilemmas of the Prevailing Family Firm Myths

As counterevidence presents dilemmas for the prevailing myths, the following overarching research findings are now known. First, the oversimplification of dynamics within and between the family and business systems had hidden much intermingling and human and material resources between the family and business (Haynes et al., 1999). Research also shows that aspects of the family affect the revenues of the business, for example, household management practices (Winter, Puspitawati, Heck, & Stafford, 1993) and the types and numbers of family employees and unpaid workers (Heck & Walker, 1993). Further, research shows that family conflict may pose an "internal threat" to the business; namely, within the framework of SWOT Analysis of the family firm (Danes, Zuiker, Kean, & Arbuthnot, 1999). Clinical case studies document that business issues may invade the family dynamics as well as family issues may overrun the business (e.g., Steinberg Case).

Exemplar Nexuses Between Family and Entrepreneurial Firms

SFBT (Danes et al., 2008) and the EVCT (Mishra & Zachary, 2014) provide unique opportunities to examine simultaneously the family system and the business system as well as explore the connections or nexuses between the family firm and the entrepreneurial firm. How are these types of firms similar or different? From a different perspective, what are the connections between entrepreneurship and family entrepreneurship?

To date, research has produced evidence of many nexuses or connections between the family firm and the entrepreneurial firm. Some possible nexuses are:

1. Family firms often emerge from entrepreneurial, innovative ideas (e.g., Danes et al., 2008).
2. Family firms must regenerate from generation to generation by utilizing entrepreneurial behaviors (e.g., Mishra & Zachary, 2014).
3. Emerging evidence that social norms are more important than economic norms; namely, family relationships are valued over money (e.g., Michael-Tsabari, Labaki, Aydinliyim, & Zachary, 2020).
4. Entrepreneurship often emerges from human environments such as friends, families, or social networks (e.g., Danes et al., 2008; Mishra & Zachary, 2014).

5. Spousal emotional support has been found to be a primary factor in entrepreneurial entries and longevity (e.g., Danes et al., 2010; Matzek et al., 2010).
6. Entrepreneurial growth is often necessitated by family growth (e.g., Heck & Walker, 1993; Michael-Tsabari, Labaki, & Zachary, 2014).
7. Both family and entrepreneurial firms are nestled in near environments (e.g., Danes et al., 2008; Mishra & Zachary, 2014).

The interconnections between family and entrepreneurial firms await further exploration and investigation (Upton & Heck, 1997; Zachary & Mishra, 2008, 2010).

The Secrets or Hidden Truths of the Family Firm

Derived from commonly used definitions and known prevalence, the SFBT offers the capacity to study the family firm from the most comprehensive view. As a result, the internal dynamics of both systems can be explored and analyzed. If aspects of both systems are explored equally, the potential findings within each system are expanded greatly as well as the interrelationships between the two systems can be explored.

See Table 5.1 for 13 major examples of secrets or hidden truths of the family firm. Note that at both the macro and micro levels, both positive and negative outcomes can result from these secrets. Each family firm secret delineated in Table 5.1 can be explored relative to the supportive research listed in the table footnote.

As one example at the macro level, the SFBT allows careful delineation of prevalence based on various definitions of a family firm, while also invoking the realities of both the family and the business systems. Thus, the prevalence of these family firms and their respective definitional differences can be explored with nationally representative sampling frame (see Table 5.1) (Heck & Trent, 1999; Winter et al., 1998).

Also at the macro level in developing countries with few or no institutional structures, family firms may assume the risk of business startups and continuing firms. Without such, many emerging market/economies and countries as well as economic areas within countries would not exist. Practitioners and family owners need to identify and recognize their contributions, in particular their assumption of risk, in their markets/economies. Although businesses may strengthen the emerging market/economies, it may also lead to a concentration of wealth and power within a specific country or area.

Table 5.1 Secrets or hidden truths of the family firm with emphases on macro and micro perspectives

Secrets or hidden truths	Exemplar positive outcomes	Exemplar negative outcomes	Suggested advice for practice
Macro perspectives			
1. Most prevalent business structure worldwide[a]	Ease of startup; locational proximity of family and business	Lack of diversity or it hinders flexible business structures	Recognize and value worldwide prevalence impact of family firms
2. Majority in most countries' economies/societies[b]	Natural and logical in most economic and social settings	May result in a concentration of wealth and low social indicators	Identify the majority segment of family firms in countries of interest
3. Vital role in assuming risk of emerging markets/economies in developing countries[c]	Allows markets and economies to flourish in countries without well-developed institutions	May result in a concentration of economic and political power	Calculate contributions of revenues, jobs, and assumption of risk within emerging markets/economies
Micro perspectives			
4. Unique family system[d]	Increases available and valuable resources	Imbalance and overlap between two systems: family and business	Identify and examine family system, its important role in family business
5. Involvement of family[e]	Family spirit and family trust	Family power may limit family involvement	Investigate involvement of family members by levels and types
6. Size/scale[f]	Family growth often parallels/generates business growth	Retrenchment or stymied growth	Identify relationship/impact between family growth and firm growth
7. Private/public[g]	Family controls their wealth	Succession issues and presence of non-family owners	Examine ownership levels, control by family members, outsiders
8. Two systems' overlap[h]	Manages change in both systems	Often not recognized	Explore internal dynamics of both family and firm as well as overlap

(continued)

Table 5.1 (continued)

Secrets or hidden truths	Exemplar positive outcomes	Exemplar negative outcomes	Suggested advice for practice
9. Systems' boundaries[i]	Emphases on family and business systems	Sometimes blurred boundaries or unrecognized	Identify effective protocol/boundaries of both family, business, and overlap
10. Emotional intelligence versus rationality[j]	Both systems address emotional and rationality	Singular purpose to the exclusion of both: family and business	Emphasize emotional intelligence within, between family and business
11. Intermingling and complex internal dynamics[k]	Effectiveness of decision-making	Difficulty of balancing both systems	Explore mixing of goals and activities between family and business
12. Harmony versus conflict[l]	Related to greater achievements	Management and communication issues	Identify conflicts and resolutions within and between family and business
13. Clinical evidence[m]	Case studies of achievements	Dissatisfaction or resentments	Identify achievements and resolve resentments within and between family and business

Citations per perspective: [a]Heck and Trent (1999), Morck and Yeung (2004), Winter et al. (1998); [b]Morck and Yeung (2004), Hareven (1982); [c]Aguilera and Crespi-Cladera (2012), Goel et al. (2012); [d]Danes et al. (2008), Stafford et al. (1999); [e]Danes et al. (2009), Heck and Walker (1993), Zachary (2011); [f]Mishra and Zachary (2014), Michael-Tsabari et al. (2014); [g]Anderson and Reeb (2003), Cramton (1993); [h]Danes et al. (2008), Stafford et al. (1999); [i]Danes et al. (2008), Stafford et al. (1999), Zachary (2011); [j]Danes et al. (2008), Labaki et al. (2013), Stafford et al. (1999), Winter et al. (1993); [k]Haynes et al. (1999); [l]Danes et al. (1999), Kaye (1991), Zachary (2015); [m]McGoldrick, Gerson, and Petry (2008)

A micro-level example occurs if the composition, age, and gender of family members are delineated within the family system and the business system. As a result, the researcher can begin to account for family members in and out of the family firm (Danes et al., 2009; Heck & Walker, 1993) and the effects on the business as well as the family. In addition, at the micro level, family firms often develop organically relative to the knowledge, skills, and experiences of family members. Once established, family firm growth may be naturally tied to the growth within the family. Another important example is reflected in the modeling of the detailed internal dynamics in the SFBT, which allows the assignment of emotional intelligence versus rationality within both the family system and the business. The emotions of family firms were significant elements in both systems (Heck & Trent, 1999; Labaki, Michael-Tsabari, & Zachary, 2013; Winter et al., 1998).

The Challenge of a Paradigm Shift

The *challenge of a paradigm shift* lies at the crux of moving the family firm field of study forward. We must recognize and understand the secrets of the family firm both for the family system and the business system. As a field of study, family firm scholars, educators, practitioners, the families, and family business owners, must shift their usual lens to encompass the comprehensive view of the family firm; meaning, the recognition of both the family system and the business system as well as their overlap and their hidden secrets throughout!

Without the recognition of the importance of the family system, we garner only a partial and incomplete view of the family firm. In fact, some effects or factors attributed to the business system may be fundamentally tied to the family system itself. Salient variables need to be identified and studied relative to the family system. For example, family business growth may be equally attributable to growth in the outputs of the business and to the growth in the number of family members supported by the business.

Implications for Researchers

Relative to both the family system and the business system, researchers must conceptualize and theorize comprehensively as well as choose appropriate sampling frame, conduct empirical surveys, qualitative data collection, and utilize appropriate empirical procedures and analyses. If data are not available for the family system, researchers must be diligent in utilizing ethnographic case studies or mixed methods and always represent or specify the family system as well as the business system. Possible bias or limitations must be examined diligently relative to research findings and their applications. This broader and detailed view must be implemented throughout our research process including conceptualizations/theories, sampling frames, measurements, analytics, interpretations, conclusions, implications, and applications.

Implications for Practice

As scholars conduct future research, the resulting teaching and practice must also encompass both the family and business systems and the interplay between each system. Our new paradigm shift must also be exercised when we might consult with family firm owners and their families.

The Implications of a Paradigm Shift

In sum, we must recognize and understand family firms with new and comprehensive conceptualization. We must uncover the secrets of the family firm both for the family system and the business system. In doing so, we have broken out from past limited thinking into a new place of increased understanding and meaningful practice. Furthermore, we assist in creating processes and procedures that will lead family firms to build long-lasting, sustainable, and harmonious family and business systems, capable of pulsating in sync with one another.

Acknowledgments I am indebted to my colleagues Elisa Balabram for her multiple reads and Lauren Aydinliyim both at Baruch College for their respective friendly reviews of this book chapter.

References

Aguilera, R. V., & Crespi-Cladera, R. (2012). Firm Family firms: Current Debates of Corporate Governance in Family Firms. *Journal of Family Business Strategy, 3*(2), 66–69.

Aldrich, H. E., & Cliff, J. E. (2003). The Pervasive Effects of Family on Entrepreneurship: Toward a Family Embeddedness Perspective. *Journal of Business Venturing, 18*(5), 573–596.

Anderson, R. C., & Reeb, D. M. (2003). Founding-Family Ownership and Firm Performance: Evidence from the S&P 500. *The journal of finance, 58*(3), 1301–1328.

Astrachan, J. H. (2003). Commentary on the Special Issue: The Emergence of a Field. *Journal of Business Venturing, 18*(5), 567–572.

Bowen, M. (1985). *Family Therapy in Clinical Practice*. New York: Jason Aaronson.

Cardon, M. S., Gregoire, D. A., Stevens, C. E., & Patel, P. C. (2013). Measuring Entrepreneurial Passion: Conceptual Foundations and Scale Validation. *Journal of Business Venturing, 28*, 373–396.

Cardon, M. S., Wincent, J., Singh, J., & Drnovsek, M. (2009). The Nature and Experience of Entrepreneurial Passion. *Academy of Management Review, 34*(3), 511–532.

Cramton, C. D. (1993). Is Rugged Individualism the Whole Story? Public and Private Accounts of a Firm's Founding. *Family Business Review, 6*(3), 233–261.

Danes, S. M., & Brewton, K. E. (2012). Follow the Capital: Benefits of Tracking Family Capital across Family and Business Systems. (Chapter 14). In A. Carsrud & M. Brannback (Eds.), *Understanding Family Businesses: Undiscovered Approaches, Unique Perspectives, and Neglected Topics* (pp. 227–250). Springer.

Danes, S. M., Lee, J., Stafford, K., & Heck, R. K. Z. (2008). The Effects of Ethnicity, Families and Culture on Entrepreneurial Experience: An Extension of Sustainable Family Business Theory. *Journal of Developmental Entrepreneurship, 13*(3), 229–268.

Danes, S. M., Matzek, A. E., & Werbel, J. D. (2010). Spousal Context During the Venture Creation Process. (Chapter 4). In A. Stewart, G. T. Lumpkin, & J. A. Katz (Eds.), *Advances in Entrepreneurship, Firm Emergence and Growth: Vol. 12* (Entrepreneurship and Family Business) (pp. 113–162). New Milford, CT: Emerald.

Danes, S. M., Stafford, K., Haynes, G., & Amarapurkar, S. (2009). Family Capital of Family Firms: Bridging human, Social, and Financial Capital. *Family Business Review, 22*(3), 199–215.

Danes, S. M., Zuiker, V. S., Kean, R., & Arbuthnot, J. (1999). Predictors of Family Business Tensions and Goal Achievements. *Family Business Review, 12*(3), 241–252.

Dimov, D. (2007). From Opportunity Insight to Opportunity Intention: The Importance of Person–Situation Learning Match. *Entrepreneurship Theory and Practice, 31*(4), 561–583.

Donnelley, R. G. (1964). The Family Business. *Harvard Business Review, 42*(4), 93–105.

Dyer, W. G., & Handler, W. (1994). Entrepreneurship and Family Business: Exploring the Connections. *Entrepreneurship Theory and Practice, 19*(1), 71–83.

Eddleston, K., Kerrermanns, R., Barnett, T., & Pearson, A. (2008). An Exploratory Study of Family Member Characteristics and Involvement: Effects on Entrepreneurial Behavior in the Family Firm. *Family Business Review, 21*(1), 1–14.

Gartner, W. B. (1985). A Conceptual Framework for Describing the Phenomenon of New Venture Creation. *Academy of Management Review, 10*(4), 696–706.

Gartner, W. B. (1990). What are We Talking about When We Talk about Entrepreneurship? *Journal of Business Venturing, 5*(1), 15–19.

Gartner, W. B. (2001). Is there an Elephant in Entrepreneurship? Blind Assumptions in Theory Development. *Entrepreneurship Theory and Practice, 25*(3), 27–39.

Goel, S., Mazzol, P., Phan, P. H., Pieper, T. M., & Zachary, R. K. (2012). Strategy, Ownership, Governance, and Socio-Psychological Perspectives on Family Businesses from around the World. *Journal of Family Business Strategy, 3*(20), 54–65.

Greenwood, R. (2003). Commentary on: "Toward a Theory of Agency and Altruism in Family Firms". *Journal of Business Venturing, 18*(4), 491–494.

Habbershon, T. G., & Williams, M. L. (1999). A Resources-Based Framework for Assessing the Strategic Advantages of Family Firms. *Family Business Review, 12,* 1–25.

Habbershon, T. G., Williams, M. L., & MacMillan, I. C. (2003). A Unified Systems Perspective of Family Firm Performance. *Journal of Business Venturing, 18*(4), 451–465.

Handler, W. (1992). The Succession Experience of the Next Generation. *Family Business Review, 5*(3), 283–307.

Hareven, T. K. (1982). *Family Time and Industrial Time: The Relationship between the Family and Work in a New England Industrial Community.* New York: Cambridge University Press.

Haynes, G. W., Walker, R., Rowe, B. R., & Hong, G. S. (1999). The Intermingling of Business and Family Finances in Family-Owned Businesses. *Family Business Review, 12*(3), 225–239.

Heck, R. K. Z. (Ed.). (1998a). *The Entrepreneurial Family.* Needham, MA: Family Business Resources Publishing.

Heck, R. K. Z. (Ed.). (1998b). *The Entrepreneurial Family: Refocusing on the Family in Business* (pp. 1–7). Needham, MA: The Entrepreneurial Family/Family Business Resources Publishing.

Heck, R. K. Z., Danes, S. M., Fitzgerald, M. A., Haynes, G. W., Jasper, C. R., Schrank, H. L., et al. (2006). The Family's Dynamic Role Within Family Business Entrepreneurship. In P. Z. Poutziouris, K. X. Smyrnios, & S. B. Klein (Eds.), *Handbook of Research on Family Business* (pp. 80–105). Cheltenham, UK: Edward Elgar Publishers.

Heck, R. K. Z., Hoy, F., Poutziouris, P. Z., & Steier, L. P. (2008). Emerging Paths of Family Entrepreneurship Research. *Journal of Small Business Management, 46*(3), 317–330.

Heck, R. K. Z., Owen, A. J., & Rowe, B. (Eds.). (1995). *Home-based Employment and Family Life.* Westport, CT: Auburn House.

Heck, R. K. Z., & Trent, E. S. (1999). The Prevalence of Family Business from a Household Sample. *Family Business Review, 12*(3), 209–224.

Heck, R. K. Z., & Walker, R. (1993). Family-Owned Home Businesses, their Employees, and Unpaid Helpers. *Family Business Review, 6,* 397–415.

Jaffe, D. T. (2014). *Working with Ones You Love: Conflict Resolution and Problem Solving Strategies for Successful Family Businesses.* CreateSpace.

Jennings, J. E., & McDougald, M. S. (2007). Work-Family Interface Experiences and Coping Strategies: Implications for Entrepreneurship Research and Practice. *Academy of Management Review, 33*(3), 747–760.

Kaye, K. (1991). Penetrating the Cycle of Sustained Conflict. *Family Business Review, 4*(1), 22–44.

Kepner, E. (1983). The Family and the Firm: A Coevolutionary Perspective. *Organizational Dynamics, 12*(1), 57–70.

Klein, S. B., Astrachan, J. H., & Smyrnios, K. X. (2002). The F-PEC Scale of Family Influence: A Proposal for Solving the Family Business Definition Problem. *Family Business Review, 15*(1), 45–58.

Labaki, R., Michael-Tsabari, N., & Zachary, R. (2013). Exploring the Emotional Nexus in Cogent Family Business Archetypes. *Entrepreneurship Research Journal, 3*(3), 130–330.

Litz, R. A. (1995). The Family Business: Toward Definitional Clarity. *Family Business Review, 8*(2), 71–81.

Matzek, A. E., Gudmunson, C. G., & Danes, S. M. (2010). Spousal Capital as a Resource for Couples Starting a Business. *Family Relations, 59*, 58–71.

McGoldrick, M., Gerson, R., & Petry, S. (2008). *Genograms: Assessment and Intervention.* New York: W. W. Norton & Company.

Michael-Tsabari, N., Labaki, R., Aydinliyim, L., & Zachary, R. K. (2020, in revision). How Do Social and Economic Norms Drive Our Behavior and Decision Making Overtime? The Natural Experiment of the Family Business.

Michael-Tsabari, N., Labaki, R., & Zachary, R. (2014). Toward the Cluster Model: The Family Firm's Entrepreneurial Behavior over Generations. *Family Business Review, 27*(2), 161–185.

Mishra, C. S., & Zachary, R. (2014). *The Theory of Entrepreneurship: Creating and Sustaining Entrepreneurial Value.* New York: Palgrave Macmillan.

Morck, R., & Yeung, B. (2004). Family Control and the Rent-Seeking Society. *Entrepreneurship Theory and Practice, 28*(4), 391–409.

Olson, P. D., Zuiker, V. S., Danes, S. M., Stafford, K., Heck, R. K. Z., & Duncan, K. A. (2003). Impact of Family and Business on Family Business Sustainability. *Journal of Business Venturing, 18*(5), 639–666.

Pearson, A. W., Carr, J. C., & Shaw, J. C. (2008). Toward a Theory of Familiness: A Social Capital Perspective. *Entrepreneurship Theory and Practice, 32*(6), 949–969.

Pieper, T., & Klein, S. B. (2007). The Bulleye: A Systems Approach to Modeling Family Firms. *Family Business Review, 20*(4), 301–319.

Ponzetti, J. J. (2003). *International Encyclopedia of Marriage and Family* (2nd ed.). New York, NY: Macmillan.

Rogoff, E. G., & Heck, R. K. Z. (2003). Evolving Research in Entrepreneurship and Family Business: Recognizing Family as the Oxygen that Feeds the Fire of Entrepreneurship. *Journal of Business Venturing, 18*(5), 559–566.

Rosenblatt, P. C., de Mik, L., Anderson, R. M., & Johnson, P. A. (1985). *The Family in Business: Understanding and Dealing with the Challenges Entrepreneurial Families Face.* San Francisco: Jossey-Bass Publishers.

Rutherford, M. W., Kuratko, D. F., & Holt, D. T. (2008). Examining the Link Between "Familiness" and Performance: Can the F-PEC Untangle the Family Business Theory Jungle? *Entrepreneurship: Theory and Practice, 32*(6), 1089–1109.

Schulze, W. S., Lubatkin, M. H., & Dino, R. N. (2003). Toward a Theory of Agency and Altruism in Family Firms. *Journal of Business Venturing, 18*(4), 473–490.

Stafford, K., Duncan, K. A., Danes, S. M., & Winter, M. (1999). A Research Model of Sustainable Family Businesses. *Family Business Review, 12*(3), 197–208.

Trent, E. S., & Astrachan, J. H. (Eds.). (1999). Editors' Notes: Family Businesses from the Household Perspective. *Family Business Review, 12*, v–vi.

Upton, N. B., & Heck, R. K. Z. (1997). The Family Business Dimension of Entrepreneurship. In D. L. Sexton & R. W. Smilor (Eds.), *Entrepreneurship: 2000* (pp. 243–266). Chicago, IL: Upstart Publishing Company.

Winter, M., Danes, S. M., Koh, S., Fredericks, K., & Paul, J. J. (2004). Tracking Family Businesses and their Owners over Time: Panel Attrition, Manager Departure, and Business Demise. *Journal of Business Venturing, 19*, 535–559.

Winter, M., Fitzgerald, M. A., Heck, R. K. Z., Haynes, G. W., & Danes, S. M. (1998). Revisiting the Study of Family Businesses: Methodological Challenges, Dilemmas, and Alternative Approaches. *Family Business Review, 11*(3), 239–252.

Winter, M., Puspitawati, H., Heck, R. K. Z., & Stafford, K. (1993). Time Management Strategies Used by Households with Home-Based Work. *Journal of Family and Economic Issues, 14*, 69–92.

Zachary, R. (2011). The Importance of the Family System in Family Business. *Journal of Family Business Management, 1*(1), 26–36.

Zachary, R. (2015). The Entrepreneurial Family, Revisited. In R. L. Narva (Ed.), *Family Enterprises: How to Build Growth, Family Control and Family Harmony* (pp. 27–37). London: Globe Law and Business.

Zachary, R., Danes, S. M., & Stafford, K. (2013). Extensions of the Sustainable Family Business Theory (SFBT): Operationalization and Application. In K. Smyrnios, P. Z. Poutziouris, & S. Goel (Eds.), *Handbook of Research on Family Business* (2nd ed., pp. 507–553). Cheltenham, UK: Edward Elgar Publishing in Association with International Family Enterprise Research Academy (IFERA).

Zachary, R., & Mishra, C. S. (2008). Family Entrepreneurship. *Journal of Small Business Management, 46*(3), 313–316.

Zachary, R. K., & Mishra, C. S. (2010). Entrepreneurship Research Today and beyond: Hidden in Plain Sight! *Journal of Small Business Management, 48*(4), 471–474.

Zachary, R. K., & Mishra, C. S. (2011). The Future of Entrepreneurship Research: Calling all Researchers. *Entrepreneurship Research Journal, 1*(1) https://doi.org/10.2202/2157-5665.1016.

Part II

Preparing the New Generation of Family Entrepreneurs

6

Can Entrepreneurship Be Continued from One Generation to the Next? The Answer to that Question Can Be Found in the Socialization Process

Matt R. Allen

In many business owning families, the story behind the founding of the business or the life of the founder can become the stuff of legends. These are almost superhuman individuals who despite insurmountable obstacles and opposition are somehow able to create something from nothing, often through sheer willpower. It is no wonder that subsequent generations are interested, and sometimes even obsessed with perpetuating the family legacy of entrepreneurial success across generations.

Can entrepreneurship as an approach or behavior be passed from one generation to the next and if so, how is it done? These two questions seem to occupy the minds of grandparents, parents and even children of business owning families. A vast majority of efforts being made to answer these questions have been focused on the business as the primary unit of analysis and research emphasis. As might be expected, suggestions coming from this research are focused more on business related outcomes and business related processes (Hoy & Verser, 1994). More recent research, however, has argued that in order to understand entrepreneurship in the family business, it is necessary to look to and understand the business family rather than the family

M. R. Allen (✉)
Babson College, Babson Park, MA, USA
e-mail: mallen4@babson.edu

© The Author(s), under exclusive license to Springer Nature Switzerland AG 2021
M. R. Allen, W. B. Gartner (eds.), *Family Entrepreneurship*,
https://doi.org/10.1007/978-3-030-66846-4_6

business (Michael-Tsabari, Labaki, & Zachary, 2014). Following this newer research stream, efforts have been made to adapt business level ideas to the family level in order to understand how the family influences entrepreneurship (Zellweger, Nason, & Nordqvist, 2012).

In spite of the progress being made in understanding the role of the family in driving or inhibiting entrepreneurship within family owned businesses, very little has been done to understand the core questions being asked by business owning families. The questions mentioned previously regarding the possibility of passing an entrepreneurial approach or behaviors from one generation to the next and how this might be done are questions that are often asked independent of the actual businesses that families might own.

Based on my interviews with business families the primary purpose behind any efforts to perpetuate entrepreneurship from one generation to the next is to benefit members of the next generation and society at large. Of course, the core family business will benefit from an entrepreneurial next generation, but not all businesses survive generational transitions and not all next generation members decide to or even have the opportunity to become part of the family business. Families are concerned with the overall wellbeing of the next generation and whether based on personal experience or the legacy of the business family, parents and grandparents see entrepreneurship as a vehicle for success and creation of new value. Many families do not care if entrepreneurial activity takes place in the core family business or outside so long as the next generation can utilize entrepreneurship to improve themselves and the world around them. In this way, the desire to perpetuate entrepreneurial thinking is not directly tied to the desire to perpetuate the business itself.

Socialization

With the assumption that the purpose of entrepreneurship is to grow or perpetuate just the family business removed, the focus shifts from the business to the family and we are allowed to address the question of the perpetuation of entrepreneurship more directly. However, the shift to the family also creates a need for different tools or a different lens through which the process can be understood. Business related tools for understanding entrepreneurship such as strategy, innovation, business orientations and processes become less relevant.

One tool or lens that is of particular interest in understanding how families can perpetuate entrepreneurship across generations is socialization.

Socialization has been described as "the comprehensive and consistent induction of an individual into the objective world of a society or a sector of it" (Berger & Luckmann, 1966) p 130. In more practical terms socialization is the process through which members of a social group, a family in this case, are taught or learn the values, ideals, behaviors, approaches and expectations of that social group. For a new kindergarten student entering the public school system for the first time, socialization might include understanding when to speak and when not to speak, how to appropriately ask a question, what to do during snack time and a multitude of other expectations related to the social group of the kindergarten class. Like all groups in society, families also have rules and expectations for family members. These are learned and taught through a socialization process.

Families are much more complex than a kindergarten class, but the overarching process of socialization is the same. Expectations and norms regarding hygiene, nutrition, etiquette, even tone in speech and the meaning of gestures are all taught and learned inside the home. More specific expectations such as curfew once one has a driver's license or expectations about performance in school are understood through a similar process. It should be noted that the process of socialization is not just a cognitive learning process, but involves emotional components as well. Similarly, the understanding created through socialization is not derived solely from being directly taught, but through a multitude of observations, experiences, conversations, interactions and reflections (Berger & Luckmann, 1966).

While the theory behind the process can be dense and complex, it is sufficient for the purposes of this chapter to understand that the socialization process exists and that from a family perspective the process is generational with the older generation socializing the younger generation through their words, behaviors, and other more subtle influences that they have on their children. Though the idea of socialization does not preclude individual will, it is generally accepted that our understanding of the world around us including how we approach things is a reflection of how we are socialized by our family and other social groups, but more particularly by our family (Mead, 1934).

Much of the recent research on entrepreneurship indicates that entrepreneurship at the individual level is in fact an approach or a way of thinking and behaving (Sarasvathy, 2008). Entrepreneurs have been shown to approach problems in a very specific way that is distinct from the approach of others. Given this, it is not a significant stretch to argue that entrepreneurship can be socialized just as other behaviors and approaches can be socialized.

Socializing Entrepreneurship

If you can accept the argument that entrepreneurship as an approach can be socialized then the next logical step is to ask the question; how is it done? The remainder of this chapter will discuss core components of the entrepreneurial approach and more specifically, how parents or even grandparents can instill that approach in the next generation through effective socialization.

Before I address the process of deliberately socializing entrepreneurship in a family, I want to first address a misconception that parents and grandparents often exhibit about this process. This misconception, while understandable, can undermine efforts to socialize entrepreneurship in the next generation. The misconception is this; that socializing is the same as teaching. While socialization might involve teaching, it is much more than just teaching or as some parents approach it, telling. Socializing encompasses all conversations, interactions, experiences and learning including, but certainly not limited to what parents directly teach their children. My research indicates, in fact, that the indirect components of the socialization process can be far more impactful than the efforts of parents to teach or tell the next generation.

Several years ago, I had a parent in my office who was a leader of a significant family business. He was bemoaning the fact that in spite of all his efforts to teach the next generation to be entrepreneurial, he could not seem to influence them in his intended direction. In fact, he mentioned to me that none of the next generation seemed to have any inclination toward entrepreneurial behavior. I was a bit incredulous of his assertion and asked him if he truly did not have a single example of entrepreneurial behavior. He responded that there was one nephew who had had some harebrained idea that had failed so spectacularly that everyone in the family still made fun of him. He then continued to describe to me how baffled he was that nobody in the next generation seemed to be understanding or acting on his efforts to help them be entrepreneurial. Note that his efforts to teach (tell) were being undermined by other aspects of the socialization process such as how he described actual efforts (harebrained), how the family understood the outcomes of those efforts (spectacular failure) and how the family responded to the efforts of this nephew (still made fun of him). This is perhaps an extreme example, but it makes the point that socialization is much more than teaching, and for effective socialization, parents will need to be consistent in all of the messages they send, not just what they are telling the next generation.

As families seek to socialize entrepreneurship in the next generation, they should focus on socializing core components of an entrepreneurial approach.

Here I will address four of those components. Families seeking to socialize entrepreneurship should focus on making sure that the approach of the family is action based, learning driven, socially oriented and autonomy focused. I will address each one of those individually.

Action Oriented—Recent research on entrepreneurial behavior strongly indicates that one of the key components of successful entrepreneurial behavior is that entrepreneurs are action focused. Specifically, that entrepreneurs prefer to act with the means that they have at hand (Sarasvathy, 2008). When it comes to pursuing an opportunity, rather than wait for the "right" timing or until certain resources are secured, entrepreneurs will act as quickly as possible using whatever resources they have available to them at that time. The key is to take immediate action toward the goal. The action oriented approach has been described as seeking to control or manage the future through action rather than try to predict the future through analysis and study (Sarasvathy, 2008). From a family perspective, this means that families socializing an action oriented approach should emphasize taking action as opposed to analyzing. Younger members of a family should be encouraged to try things out and experiment with ideas in an effort to understand for themselves.

One family that I interviewed indicated that a key aspect of their nurturing an action oriented approach was to assume that all ideas are good ideas until they are proven otherwise by taking action. In this family even if the parents feel that an idea will likely not be successful or has even been tried before, they deliberately refrain from expressing their opinions and instead encourage their children to try it out and see for themselves what the outcome might be. Obviously, this approach is not pursued when the idea might affect the well-being of the child, but overall, as an approach, it encourages an experimental attitude where members of the family feel empowered to test and try new ideas.

Learning driven—Following on the idea of being action oriented, families seeking to socialize entrepreneurship do not emphasize action for action sake. Action has a purpose and that purpose is to learn. There are many different ways to gather information, but entrepreneurs prefer to gather their own information through their own actions. From the entrepreneurial perspective, the best way to learn about something is to try that something out for yourself so that you can better understand. In a general sense, this means that families should be focused on what is learned from actions taken. This can be difficult in a world that is often hyper-focused on the outcome and not the learning involved. A family focused on learning from action would place more emphasis on the learning that took place in a school class than the grade achieved. This is true regardless of whether that grade was considered to be good or bad. When the focus is on learning, failure becomes more of an opportunity to learn than an experience to be avoided. All experiences represent the chance to learn more and be more prepared for the next action to be taken.

When I worked at IBM, they had an unwritten policy that any manager who had the potential to reach an executive level in the organization should first have the opportunity to manage a declining business. They recognized what entrepreneurs know to be true, failure is actually an opportunity to learn and grow. Parents often struggle with supporting a learning driven approach. The desire to see their children achieve great things can lead to an effort to avoid failure at all costs. I awoke very early one morning to find a car straddling a large landscaping boulder in my front yard. As I stepped outside to make sure that everyone was okay, I discovered that the driver was a young teenager. His father had already arrived on the scene and while the teenager sat several meters away from the activity around the wrecked vehicle, the father was in the middle of the action giving instructions to everyone around him and offering the contents of his wallet to all involved in a tremendous effort to make this mishap "go away" for his son. While the accident might represent a small tragedy in the life of this teenager, the larger tragedy was that he would never have the opportunity to learn from his mistakes and would be no better prepared for what comes next as a result.

Social process—Many people think that the process of entrepreneurship is a lonely one with the lone-wolf entrepreneur conquering markets and obstacles as an individual superhero. The reality is actually much different. Entrepreneurs are inherently social. Not necessarily for the joy of social engagement, but because the more others are engaged in the process the more information, experience and knowledge is applied to the problem increasing the likelihood of success. Engaging others in order to gather more information, see things differently or get access to more resources or advice is a key component of the entrepreneurial process (Sarasvathy, 2008).

Families looking to promote a social approach to problem solving need to help younger members of the family feel comfortable both asking for and giving help. Some families will use the dinner table to let each family member share their current problems or needs and then listen as other members of the family offer advice, support or help. Others will consistently and effectively use a board of directors, board of advisors or advisors in general to make better decisions.

Growing up, my father often joked that because he was an accountant by trade he was somehow not cut out for many activities that involved fixing things or building things around the house. While that was not really true, I do remember that whenever we ran into something that he was not able to accomplish on his own, he always knew someone he could turn to in order to get the help that we needed. I remember as a kid thinking: My dad must know just about everyone because no matter how complex the task, he could name someone he knew who was an expert at that particular activity. As I matured, that capability in my father helped me even further as every one of my multiple summer jobs over my teenage years came from a connection provided by or suggested by my father. While small activities like these might seem trivial, as part of the socialization process they have powerful outcomes in how the next generation approaches life. As a result of my experience with my father and his network of experts, my first reaction when I run into a problem I can't solve is to ask myself who I can call, text or email to get help.

Autonomy focused—The above three components of the entrepreneurial approach have one thing in common; they all require a certain level of autonomy for the younger generation. When thinking about the socialization process, many parents assume that it can and should be tightly controlled in order to get maximum results. That is, parents and grandparents should seek to control and manipulate every experience and activity in order to make sure that the outcome is exactly what was originally intended. This misconception ignores the fact that we are individuals in addition to being a part of a social group. Though the socialization process is mostly generational, meaning that it moves from the older to the younger generation, the younger generation does have the opportunity to react to the social cues and teaching being presented to them. Socialization is a two-way interaction and parents need to accept this in their efforts by recognizing that the learning involves a give and take from both generations. The younger generations will first understand and then internalize the norms of the family.

A friend of mine once complained to me that he had spent thousands and thousands of dollars preparing his daughter for acceptance to an Ivy League university to be followed by an illustrious business career. No expense had been spared in private schools, tutoring, service trips and music lessons. In the end and after all of these expenses, the daughter had chosen to skip the university and take a job working with boats and tourists at the "lake". I am not arguing that one or the other of these options was right or wrong. I am just using this example to illustrate that family members do have some autonomy to act on their own in spite of efforts to socialize them in another direction. In this case, the father, in hindsight, felt that perhaps the deviation from the plan on the part of his daughter was because of and not in spite of all of his efforts to control her life path. I would tend to agree.

Research on innovation indicates that when dealing with entrepreneurial situations, managers should exert less rather than more control (Allen, Adomdza, & Meyer, 2015). The worst kind of control to exercise in these situations is referred to as process control which in layman's terms can be described as micro-managing the entire process. Instead, managers should focus on outcome control where they communicate the end expectation and allow the employees to find their own best path toward the expected goal.

Families will react similarly. Some level of autonomy provides room for trying new and innovative approaches to solving problems. It also allows individuals to discover their own talents and capabilities and apply them in their own way rather than in the way prescribed by parents. As families embrace an approach that provides autonomy to family members allowing them to figure out their own path to reach key goals and expectations, family members are more likely to embrace entrepreneurial approaches.

Conclusion

In conclusion, entrepreneurial approaches can indeed be passed from one generation to another. The process through which this takes place is referred to as socialization and takes place in the family, not the family business. Families that hope to instill an entrepreneurial approach in the next generation should work to socialize approaches exhibited by entrepreneurs. Specifically, parents and families should focus on promoting an orientation toward action rather than analysis, a focus on learning through successes and mistakes rather than outcomes, seeking advice from and recruiting other people to help with problem solving and fostering autonomy for individual decision making rather than tight management of every part of the process. As families actively pursue these approaches by deliberately and consistently socializing the intended behaviors and approaches in every part of family life, they will prepare the next generation to be more entrepreneurial. This process does not guarantee that all members of the next generation will found new businesses, but it will promote entrepreneurial behavior and thinking and will increase the probability of entrepreneurial success.

References

Allen, M. R., Adomdza, G. K., & Meyer, M. H. (2015). Managing for Innovation: Managerial Control and Employee Level Outcomes. *Journal of Business Research, 68*(2), 371–379.

Berger, P. L., & Luckmann, T. (1966). *The Social Construction of Reality*. New York, NY: Anchor Books.

Hoy, F., & Verser, T. G. (1994). Emerging Business, Emerging Field: Entrepreneurship and the Family Firm. *Entrepreneurship: Theory and Practice, 19*(1), 9–23.

Mead, G. H. (1934). *Mind, Self and Society.* Chicago: The University of Chicago Press.

Michael-Tsabari, N., Labaki, R., & Zachary, R. K. (2014). Toward the Cluster Model: The Family Firm's Entrepreneurial Behavior over Generations. *Family Business Review, 27*(2), 161–185.

Sarasvathy, S. D. (2008). *Effectuation: Elements of Entrepreneurial Expertise.* Cheltenham, UK: Edward Elgar.

Zellweger, T. M., Nason, R. S., & Nordqvist, M. (2012). From Longevity of Firms to Transgenerational Entrepreneurship of Families: Introducing Family Entrepreneurial Orientation. *Family Business Review, 25*(2), 136–155.

7

Tilling the Soil—And Wait and See How the Next Generation Develops

Stefan Prigge and Peter Klein

Introduction

How does the family, as a system, establish, develop, promote, support, and teach entrepreneurship as a behavior, belief, or value across generations? We do not know any patent solutions for this. But we have talked to some family entrepreneurs specifically for this chapter. Looking at it as a whole, this results in an approach that is also supported by our general experience with family businesses: Tilling the Soil—and Wait and See how the Next Generation Develops. By this, we mean that neither explicit nor implicit pressure should be exerted on the next generation to assume a specific position or role in the family business. Rather, the adult generation should have confidence in the soil in which the next generation is growing up, which is doubly biased in favor of entrepreneurship and family businesses: they are clearly better informed about entrepreneurship than their peers, and they have experienced what it is like to be an entrepreneur by growing up in an entrepreneurial family, and they have most likely been given a positive image. Then we will have to wait and see what fruits will grow in this field. If there was a predisposition to entrepreneurship, it was most likely activated by the environment. This does not necessarily have to happen (immediately) in the family business. But

S. Prigge (✉) • P. Klein
Institute for Mittelstand and Family Firms, HSBA Hamburg School of Business Administration, Hamburg, Germany
e-mail: stefan.prigge@hsba.de; peter.klein@hsba.de

© The Author(s), under exclusive license to Springer Nature Switzerland AG 2021
M. R. Allen, W. B. Gartner (eds.), *Family Entrepreneurship*,
https://doi.org/10.1007/978-3-030-66846-4_7

even if the junior generation becomes entrepreneurially active outside the family business, the family business will benefit from the experience gained there, which the members of the junior generation can contribute, for example, as shareholders or on the supervisory board.

We will explain and justify this approach in the following three steps. Furthermore, we will also show how this—rather abstract—concept can be put into practice by referring to our discussions.

1. Why it is so important that no coercion whatsoever be exercised. What can happen when it is exercised?
2. How to cultivate the field in a way that promotes entrepreneurial mindsets of the next generation without putting pressure on them?
3. How diversified can the harvest result be from the cultivated field, that is, how varied can the degree of entrepreneurial mindsets and the connection to the family business be over the decades in the adult life of the following generation?

Even though this contribution is essentially based on discussions and experience, and is aimed at family entrepreneurs, there are also links to theoretical approaches that family business research has developed in recent years. First and foremost, the concept of transgenerational entrepreneurship (Habbershon & Pistrui, 2002; Habbershon, Nordqvist, & Zellweger, 2010) should be mentioned here. According to Habbershon et al. (2010, p. 1), transgenerational entrepreneurship is "the processes through which a family uses and develops entrepreneurial mindsets and family influenced resources and capabilities to create new streams of entrepreneurial, financial and social value across generations". Our concentration will be on developing entrepreneurial mindsets among the next generation. A feature of the transgenerational entrepreneurship that we find particularly appealing is that it focuses on the business family (Zellweger, Nason, & Nordqvist, 2012, pp. 138–139) and not the family business.

Our observations also show a relation to the concept of psychological ownership. This approach developed by Pierce, Kostova, and Dirks (2001) explains how the (positive) feelings of ownership arise independently of an actual (legal) power of disposal over a good. Although this theory was developed from the behavior of employees in companies, the findings can easily be transferred to actors in family businesses.

Pittino, Martínez, Chirico, and Galván (2018) make the link between psychological ownership and entrepreneurial behavior. They claim that in family firms, psychological ownership leads to a sense of stewardship toward the family business and the perception of a common purpose which in turn are considered a source of entrepreneurial behavior. Another link to this train of thought leads to the "I" in the FIBER scale proposed by Berrone, Cruz, and Gomez-Mejia (2012): to operationalize the socio-emotional wealth (SEW). "I" stands for identification of family members with the family firm.

Why it is So Important That No Coercion is Used

An experienced family entrepreneur told us, with a view to his children, but also with a view back to the time when he and his brothers were the next generation, that there had to be a basic inclination toward family business; this could not be forced.

This statement sums up very well what we were told in unison in our discussions: no compulsion. This is a rather recent development if one looks at the recent history of entrepreneurial families and family businesses. In this context, "compulsion" can take many forms and can also be implicit and subtle. Another experienced family entrepreneur describes the expectations his parents had of him and his siblings, all born in the 1950s and 1960s:

> And it has always been clear somehow, the children have to go to the company, as it was the case in the past and perhaps it is still the case today with many of them. Which later on led to severe complications.

As the youngest of the siblings and straggler, he himself was given comparatively large freedoms, but he too began working in the family business rather reluctantly than enthusiastically. After four years in the family business, however, he pulled the ripcord and told his mother, the matriarch, that he was giving up his position in the family business because his personal interest belonged to another industry. He would rather do that and believed that he would be better off there. In the back of his mind, he already had the idea of starting his own business in his favorite industry, clearly indicating that an entrepreneurial mindset had been developed. His mother found her son leaving the family business extremely difficult, but in the end, she supported it fully.

The fact that she supported it in the end was certainly also due to her experiences with his older brother, whose case excellently illustrates the power of implicit expectations. By the way, it is significant that this is about the eldest son and not about the eldest child, the daughter.

But he already felt himself already chosen and determined to succeed in family business leadership. And since then, apparently my parents have made a lot of mistakes over the years. Because they didn't make it openly enough and therefore laid the foundation for great disappointments in the future, which ultimately led to the separation.

This case shows very clearly that even what is only hinted at, even unspoken, and traditions, can shape the expectations and assessments of the next generation and thus also exert pressure. The separation cited above ultimately dragged on for many years, placed a heavy burden on the family and the company, and finally ended with the eldest son's complete withdrawal from the company, that is, also as a shareholder. What had been intended to create and develop the identification of the eldest son with the family firm destroyed it. As a consequence, the family wrote into their family constitution that any involvement of family members on an operational level or in management outside of internships is only permissible as CEO. Today, the family's basic understanding is that a non-family CEO is desirable—and is currently being practiced. This is also manifested in the family constitution, in which high hurdles have been set for a family CEO. The own experiences of our conversation partner led him and his sister to introduce the family business to their children in a completely different way, namely casually.

Even though we have discussed the forms and consequences of coercion using only a single concrete example, we are convinced that this is not an isolated case. Coercion, even in its subtle variations, should be avoided, which is not at all easy, because the adult generation does not necessarily always have to notice when it behaves in a way that could be interpreted by the offspring as coercion.

The wait and see in our motto refers back to casualness. Yes, the parent generation can cultivate the field toward pro-entrepreneurship, but rather through information, example, and nudges, without coercion. This is what the next section is about.

How to Cultivate the Field in a Way That Promotes Entrepreneurial Mindsets of the Next Generation without Putting Pressure on Them

It goes without saying that the family and family life shape tremendously the children growing up in this ecosystem. The ecosystem of a business family is special, such that it is biased in favor of entrepreneurship (transgenerational entrepreneurship), when benchmarked with the typical family ecosystem. The young business family member grows up in his or her family where the family firm is a "family member", supporting the development of psychological ownership and identification with the family firm. Thus, the young family member is more strongly exposed to an entrepreneurial mindset than the average adolescent is. He or she knows more about the freedom, responsibility, pride, and wealth, but also about the workload, pressure, and failure than their contemporaries that being an entrepreneur could be about. They can very closely observe whether their parents and other relatives experience their role in the family firm as positive or negative. In those cases where the parents are interested in igniting the entrepreneurial flame in their offspring, we can assume that for them the advantages outweigh the disadvantages of being an entrepreneur. This gives becoming an entrepreneur a positive connotation. As a result, even without exerting explicit or implicit force, this family ecosystem—the soil—is biased toward an entrepreneurial development of the children, compared to their contemporaries who do not grow up in a business family, in two ways: First, they dispose of more information about taking an entrepreneurial path in life; second, this information paints a positive picture of the life as an entrepreneur.

How can the parent generation cultivate the field toward entrepreneurial mindsets without pressure or coercion? This is where important approaches and ideas come in, which were perceived by our discussion partners as positive but unobtrusive:

One interviewee summed up very aptly the point of view that we want to present here with the following key words: In childhood and adolescence, dealing with the family business should always be playful, parents can arouse interest in the family business, and they can enable (but not force) their children to participate. In her specific case, her curiosity was aroused by the fact that her father characterized the company to the children with the words, "that's what is feeding you". The family business and the father's office were not an isolated world. Participation and involvement at a childlike and playful level were automatically achieved by voluntarily going to the office at the age of 10–12 years. The bagging of letters during mailings, and a few years later, as a teenager—going to business appointments and business lunches, or temporarily operating the telephone gave her a realistic experience of working in a family business, which in turn was a great help in making decisions about her own professional future. Even though she does not currently work in the family business, she developed a strong identification with the company.

To cultivate the field in family life, the thoughts of an experienced family entrepreneur who can draw from his own previous role as the next generation as well as from his current role as a family man can be well complemented. As a basic prerequisite, he sees that entrepreneurship and being an entrepreneur must have a positive connotation in the family. An important role for him is played by his wife, their children's mother. She must not complain about the workload, but must also be pro-entrepreneurship. As a family entrepreneur, he would draw a positive but realistic picture at home with his family. He would make it possible his children to experience the great creative possibilities and freedom that come with entrepreneurship. But the realistic picture would also include the great responsibility, the considerable workload, and the need to constantly adapt to market changes. However, he would not take extreme anger home with him. In the end, he hopes that this environment sparks an entrepreneurial spirit among his children (transgenerational entrepreneurship), in the best case linked to their family business (psychological ownership and identification).

In family life, the family business is practically at the dining table. This is how another experienced family entrepreneur described it, who can also report from his own time as next generation, as well as about the growing up of his children and his sister's children. He remembers his time at home as follows:

> Yes, with us it was, how do you say it, the company … at the dinner table. (…) That was always somehow present, everything happened at our home. It was mega present. Both of them, my father was the operative manager, my mother was, how should I put it, the backbone, so to speak, owner. And both of them, she at home and he in the company, managed the company together.

As in the two cases described above, it could happen that the parents are operationally active in the family business. Then the connection to the family business is certainly strongest, and with it its radiance into the family and to the offspring, helping developing identification and psychological ownership. The same family entrepreneur who last had his say is not himself operationally active in the family business, but is a shareholder and representative of the family on the supervisory board. (The family is no longer operationally active in family businesses at all.) Given the greater distance, how did he introduce the family business to his children?

> I have never pushed the issue of family business. So, it was always clear to both kids that the company was there. They were also totally aware of what they [the company] were doing and how they were doing it and everything, but we never talked about whether one would work in it or how it would be with the shares when the kids grew up or whatever. Of course, they heard all this when there were advisory board meetings and, in the past, we all lived in [a certain town in Germany] and before the meetings there was always dinner at my mother's house. So, there has been some translation, but I tried to make it relatively low-threshold and not so big a topic. And I have to say that I am fascinated by how it has worked with my children.

About his sister as a mother, he reports that she too drew the consequences from the short leash that applied to her and her two brothers, which had led to the most serious upheavals in the family:

> She certainly did not push them into this function, because she probably had the same experience that I had and the consequence of what followed. And she also let them have that. (…) That must have been extremely free.

The sister's two children have also become active shareholders, who also take additional care of the family business as a member of the supervisory board and organizer of family governance, respectively. Thus, all four members of the next generation formed a strong identification with the family business.

Low-threshold accesses, as described by the first interviewee in this section from personal experience, are very suitable for establishing casual contact with the family business and forming psychological ownership in a gentle way: accompanying father or mother to the company, discovering the company independently. Ideally, of course, the initiative for this should come from the next generation. There are also organized formats such as the classic internship and family days. The more organized the format, the more difficult it is to avoid even subliminal pressure.

An interesting idea arose from a conversation with a family entrepreneur, where his children and the children of his siblings are now in their teens or are about to be. The family business is of medium size and is, despite several regional locations, very strongly anchored locally. The charitable foundation named after the parents of the family entrepreneur is also active in this local area and is also run by family members. His as-yet-untried idea is to find out whether the young people are interested in developing their own projects within the foundation and would be given a budget to do so. Ideally, the next generation would have the opportunity to test for themselves the extent to which entrepreneurial spirit lies dormant in them (transgenerational entrepreneurship). At the same time, they would get to know other facets of the family business, namely that parts of the profits flow into this foundation and how the company and foundation radiate into the local environment (psychological ownership and identification). Of course, the art here again is that no pressure is built up as a result.

How Wide the Range of Harvest Results from the Cultivated Field Can Be

So, what are the results of this long leash policy? First of all, it can be assumed that the greater freedom will lead to happier life plans for the offspring. This is of course an enormously important criterion for parents, probably even the most important criterion of all. But this chapter is about entrepreneurship and family businesses, so this aspect will be the focus of the discussion of the results.

As a further preliminary remark, it should be noted that the future relationship of the younger generation to the family business can take very different forms. The idea may still be determined by the "classic" concept of the next generation, who in the course of time will take over leading management positions in the family business in addition to their shares. The following examples will show that there are also quite different forms which also contribute to the success of the family business. It should also be noted that the relationship of the former next generation to the family business is not static during the several decades of adult life, but can change and often actually does change.

As reported above, one of our interlocutors has left the family business "with pain" after four years in managerial positions to work in his desired industry after the "family leash" was too tight. However, he then returned to the company in a responsible position after the death of his mother, the matriarch. In order to represent the family on the supervisory board and its committees, he gave up his own small company in the industry of his choice to be able to concentrate fully on this role, documenting a strong identification with the family firm.

In the case of his nephew, growing up in an entrepreneurial family may have favored the fact that he was very active in business and also very successful in business, but not in the family business, but in start-up companies that have no connection to the family business. Today, alongside his activities in the start-up sector, he is the second family representative beside his uncle on the supervisory board and its committees. In this way, he contributes valuable knowledge and contacts there which he has acquired outside the family business. The same applies to his uncle. Thus, both could be taken as examples where an entrepreneurial mindset led to entrepreneurial activities outside the family business, but the strong identification brought them back to the family business that they support in governance positions.

In the two examples above, the family members hold positions on the supervisory board but not in management. But here, too, there is an interesting example among our discussion partners. The discussion partner belongs to the older next generation in terms of age. The German family-owned company processes and trades herbal raw materials. Despite his positive basic attitude toward the family business, his interest was initially in sports management, which he studied in the USA. Nevertheless, he returned to the family business afterwards, because he enjoys working with his father and brother and likes to combine work and private life. Now he is responsible for the trading of new product segments in the company's USA branch. Trade as a business object is more open and flexible than production. Together with the USA location, this gives him a lot of business freedom. This is a good example of how the right dose of psychological ownership and identification during childhood and adolescence can lead back to the management of the family business without any pressure and even allowed for a "detour" via sports management studies.

Even if we put a lot of emphasis on casualness, understood as the absence of any kind of force, it goes without saying that every family member must have sufficient qualifications for the position in question. The shareholder position is the formal role in the family business that requires the least qualification. For positions in management and supervisory boards, the requirements would increase accordingly. One of our interviewees aptly sums up the tension between casualness and the qualification requirements of the next generation:

> We are also all agreed that we say: it doesn't really matter what each family shareholder does. Nobody has to go into the role 'company' in any way. Everybody just has to get a decent education and if they do a different education, i.e., not

in an economic, technical, whatever profession or education, they have to do something to fulfil their role as shareholder. In other words, he must be committed to it, he must also acquire the appropriate knowledge. So if someone should really become a physician, which is currently not the case, he has to attend seminars or something similar so that he can fulfil his role as a partner in the company. We also support this.

Conclusion

How does the family, as a system, establish, develop, promote, support, and teach entrepreneurship as a behavior, belief, or value across generations? We do not know any patent solution for this. But we have talked to some family entrepreneurs specifically for this chapter. Looking at it as a whole, this results in an approach that is also supported by our general experience with family businesses: Our discussions confirm that family entrepreneurs are concerned with awakening feelings of ownership and thus psychological ownership at an early stage, especially in the next generation (learning to love the family business), developing them (making them part of the identity) and cultivating them further (taking possession, decision-making power and assuming responsibility).

In order to maintain and support transgenerational entrepreneurship in their families, family business owners and leaders should be aware of the fact that they provide to their children the most direct view on what life is like being an entrepreneur one could think of. Thus, if they as a family business leader are happy with their life in that position, they will emit the positive sides of being a family business leader automatically at home in their family life. It can easily be counterproductive to put pressure on children, both explicitly and implicitly, by letting them know or feel what the parent's favorite outcome in their future role in the family firm would be.

Following these suggestions might lead to benefits, but there is no guarantee. Family business owners and leaders should trust that by growing up in an entrepreneurial family, the casual experience of what it means to be an entrepreneur will lead the next generation to be entrepreneurially oriented, provided your children have the appropriate "hereditary" traits. However, this does not necessarily have to happen within the family business. But even then, the family business can benefit from the experience gained there. And if they do not dispose of the appropriate "hereditary" traits, at least you would not have forced your children into a way of living against their preferences. In both cases, with and without managerial involvement of the next generation in the family business, probability is high that the approach will result in a strong identification with the family firm.

References

Berrone, P., Cruz, C., & Gomez-Mejia, L. R. (2012). Socioemotional Wealth in Family Firms: Theoretical Dimensions, Assessment Approaches, and Agenda for Future Research. *Family Business Review, 25*(3), 258–279.

Habbershon, T. G., Nordqvist, M., & Zellweger, T. (2010). Transgenerational Entrepreneurship. In M. Nordqvist & T. Zellweger (Eds.), *Transgenerational Entrepreneurship: Exploring Growth and Performance in Family Firms across Generations* (pp. 1–38). Cheltenham, Gloucestershire: Edward Elgar Publishing.

Habbershon, T. G., & Pistrui, J. (2002). Enterprising Families Domain: Family-Influenced Ownership Groups in Pursuit of Transgenerational Wealth. *Family Business Review, 15*(3), 223–237.

Pierce, J. L., Kostova, T., & Dirks, K. T. (2001). Toward a Theory of Psychological Ownership in Organizations. *Academy of Management Review, 26*(2), 298–310.

Pittino, D., Martínez, A. B., Chirico, F., & Galván, R. S. (2018). Psychological Ownership, Knowledge Sharing and Entrepreneurial Orientation in Family Firms: The Moderating Role of Governance Heterogeneity. *Journal of Business Research, 84*, 312–326.

Zellweger, T. M., Nason, R. S., & Nordqvist, M. (2012). From Longevity of Firms to Transgenerational Entrepreneurship of Families: Introducing Family Entrepreneurial Orientation. *Family Business Review, 25*(2), 136–155.

Part III

Developing Entrepreneurial Leaders

8

Sustaining a Multi-Generational Family Enterprise Through Ambidextrous Leadership

Allan R. Cohen and Pramodita Sharma

Introduction

Why do some family enterprises flourish generation after generation, while others discontinue after succeeding for one or two generations? Business families[1] that enjoy transgenerational success invest efforts and resources to develop

---

This chapter is largely based on material from Cohen and Sharma, *Entrepreneurs in Every Generation: How Successful Family Businesses Develop Their Next Leaders, Berrett-Koehler, 2016*, with additional conceptualization and examples. We are grateful for the encouragement and thoughtful comments by Michael Tushman.

---

[1] Nason, R., Mazzelli, A., & Carney, M. (2019). The ties that unbind: Socialization and business-owning family reference point shift. *Academy of Management Review*, 44(4): 846–870.

A. R. Cohen (✉)
Babson College (Emeritus), Oakland, CA, USA
e-mail: cohen@babson.edu

P. Sharma
University of Vermont, Burlington, VT, USA
e-mail: Pramodita.Sharma@uvm.edu

ambidextrous leaders[2] who are equally deft at proactive *explorations*[3] seeking novel solutions, all while imposing discipline to accomplish fundamental organizational tasks efficiently and effectively—*exploitation.* Entrepreneurial explorations encourage experimentation and organizational renewal while opening possibilities for transgenerational engagement. Performance expectations monitored through governance systems and structures inject accountability to balance explorations with income generation from existing capabilities. The why and how of this yin and yang of openness to new possibilities while adhering to traditional competencies[4] enable the development of entrepreneurial skills from one generation to the next.

In simplest terms, transgenerational continuity of a family enterprise must meet two conditions: a viable business with products or services of interest to customers, and at least one capable family member willing to run the firm efficiently while adapting it to ensure its sustainability. When more than one family member is interested in the business, mechanisms become essential to situate interested family members in appropriate roles within or outside the family enterprise, and manage leadership and ownership transitions across generations.

The overlay of the economic and societal systems of business and family can be challenging particularly when a thriving multi-generational family enterprise lies at the core. Business family becomes a ripe arena to develop human skills and for family dramas to play out. There is plenty of room for conflict as each family member learns how to be live with others of equal power but varied levels of skills and talents, determine what interests will be supported and reported, experience feelings of being part of in- and out-groups as partners, special others, and offspring are integrated into families. Amidst all these complex human overlays of relationships and interactions are opportunities to build entrepreneurial and leadership skills of family

---

[2] Lubatkin, M.H., Simsek, Z., Ling, Y., & Veiga, J.F. (2006). Ambidexterity and performance in small- to medium-sized firms: The pivotal role of top management team behavioral integration. *Journal of Management*, 32, 646–672.

Raisch, S., Birkinshaw, J., Probst, G., & Tushman, M.L. (2009). Organizational Ambidexterity: Balancing Exploitation and Exploration for Sustained Performance. *Organizational Science*, 20, 685–695;

Rosing, K., Frese, M., & Bausch, A. (2011). Explaining the Heterogeneity of the Leadership-Innovation Relationship: Ambidextrous Leadership. *Leadership Quarterly*, 22, 956–974.

Tushman, M.L., Smith, W.K., & Binns, A. (2011). The Ambidextrous CEO. *Harvard Business Review*, 89(6): 74–80.

[3] March, J.G. (1991). Exploitation and Exploration in Organizational Learning. *Organization Science*, 2(1): 71–87.

[4] Gupta, A.K., Smith, K.G., & Shalley, C.E. (2006). The interplay between exploration and exploitation. *Academy of Management Journal*, 49(4): 693–706.

members encouraging explorations of new possibilities and exploitations of current ways of thinking and doing.

For the remainder of this chapter we will discuss what is known about the best practices to seamlessly balance the exploration and exploitation of new ideas, while building on the core values and identity of the controlling family. We acknowledge that there is no perfect formula that guarantees success along every dimension. Maybe, at best it is genuine humility and the willingness to acknowledge mistakes and work on them when getting in the way. The most successful business families don't get it right all the time. Yet by using structures and processes in their family enterprises, they find ways to develop family members' ambidextrous entrepreneurial and leadership skills and mind-sets needed to build capacity for growth and continuity.[5]

Before we discuss the best practices related to exploration and exploitation ambidexterity, it is important to note that each long-lived family enterprise grows in its unique ways over time. Some may persist in the same location and industry for generations, while in other cases everything changes except the core values and the approach to integrating continuity and change. For example, Nishiyama Onsen Keiunkan in Japan is the world's oldest hot spring inn. For over 1300 years, it has been located at the foot of the South Japanese Alps with the hot spring water flowing directly into the inn. The same family has operated it for 52 generations. Although it has made modifications over the years, the traditional features have always been retained. This represents a family business at one extreme of stability. Others, like the Murugappa Group, bear little resemblance to their original industry, having had to adapt to remain economically viable, and learned to run multiple businesses. Started as a money lending and banking business in Burma (now Myanmar) in 1900, by 1915 it had diversified into rubber plantations, textiles, insurance and stock brokerage in Ceylon (now Sri Lanka), Malaya, and Vietnam. With continuous expansion through acquisitions, joint ventures, new product launches, and green-field projects, and annual sales of over a billion US dollars since 2003, the Group is now one of India's leading business conglomerates. It covers 28 businesses including 9 listed companies in diverse industries such as abrasives, auto components, bio-products, plantations and sugar. This requires the ability to mix the discipline and skills of operational excellence with genuine exploration and innovativeness.

---

[5] Raffaelli, R., Glynn, M.A., & Tushman, M. (2019). Frame flexibility: The role of cognitive and emotional framing in innovation adoption by incumbent firms. *Strategic Management Journal*, 40(7): 1013–1039.

For a small company like the Japanese inn, only one family member per generation with interest and ability in the business is necessary, although strong traditions of primogeniture prefer the oldest male family member. Over the years, it sometimes became necessary to place a son-in-law or even adopt an adult male as a son to lead the business. More recently, in some cases daughters have been elevated to lead their family enterprises, at times with results far more positive than even they had expected.

In business families that succeed generation after generation, opportunities to build skills to continuously explore for innovative opportunities and know when and how to exploit the value of identified opportunities become part of family practices, the way children are raised and the family goes about being a family. In addition, astute long-lived enterprising families embed innovative learning opportunities within their business. Company policies and practices are designed to solicit new ideas and encourage experimentation. Such opportunities are extended to family and non-family members alike and become part of the DNA or culture of the enterprise, thereby expanding both the temporal and contextual domains[6] in which the ambidextrous skills of entrepreneurial exploitation and exploration are developed.

There is now increasing realization that business families can provide conditions to engage next generational family members within and outside their family enterprises, while bringing creativity into their business and enhancing the entrepreneurial leadership skills of these members.[7] Successful business families provide more choices and autonomy to family members *and* employees at every level; encourage pursuit of individual interests even when they do not appear to fit narrow, traditional roles within the current family businesses; offer rich developmental opportunities as part of employment and often as part of family membership; encourage outside education and employment or internships as part of broadening learning and perspective; and include non-family members in responsible managerial ranks including overseeing training and development of family members. Nothing guarantees that every capable family member will be attracted to work in the family enterprise, but it is possible to alter the odds of positive results for such engagement.

---

[6] Ibid.

[7] Bloemen-Bekx, Van Gils, A., Lambrechts, F., & Sharma, P. (2019). Nurturing offspring's affective commitment through family governance mechanisms. *Journal of Family Business Strategy*. https://doi.org/10.1016/j.jfbs.2019.100309.

Explorations

Business families that thrive over generations are often anchored by a shared dream of excellence in quality of products, lowest prices, fastest delivery, identity, aspiration, emotional engagement, and so on. Research on personality traits suggests that entrepreneurs score higher than non-entrepreneurs in *openness to experiences*.[8] Enterprising families find ways to inculcate a desire to learn while doing something different into the mind-set of family members at a young age. Efforts are made to modify the specifics of this anchoring dream to align with the core strengths and interests of each generation, sometimes leading to new lines of business, novel products, renewal of processes to identify and reach new market segments—in short, innovation. This modification opens opportunities to engage family members in ways not previously imagined. As illustrated in the examples included below, long-lived enterprising families expend a lot of thought, attention, time and resources to build the self-efficacy and entrepreneurial skills of next-generation members by enabling varied learning opportunities, at different life stages.

For example, Gerry Ettinger founded Ettinger in 1934 to create innovative high-quality leather goods that would be known not only in the UK, but around the world. His grandson, Robert Ettinger, recalls his winding preparatory path before joining the family business in 1985. He studied in Austrian and French boarding schools, where he learned languages and discipline. While the former enabled him to expand his horizons beyond his country, the latter instilled the importance of structures in him. Schooling was followed by an apprenticeship in a German marble stone family business with an aim of understanding craftsmanship. This was followed by working at Mappins Fine Jewelers in Canada, which helped him to learn about the business of the luxury industry. For a few years, he was a professional skier and a ski instructor, before joining the family business. Though his father did not force him to join the family business, he had the foresight to groom him through these opportunities and experiences, while letting him free to learn on his own.

In another example of age appropriate skill development opportunities, Robert Tracy, a father of eight was 34 in 1960 when he started a modest powdered-milk delivery service in Mount Sterling in western Illinois. Today, Tracy's Dot Foods Inc. is the largest food redistributor in the U.S., delivering more than 134,000 products to distributors across the country, employing over 4300 workers, with sales exceeding $8.1 billion. Joe Tracy, son of Robert

---

[8] Zhao, H., & Seobert, S.E. (2006). The big five personality dimensions and entrepreneurial status: A meta-analytic review. *Journal of Applied Psychology*, 91: 259–271.

and Dorothy, and the current President and Chief Operating Officer of Dot Foods, recalls observing his father's love of talking with employees and customers. And, every other month, his mother would invite a different group of customers to the company to listen to what they were doing right and their views about how Dot Foods could improve. In an interview with *Family Business Magazine*, he explains how dinner conversations in their family reinforced the notion that while family harmony was the Rule #1, it was also okay to disagree and debate with candor without being destructive:

> We love to debate and don't shy away from conflicts.... Our parents often didn't see eye-to-eye. We learned from listening to them argue at the dinner table that people could have different perspectives and still share a common vision. Our comfort level with disagreements was a good preparation for the business. [Joe Tracy, President and COO, Dot Foods Inc.].[9]

It is not necessary for such quality family time to be spent around meals, however. Each family is unique and can arrange some form of regular get-togethers that facilitate the flow of conversations. Stories and dreams can be shared and listened to during walks or drives, vacations or celebrations, or even during sad family gatherings. The rhythms of some families naturally carve out times for easy flowing conversations. In such cases, all that is needed is to be an active participant and think of ways to deepen the experience and mutual learning. In cases where the current rhythms of a family do not encourage such conversations, there is a unique opportunity to organize new activities that bring the family in close range to listen to and observe each other.

As societal values change, family firm leaders at times have to contend with difficult mind-set shifts. Curt Carlson founded the Carlson Company in 1914, and provides an illustration of such challenges. Curt led his enterprise for sixty years and grew it to be one of the largest privately held hospitality and travel enterprises in the world, with annual revenues exceeding $8 billion. An old-school entrepreneur, he felt the leadership position was a man's domain. With no sons of his own, and despite his daughter Marilyn's interest in and aptitude to run the family business since she was young, it was only a year before he died at 84 in 1998 that he named her his successor. When he was in his seventies and became ill, Curt appointed his son-in-law as CEO for a brief period, only to reclaim the leadership once he recovered. Might this interim appointment of his son-in-law as CEO signal his struggle to renegotiate the concept of family and gender roles that he had grown up with?

---

[9] Stone, D. (2013). Big family, big business. *Family Business Magazine*, November–December.

In order to manage his internal struggles and beliefs around gender and leadership, Curt became an avid student of family business and eventually named his daughter Marilyn as his successor, while also creating a nine-member board, with three members each elected by the two daughters and another three independents. Although he was unsure whether or not any of his daughters could or should lead the company, it is interesting that this dilemma did not stop him from encouraging developing the skills and self-efficacy in his daughters. When interviewed by *Women Corporate Directors*, Marilyn noted how he imbued the desire to excel in her by pushing her to 'strive for an A rather than A-; to run for President rather than Vice-President.'[10]

At age 12, when Marilyn Carlson Nelson announced to her parents that she no longer wanted to attend Sunday school because of its dull curriculum, her father insisted, "if you don't like it, fix it!", asking her to make a list of how to fix it. Later, her mother drove her to the superintendent of Sunday school to present her concerns and ideas. Taking her seriously, the superintendent asked her to form and lead a group of students to fix the program.[11] The effect of this learning moment was so profound for her that when she was inter-viewed after ten years at the helm of one of the largest hospitality companies in the world, she recounted it as one of the important learning moments of her life.[12] Her father had challenged her to think of ways to improve the Sunday School rather than turning a blind eye on the problem she identified, thus encouraging her to think of new solutions to identified problems. Her parents set in motion an opportunity to learn to articulate her ideas, work in a team and take responsibility of making a meaningful difference in her com-munity—all without them providing the solutions directly. Instead, they used the moment to let her experience the entrepreneurial learning. Stretch goals like these are part of everyday norms in enterprising families.

In 2013, Diana Nelson, third generation of the Carlson family, took over the role of board Chair from her mother who held the job for ten years after the founder died. While these leadership transitions appear seamless now, there were some challenging moments for the incumbent leaders in making these decisions. Curt expected Marilyn's son and his namesake, Curtis Carlson Nelson, to succeed his mother as a CEO. And, Curtis did serve as the presi-dent and chief operating officer of the company for some time. But the board did not select him to lead the company, citing poor performance and

---

[10] Spector, B. (2013). A new era at Carlson. *Family Business Magazine*, September–October.

[11] Spector, B. (2013). A new era at Carlson. *Family Business Magazine*. September–October.

[12] Spector, B. (2013). A new era at Carlson. *Family Business Magazine*. September–October.

substance abuse. Instead, his sister, Diane was selected for the top job. Even for one of the most enterprising companies in the world, the family concepts of gender and blood relationships seem to be deep rooted over generations. In her 2008 book, Marilyn expresses sadness in having to let go of her dream of passing the leadership of her father's business to her son but expresses confidence and delight that her daughter is in the job.

There are no short cuts to embed a habit of exploring for ideas and opportunities. The pathway of mindful training is winding and dotted with challenging stretch goals not only for the junior generation but also for the incumbent leaders. Long leadership tenures in family enterprises necessitate incumbent leaders to cope with changing norms and expectations across generations. Continuous reflections, peer learning, and experimentation combined with governance pathways like family meetings and councils, enable the negotiation of challenges along the way. Table 8.1 summarizes some key

Table 8.1 Building family members' ambidextrous skills

Explorations
Parenting structures
- Support for individuals pursuing their best talents and developing skills
- Support for real choice in terms of careers
- High expectations and standards for performance

Communication patterns
- Talk at the family table
- Openness of perspectives
- Enthusiasm for business possibilities
- Common vision and values

Roles and Opportunities to build skills
- Paid age appropriate summer jobs and internships
- A series of progressively larger jobs within the business
- Managerial responsibilities with clear accountability for outcomes
- Imaginative assignments within or at the margins of existing enterprises
- True mentoring and career advice from senior family and non-family managers

Exploitations
Vision to grow through innovation and renewal
- Articulate family values driven vision and purpose of the family enterprise
- Access to run ideas by family and non-family experts
- Opportunities to hear and share different perspectives

Professional structures, systems and training
- Governance systems to clarify decision making authority and responsibility
- Capabilities to draw data driven decisions aligned with the stated vision
- Clarity of objectives and milestones

Family and/or non-family member teams
- Empowered with time and resources to experiment with new ideas
- Continuous learning expected and honest mistakes encouraged and documented
- Accountability for results; Performance evaluations by self- and others and corrective actions

insights and actionable items in family and business contexts to develop family members' confidence and ability to explore and exploit entrepreneurial possibilities.

Exploitations

As important as it is to explore, identify and develop new opportunities that fit with values and aspirations of the business family, it is equally important to preserve the core competencies that ensure the business continues to perform well, and when possible improve processes and practices that account for the bulk of revenue and profitability. Family enterprises with too many undeveloped new ideas incur exploration costs without its benefits, and those focused exclusively on exploitations get trapped in suboptimal or diminishing returns of investments.[13] Even startups have to deliver on basic operational tasks, not just a declared vision. For example, crucial for sustained life of the organization are tasks like generating and maintaining knowledge of and service to customers or clients, establishing and keeping supply lines open and processing/operations costs in control, quality ingrained, product features closely connected to market needs and desires, sources of capital preserved with proper trust, and so on.

Entrepreneurial leaders enjoy starting something new and inspiring others to energetically follow along. Wherever a gap exists, an opportunity awaits. As the Covid-19 pandemic engulfed the world restricting travel, some families have made it a habit to conduct regular virtual calls not only to stay connected with family and customers, but also to brainstorm business development ideas. Many business families struggle to know where to begin to develop a structure where family members could step out from their familial roles to discuss the business as colleagues. A few illustrative examples are shared below. "Rita Marquez",[14] a young Latina whom we knew as a bright Babson College student, became very concerned about the unfolding dynamics among her business family that included her parents (founders), brother (now CEO), and two sisters (one VP of sales living in the US, and one CEO of a division). Rita, the youngest sibling, was serving as CEO of another division in another Central American country, a stretch job for her since she was a recent graduate and the youngest in the business. Here's how she described her concerns:

---

[13] March, J.G. (1991). Exploitation and Exploration in Organizational Learning, *Organization Science*, 2(1): 71–87.

[14] Disguised name.

All my brothers and sisters involved in the family business will be in [our home country] this weekend. Thus, I wanted to use this opportunity to have a family meeting as there have been many unresolved problems that need to be fixed. How do I make it a proactive session instead of a session where feelings will be hurt?…

My family never talks about problems; people don't like to openly talk about their feelings. My dad transferred the baton as CEO to my brother. This decision had the support of all family members. He did it as we were pressuring him to pass it on. We were getting quotes from consultants. However, he did it without a consultant. Without telling anyone in the company, in his speech at the Christmas dinner, he passed the baton over to my brother "*Hector*". My brother has implemented new projects that have allowed the company to maintain sustained growth in a very rough economy. And, my father has remained in the company as legal advisor/supervising stores/public relations. Two years after this, *Hector* was diagnosed with very delicate health issues. My brother is actively involved with many charitable organizations and is the chapter president in some cases. This has forced my mother and my father to get more involved in the business and the power has changed again towards the founders. Currently my mother's and my dad's health have declined due to stress and pressure. They complain about my brother's absence and the workload they are carrying, as he is not focusing on the business, as he should. On the other hand, my brother complains about my parents doing things without his consent…

I have called a three-hour family meeting on Sunday. I need to create a dynamic that will allow me to reveal these problems without talking about it directly. I need to trust the process, but I have no idea what dynamic to create, or how to go about it. **HELP SOS.**

The challenge of getting things done without talking about them directly is challenging in any context and particularly so in business families with little experience in such delicate family discussions. Yet, coming out of the meeting, she reported great progress, summarized as follows:

1. Quantitative evaluations for family members (a completely new idea, embraced by all)
2. Regular board meetings for Division 1 (even months) and Division 2 (odd months)
3. Become headhunters. Develop in-company programs to identify and grow high potential managers and use internships to engage new employees
4. Use intra-departmental quality circles to be in continuous improvement and cross-learning mode
5. Boosting growth in private label for the two major product areas

Three months later Rita reported:

> Last week, we had our first board meeting after the intervention. All the family members presented their quantitative [self-] evaluations. I think it was a great start because it helped us to focus on the priorities the company is expecting of us, and we could see the improvements immediately. From this experience I would encourage all family businesses to be more quantitative with their family members' evaluations, and actually have evaluations.

A recent update from Rita was even more encouraging. The overall business was thriving and she personally was growing and doing very well.[15]

While this example highlights some first steps toward developing a system for family members to come together to share their ideas and deliberate on roles and entrepreneurial possibilities, with accountability, our next example focuses on the unfolding of innovation while maintaining exploitation at Menasha Corporation, a fifth-generation company.[16] This billion-dollar packaging company was founded in 1852 and has evolved from retailing of dry goods into manufacturing wooden tubs and containers, through owning, managing and selling timberlands into brown corrugated box production, then promotional displays and now manufacturing of consumer goods packaging. It had its ups and downs over the years, but developed entrepreneurial solutions that have allowed the company to survive and thrive. Formal leadership, for example, alternated among family and non-family members, depending on how well the executives did at steering the company. Though they were good at exploration and innovation, several were poor at execution and were replaced by family or non-family members.

Throughout Menasha's history, employees had been empowered, encouraged and motivated to continuously implement innovations at all levels in the company—design, sales, manufacturing and internal systems. There is a strong training program in which the fundamentals of innovation processes, experimentation and evaluating new ideas are taught using the latest available knowledge.

---

[15] Information provided by Rita Marquez and included in Cohen and Sharma, *Entrepreneurs in Every Generation*.

[16] This description is based on the article, "Generation to generation innovation at Menasha Corporation," by Sylvia Shepherd, (chair of the Smith Family Council and a fifth-generation owner of Menasha Corporation,), *Family Business Magazine*, 2013, and personal interviews with her by Cohen and Sharma, 7/8, 8/12, 2014.

Leadership is the other factor which has had an impact on their culture of innovation. Once again, the expectation is that the leaders will provide financial support and allow time for innovation to be successful. While as a private corporation, Menasha is financially frugal and tends to avoid big risks, calculated risk taking by employees is encouraged. The business family believes that if you aren't constantly experimenting, trying new things, you aren't doing your job. But many experiments fail, and that is also acceptable as long as lessons learned are clearly articulated. Menasha leaders are "hands on" and are willing to get down in the trenches and provide support wherever it is needed, while avoiding micro-managing their teams. Innovative employees are recognized and celebrated. Employees are encouraged to communicate between business units and among each other, learning how innovative practices or products in one area can be utilized in another. Open communication is practiced and reinforced.

A useful fifth-generation innovation was the creation of the Smith Family Council, aimed at improving communications among the business, board, and other family members. With over 150 family shareholders, this structure is a necessary component allowing for future entrepreneurial decisions related to issues such as major investment, dividend policy, liquidity options, family member roles in and out of the business, and so on. Looking at the history of encouraging entrepreneurial behavior, we can see many of the universal elements of organizations that encourage innovation and some others particular to family business.

Not every company is fortunate enough to have a long history that supports flexibility, initiative from below, willingness to try new things, experience and an understanding that the family is not the sole possessor of knowledge and good ideas, plus decentralization and reliance on teams, but this one serves as a vivid example of what is possible when the mechanisms can be established and accepted.

As families grow larger over generations, inevitably a gap develops between the opportunities available in the business and the diverse interests of family members. Many contend with the 'roots and wings' question, that is, how to ensure that the family stays close and connected to its core values and to each other, while enabling opportunities for each individual. Another recent trend is for family members to transition out of operational roles into governance roles.

The Kanfer family,[17] manufacturers of Purell hand sanitizers, is another exemplary entrepreneurial business family that has moved to family investor

[17] Schupak, H. (2016). Clean hands and giving hearts. *Family Business Magazine*.

roles while the business operations are managed by non-family professionals. The family board has carved out policies that allow family members to conceptualize and propose new ventures in areas of their interest, as long as the venture aligns with the values of the Kanfer family. The family invests a portion of the seed funding needed and the proposer must invest his/her own or outside funding for the rest. This is a fine example of how one family is attempting to encourage entrepreneurial explorations and exploitations over generations.

Each business family and its enterprises are unique and thus each family has to carve its own pathways to ingrain the freedom to explore and the accountability to exploit entrepreneurial ideas, and provide opportunities for interested family and non-family members to build their ambidextrous skills. But like Curt Nelson, family leaders who continue to learn from others and reflect on variations that would work for them, tend to balance the continuity and change dilemma effectively to succeed over generations. With long-term orientation and overlap of family and business, unlike their non-family counter-parts, leaders of business families are nicely positioned to take advantages of the extended temporal depth and contextual breadth to develop ambidextrous entrepreneurial skills of their family members.

Concluding Insights

Ambidextrous family leaders find ways to balance the explorations and exploitation of innovations by their enterprises across generations. In general, enlightened leadership that supports openness to experiences and welcomes entrepreneurial ideas and initiatives by family and non-family members are most attractive to diverse family members and keep them involved once they are in. Commitment to adaptation makes room for diverse interests that are not automatically easy spinoffs from existing businesses. Using the multiple contexts of family, community and business enterprise (see Table 8.1), it is possible to increase the probability to develop the ambidextrous skills and talents of family members, and increase the likelihood of next-generation engagement. Like the Kanfer family, creative ideas can be used to retain the core of the family business while encouraging new ventures by family members that are at least partly financed by the business family. Yet ways to sustain traditional practices that meet demands for operational excellence prevent avoidable execution failures. The challenges, however, are ongoing, providing opportunity for family members with diverse talents and interests to find connection and commitment.

We discussed a few strategies proven useful to cultivate and transmit the entrepreneurial mind-set across generations, even as the nature of business and external environment continues to evolve. Using examples, we describe how the family communication patterns, parenting structures and family member roles evolve over time to build intergenerational solidarity in pursuit of exploring entrepreneurial initiatives. And, clarity and refinement of family's vision and identity for business, professional structures and talented family and non-family teams ensure strategic exploitations of identified new ideas to create value over generations of family leadership.

9

The Importance of Externally Focused Self-awareness to Family Entrepreneurship

Scott N. Taylor

We have learned much in recent years about the influence positive emotions and positive relationships have on our ability to be innovative, creative, and empathetic (e.g., Boyatzis, Rochford, & Taylor, 2015). Innovation, creativity and empathy are at the heart of thinking and acting entrepreneurially (Shalley, Hitt, & Zhou, 2015). Therefore, entrepreneurial activity in a family is likely contingent on the nature of the relationships in the family. In my years as an executive coach working with family businesses and businesses that are family led, I consistently observe one sobering reality: even though family members have spent their lives together, it does not mean that they know what the others *really* want. This may shock some, especially those who would claim that their family dynamics are positive and healthy, and have been so for many years. Others may be surprised because "In our family we share everything about everything." Perhaps, but what I find is that often family members *believe* they know more than they actually do know about each other, especially when it comes to what a family member *ideally* wants out of life, work, family and what the member's *ideal* moments have been and what they hope they will be, going forward. As a result, the relationships and emotions in the family are not as positive as they could be which influences the level of family entrepreneurship.

S. N. Taylor (✉)
Babson College, Babson Park, MA, USA
e-mail: staylor@babson.edu

© The Author(s), under exclusive license to Springer Nature Switzerland AG 2021
M. R. Allen, W. B. Gartner (eds.), *Family Entrepreneurship*,
https://doi.org/10.1007/978-3-030-66846-4_9

These observations became more poignant for me when I joined Babson College where almost 50% of our undergraduate students and over 60% of our graduate students come from family businesses. We find that by the time these students graduate, too often there is a disconnect between what the students hope happens to them in relation to the family business versus the expectations or perceptions the family has for their graduating students. For example, the student wants to have nothing to do with the business while the family eagerly awaits the student's return to take over a major part of the business. Alternatively, the student is anxious to use family finances to start a new line in the family business and the family is excited for the student to return— counting inventory—right where the student left off before heading out to college. In many cases, the students' aspirations go unshared, which creates misperceptions about the other. The misperceptions—a lack of awareness as to what each other really wants—exist because families often fail to have discussions that would build collective awareness about the hopes and dreams of the other. Instead, family members make assumptions about each other, or worse, impose their own hopes and dreams on others in the family.

When we see others as something other than for who they really are, we have stepped into the zone of self-deception, the antithesis of self-awareness (The Arbinger Institute, 2019). If I see you as an incompetent accountant and your actual capability is indeed exceptional, then I have falsified reality by way of my self-deception. In some cases, I may do this because I have bad information, which led to my inaccurate assessment. In other cases, I may not like you as a person or I may distrust you, and this leads to seeing you as something you are not. Whenever we see someone as a vehicle, object, or a means to an end, or something to be acted upon, for example, we have self-deceived because the reality is that another person is none of those things. Human beings (i.e., our employees, our family members, etc.,) are actors, not objects to be acted upon.

I have been researching leader self-awareness for over 20 years. I have asked hundreds of leaders how they define self-awareness. The most common answers I receive are an awareness of one's strengths and weaknesses, an understanding of one's identity, values, goals, personal preferences, clarity about one's personality, and so on. These are indeed all part of the definition of self-awareness (i.e., a knowledge of the self and the self's resources), but they are only half of the definition of self-awareness (Taylor, 2010). It is correct to say that self-awareness is an awareness of self and all the capabilities that self has to offer. Think of this aspect of self-awareness as being the *internally focused* part of self-awareness. However, there is more. The often forgotten, second part of self-awareness is the part of self-awareness that also resides within the individual but is *externally focused*. This second component is the ability to anticipate how others experience us (Taylor, 2010). This is the part of self-awareness that is often missing in discussions of leader self-awareness, and yet it is so critical to leading others effectively (e.g., Sturm, Taylor, Atwater, & Braddy, 2014; Taylor, Wang, & Zhan, 2012) and avoiding the forms of self-deception described earlier.

To illustrate the importance of this second component of self-awareness, the ability to anticipate how others experience our leadership, let me share a story from U.S. history:

> Charles Francis Adams, the grandson of the second president of the United States, was a successful lawyer, a member of the U.S. House of Representatives, and the U.S. ambassador to Britain. Amidst his responsibilities, he had little time to spare. He did, however, keep a diary. One day he wrote, "Went fishing with my son today—a day wasted!" On that same date, Charles's son, Brooks Adams, had printed in his own diary, "Went fishing with my father today—the most wonderful day of my life" (Pinnegar, 1994, p. 82).

If Charles was not aware of the impact fishing with dad had on Brooks Adams, I seriously doubt father and son had many other fishing expeditions after dad's "wasted day." On the other hand, imagine if Charles could anticipate accurately how his son experienced fishing with dad. Let me provide an example of the same idea from my own family experience.

My wife worked for Disney World. She loves all things related to the Disney Parks. In fact, one of the most memorable discussions we had in our courting days was on *if* we were to marry and *if* we were fortunate enough to have children, would take them to Disneyland or Disney World. I, for one, did not feel as if my youth was deprived in never having had the opportunity to go to either park. On the other hand, it became very clear that my chances of marrying this former Disney employee may very well be contingent on my agreeing that for certain we would take any and all future children to the Disney Parks one day (not really, but it was certainly on her "bucket list"). I agreed that this would be a fun family adventure, on the condition that we not take our children to Disney World or Disneyland until they were old enough to remember the experience (i.e., we are not taking our 1 year old child to a Disney park!).

After marriage and four children joining the two of us, the defining moment finally came when our youngest was five years old. The long anticipated family adventure had arrived. Team Taylor was heading to Disneyland. I could not tell who was more excited, my wife or our four children.

It was at this time when I came across the story of Charles Adams and his son Brooks. I decided I should test my own level of external self-awareness. I came up with the brilliant idea of using our trip to Disneyland as just the way to do so. This would be a social experiment of sorts. I would observe my children closely during our week at Disneyland. At the end of the week, I would try to predict with perfect accuracy what the high point of the trip was for each child. Could I do it? Could I be that observant and in tune with each child to guess accurately? I felt quite confident I could do so. By mid-week, I had each child pegged. I was able to use the rest of the week to confirm my predictions. For our oldest son, I had no doubt that his peak moment of the week was the Magic Mountain ride. He could not get enough of that ride! He even had a dream about it one night in the hotel room. For our daughter it was the Carrousel ride. This was clearly her greatest moment of the week. And so on with the other two.

After the week was over and we were heading home, it was time to assess my level of self-awareness. On the plane ride home, I took time with the children (one by one in order to not bias my sample by having them hear each other's story), and asked him or her to share their high-point moment for the week at Disneyland. I eagerly listened as they shared their peak moment stories and compared what they shared with what I had predicted they would share. To my surprise, I got all four predictions wrong. I could not believe it. What made matters even more devastating (but spurred my interest in leader self-awareness—especially my own—even more) was that all four children told me the same story. They collectively said, "Dad, we had a great time at Disneyland, but if you want to know the best moment, it was at the end of the day we would come back to the hotel and go swimming." Really? We spent all that money and time at Disneyland and their best moment that week was swimming at a hotel pool? Out of (a prenuptial) agreement, we went to Disney World a few years later, but we have not been to either park since. However, I will tell you this. Team Taylor has done *much* swimming since that trip to Disneyland. My children love to swim and that awareness has had a significant impact on how we as parents have chosen to spend our time with our children. We do not go on vacation where there is not a pool nearby.

One of my contributions to the research literature on leader self-awareness has been to bring back a focus on seeing self-awareness as more than just "know thyself". Self-awareness is also one's ability to anticipate how others experience us (Taylor, 2010). This ability to predict accurately seems particularly important in the manager-direct report relationship (Taylor et al., 2012), even more important than the manager seeing him or herself the same as he or she is seen by others.

Externally Focused Self-Awareness in the Family Business

Now consider your family business. Can you anticipate accurately how family members experience you and your leadership? Can you anticipate accurately what role your family members want to have in the family business in the near future and in the long-term? Notice I am not asking what role you want them to have in the business or even what they may have told you the role is they want to have. These questions focus on assessing how accurately aware you are of what others *genuinely* want.

Let me offer some ways to help you assess and develop your externally focused self-awareness. Consider having a one-one-one discussion with members of your family around the questions noted below. This is an active listening session rather than a time for you to give them feedback. Ask them the following questions, but before you do, I want you to predict what they will say in response to each question. Write your predictions down for each person you interview and then go have the interview. The key with these interviews is to have the family members share stories with each question. You are trying to predict the stories each person will share.

1. There are difficulties and peak moments within every family. I want you to consider a high-point moment. A moment or experience in our family that for you was a peak moment where you felt the most joy or sense of connection or happiness as a member of our family. Share that moment with me.
2. Think of someone you know whom you would consider an outstanding leader. Tell me the person's name and share a story about this person that for you exemplifies why you consider this person to be an outstanding leader.
3. Share with me one thing that you believe you are really good at doing in your life or at work. After you have thought of that one thing, share with me a story of doing that one thing and the impact you think it had on you and/or others.
4. If you had your ideal life and work ten years from now, what would it be like? What would you be doing? Who would you be doing it with?

After making predictions (as accurately as possible) as to what stories each family member will tell and after interviewing each person, compare what you predicted they would say versus what they actually said? How did you do? Were you able to anticipate what others would say?

If you struggled, you are not alone. In reviewing how self-awareness has been defined and taught, I found that most leadership and management education only define self-awareness in terms of the first, internal aspect (i.e., knowledge of self). We were rarely asked to think about self-awareness in terms of our ability to anticipate how others experience our leadership. What this has created are many leaders who think that as long as they have themselves figured out (the internal aspects of self-awareness; e.g., they know they do not like fishing) then they have leader self-awareness figured out. In too many cases, these leaders feel like they have done the self-work needed to lead others (e.g., they took personality assessments, they know their strengths, etc.). Nevertheless, without developing and strengthening their being attuned to how others experience them, they make assumptions about others that might not be correct. In family business, this can be even more challenging given the duration and level of intimacy of family relationships.

With misperceptions and assumptions in place, long-term patterns of relating can get us in trouble in terms of our creating a reality about ourselves, our impact on others and how others experience us that are not correct, and are a falsification of reality. When confronted with the contrary (e.g., the reality experienced by others), these leaders resist the counter reality and use defensive routines to discount it (e.g., stating others are wrong or misguided or being irascible and difficult), when in reality it is the leader that is misguided. Suppose Charles Adams assumed that because he considered the day fishing a day wasted that his son did as well. Imagine his response years later when he learns his son wants leave the family business to open a bait and tackle shop to sell fishing supplies and run fishing expeditions.

Linking Family Entrepreneurship to Self-awareness

Research shows that emotional and social intelligence competencies, like self-awareness, are critical to entrepreneurship (e.g., Humphrey, 2013; Zakarevičius & Župerka, 2010). For example, Humphrey (2013) claimed that entrepreneurs high in emotional and social intelligence will be "more successful at handling intense emotions when working with family members" as well as enable the family entrepreneurs to be more "successful at motivating and leading their employees", "helping their employees cope with workplace stresses" and "be more innovative" (p. 287). A lack of self-awareness will restrain the entrepreneurial process and could cause the family to miss the very things that will effectively sustain the family venture.

For example, few daughters become successors of the family business (Overbeke, Bilimoria, & Perelli, 2013). Could the dearth of daughter successors to family businesses result from a lack of self-awareness that leads to misperceptions family business leaders have made about their daughters? This may be why one set of researchers stated that daughter successors are often "invisible" as potential successors. What did make for successful father and daughter succession? One set of researchers found that "shared vision between father and daughters is central to daughter succession....when fathers and daughters share a vision for the future of the company, daughters are likely to be...successors" (Overbeke, Bilimoria, & Somers, 2015, p. 1). Shared vision occurs when there is a high level of shared understanding that comes from mutual awareness (Boyatzis et al., 2015).

Returning to our Babson students who come from family businesses, imagine if family members (and the students) were accurately attuned to each other. Important aspects of family business like succession planning, conflict management, talent management, delegation, trust, and so on would become much easier and more efficient. This clarity of shared vision and understanding would foster positive emotions and positive relationships to enable stronger family entrepreneurial activity.

What is the Antidote for Low Self-awareness?

One of the greatest antidotes to low external self-awareness is to see people as people, to see others as they really are. This requires us to look outside of ourselves and invest in getting to know others, including their hopes, dreams, beliefs, values and desired future. As we do, as we care and learn about others in this way, we start to become more accurate in anticipating how our leadership (parenting, coaching, etc.,) affects them.

What I am describing here is seeing the other more holistically and accurately. Recent research shows we do so when certain networks in our brain (e.g. the default mode network) are activated. These networks enable our empathetic cognition that in turn assist us to see others more accurately and holistically, to receive feedback from others more willingly, and to connect with others in more meaningful (prosocial) ways (Boyatzis, Smith, & Van Oosten, 2019). More accurate estimate of how others experience my leadership is how I became aware that my children love to swim, for example. Because I know that my children love to swim, one of the best recognitions I can give them for their efforts in school and at home is to take them on a swimming trip. I know that recognition will have a stronger, more positive impact than other choices I could make to acknowledge their effort.

On the other hand, it is not enough to invest in these relationship-building efforts just once. People change. As my children got older, their interests in what they like to do as a family changed. Thus, I needed to stay in tune with their changes to understand how I could be the best possible father for them in our family and more effectively influence them in positive ways. Therefore, the development of externally focused self-awareness needs continual investment on our part in order to stay in tune with the changes of the other. We can foster this growth by engaging in ongoing developmental discussions as part of the family business.

How Do We Get There? Developmental Conversations

Family business members are generally good about ensuring they have ongoing conversations about business issues and conversations about family issues. I find (and research supports; e.g., Pounder, 2015) the challenge comes in the interrelationship between family issues and business issues. This is certainly not a new challenge to research on family business (e.g., Levinson, 1971). One of the ways we seek to help our Babson students who come from family businesses to wrestle with potential awareness gap and the interrelationships between them, their families and their family business is via a new course called *The Amplifier*. This course grows the external focused aspect of self-awareness between a family business leader and a Babson student by helping them engage in developmental conversations with each other. For example, we invite the students to do the following over the course of a semester.

1. We ask the student how they define a leader. After writing out their definition and sharing with a peer student, we ask the students to ask the same question of their family business leader. Before they have the conversation with their family business leader, we ask the students to predict what they think their family leader will say. We also ask the students to ask their family business leader to predict how the student defined what constitutes a leader. After they each share their definitions with one another, they compare how they predicted and what they learn about each other from how

they defined and how attuned they were to how the other would define a leader.

2. Following the pattern above of defining and predicting and then sharing, we ask our student to write out what their ideal work and life would look like 10–15 years from the present date. We tell the students this is not about writing out what their goals might be over the next 10–15 years but instead to write out their dream for a desired future, their ideal self or vision statement. Again, once written, the students ask their family business leader to do the same and then they predict what the other wrote and share what they each wrote.

3. Following the pattern with the last two developmental conversations, we have the students do the same with listing their top five values and identifying whom they would have on a personal board of directors if they could choose anyone as personal advisors to support them in their growth and development in the contexts of their life and work.

I have found in both my coaching work with family businesses and with students that these type of developmental conversations create positive, generative discussions that change how we see the other (Taylor, Passarelli, & Van Oosten, 2019); we come to see others more holistically and more accurately (Boyatzis et al., 2019). As we do, our self-awareness increases; and with more accurate awareness, we are in a position to influence each other in more positive and generative ways. Developmental discussions lead to higher levels of shared awareness that in turn leads to positive relationships and emotions that then foster innovation and creativity (Taylor et al., 2019). This results in increased entrepreneurial activity in family businesses.

Conclusion

One of the overarching questions of this book asks how a family, as a system, can establish, develop, promote, support or teach entrepreneurship as a behavior, belief or value across generations. My response is that entrepreneurial activity in a family is most likely to occur and *maintained over time* when the nature of the family relationships are overall positive and closely connected. One of the ways to create such relationships is to invest in the development of externally focused self-awareness in the family.

References

Boyatzis, R. E., Rochford, K., & Taylor, S. N. (2015). The Role of the Positive and Negative Emotional Attractors in Vision and Shared Vision: Toward Effective Leadership, Relationships and Engagement. *Frontiers in Psychology, 6*, 670. https://doi.org/10.3389/fpsyg.2015.00670

Boyatzis, R., Smith, M., & Van Oosten, E. (2019). *Helping People Change: Coaching with Compassion for Lifelong Learning and Growth*. Boston, MA: Harvard Business School Press.

Humphrey, R. H. (2013). The Benefits of Emotional Intelligence and Empathy to Entrepreneurship. *Entrepreneurship Research Journal, 3*(3), 287–294.

Levinson, H. (1971). Conflicts that Plague the Family Business. *Harvard Business Review, 71*(2), 90–98.

Overbeke, K., Bilimoria, D., & Perelli, S. (2013). The Dearth of Daughter Successors in Family Businesses: Gendered Norms, Blindness to Possibility and Invisibility. *Journal of Family Business Strategy, 4*, 201–212. https://doi.org/10.1016/j.jfbs.2013.07.002

Overbeke, K. K., Bilimoria, D., & Somers, T. (2015). Shared Vision between Fathers and Daughters in Family Businesses: The Determining Factor that Transforms Daughters into Successors. *Frontiers in Psychology, 6*, 625. https://doi.org/10.3389/fpsyg.2015.00625

Pinnegar, R. D. (1994). The Simple Things. *Ensign, 24*(11), 80–82.

Pounder, P. (2015). Family Business Insights: An Overview of the Literature. *Journal of Family Business Management, 5*(1), 116–127.

Shalley, C. E., Hitt, M. A., & Zhou, J. (Eds.). (2015). *The Oxford Handbook of Creativity, Innovation, and Entrepreneurship*. New York, NY: Oxford University Press.

Sturm, R. E., Taylor, S. N., Atwater, L. E., & Braddy, P. W. (2014). Leader Self-awareness: An Examination and Implications for Women Leaders. *Journal of Organizational Behavior, 35*, 657–677.

Taylor, S. N. (2010). Redefining Leader Self-Awareness by Integrating the Second Component of Self-awareness. *Journal of Leadership Studies, 3*(4), 57–68.

Taylor, S. N., Passarelli, A., & Van Oosten, E. B. (2019). Leadership Coach Effectiveness as Fostering Self-determined, Sustained Change. *The Leadership Quarterly, 30*(6). https://doi.org/10.1016/j.leaqua.2019.101313

Taylor, S. N., Wang, M., & Zhan, Y. (2012). Going beyond Self-other Rating Agreement: Comparing Two Components of Self-awareness Using Multisource Feedback Assessment. *Journal of Leadership Studies, 6*(2), 6–31.

The Arbinger Institute. (2019). *The Outward Mindset*. San Francisco, CA: Berrett-Koehler Publishers.

Zakarevičius, P., & Župerka, A. (2010). Expression of Emotional Intelligence in Development of Students' Entrepreneurship. *Economics & Management*, 865–873.

Part IV

Advancing Family Entrepreneurship

10

Antecedents to Entrepreneurship: How Successful Business Families Nurture Agency and Kindle the Dreams of the Next Generation

Ivan Lansberg and Fernanda Jaramillo

Entrepreneurship means the act (or acts) of turning an aspiration into a viable, sustainable business through creation or by identifying and then fulfilling the need for reinvention in an existing enterprise. While the entrepreneurship literature recognizes the existence of an *ecosystem* that enhances the very likelihood of entrepreneurship (government programs, small-business-focused NGOs, microcredit agencies, etc.), it has, for the most part, neglected the family as a powerful contextual force in the successful development of new enterprises or in the reinvention of existing ones. And yet, since time immemorial, the family has acted as the natural incubator in which entrepreneurial ideas are conceived, hatched, and nurtured. Whether *pushed* into entrepreneurship by hardship and sheer force of circumstance or *pulled* into it by the pursuit of an imagined business possibility, it is often an entrepreneur's

The authors would like to acknowledge the invaluable editorial contributions of Simon Lansberg-Rodriguez to this chapter.

I. Lansberg (✉)
Lansberg, Gersick & Associates, New Haven, CT, USA

Kellogg School of Management, Northwestern University, Evanston, IL, USA
e-mail: lansberg@lgassoc.com

F. Jaramillo
Lansberg, Gersick & Associates, New Haven, CT, USA
e-mail: jaramillo@lgassoc.com

© The Author(s), under exclusive license to Springer Nature Switzerland AG 2021
M. R. Allen, W. B. Gartner (eds.), *Family Entrepreneurship*,
https://doi.org/10.1007/978-3-030-66846-4_10

family—with its complex array of personalities, expectations, obligations, resources, relationships, dynamics, and dysfunctions—that stimulates and guides the transformation of individual aspirations into viable businesses. That families naturally vary in their capacity to stimulate entrepreneurship (and, likewise, individual family members differ in their own innate entrepreneurial abilities and predispositions) raises the question of how best to promote and bolster entrepreneurial qualities across a wide range of families, businesses, and, crucially, the unique characteristics that make up these intimate networks. This chapter focuses on the practical nurturing of *agency* as it relates to successful entrepreneurship. Our objective here is to understand the origins, commonalities, and potential applications of familial practices that we have documented in the course of over thirty-five years working with business families.

Agency Within Family Enterprise

Before the Industrial Revolution, most production of goods and services took place in a home environment and children grew up having direct exposure to their parents' work (Mintz & Kellogg, 1988). Children over time became de facto apprentices, learning the skills of their family's trade out of necessity, duty, or even via osmosis by observing and mirroring those around them.[1] All these trajectories can, and do, prepare the members of new generations to maintain the family's business, without necessarily entrusting them with the *agency* that is so foundational to entrepreneurship.

Like freedom, agency results from mutual, intergenerational trust and respect: in exchange for meeting or surpassing expectations (behavioral, familial, academic, or otherwise), younger family members are given the space to form their own opinions, try new things, and take basic risks with the tacit or explicit understanding that these expectations persist. If the family honors this informal social contract, it creates an early sense of autonomy and strengthens that very trust and respect by giving those principles tangible value. Freedom is expressed through actions: driving to the mall, enrolling in an elective music course. Agency goes further by giving these actions an *effective purpose*: driving to the mall *to buy swim goggles*, enrolling in an elective music course *to learn about rock and roll for college credit*. By allowing younger family members not just the *how* of freedom but the *why* of agency, families arrive at an antecedent understanding of entrepreneurship: that freedom

---

[1] This was especially the case in framing the sector that has most powerfully forged the traditions, customs, and laws that are foundational to the archetypal construct of the family enterprise.

demands effective purpose. As these moment-by-moment choices, reasons, and effects accumulate, a direct relationship between agency and responsibility is further defined by family encouragement to pursue *particular* effective purposes: values expressed as *an understanding of privilege as a platform for responsibility and opportunity*.

While the interplay between various kinds of agency and their definitions remain subjects for academic debate, especially in philosophy and sociology (i.e., beyond the practical scope of this chapter), it is useful, especially when encouraging entrepreneurial thinking in younger members of rising generations, to differentiate between the *collective* agency of a group (an enterprising family, in this case) and the *individual* agency of each family member that group comprises (or may yet comprise). Seniors who express *relational* agency by remaining cognizant of the potential dynamics between their own individual agency, the collective agency of the family business, and the individual agency of young family members—and who *act* in a way that acknowledges the validity of the latter—demonstrate and *imbue* the very trust and respect necessary to align intergenerational values and promote successful entrepreneurship.

Privilege, recognized or not, often informs how a family enterprise will carry out its collective agency (or the individual agency of each member). When a mature family enterprise—one in its second generation or beyond—establishes among its members an intergenerational understanding of privilege as a purposeful platform, individual freedoms permitted by the family's means are imbued with effective purpose.[2] Viewed through this prism, freedoms that may otherwise be misused instead invite imagined productivity and demand demonstrable accountability. In the best of cases, the same platform lays a motivating foundation which elevates freedom of choice into agency with a conscience. Entrepreneurship, as an act, relies on the detection or creation of opportunity, but *successful* entrepreneurship requires the entrepreneur to act responsibly.[3] As seniors endeavor to foster entrepreneurial thinking in members of the younger generation, this paradigm is best expressed clearly, and in sequence: privilege is a platform for responsibility, *then* opportunity. By prioritizing responsibility, seniors are practicing the very

---

[2] While many of the antecedents we will review in this chapter have broad applicability to entrepreneurial families at all levels, this chapter will focus on *mature* business families in which there is an existing enterprise, an established baseline of wealth.

[3] There are, of course, mature family businesses with vastly different circumstances, including means and the degree of privilege enjoyed by their respective members. Some of the practices detailed in this chapter are not practical for *all* family businesses—our focus here is families who would be able to weather an immediate absence of profit. It is not our intent to *prescribe* practices to any families—*especially* those with urgent, existential concerns. (Simulating further necessity, for instance, would likely cause a needy family undue strain.)

values they are attempting to perpetuate, effectively modeling—not merely espousing—expectations for the next generation.

The most illuminating biographies of entrepreneurs (and histories of legendary business families) point to common familial **antecedents** that catalyze their agency. Taken alone or in a group (few families will implement *all* these suggestions), these antecedent practices are general enough to be meaningfully, transparently—even harmoniously—applicable to everyday activities and situations, yet focused enough to thoughtfully stoke the agency that leads to entrepreneurship. While that same versatility means that there is no "best" order in which to sequence or prioritize these practices, we believe their inherently relational nature—how they influence and are influenced by the complex, initially disparate authority dynamics of family, parenting styles, and developmental stages of a given family—demands an integrated understanding of privilege as a purposeful platform, shared between practitioner and tomorrow's entrepreneur.

These antecedents are as follows:

1. Modeling
2. Conveying an honest family narrative
3. Persevering together
4. Nurturing and giving permission to dream
5. Fostering curiosity
6. Conveying scarcity in a context of abundance

The intertwining nature of responsibility, opportunity, and agency makes feasible these antecedents across individual stages of life. For instance, John D. Rockefeller Jr.'s caveat for his children's allowances—that they give ten percent to charity, save another ten percent, and hold themselves accountable with a checkbook for the rest—worked as a transparent conveyance of scarcity that let the next generation exercise their agency at an impressionable age. Similarly, the Ochs-Sulzburgers of the *New York Times* have managed to entice the interest and agency of succeeding generations so that their diverse talents, dreams, and aspirations found expression and aligned with the institution's need for continuous reinvention. The transformation of a newspaper business into a global digital news and information platform could not have been accomplished without evoking and harnessing the individual and collective agency of their descendants.

Our basic thesis is that these practices are *antecedents* to entrepreneurship that serve to empower succeeding generations with the agency to innovate in line with a consistent set of values. Likewise, an intergenerational understanding of privilege as a platform for responsibility and opportunity is a versatile concept which begets adaptability in families at even starkly different points in their shared history. The individual merits of these practices are affirmed through the lived experiences of each generation, and, over time, compound into a balanced set of coalescing, self-correcting principles that imbue and sustain entrepreneurship, respectively, with viability and durability.

We arrive, then, at the answer to *why* families cultivate successful entrepreneurship: responsibility and opportunity. To understand *when* and *where* these moments occur, we must examine each antecedent practice in its singular capacity as a crucial ingredient in a handed-down recipe for family entrepreneurship. After exploring these practices in detail, we will turn to **entrepreneurial funds** as a specific, practical example of how the same strategies are expressed, sustained, and consistently guided by the fundamental values of a family business after it has integrated members of the next generation.

It is not our intention in the next section to comprehensively categorize these practices, but rather to describe the myriad ways in which families foster entrepreneurship and engage their members in the process of value creation: social, financial, emotional, and otherwise. While some details might come off as idealized, the approaches documented in this chapter reflect recurring themes and actions that we have observed in a diverse array of families around the world.

Modeling

Children are experts at fun. Put a five-year-old in a room full of people: she will scan the situation before moving—like a moth to a flame—directly toward the source of fun. From an early age, through exposure and invitation, children from business families can likewise intuit whether their parents and other family seniors (grandparents, aunts, uncles) genuinely enjoy their work (regardless of whether that work takes place in the business, its governance, or with the family). When seniors discuss their day over dinner or take business phone calls in a shared family space, or when they explain what they do and why it matters, or anytime they share the personal joys and sacrifices of their work, the young ones absorb powerful messages about the role of work in the lives of their seniors. These early, familiar impressions can help the next generation make sense of their own agency and give shape to their *own* psychological relationship to work. In time, questions about the meaning of work begin to emerge: *How will I engage with work in my life? What is meaningful work to me? What are my aspirations? How hard am I willing to work to realize them?*

When parents exhibit a genuine enjoyment of work through, say, a frequent and discernable display of being in a state flow (Csikszentmihalyi, 1990), their focus and engagement project a sense of fulfillment and excitement—a direct engagement with life and its vast array of possibilities. The enthusiasm of familial role models conveys how meaningful, purposeful work can be not only a viable but also an *enjoyable* path to self-actualization. A demonstrated passion for work, especially when coupled with stories about how the aspirations of past generations informed actions that yielded viable business opportunities, can be a powerful—and indeed, a *contagious*—stimulant of the entrepreneurial imagination of the next generation (Jaskiewicz, Combs, & Rau, 2015).

Ask next-generation members engaged in entrepreneurship: *Did your family influence your career choice? And if so, how?* More likely than not, you will hear moving accounts of incidents that left a deep imprint on the minds of young family members—inciting moments, often of the day-to-day variety, that inspired them with the personal possibility of entrepreneurship.

Years ago, our firm worked with a retail family whose flagship store was so successful that customers had begun to complain about long checkout lines. The store was in an ideal location in a popular New England town, but nevertheless struggled to expand beyond its current footprint. At the family's regular Sunday lunches, the company's founder, a charismatic entrepreneur in his eighties, loved to talk with his grandchildren about his work, the store he built, and its strategic and operational challenges. As complaints added up, the founder created a task force with three members of his staff (including two sons who worked in the business) to explore ideas on how best to tackle the problem of lengthy lines. At lunch the following Sunday, he brought the situation to the attention of his seven grandchildren: *"Can you guys help me solve a problem with the store's cash registers?"* After listening intently, the grandchildren immediately began brainstorming, but nothing seemed to offer much hope in the way of a solution. A week later, his fourteen-year-old granddaughter was at a store in a nearby town with her mother buying a Father's Day present for her father. Suddenly she notices how the cash register stations at this store were *streamlined*—and she realized that, by redesigning her family's checkout stations to be similarly narrow, the same space could accommodate *two* cashiers instead of one. The girl was so excited that she immediately blurted: *"Mom, guess what! This is the solution to Grandpa's problem!"* She even asked to be dropped off at the store on their way back so she could share the insight with her grandfather. When he heard the news, the grandfather jumped up and exclaimed: *"This is it! You solved it!"* He then convened a meeting with the taskforce and invited his granddaughter to personally explain the design to senior executives (who, needless to say, were mildly embarrassed for not having thought of this themselves).

Within a month, the entire store was remodeled per her suggestion. Every time she rode the bus back from school, she couldn't wait to hop off so she could check on how *her* idea was being implemented. After college and graduate school, the granddaughter joined the family enterprise and has been responsible for developing the company's online platform—now one of the most lucrative parts of the family business. And to this day, she describes this as being an indelible moment in her development. Moreover, two of the founder's children and five of the twelve grandchildren went on to start their own companies. Their grandfather's zest for entrepreneurship, his willingness to recruit his grandchildren's opinions in improving the store, and his delighted response upon being presented a useful solution captured their imaginations and helped to fuel their entrepreneurial dreams.

This kind of modeling is especially meaningful in family companies where the work of its seniors is interwoven with a shared family identity that goes back generations. When a young member of a prominent business family goes to school, their peers might ask about their possible connection to a business, its products, or services with which they share a name. How a family's seniors frame their own work experiences and personal connection to an existing enterprise affects how the next generation responds to these kinds of inquiries. When a family's seniors have modeled sincere enthusiasm for their work and investment in the family enterprise, the next generation is likely to respond to these inquiries with pride of association—reinforcing how belonging to an enterprising family is significant in the outside world.

Conveying an Honest Family Narrative

Business families can empower new generations of entrepreneurs by humanizing their founders and acknowledging their high and low points as distinct, informative chapters within their collective, *ongoing* narrative. As essential as conveying the flaws, contradictions, occasional luck, and privileges of founding figures is carving out a tangible place in which members of young generations can visualize themselves. *What will be my role in the family narrative?* The answer to this question must not be overshadowed, let alone informed by another figure, lest the prospective entrepreneur lose their agency. Psychologist Marshall Duke of Emory University (Feiler, 2013) has identified three arcs typical in family narratives and researched their effects on a child's sense of identity, place within a community, and ability to overcome challenges.

Ascendant family narratives follow the rags-to-riches trajectory of unbroken upward mobility, while descendent narratives detail an opposite, *we-used-to-have-it-all* trajectory of inevitable decline. The preordained slopes of both the ascendant and descendent narratives set expectations that, either way, subvert one's agency by inviting complacency and applying pressure to buck a high-stakes, historic trend.

The third narrative, Duke argues, is the one that provides the most constructive and comprehensive sense of belonging to a community: the *oscillating* family narrative. This narrative avoids the pitfalls of broad mythologizing and the extremes of expectation (or its absence) by following a family's journey through its high, low, and average points. Successes, failures, and everything in between are acknowledged, reflected upon, and celebrated. It's an honest approach and one that Duke points to as a way to imbue children with a sense of belonging to something larger than themselves, along with all of the support therein. This is an identity with agency: the potential to realize self-actualization in a way that is *informed* by family history, or a founder's entrepreneurial aptitude, but not *dependent* on it.

Every family enterprise has an origin story (Jaskiewicz et al., 2015). While the contours of these stories vary considerably among families, their distinct potential to frame the foundational narrative's pertinent entrepreneurial activity—and, by extension, shape the next generation's perspective on entrepreneurship—is invariable. Embedded in these stories are messages that become integral to the culture of the family and its enterprise. They motivate a sense of shared family identity and establish a point of reference for understanding one's own privilege in a business family (thus creating a basis for understanding privilege as a platform for responsibility and opportunity). These stories contribute greatly to the motivating foundation on which succeeding generations shape their values, aspirations, and dreams. These stories also encourage family members to take risks by legitimizing that failure is part and parcel of being an entrepreneur and not necessarily indicative of a lack of capacity, intelligence, or talent.

The formative potential of a business family's origin story to supply entrepreneurial touchstones, anchor familial identity, and broadly color a family's (usually far more nuanced) narrative can exacerbate the tendency to self-mythologize. It is common for business families to romanticize the actions and intentions of their founding figures through selective details and generous retrospect. Founders are portrayed as heroic, innately shrewd figures—larger-than-life personalities to be imitated and revered. These reimagined accounts, so often rooted in the narcissism of founders, can have pernicious effects on succeeding generations, begetting future narcissism, or conversely, bequeathing a sense of comparative inferiority. Rather than establishing a motivating foundation, idealized origin narratives instead take on an oppressive, stifling weight since no one can ever measure up to the entrepreneur who made it all possible. By perpetuating the notion that the founders were uniquely visionary, these narratives can also inspire complacency and even dependency by suggesting a standard of excellence, tenacity, or good fortune that cannot be replicated. Faced with shared negative memories or contradictory accounts as to a founder's *actual* nature—as a spouse, parent, sibling, or boss—these narratives can also engender hypocrisy, resentment, or detachment. Likewise, origin stories that are refined to the point of neglecting or excising the contributions of others also invite resentment—not only from those individuals but also from younger family members who may be disincentivized from participating in the enterprise by perceived erasure and inequity.

When business families edit their narratives for blemishes or circumstantial factors, the resulting myth typically exaggerates the founder's entrepreneurial qualities to an unattainable degree—which, in turn, makes the entrepreneurial potential of heirs pale in comparison. In needlessly eroding the self-esteem of the next generation, a mythologized origin story can bring about a self-fulfilling prophecy of decline. If the promise of entrepreneurial self-actualization is a mirage, the reasons for one's agency become, at best, shadows of some impossible ideal. The most effective stories also recognize that there were others who contributed to the founder's success—the spouse with a formidable product idea, the sibling who stepped in to shoulder an early burden, or the cousin who provided seed capital.

This is not to deny that many founders are truly remarkable individuals or to belittle the exceptional achievement that is building a successful business. The reality is that only a small fraction of entrepreneurial ideas ever see the light of day. Yet the success of a business is never attributable to a single cause. Origin stories that celebrate their founders' achievements, while also acknowledging their *humanity*—with all its typical complexities—are simply more relatable, and therefore accessible, than narratives that eschew potentially unflattering details. Such honest chapters serve another basic truth: entrepreneurship is *hard*. Narratives that ascribe a founder's entrepreneurial success to a *mix* of factors including hard work, sensing then seizing an opportunity, and persevering in the face of adversity (be it internal or external) provide an authentic, three-dimensional view of entrepreneurship. This conveys mutual trust and respect between generations and makes central to the family's identity the promise of potential: "*You too can overcome personal struggles and build something significant.*" Like every piece of an oscillating family narrative, foundational chapters have the distinct ability to inspire younger generations, invite them to aspire to greatness, and reassure them that their own place within the story, while yet to be written, brims with infinite possibility. By providing a narrative anchor of entrepreneurship, business families encourage their younger members to use their agency to the same (or better) end.

Persevering Together

By using an oscillating narrative framing device and incorporating transparency into their origin stories, families communicate a more complete vision of entrepreneurship. As these stories are shared, the founder's accomplishments and travails take on meaning and contribute to a family's communal identity. Past entrepreneurship remains a model for aspiring members of future generations and is complemented by context that delivers some of the earliest lessons about entrepreneurship: its inherent difficulty, the universal potential of self-growth, and the importance of *persevering together*.

Successful entrepreneurship requires a great deal of endurance, discipline, and what are often decades of patience and delayed gratification. What distinguishes families that are successful in these efforts is their *shared* enduring of these challenges. As a practicable antecedent, persevering together is accomplished by creating an environment that simultaneously celebrates and appropriately contextualizes hard work and dedication. For instance, seniors who share ongoing business challenges with their children and solicit their ideas integrate those issues into everyday family conversation with inclusivity, cooperation, and curiosity. Over time, merely talking about one's work with the family becomes a small ritual from which shared identity is affirmed, engagement is rewarded, and, through intergenerational support and guidance, early entrepreneurial ideas are made accessible—even exciting!

Another entrepreneur we know was looking for a bonding experience to share with his thirteen-year-old son. After exploring various options, they chose a challenging hike in the Andes Mountains near their home city. The adventure required weeks of preparation: they trained their endurance, acquired the right gear, and studied the various routes up the 10,000-foot mountain they'd picked. When the day finally arrived, climbing conditions were perfect—until they weren't. A sudden downpour and high winds soaked them to their bones and turned the trail beneath their feet into a treacherous mudslide. But the father and son were determined. For hours, they braved the elements until the storm subsided and the day again transformed into one of intense heat, unbearable humidity, and an onslaught of mosquitos. By the time they reached the halfway point, they were both exhausted and increasingly frustrated. The son would not stop complaining and the father lamented that they had come at all. After a heated argument, the father was fed up. He called his helicopter pilot to rescue them from their seemingly misguided adventure. Once aboard, the son asked if they could see the view from the summit before going home. The father reluctantly accepted and the pilot flew them to the top. When they hopped out for a look around, the son was thoroughly disappointed by what he saw: "*Is this it? We did all that work for... just this?*" The father explained that if they had arrived at the summit the hard way, if they had *persisted*, the same view would look very different. They tried again two years later. This time, with a new understanding of the collaborative effort it would take (and slightly better weather), they finally earned their breathtaking view.

Business families that foster entrepreneurship expose their children to the value of perseverance in a variety of ways. Sometimes it's something as simple as sharing household chores. One successful business couple with whom we've worked gives their staff at home the weekends off precisely so their children must themselves do the same chores instead. Their mother mentioned that before they started doing this, her children didn't understand how the clothes they left all over the floor saw its way back into their closets washed, ironed, and folded. Their goal was to dispel any magical thinking as to the real work required to maintain a home—regardless of who was doing the work. In this environment, children grow up appreciating that there is dignity in all work.

Other families convey a similar signal through involvement in their children's extracurricular activities. Parents and seniors in these families invest themselves in these activities—arts, athletics, or otherwise—and genuinely care about them. Expanded efforts in these spheres—instead of, say, ferrying young soccer players to practice and back, actually *coaching* or *managing* the team—imbue shared perseverance with real communal value. These efforts give rise to shared, personal stakes for each family member and contribute to a mutual understanding that they're all in it together—an actual team. But like any team, family members each have a role with their own responsibilities (parent, child, etc.) and must often gauge the level of their involvement, so as to not overstep. Parents who refrain from doing work *for* their children, and instead work *in parallel* to them, promote an environment in which everyone is accountable for their specific part in what is understood to be very much a collective effort. Families also harness natural opportunities allowed by their enterprises to encourage perseverance and resiliency through activities relevant to the business, including summer jobs, internships, special assignments, and site visits, as well as opportunities to benchmark with peers in other entrepreneurial families. These initiatives are most effective, however, when carefully designed with clear objectives and rules of engagement.

Nurturing and Giving Permission to Dream

How do entrepreneurial aspirations form in the minds of the next generation? At what age do children in business families begin to fantasize about starting their own business? Or joining an existing enterprise? Even making it their own? In our experience, these aspirations often form early in childhood—particularly in families in which the business has a prominent role in everyone's individual experiences and whose seniors have communicated the role entrepreneurship and the business took in realizing their own aspirations. Typically, early forays into entrepreneurship are driven by a blend of playful activities as well as the wish to make some money on the side. Consider the myriad ways in which children learn the basics of starting with an idea that becomes an activity that earns a little money, which they can then spend on what they'd like (often without parental approval—an added incentive). When we think of activities through which children can make money while still having fun, our minds often go to lemonade stands, bake sales, babysitting, mowing lawns—and other clichés. But to a young person, the concept that there are people in the world who would pay you to do what you genuinely enjoy can amount to a *revelation.*

The first time a child in a business family asks about a particular occupation or profession, he or she will be more attentive to *the way* in which the parent responds than to the content of what the parent conveys. The content of the children's vocational aspirations will typically evolve and change as they develop. But the extent to which they feel free (or not) to explore their interests and shape their aspirations as they see fit will be constant throughout their development. Children carefully track the extent to which they have permission to pursue their own interests and aspirations—especially in business families where the subtle (and, often, not-so-subtle) expectation is for the children to work for the family company. Too often are companies portrayed as "sacred cows"—institutions to be insulated from family influence, regardless of how potentially beneficial—and the aspirations of younger generations that aim to alter the company's current direction or business model are looked down on by their seniors.

Self-determination is one of the most alluring aspects of entrepreneurship. Indeed, many entrepreneurs do not fit neatly into the hierarchies already present in their everyday lives. When one's role in a system is replaced by the possibility of creation—something *new*, imbued with personal meaning—the inherent risks of hierarchical nonconformity are thrilling. But how is this taught? More challenging yet, how does one teach young entrepreneurs to harness their (potential) skepticism of authority while simultaneously encouraging them to comply with the requirements, guidelines, and, especially, the accountability needed to operate within the platform of opportunity that the family provides? The answer may well lay in the paradoxical organizational dictum as applicable to families as it is to businesses: *differentiate before you integrate*. By encouraging differentiation early in the development of their children, by valuing their unique identity, perspective, and point of view, and, especially, by supporting (if not requiring) that they work outside the family enterprise before they have access to the opportunities it offers, families can nurture the independence needed to elicit sustainable *interdependence*. And in so doing, build their capacity to manage the never-ending tension between the "I" and the "We."

Families that stimulate entrepreneurship understand the continuity of the enterprise will invariably depend on its ability to adapt, evolve, and transform itself. Therefore, the signal to the next generation must convey *both* the need to respect the business that exists while still recognizing not only that change is necessary for survival but also that change is most effective when it is driven by the genuinely shared dreams of the next generation. The essence of this message is a paradoxical synthesis: *a tradition of change*. Succeeding generations are told to honor what has been built *but to evolve it in a direction that works for them*. In other words, the dream will need to be feasible.

When seniors actively listen to their children's aspirations and support their being shaped into viable, real-world possibilities, their children in turn sense that their interests are taken seriously and that their family is willing to support their aspirations and choices. When this process works effectively, it is typically because seniors have not abdicated their responsibilities to offer counsel or leverage their own experience to help their children succeed. (How to offer support without becoming intrusive, however, is part of the artistry of parenting.) If they are to ultimately succeed, entrepreneurial aspirations must pass two fundamental tests: first, they must be suitable for the next generation and reflect their priorities, values, and interests; and second, they must be viable in the world. Families that foster entrepreneurship facilitate both by validating their children's aspirations and by simultaneously providing information and opportunities for their children to test the extent to which their aspirations are realistic. The former is usually accomplished by listening to and supporting their children's ever-evolving interests; creatively stimulating possibilities; and conveying the importance of leading productive and meaningful lives. And the latter is usually accomplished by encouraging them to systematically gather data as to what aspirations work and which ones don't. It is often difficult for seniors to play devil's advocate against their children's entrepreneurial ideas. Despite the usefulness of the exercise, it is undoubtedly challenging for seniors to perform this function without seeming overly critical. And yet, we know from experience that change is best accomplished when it is driven by the aspirations of those who will have to live with the consequences of the choices that are made.

Fostering Curiosity

Entrepreneurial aspirations and dreams serve to define the destination for a process of change. They help to answer the most fundamental questions a business family must address: *What do we want for ourselves, for our family, and for our enterprise?* But the effective operation and realization of aspirations require not just a destination but also a *path*. To nurture the entrepreneurial drives of their heirs and empower them with the agency to pursue their aspirations, families mentor them to understand viability—how business ideas ultimately translate into tangible enterprise. Seniors, for instance, might help young family members deconstruct how the family's business came to be: why and how the original idea was conceived, who thought of it, what specific actions were taken to tangibly express the idea, what mistakes were made, and how those mistakes informed the evolution of the original concept. Detailed descriptions of the enterprise's history are instructive, and every specific is a potential reference point for entrepreneurial inspiration.

When the aspirations of the next generation emerge—the lemonade stand, or high school startup—similar rigor can be applied in unassuming, even playful ways. It's possible to discuss these basic pragmatics in engaging ways: defining the needs of a potential customer; devising a viable strategy for servicing those needs; considering raw materials and the costs of production; experimenting with different pricing strategies to make a profit; and reflecting on strategies that failed or led to unanticipated outcomes. Seniors who focus on framing questions—rather than providing answers—are most effective at stimulating an ongoing, curiosity-energizing dialogue with their children.

One proactive approach that families take to instill an early sense of entrepreneurship and incentivize its exploration is to gamify activities that promote entrepreneurial thinking. For instance, parents who offer their children a modest reward for every five suggestions for improving the business (that are then implemented, say) are providing a consistent feedback loop that rewards innovation, cultivates a habit of critical assessment, and gives structure to contribution and involvement. In other words, early entrepreneurial mentorship need not be overbearing or reliant on a child's innate curiosity about business: just as a simulation video game imbues the player with a sense of control and offers constant feedback on their ability to, say, run a city or manage a soccer team, seniors can empower children to discover their voice and, indeed, *agency* through tasks and exercises that have been gamified—with constant feedback and a modicum of influence and consequences—to teach entrepreneurship. Consistent, specific feedback can be applied to many activities as a way to form early links between curiosity, effort, risk-taking, and self-affirmation. A reliance on interpersonal feedback can be problematic, as even the best-intended assessments can be construed as loaded with judgment. It is therefore preferable that any feedback emerge naturally from the relevant task or activity's own mechanisms—self-sufficient gamification.

Conveying Scarcity in a Context of Abundance

Families that effectively propel the entrepreneurial aspirations of their children are often attentive to the value of things. They often ensure that their children become thoughtful consumers and do not take the expenses underlying their lifestyle (lavish as it may sometimes seem) for granted. This amounts to a potential antidote against entitlement. It often seems surprising how long it can take for them to spend the money that they in fact have available. A client once explained to us: "*Our challenge as seniors is raising wealthy children with middle class values.*" Their objective was to ensure that their children understand the value of money and the utility of disciplined budgets and expenditures. Nevertheless, a family's financial restraint can prove vexing to members of the next generation—causing feelings of relative deprivation, even resentment—if they interpret their seniors' efforts as *withholding*. (Particularly the case when their peers—and their families—don't subscribe to the same values.) Seniors who make (transparently) genuine efforts to provide thoughtful, rewarding alternatives are most likely to overcome those negative reactions.

The dilemma of conveying scarcity in abundance is routinely illustrated when families convene to plan their yearly reunions—and often sharpened by the ensuing debate over venue, budget, and logistics. Typically, families that manage these competing tensions well are able to prioritize frugality and responsibility above luxury and excess. These families understand that coming together and conveying their stewardship over their own platform of privilege provides the primary driver for the gathering. (And when they *do* splurge, there is some collective awareness that it is an exception that requires an added explanation.) It is the antithesis of magical thinking, as it pertains to the family's economics. However, families that strike an optimal balance between abundance and scarcity well are also able to communicate to the next generation openly that the responsibility for their individual destiny is their own and not the family's. Although it is a communal effort, it is one's own agency that leads to self-determination.

An awareness of relational agency can inform seniors on how to successfully navigate the boundaries of collective and individual agency, and to manage the limitations of aligned values. That is, once an aspiring entrepreneur reaches a certain point or position, or is otherwise empowered, other responsibilities become more important. Families can assume what is effectively the opposite of helicopter parenting: supporting their children while stopping short of sheltering them from the consequences of their choices. At every level of wealth, life poses children with challenges. It is from these challenges as well as the perceived adversity they invite that often functions as the motor that fuels growth and maturity. Human development is dialectical in nature—our growth and maturity results from opposite vectors—whether the stress and resistance that strengthen our skeletal structure and muscles that hang from it, to the cellular and biome ecosystems, our very existence is the manifest expression of oppositional processes that propel us forward in life. Our psychology is no different. All one needs to do to see this in action is to observe how an infant persists in mastering how to walk. The exhilaration of agency and self-determination temper the inevitable risks of falling. Families that fuel entrepreneurship encourage measured risk-taking. More importantly, they understand, as Maslow did, that self-actualization requires perseverance in the face of adversity.

Entrepreneurship Funds: At the Right Time and in the Right Way...

While the antecedent practices described in this chapter can be applied to any business family in any stage of development, it should be noted that there is a relational aspect at their core between the next generation of entrepreneurs and the family members involved in the business. The challenge, as the family grows and the system becomes more complex, is how to institutionalize these practices for the benefit of the family at large.

One such practical application is the use of entrepreneurial funds to promote entrepreneurship through the education, support, and funding of entrepreneurial initiatives of members of the family using its own resources. This system benefits from the cultivation of shared values and, especially, the early establishment of links between privilege, responsibility, and opportunity.

Entrepreneurship funds, as in venture capital allocated for the entrepreneurial pursuits of family members, offer many opportunities consistent in a platform of coalesced opportunity and responsibility. These funds involve family members, diverse and dispersed, who cannot be accommodated into the core business because of limited positions, as well as those whose aspirations diverge from traditional positions in the enterprise. This structure acknowledges and supports the entrepreneurial spirit of family members for whom there is no natural fit within the existing core business. By fostering this spirit within a culture of inclusivity and shared responsibility, funded family members (or those given access to family resources) can create new opportunities for the family as a whole through emergent companies. Entrepreneurship funds also benefit from a self-perpetuating, self-sustaining dynamic as younger family members attain seniority. When a family invites its prospective entrepreneurs to align their personal aspirations with the family's shared vision for the core business and provides a platform dedicated to realizing that very alignment, it signals the ultimate permission to dream. This is also where early, lifelong efforts to align guiding values pay dividends, as the family may already share a company vision. Entrepreneurial funds also give members a distinctly practical education (complete with experience) unavailable in an MBA or any other classroom. Crucially, these funds also create an invaluable opportunity for the emotional links between generations to be *strengthened*—which, in turn, bolsters the chances at continuity. Every family member benefits from a system that facilitates the discerning allotment of shared resources to empower, align, and integrate the aspirations of the individual into the collective enterprise. Entrepreneurial funds enable families to ratify inclusivity, creativity, and affirmation as channels for self-actualization and a self-sustaining community—a forceful embodiment of persevering together.

But entrepreneurial funds are not without risks. There exists the concrete risk of a business family jeopardizing significant financial resources should funded ventures fail as well as the possible establishment of damaging fault lines—competitively differentiated between "winners" and "losers." These risks have the potential to create inequalities (material and perceived) between family members, not to mention tension and disharmony. Conflicts of interest that erode the original business's financial returns could also emerge down the line, such as unforeseen financial dependencies and the possibility of two competing companies run by the same family.

Therefore, there are best practices—*advanced* practices—for entrepreneurial funds that use the antecedent practices as a powerful foundation to mitigate risk and help preserve guiding values. The first of these is to clearly define the fund's purpose from the outset and to align all related rules, policies, and practices with the interests of the family, the owners, and the business. This includes clear ownership exit mechanisms to free up financial resources for future investments. Next, families should formulate investment policies that provide *transparency*, which, crucially, perpetuates a culture of honesty and feedback, including the real possibility of failure. These policies include the maximum investment or participation of the fund in any venture; valuation and exit mechanisms; a concrete understanding as to how the fund will be governed; and guidelines for how a funded firm can (or can't) become a supplier for the family business (as well as a plan for managing that potential relationship). It is important for every family member to adhere to these rules and to model for one another their embrace of this social contract as the underpinning for cooperative realization. Likewise, the mutual responsibilities and accountability between stakeholders signal the willingness to help aspiring entrepreneurs help themselves with access to tangible but limited resources.

Among practices that aim to specifically promote thoughtful governance is instituting a dedicated governance body for the entrepreneurship fund (e.g., an investment committee). These would preferably include external, independent members experienced with early stage investments who are tasked with exercising due diligence and performing analysis to minimize the risk of failure. These funds also benefit profoundly from rigorous and impartial project evaluation processes including deep feedback. This fosters curiosity through immersion and contextual, practical coaching. Importantly, it helps teach relatively inexperienced entrepreneurs while extending the lessons to future aspirants. Another key practice is to provide prospective entrepreneurs with business resources. These resources may include explicit instruction and access to mentors. Many businesses also use apprenticeship programs that integrate finance studies, law studies, and hands-on experience into a curriculum that is informed by family culture and values.

One practice that begs additional care is strategic funding, such as using loans instead of direct investments. While this may protect fund assets and limit financial risk to the family business, it also shifts the risk directly to the entrepreneurs and limits (possibly even undermines) the shared building of values that have hitherto found common understanding and expression. It is also critical to set realistic expectations with aspiring entrepreneurs—they must understand that most ventures are likely to fail. Business families must be prepared to handle such failures without reproaching, alienating, or ostracizing the entrepreneur, yet still impose any predetermined, agreed-upon consequences. The idea is to *learn* and *improve*.

Entrepreneurship funds harness the utility of responsibility and opportunity, understood through a lens of privilege as a platform. They represent advanced practices that build upon and perpetuate antecedent practices that cultivate entrepreneurship through all stages of life across generations of family enterprise. Over time, as their identity intertwines with their embraced values, a successful family business will generate wealth. But the *purpose* of this wealth is determined through the myriad ways in which the family collaborates to stimulate entrepreneurship and the endless potential of its younger, dreaming generations.

Entrepreneurial Challenges Ahead

Enduring family companies have historically dwelled in the relative shelter of strategic niches wherein the shelf lives of ideas and product life cycles have similar longevity. This often coincides with the tenure of enterprise leaders. Even for traditional family companies, however, both the competitive barriers around these niches and the lifespan of strategic ideas are shrinking at unprecedented rates. Succeeding generations are rapidly confronting the challenge of having to reinvent the family business several times during their tenure, making the need to ensure the continuity of these enterprises through effective entrepreneurship all the more critical.

The continuity of family enterprises, however, will increasingly involve much more than innovation and entrepreneurial drive. More than ever before it will require increasingly urgent conversations about the purpose and sustainability of these enterprises. As a young entrepreneur from a business family we know asked at his family's assembly recently: "*Why are we selling a product I wouldn't feed to my own kids?*" It was a profound question and a direct challenge to the family to reassess and realign their business with their values. If the overarching objective is continuity, questions like this can be pivotal. Realignment requires courage—not only to speak but also to listen. Not only to express a new generation's energy, idealism, and values but also to consider the voices of prior generations for whom the existing business platform constitutes a source of pride as well as a bird in hand: the certitude of a business that is rather than one that could be. It is our aspiration that familial practices depicted here can ultimately contribute to revitalizing and reasserting a shared understanding of how best to use the platform for responsibility and opportunity that the family enterprise offers.

References

Csikszentmihalyi, M. (1990). *Flow: The Psychology of Optimal Experience*. New York: Harper & Row.

Feiler, B. (2013, March 15). The Stories that Bind Us. *The New York Times*.

Jaskiewicz, P., Combs, J. G., & Rau, S. B. (2015). Entrepreneurial Legacy: Toward a Theory of How Some Family Firms Nurture Transgenerational Entrepreneurship. *Journal of Business Venturing, 30*(1), 29–49.

Mintz, S., & Kellogg, S. (1988). *Domestic Revolutions: A Social History of American Family Life*. New York: The Free Press.

11

Who Do *You* Think You Are? Who Do *They* Think You Are? The Golden Cage and the Silver Spoon

Vincent Lefebvre

I would like to invite you to take a couple of minutes to think about the typical situations when you were exposed to information relative to family businesses in your daily life. The popular culture and the public media discourse convey a large amount of information relative to family businesses through various channels such as newspapers, books, television shows or series, films, legends, and myths. I would like to also ask you to remember some of the situations when you discussed family businesses with your colleagues, friends, and family members.

How would you categorize these inputs: reality, cliché, partial reality, or partial cliché? Are they in line with what you think about family businesses? Are they coherent with your *personal representation* of what family businesses are and of how business family members usually behave in their family and business lives, respectively? Do you think that everyone would have categorized these inputs in the same way? Can we consider that the way our popular culture pictures family businesses and business family members is actually an insight into the *collective representation* regarding multi-generational family businesses in our societies? According to the school of social representations in social psychology, individuals hold personal representations relative to people, situations, and abstract notions that they build in interaction with their

V. Lefebvre (✉)
Audencia Business School, Nantes, France
e-mail: vlefebvre@audencia.com

wider cultural, economic, and political environments. What we think about the world and how the world is represented by popular culture are thus in constant dialogue and mutual influence.

How do you think a successor, heir, or next generation entrepreneur of a multi-generational family business deal with these representations while preparing to take a leadership role in the family firm? The successor's position is at the crossroads of different social representations, each promoting a particular understanding of who should be a successor and how she should behave in order to belong. Thinking about oneself as a successor, an heir, or a next generation entrepreneur entails different social roles to which popular culture attaches different sets of expectations. Tensions may surface, throughout the successor's journey, between how one perceives one's role and mission, and how others (including business family members, employees, and external stakeholders) envision them. Popular culture and public media discourse nourish these representations and offer an insightful scene of how successors, heirs, or next generation entrepreneurs are constructed as modern villains and heroes.

In this chapter, we start by exploring the collective representation of family businesses and successors/heirs/next generation entrepreneurs provided by two channels. The first channel contributes to public media discourse: we focus here on national French newspapers. The second channel belongs to the popular culture and its audience is much wider than that of national newspapers: we focus here on comics, specifically on Bande Dessinée (BD) in the French and Belgian tradition.

After exploring these two main channels conveying collective representations about family businesses and successors, we will try to answer the above question relative to how successors deal with these multiple and sometimes conflicting representations, coming from different sources? Multi-generational family business successors not only deal with the social representations provided by public media discourse and popular culture; they are also confronted to the social representations of their different interlocutors and audiences as individuals and group members. Multiply embedded in personal and professional groups and networks, successors face people with different representations regarding family businesses, successors, and succession. This is what we call the *golden cage of successors*. To get out of this cage, we believe that successors must choose whom they want to become by openly confronting others' expectations and imaginary; they could do this by using their own characteristic tool: a *silver spoon*.

The Golden Cage of the Successor's Social Representation

Public media discourse and popular culture generates what we may analyze as the social representation of family businesses and successors. The metaphor of the successors' "silver spoon" is at the core of this social representation. Does this metaphor of a wealthy past and future accurately describe the life of every family business and that of every successor? How do French national newspapers and BDs speak about multi-generational family businesses and how do they picture successors?

National Newspapers and Metaphors

Newspapers are an especially powerful producer and reproducer as well as circulator of public discourse on entrepreneurship, as they persuade 'our consent to ways of talking about reality that are often regarded as normal and acceptable beyond the confines of media.' (Achtenhagen & Welter, 2011, p. 765 citing Macdonald 1995, p. 3)

Every week, the French national press evokes family business successors, heirs, or entrepreneurs. If we enlarge the search to regional press, new articles are published on these topics nearly every day. We conducted a search on the database Europresse on January 20, 2020.[1] We searched for all the articles mentioning the words "family business(es)" and "successor" or "heir" or "entrepreneur" in the whole text. For the last year (2019), we found 60 articles in French national newspapers and 341 articles in regional press newspapers. We then focused on national newspapers to examine what is said about multi-generational family businesses and successors and how journalists picture them through metaphors. The decision to highlight metaphors when exploring social representations is in line with the very definition of social representations, which associate a word and an image, according to Moscovici and Duveen (2000). Also, metaphors are highly informative about how people think and feel about others, and about the world they live in (Moscovici & Duveen, 2000).

There are so many possible ways in which one may speak about a phenomenon: we found all the common metaphors usually employed to describe family business succession and leadership transfer, such as the metaphors of

---

[1] The exact search request in French was the following one: "TEXT= 'entreprise* familiale*' & (repreneu *lsuccesseu*lheritier*lentrepreneu*)."

"passing the baton," "taking the succession of," "holding the reins," "piloting the takeover of the business." We picked out from the 60 articles several citations that we thought evocative and we categorized them to illustrate the large variety of representations provided by newspapers.

- Old companies facing next generations' difficulties and the risk of losing an "ancestral" know-how

  - "The Simon Marq workshop in Reims, one of the oldest and most emblematic workshops of master glassmaker in France, has been placed in court proceedings. Founded in 1640, the family business had saved the stained glass windows of Reims cathedral from German bombing in 1917" (Le Figaro, 09/17/2019).
  - "Textile manufacturers have made a reason. Their children will not take over the family business and they are delighted" (Libération, 07/17/2019).

- The dynastical succession of heirs

  - "*In a family business, you find your place when you achieve something. Nicolas did it. There is no longer any doubt about his ability to bring the necessary renewal*" (…) Nicolas Houzé was then 23 years old and he was aware that his heir label was not worthy of his favor (Le Figaro, 04/15/2019).
  - "*Economics studies intended to ensure the family dynasty of entrepreneurs*" about Rebeca Horn (Le Figaro, 06/10/2019).
  - "*The heir, who, at 46 years of age, is the CEO of the family business 12th capitalization of the Paris stock exchange*" (Le Point, 02/14/2019).

- When successors are entrepreneurs endowed with an entrepreneurial mindset

  - "*Yann Bucaille was the perfect son of a good family who always succeed in his projects. Baccalauréat at Saint Louis de Gonzague (Franklin), a diploma from EM Lyon, the takeover of the family firm Emereaude, a specialist of transport and distribution of polymers*" and he became an "*entrepreneur*" by launching a foundation linked to sailing activities to support people with disabilities (autism, trisomy…) and to find a job, in partnership with restaurants (Le Figaro, 01/04/2020).
  - "*We will have to succeed being multicentric while maintaining our values and entrepreneurial mindset*" (Le Figaro, 06/11/2019).

– "*When he decided to take over the family business in 1992, the company only interested a few antique dealers and the spiders who wove their webs. (…) The entrepreneur's next objective, for the summer of 2020: the enlargement and fitting out of 2000 m² for exhibitions*" (Le Point, 07/18/2019),

- Inheritance as a trap, a burden, or an obligation

  – "'*What are you going to become my daughter? A bitch?*' said the one who wants her to take over the family business." A family business owner-manager to his daughter who refused to take over the family firm to become (famous) French actress (Libération, 01/10/2020).
  – "*Some leaders who find it difficult to pass the baton go so far as to pretend to prepare their succession but set traps for the heirs*" (Le Figaro p. 43, 11/06/2019),
  – "*Family businesses seem so vital to the economy that many states have put in place special tax systems to facilitate the passing of the baton to the next generation and to prevent their heirs from being forced to sell, because of not being able to financially assume the price of succession*" (Le Figaro p. 40, 11/06/2019),

- Being a discreet family business
  – "*The latter wishes to clarify that the how to manage the 'Castel Group' label embarrasses her because it implies a financial logic whereas it is a family business*" (Le Monde, 05/24/2019).
- The annuitant

  – "*The Murphy couple are atypical American renters, heirs of wealthy East Coast families, passionate about art and culture*" (Libération, 08/24/2019).

As we may easily grasp from these citations, when national French newspapers picture successors ad "heirs," they insist on notions such as "dynasty," "know-how," and "success" over several decades or centuries. When successors are depicted as "entrepreneurs," notions such as "entrepreneurial mindset," "new ideas or projects" are evoked. Finally, when successors are presented as "successors," notions such as "legitimacy," "legacy," "inheritance," "tax troubles," and "family pressure" are put forward.

Journalists use the term "heir" when they talk about "dynasty" and wealthy family businesses. They talk about "entrepreneurs" to qualify those new generation leaders who aim to build something new or to engage in renewing the family business. Succession is pictured as a challenging process, both for family and financial reasons.

Largo Winch BD: The Everyday Life of a Family Business Successor

If newspapers contribute to the social representation of multi-generational family businesses and successors, what about BD? In France, a total of 30.4 M of books have been sold in 2016, of which 8.4 M were BDs, comics, and mangas (SNE & GfK, 2017). Over the last 10 years, the sector of BDs, comics, and mangas had an average growth rate of 20%. The BD is strongly anchored in the French popular culture, every generation reading BD, adults as well as adolescents. The total number of BD read per year is 450 million (Bonneau & Guillaudeux, 2011), more or less the amount of Harry Potter books sold all around the world in a year.

We decided to focus here on a particular BD—Largo Winch. This because Largo Winch is the first *business comics* created by Jean Van Hamme in 1990 and first edited as a book in 1977 (Reyns-Chikuma, 2009). The last Largo Winch BD book has been printed in 300,000 units in November 2019, only for the first edition. In comparison, we may notice that the *Figaro*, the most printed national newspaper in France, counts 321,157 units ("Le Figaro – ACPM," 2018). If we take into account all the Largo Winch 22 books, 11 million BD books have been printed just for the French version. The books have also been translated into 17 languages.

The main character of the Largo Winch BD is the heir of a trust valuated $1 billion. Largo has been adopted by the founder of the "group W," Nerio Winch. He grew up far from the group and his father. No one knows him in the company, so when his father dies at the very beginning of the story, nearly nobody among the company's executives may imagine that the company has a designated heir and that this heir will be willing to take the lead of the family business. Based on these elements, we may assume that Largo Winch BD nourishes the social representation of family businesses and successors. Additionally, we assume that Largo Winch, as the main character of this BD, contributes to the social representation of family business successors in France.

Going through the first Largo Winch books, we identified several suggestive quotations and situations relative to the Largo's family business and to succession. We cite these quotes chronologically, in their order of occurrence in the BDs:

- The company's board does not consider Largo as a legitimate leader: "*Do we have to understand that you actually hope to manage the group?*" Buzzeti, member of the board—(Francq, Van Hamme, & Spear, 2008b)—(T2, p. 7, i1)

- In a childhood memory, Largo Winch remembers how he used to skip school and his father telling him: "*You don't belong to yourself, Largo, you belong to the future I've laid out for you*" Nerio Winch—(T2, p. 13, i6)
- In a childhood memory, Largo Winch remembers the "secret time" when his father used to teach him about how to manage the company in a way that Largo rejected from all his heart: "*I don't want to be your heir*" (T2, p. 44, i7) and "*You taught me the art of corruption and blackmail*" (T2, p. 45, i3)—Largo Winch (young)
- After the death of his father, Largo Winch faces bureaucracy issues and the visit of an IRS agent looking for inheritance tax. This agent says to him: "*Due to this and in application of the federal tax and recovery code article 31, the inheritance tax that you owe to the treasury amounts to exactly $1,382,614,277.37.*" IRS agent—(Francq, Van Hamme, & Spear, 2008a)—(T3, p. 16, i8)
- After a board meeting, the CFO shouts at Largo Winch and says to him: "*Who do you think you are, eh? You're nothing more than an instrument in Nerio's hands, played for the survival of his group. I was the one Nerio entrusted with the responsibility of the W group*"—M. Cochrane, CFO—(T3, p. 31, i3)
- At the end of the first three BD books, Nerio Winch appears as a spectrum and says to his son: "*You'll accept my inheritance because, you see, I didn't choose such a bad heir after all*"—Nerio Winch as a spectrum—(T3, p. 46, i3)

These citations give us interesting insights into the everyday life of successors:

- During childhood and adolescence, business family members teach successors about the company and about how to manage it effectively;
- Business family members tell successors that their life is that of a steward: their destiny is not in their hands, but belongs to the family and to the family business;
- During the family business takeover, successors face several obstacles: the board does not trust them, people want their position, IRS asks for inheritance tax.

In one of the following tomes, there is "a large interview" of Largo Winch. In this interview, he presents the numbers of the last year and emphasizes the growth of the family group: the group's valuation in the first BD book is

$10 billion, whereas in the 13th book the company is valued at nearly $30 billion. At the same time, Largo Winch creates a foundation, saves numerous jobs within the group through outplacement solutions, during an important economic crisis. In short, he demonstrates that he is performing above the expectations as a family business leader (Van Hamme, Francq, & Saincantin, 2014, pp. 5–7)—(T13, pp. 5–7).

This story builds a particular representation of the family business, that of a successful and sustainable company. In Largo Winch, a family business can and should combine growth and sustainability. A successor is expected to renew the entire company, making it more sustainable but also to develop its activities by generating an impressive growth. The creator of the BD explains why he imagined the personality of Largo Winch as he did and why he voluntarily selected a particular life path for his hero. He totally assumes the social representation of family business and succession that he built in the BD: "*As the public appreciates wealthy people but not those who love money, it should be made to feel guilty. Largo is an orphan, adopted by a multi-billionaire and has asked nothing of anyone. He despises money while being rich, it's a bit hypocritical but it makes him nice*" (from Jean Van Hamme, author of Largo Winch) (Reyns-Chikuma, 2009, p. 52),

We pointed out here that the social representations of family business, succession, and family business successors embrace opposite ideas and images of wealth, burden, constraints, and opportunities. Because of the multiple constraints and opportunities attached to their role, successors may be confronted to intense ambivalent emotions (Radu-Lefebvre & Randerson, 2020). Assuming that the social construction of reality draws *together* on these multiple representations can enable us to better understand the multi-faceted phenomenon of family business succession along with the particular challenges faced by successors when trying to navigate the ambivalent landscape of family business social representations.

Becoming Who You Want to Be or Who They Want You to Be?

We previously introduced the idea of the golden cage of social representations relative to family businesses and family business successors. To be able to become who they want to be, successors cannot escape from this cage as this cage *is* the only reality they know, the reality they live in; they can only struggle to find their place *within* the golden cage of social representations. In the first part of this section, we explore this golden cage to understand how different levels of representations, personal and collective, combine to create commonly shared understandings in a particular society.

Following social psychology literature on social representations (Doise, 1985; Jodelet, 2003; Moscovici, 1981), several kinds of representations coexist and communicate with each other in a particular society: the representations held by individuals, groups, and society as a whole. We may say that there are several sub-cages within the main cage represented by the whole society; these are the subgroups to which individuals belong or the groups to which they would like to belong in the future. In every group, there is a specific representation regarding people, social roles, and events. If we take the social representation of the successor and consider it as a golden cage with multiple sub-levels, we may start with a simple observation: successors are embedded in different personal and professional subgroups, each of them functioning as a network through which descriptive and normative information circulates continuously (Birley, 1985). From a family business perspective, we can also take into account two other subgroups: the family and the family business. The successor is at the intersection of these groups. The golden cage of social representations is an assemblage of these different cages, each belonging to a particular group (Fig. 11.1).

Taking into account the golden cage of social representations, two questions should be addressed by family business successors:

- Who do you think you are? An heir, a successor, or a next generation entrepreneur?
- And, who do you think that they [people belonging to the various groups cited above] think you are?

By answering the first question, successors may explicitly decide who they are by self-categorizing themselves and by positioning themselves within the golden cage of social representations. By answering the second question, they may find out if there is a gap between their self-perception and the others' perception of themselves. We can formulate these two questions in another way: Does your personal identity fit your social identity? And what consequences may this generate on your behavior (Tajfel & Turner, 2004)?

As succession is a process, distinguishing these two perspectives and perceptions is crucial not only at the beginning of the process but also throughout its various stages. We should ask successors these two questions in future tense:

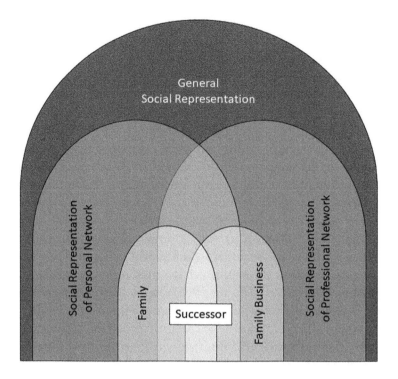

Fig. 11.1 The golden cage of social representations

- Who do *you* want to become?
- Who do *they* want you to become?

The two questions above suggest that there is an identity dynamics within the succession process, whereby a change in the successor's position within the cage is always possible. Personal and social identities are not frozen, there can be an old self and a potential new self (Turner, 1995) and there is always an escape door in the golden cage of social representations. But to open this door, successors would need to engage in what anthropologists called a rite de passage (Van Gennep, 1960).

A rite de passage is not a lonely journey but rather a visible and recognized path by others, by the community involved in the successor's identity change. Entering into a rite de passage can also enable individuals to match their self-perception with the others' perception and representation regarding who they should be and become. In Fig. 11.2, we illustrate an identity change from successor to next generation entrepreneur, at the intersection of social representations. To be a legitimate successor means to effectively fit the

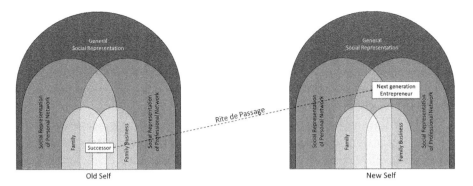

Fig. 11.2 The successor's rite de passage or the art of playing in a cage

expectations of the family and the family business groups regarding the social representation of who should be a successor and how she should behave. If a successor later wants to become a next generation entrepreneur, this aspiration must fit the social representation of his professional network and that of his personal network regarding what an entrepreneur is and how she should behave. The two identities can be bridged by a rite of passage involving a progressive autonomization in relation to the family and the family business' social representations and an increased embeddedness in one's professional and personal networks.

The Next Generation Entrepreneur in Practice

In the previous sections, I highlighted how social representation locks up in cages successors of family business and how a liminal experience can bring them out. Our purpose is first to make heirs, successors, and next generation entrepreneurs realize that cages existed then that the way to open them and get out is by reaching new self: more entrepreneurial new self.

By training successors, I had the opportunity to share this view with many successors. When I collected the press articles for this chapter, I did my research at a national level but also had a look at the regional level. I had the surprise to find a citation in the regional press evoking a "new generation of entrepreneur" which was actually a trainee of the program designed for family business successors I teach in. I decided not to include regional press within the present study because such citation is not neutral: this successor was influenced by prior discussions we had together in class regarding the iron cage of successors. This citation shows how a successor perceives himself today primarily as a next generation entrepreneur, which was not the case when he first attended the program. This illustration made me realize the importance of the role of trainers in contributing not only to the circulation of social representations but also in how successors and entrepreneurs make use of these social representations when defining who they are and how they present to others, in the public space.

In the following paragraphs, I would like to propose a process for family business successors and heirs who would like to become a next generation entrepreneur. This process of becoming involves an active dialogue between extant social representations, normatively designating who a successor should be, and the successor's unique self-perception and desires relative to who she may want to be(come). The different steps of this process invite to both a self-assessment and a mapping of extant social representations; then, an effort to identify the constraints and limitations of these social representations along with the barriers that successors themselves accept to not cross in order to belong. Finally, this process requires courage: that of daring to dream about oneself as different, a next generation entrepreneur ready to cross the risky "rite de passage" to become someone "new," an individual aware of her iron cage(s) and ready to openly confront the script written by others.

1. Take a pencil or colors and draw your personal representation of what an heir or a successor means in general in your culture and for your family, your family business members, your personal network, and your professional network. *What the cages look like.*
2. Categorize the different characteristics of the different social representations you have identified at stage (1): make two groups of characteristics—those you agree with and those you totally disagree with. *How an heir or a successor looks like in your own perception?*
3. Create your new self-representation. Think about your own dreams, desires, and aspirations. Think about yourself as unique, think about how you would like to live your life, how you would like others to see you, and what could truly make you feel accomplished and happy. Build your future self-portrait as freely as possible. *How is the cage you want to live in?*
4. Anticipate your "rite de passage" and list events you must pass through in order to enable you to become who you want to be. Envision the concrete actions you should initiate in order to make possible—for you and for others, watching you and evaluating you—the transformation from the old self to your new self. *How to become a next generation entrepreneur?*
5. Elaborate a new succession planning including actions that will offer you the opportunity to cross of liminal space between new and old selves while

also involving others—mainly, family and family business management within the process. The aim is to gain others' support and approval by showing them the benefits that they could gain from supporting your efforts directed toward becoming a next generation entrepreneur. *How to obtain external validation as a next generation entrepreneur?*

6. Act as an entrepreneur: the family business is a set of resources; sustaining and growing the family business is your opportunity; transforming the organization is within your power.

Like any company, all families and successors are different, so are their respective cages and silver spoons. By enhancing their self-awareness regarding their personal representations and those shared by others and by boldly daring to imagine and set up a desirable new self, successors may design their own pathway to become the next generation entrepreneurs.

For business support, trainers and professors, my advice is to take into account the fact that successors do have "silent" entrepreneurial aspirations which they may not (want to) express within the classroom. Imagine that the unspoken expectations of successors concerning who they want to be(come) are ten times bigger than what they publicly say to others, including what they share within the classroom. My recommendation for you is to actively use social representations to help successors position themselves, which may offer an opportunity to use a neutral way of "drawing" the cages they live in. When these cages are clearly represented, one may use entrepreneurship as a leverage to open up the cages and let the successor act as a new generation entrepreneur by re-founding the family business and acting as an entrepreneur. By doing so, next generation entrepreneurs may mobilize the family business as an entrepreneurial resource and then act as an entrepreneur to find a way to sustain and/or develop the family business and re-found the organization by creating their own new one. However, helping successors to develop an entrepreneurial mindset and entrepreneurial competences to solve their identity issue is not enough. Don't forget they will also face challenging external evaluations both within their family and their family business: make sure the new self which successors aim to enact fits the expectations of other stakeholders or, if not, make sure that the successor is able to cope with adversity and build an agenda for gaining others' support through effective communication and action.

Conclusion

Family business successors, heirs, and next generation entrepreneurs should take into account the golden cage of social representations. Facing the everyday clichés of the silver spoon and the social representations of multigenerational family business as conveyed by the public media discourse and the popular culture, along with facing the expectations of the business family and the family business regarding whom they should be and whom they should become is part of their legacy. Playing within this cage and adapting one's own position to match others' expectations with personal aspirations is probably the main challenge of family business succession.

If the silver spoon is the family business successors' legacy, they should learn to use it as a tool to create their own path within the golden cage of social representation.

References

Achtenhagen, L., & Welter, F. (2011). 'Surfing on the ironing board'—The representation of women's entrepreneurship in German newspapers. Entrepreneurship and Regional Development, 23(9–10), 763–786. https://doi.org/10.1080/0898562 6.2010.520338.

Belouassaa, M. (2020, January 10). Mamie fait de la résistance. Libération, p. 32.

Birley, S. (1985). The Role of Networks in the Entrepreneurial Process. Journal of Business Venturing, 1, 107–117.

Bodescot, A. (2019, November 6). Quand les entreprises familiales changent de génération. Le Figaro, p. 40.

Bonneau, J., & Guillaudeux, V. (2011). L'enquête sur la lecture de bandes dessinées en France. Etudes et Recherche de la Bpi et le Département des études, de la prospective et des statistiques (DEPS) du Ministère de la culture et de la communication (MCC), avec le soutien du Service du livre et de la lecture (MCC/Direction générale des médias et des industries culturelles)

Doise, W. (1985). Les représentations sociales: définition d'un concept [Social Representations: Definition of the Concept]. Connexions, 45, 243–253.

Duponchelle, V. (2019, June 10). Rebecca Horn, la magicienne de l'art. Le Figaro, p. 27.

Emery, A. (2019, July 18). L'illuminé Régis Mathieu. Le Point, 2446(2446), 141–143.

Francq, P., Van Hamme, J., & Spear, L. (2008a). Largo Winch – Takeover Bid (T3) a Business Blues (T4) (Vol. 3 & 4). Canterbury, Kent: Cinebook Ltd.

Francq, P., Van Hamme, J., & Spear, L. (2008b). Largo Winch – The Heir (T1) & The W Group (T2) (Vol. 1 & 2). Canterbury, Kent: Cinebook.

Fulda, A. (2019, April 15). Nicolas Houzé, une force tranquille. *Le Figaro*, p. 38.

Galinier, P., & Neiman, O. (2019, May 24). Pierre Castel, vin bon marché, triomphe discret. *Le Monde*, p. SPA2.

Jacquot, B. (2019, November 6). Le dirigeant doit se prépa rer avec toute sa famille. *Le Figaro*, p. 43.

Jodelet, D. (2003). 1. Représentations sociales: un domaine en expansion. In D. Jodelet (Ed.), *Les représentations sociales* (7th ed., p. 45). Presses Universitaires de France.

Le Figaro – ACPM. (2018). Retrieved January 23, 2020, from https://www.acpm.fr/Support/le-figaro

Leclair, A. (2020, January 4). Yann Bucaille-Lanrezac, capitaine JoyeuxYann Bucaille-Lanrezac, capitaine Joyeux. *Le Figaro*, p. 30.

Lentschner, K. (2019, June 11). Nouvelle génération, nouveaux défis pour Urgo. *Le Figaro*, p. 24.

Malagardis, M. (2019, August 24). Sara et Gerald Murphy, la Riviera sans retour. *Libération*, p. 2l3l4.

Moscovici, S. (1981). On Social Representations. *Social Cognition: Perspectives on Everyday Understanding, 8*, 181–209.

Moscovici, S., & Duveen, G. (2000). *Social Representations: Explorations in Social Psychology* (1.publ). Cambridge: Polity Press.

Naulin, M. (2019, September 17). Maîtres verriers: un avenir très fragile. *Le Figaro*, p. 34.

Parrino, B. (2019, February 14). Alexandre Ricard, prêt à la bagarre. *Le Point, 2424*(2424), 58–62.

Radu-Lefebvre, M., & Randerson, K. (2020). Successfully Navigating the Paradox of Control and Autonomy in Succession: The Role of Managing Ambivalent Emotions. *International Small Business Journal, 38*(3), 184–210.

Reyns-Chikuma, C. (2009). La BD d'affaires en France, une autre exception française? L'exemple de largo winch. *Neophilologus, 93*, 43–57.

Rizzitelli, R. (2019, July 17). A Clamart, il n'y a plus de maille à se faire dans le tricot. *Libération*, p. 14l15.

SNE & GfK. (2017). *La Bande dessinée, une pratique culturelle de premier plan: qui en lit, qui en achète?*

Tajfel, H., & Turner, J. C. (2004). *The Social Identity Theory Of Intergroup Behavior*. In J. T. Jost & J. Sidanius (Éds.), Political Psychology (0 éd., p. 276–293). Psychology Press. https://doi.org/10.4324/9780203505984-16.

Turner, V. (1995). *The Ritual Process: Structure and Anti-Structure*. New York: Aldine de Gruyter.

Van Gennep, A. (1960). The Rites of Passage, trans. MB Vizedom and GL Caffee. London/Henley: Routledge & Kegan Paul.

Van Hamme, J., Francq, P., & Saincantin, J. (2014). *Largo Winch – Cold Black Sea (T13)* (Vol. 13).

12

From Family Businesses to Entrepreneurial Families: Tacit Knowledge at the Core of Entrepreneurial Learning

Luis Díaz-Matajira

In the context of family businesses, tacit knowledge transfer plays a key role for the next generation to informally learn skills and knowledge for the future family and business continuity. This is because the involvement of family members in the family business system provides a permanent opportunity to develop a balance in family entrepreneurial system. Qualitative research based on the STEP Project for Family Enterprising has shown that tacit knowledge appears to enhance firm performance and more specifically the pursuit of new ventures and general business opportunities. This specific knowledge is usually developed from an early age, through living within the family and working in the family business (Chirico & Salvato, 2008). This is due to the process of entrepreneurial learning (Konopaski, Jack, & Hamilton, 2015), a process that facilitates the transfer of knowledge allowing the transformation of the family business into an entrepreneurial family; this is what a Colombian family businessman says: "*My family's legacy is not made of company shares, it is made of entrepreneurial spirit and skills.*"

L. Díaz-Matajira (✉)
School of Management, Universidad de los Andes, Bogotá, Colombia
e-mail: luidiaz@uniandes.edu.co

Scholars call this process transgenerational entrepreneurship, or *"the processes through which a family uses and develops entrepreneurial mindsets and family influenced capabilities to create new streams of entrepreneurial, financial and social value across generations"* (Habbershon, Nordqvist, & Zellweger, 2010; Zellweger, Nason, & Nordqvist, 2012: 137). This means that family businesses may follow a path over time in which they create a system of entrepreneurial initiatives gravitating around the family instead of a group of family members gravitating around a business. This approach led us to focus on the entrepreneurial family instead of the family business.

By focusing on the family and its prevalence over time, in this chapter, I argue that the family as a system becomes an entrepreneurial learning organization in which tacit knowledge is at the core of such learning. This allows for entrepreneurship to emerge not only at the core of the nuclear family, but beyond it. As the firm and family life cycles may not overlap, it is important to focus on the family as a dynamic system with a long-term perspective that goes beyond the traditional approach on family business continuity (Habbershon et al., 2010; Thomas Zellweger & Sieger, 2012; Nordqvist & Zellweger, 2010).

The chapter organizes in the following structure: first an exploration of the family as a system, followed by the role of tacit knowledge in the entrepreneurial learning process as a central feature of a balanced family system, concluding with some lessons for practice.

The Family as an Entrepreneurial System

The family as a system can be understood as an emotional network of interlocking relationships, with a multigenerational and historical framework that creates patterns of interactions among family members (Jaskiewicz et al., 2019). According to Olson's (1986, 2000; Olson, Russell, & Sprenkle, 1983) circumplex model, a balanced model of family system implies a specific combination of three dimensions: cohesion (emotional bonding), flexibility (change in roles and relationships), and communication (speaking and listening skills as well as clarity, continuity, and respect). This means that we cannot look at the family as an integrated unit (or group) when making decisions regarding the business or their entrepreneurial activity. We have to consider the role of each family member (as well as their own interests and values) and the forces behind interaction among family members.

Davis (2007) suggests two major forces behind family members' interactions: the togetherness force and the individuation force. This lead to an idea that families may promote an entrepreneurial activity in a coordinated way (following a togetherness idea as a closed family) based upon the family entrepreneurial orientation or they can allow this process to be more open and democratic (allowing the individuals to pursue their own interests), and thus allowing for a multiplicity of entrepreneurial endeavors, as some scholars have shown (Rosa, Howorth, & Discua, 2014). By looking at entrepreneurial families and the family as a system we can have a better understanding of how an entrepreneurial legacy allows family continuity and family value creation over time. This means to see the family as an entrepreneurial system.

How can you assess if yours is an entrepreneurial family? An initial assessment comes by observing if family influence goes beyond a single-family business. Does the family promote entrepreneurship? Are the new entrepreneurial initiatives emerging as family endeavors or as individual activities? Examples from Colombian entrepreneurial families illustrate this (see Tables 12.1 and 12.2).

In summary, looking at the family business is not enough to understand transgenerational entrepreneurship, as business life cycles may not coincide with individual and family life trajectories. By looking at the family as an entrepreneurial system we can observe continuity (Colli, 2011; Miller & Le Breton-Miller, 2005) and have a better understanding of how families create value by using their own resources or allowing family members to develop their own entrepreneurial initiatives, thus facilitating entrepreneurial legacy to perpetuate.

Individual family member's entrepreneurial efforts may appear to be unrelated from their original family business; however, those initiatives mainly were built upon some form of family unique resources. The initial family business may disappear, but the family prevails through the family legacy of value creation (economic, social, family, entrepreneurial value).

For Hamilton (2013), entrepreneurial families are ideal organizations for understanding the development of entrepreneurs, as their members are, during their whole lifetimes, "*embedded in participation in practice in multiple, overlapping work—and family based communities of practice*" (Hamilton, 2013: 120). Moreover, this entrepreneurial learning enhances family cohesion, thus continuity. In the Colombian families studied there seems to be a key factor behind such process entrepreneurial learning: a knowledge succession process with a special focus on tacit knowledge, the kind of knowledge behind family cohesion, too.

Table 12.1 Family and individual entrepreneurial initiatives in Colombian families

Family[a]—industry	Generation (# members)	Entrepreneurial initiatives at the family level	Entrepreneurial initiatives at the individual level
Banking and insurance	1st (1)	Creation of family business (FB) and acquisition of related firms	
	2nd (4)	Growth and diversification	Creation of 3 new businesses
	3rd (15)	Involvement in other firm's boards and creation of family foundations (FF)	Creation of 5 new businesses
Energy	1st (1)	FB creation and acquisition of related firms	
	2nd (5)	Growth and diversification	Creation of 1 new business
	3rd (8)	Involvement in other firm's boards and FF creation	Creation of 2 new businesses
Poultry (see details in Table 12.2)	1st (1)	FB creation	
	2nd (5)	Growth and product diversification	Creation of 3 new businesses
	3rd (10)		Creation of 2 new businesses
Agroindustry	1st (3)	Creation and acquisition of related firms	
	2nd (15)	Growth and diversification Creation and acquisition of related firms	
	3rd and 4th (30)	Involvement in other firm's boards and FF creation. Creation of seed fund	Creation of several new businesses (with family seed fund support)

[a]Family names are omitted for confidentiality reasons

Tacit Knowledge and Entrepreneurial Learning

Michael Polanyi introduced the concept of tacit knowledge into academic literature with his famous statement "*we know more than we can tell*" (Polanyi, 1966: 4), which refers to the human capacity to acquire knowledge beyond what we are able to explain and communicate. Polanyi (1966: 6) also pointed out that the effectiveness in transferring tacit knowledge depends on the "pupil's intelligent cooperation for catching the meaning of the demonstration."

Table 12.2 *Family Egg-Makers*

The Colombian poultry industry started to develop during the 1940s, but it was between 1960 and 1980 that it grew faster than the rest of the Colombian economy. While Colombian GDP grew at an average rate of 6% in this period, the poultry industry grew over 11%. With regard to the egg production subsector, in 1970 egg production was around 1 million units per day, while in 1977 it was 3.1 million units per day, and by 1987 the production was over 11 million units per day, but this process required to overcome crisis at the beginning of the 1980s. The development of the egg production sector depended highly on how to face the rising costs.

Family Egg-Makers began operations in 1972, when General González decided to start his own business and retire from the Colombian Armed Forces. A few months before he made the decision, he bought a farm nearby Bogotá (Colombia's capital) where he started operations with 5000 chickens, and a cage for egg production, with a plan to eventually have 15,000 animals. The farm was consuming most of his time and financial results were good. He stated himself *"each egg cost 14 cents and was sold for 18 cents."* The farm was doing well, and General González had the full support of his family. He was married and had five children, one son, the eldest, and four girls. At the beginning, he took his wife and kids to help him in the production process. They went every weekend to the farm to vaccinate, beak trimming, and take care of the chicken. They arrived at 5:00 a.m. in the morning on Saturdays and helped during the whole morning. General González then recalls: *"When they finally got the first egg production*, our dream, we did not know what to do next."*

Then, their house became a 24/7 convenience store for selling eggs and all who lived there helped with sales. Laura, the eldest of General González's daughters, stated: *"We were having breakfast, lunch or dinner and the doorbell rang. It was someone looking for eggs. Then my mom or my grandma sold them."*

Juan González, the General's eldest son, was very interested in the business from the very beginning. He felt motivated and wanted to actively participate in it. He even asked his father to let him run the vaccination process. General González remembered that sometimes he left his son in charge of the farms at a very young age (sixteen years old). It was a "double command," he stated, a term used in the Army to say that even if there is a clear boss, there is someone authorized by him to make decisions.

After his graduation from a Bachelor in Business Administration in 1982, Juan had a dilemma: to continue and join the family business full-time or to gain working experience somewhere else. Juan decided to work for his father at *Family Egg-Makers*, given that he cared about the business, had business knowledge from his working experience since he was a kid, and had the educational background and skills from college. The General remained as general manager, Juan was left in charge of new initiatives and marketing. His sisters also joined the business, following a process of innovation, growth, and diversification in products and markets. By 2012 *Family Egg-Makers* became market leaders selling over 10 million units per month.

Later on Juan and two of his sisters, each decided to invest in their own entrepreneurial business (not related to poultry) in order to build their own new family businesses. After conflict among family members, they changed the family protocol in order to allow next-generation members to be involved in the business, but most importantly to support their own initiatives, which allow initially two next-gen members in creating their own businesses (advertising and restaurants). While *Family Egg-Makers* may disappear or be sold over time, González entrepreneurial family seems to have the bases to prevail.

Thus, the knowledge recipients must be willing to understand what is told beyond words.

In the context of family businesses, Chirico and Salvato (2008: 172) state that the "*processes of knowledge accumulation and integration take vivid forms in family firms, in particular when tacit knowledge is involved. Living within the family and working within the business from an early age allows family members to develop deep levels of firm-specific tacit knowledge.*" This is due to the fact that growing up with the business develops an affective commitment that improves the next generation's will to provide support to change (Chirico & Salvato, 2008: 175). In fact, both commitment and will to learn, which could be features of entrepreneurial families, are motivations that may improve tacit knowledge transfer. In entrepreneurial family systems, there are strong social interactions beyond the workplace and strong bonds of trust developed among family members based upon lived-values; thus, they become a natural scenario that facilitates tacit knowledge transfer. Therefore, family members, as they grew up with the business, are in a privileged position compared to even longtime non-family employees to learn and understand more about the company and to develop entrepreneurial skills.

Based on Wagner and Sternberg's (1985) areas of tacit knowledge, managing oneself, managing tasks, and managing people, Insch, McIntyre, and Dawley (2008) define three dimensions in which individual tacit knowledge is present: a *cognitive* one, which includes values, beliefs, and ideas that are usually taken for granted, that contributes to the development of self-motivation and self-organization skills to accomplish goals; a *technical* knowledge, which includes the specific know-how for developing certain activities; and a *social* one, which involves an understanding on how to interact with others, either in a general social interaction or in a task-related one.

For instance, the second-generation CEO (and her siblings) of a family business (in the insurance sector) learned discipline (cognitive), how to seek business opportunities (technical) and how to manage social relationships (social) by waking up early morning once a week, traveling with his father around the country being their father shadow during business and board meetings while he made new businesses. At the same time this experience enhanced family cohesion.

In entrepreneurial families, I argue that the accumulation of tacit knowledge from one generation to the other is more feasible, given the emotional and long-standing ties among family members and the kind of knowledge dimension they are living.

Tacit knowledge could bring positive outcomes to Family Businesses, related to entrepreneurial performance to the extent that it may assist them in the identification-enactment process of entrepreneurial opportunities (EOPs). An entrepreneur builds on his past experience and information in order to recognize what is new and complementary to the new information. The discovery of EOPs is influenced by an individual's differences but in a different way that the literature has treated until now: not due to special attributes that make them better able to recognize opportunities, but because idiosyncratic prior knowledge makes people better able to discover certain opportunities than others. These are conditions that are met by entrepreneurial families with at least a couple of generations at hand.

Smith, Matthews, and Schenkel (2009) point out that opportunity identification depends on two things: the opportunity's attributes and the entrepreneur's knowledge. They apply the categories used for knowledge (tacit or codified) to entrepreneurial opportunities. A "codified opportunity" is then a well-documented, articulated, or communicated profit-seeking situation in which a person attempts to exploit market inefficiencies. While a "tacit opportunity" is a profit-seeking situation difficult to codify, articulate, or communicate relating to a market inefficiency and tied to major improvements or new innovations of products, and so on, the market here is severely unexploited or non-existent. If the opportunity is tacit, then its discovery is feasible if the entrepreneur has prior knowledge and experience, otherwise the opportunity is overlooked. On the other hand, if the opportunity is codified, the entrepreneur's prior knowledge will contribute to establish a more focused search, but if he/she has no prior knowledge, then, a systematic search for the opportunity must be performed. This process would be enhanced in the context of entrepreneurial families, due to the processes of knowledge transfer mentioned above. In the end, the greater the number of profitable opportunities that an entrepreneur can identify, the greater the number of real profitable investments and ventures he will perform.

The concept of entrepreneurial learning (EL) is helpful for understanding these knowledge and values transfers; EL, understood as the process of acquiring the skills and knowledge necessary to initiate, manage, and develop a venture (Corbett, 2005; Politis, 2005) has recently been proposed as a mediating variable between entrepreneurial orientation and firm performance and between "familiness" and firm performance (Cheng, Ho, & Au, 2013). If this is so, EL becomes a pivotal notion in examining the process by which the involvement of the next generation in the business affairs of entrepreneurial families is ensured.

EL may be approached from opposite directions by focusing either on the individuals or on the social settings in which they participate during the course of their lives. The EL methods proposed by Cheng et al. (2013) may be considered to occupy the middle ground between these poles. They also provide a helpful categorization by referring to *Communities of Practice* (CoPs), which play a creative role and encourage intergenerational learning processes.

In the first approach, the unit of analysis is the individual, who accumulates a "stock of experiences" and on whom the entrepreneur then relies to run the business (Minniti & Bygrave, 2001; Reuber & Fischer, 1999). The second approach, on the other hand, involves a socially situated learning perspective provided by the CoP. A particular set of relations between people and social activities, occurring in the world over time, constitutes an intrinsic condition for the existence of knowledge.

CoPs are social settings that enable learning to take place in circumstances where knowledge is conceived of as a social phenomenon. Some examples of CoPs are the family itself (in its informal meetings as lunch, or traveling); the family business (if children and teenagers have played a role within it); other organizations where family members have worked; social networks and organizations where family members can be part of; and the educational CoP where formal education takes place (schools, vocational training establishments, college, etc.). See Table 12.3 for CoP examples in Colombian cases.

Entrepreneurial learning is the result of social participation. It is not just the result of daily experiences and of encounters with others but of "a more encompassing process of being active participants in the *practices* of social communities and constructing *identities* in relation to these communities. Participating in a playground clique or in a work team is both a kind of action and a form of belonging. Such participation shapes not only what we do, but also what we are and how we interpret what we do" (Wenger, 1998: 4).

"Community" here refers to "a way of talking about the social configurations in which our enterprises are defined as worth pursuing and our participation is recognized as competence." "Identity," on the other hand, is "*a way of talking about how learning changes who we are and creates personal histories of becoming in the context of our communities*" (Wenger, 1998: 5). This learning process creates entrepreneurial identities-in-practice. These identities change over time. For example, in the past an incumbent founding entrepreneur might have been labeled a "risk-taker" before becoming an established manager, then "the owner," and finally, once retired, a peripheral participant—probably as a board member—known for his or her "wisdom." Intergenerational encounters such as these bring together different histories of practice through which the future is negotiated and developed (Hamilton, 2013) as the example of the *Family Egg-Makers* illustrate.

Formal business education focuses on developing management skills, not on the roles of family member shareholders. This educational CoP is just one

Table 12.3 CoP in two Colombian cases—some examples of narratives

---

From first to second generations

Banking family

After buying the Bank my dad came and said, "It is different to be a banker than to be an insurer. As an insurer, you have to ask for money, as a banker people ask you for money."

I graduated from college in 1974. My brother Mario started working in our firm in 1976, and that was the first time a Pacheco had come to work in the company. I came later in 1981.

Succession was not hard. The day he said he was going to leave, he just left. He stayed on the boards for as long as he wanted. We always respected him and what he did until he died.

Agroindustry family

My uncle León, who was single at the time, first entered the coffee business by buying coffee, milling it, and then selling it to large exporters. Afonso joined him and my father Luis kept his steady job in order to back his brother's ventures. During the 1940s they had several partnerships with other coffee brokers and even ventured into the hardware business. The three then agreed to focus on exporting coffee.

One of the most outstanding family policies is that concerning the non-employment of family members in the companies. It came about due to the unfortunate experience that resulted from all second-generation cousins and their in-laws having a "right to work" in any of the family's companies.

When the founding brothers had reached their eighties and succession rules had to be settled while they were still alive, a consultant in family companies advised the family about succession issues. Then the first two generations agreed to a protocol whereby, from then on, third-generation members would not have a "right to work."

From second to third generations

Banking family

We have an annual meeting with all members of the family, and those who are interested ask about what's going on in the firm.

Another thing is that my dad never made a business out of the Bank, but now we, his children, have to learn to do business on our own.

In the family there is a culture of study, work, dedication to do something good. This family has always honored those who do well and have degrees.

Well, our vision began to change the day my grandfather decided that the third generation would not work in the company. We have attended some seminars on our own part, but I feel that, at least, we should have been trained to be good members of the board.

Agroindustry family

The three families felt it was a must to teach our values from childhood. They always respected each family's way of educating their children…but everyone instilled values and principles in their siblings from early childhood. But most of all they educated by example.

(*continued*)

Table 12.3 (continued)

Mariana studied business administration; she has an MBA and is very business-minded, while my daughters are art majors and are not like most of their cousins. While I had little choice but to work in the family business, since it was my father's wish that I did so, I have tried to be very cautious with my daughters about the FBs, to the point where they appear to be emotionally detached on the subject when compared with some of their cousins.
While working in the FB, I was setting an example to my daughters, nephews, and nieces about the commitment to a legacy. This is the only way, I think, that we can educate the third-generation family shareholders to be responsible. Reaching an agreement on the protocol while the three founding brothers were still alive is the greatest accomplishment of the second generation.

Source: Based upon Hamilton (2013), González, González, and Díaz (2010)

of the many CoPs that a successor candidate experiences on the way to learning how to fulfill either of these roles. The entrepreneurial identity-in-practice that the individuals develop through their participation in the CoPs mentioned in this chapter helps establish their entrepreneurial preparedness.

In summary, this process of entrepreneurial learning facilitates the transfer of tacit knowledge allowing the transformation of the family business into an entrepreneurial family, recalling the agroindustry family business leader: "*My family's legacy is not made of company shares, it is made of entrepreneurial spirit and skills.*"

Therefore, family business should identify on one side the key type of tacit knowledge behind their entrepreneurial legacy (cognitive, technical, and social ones) and identify the CoP its family members are part of. An emphasis on family meetings, shared experiences, and early involvement of next-generation members will enhance family cohesion while transferring critical knowledge to become an entrepreneurial family.

References

Cheng, J. C., Ho, F. H., & Au, K. (2013). Transgenerational Entrepreneurship and Entrepreneurial Learning: A Case Study of Associated Engineers Ltd in Hong Kong. In P. Sharma, P. Sieger, R. S. Nason, & K. Ramachandran (Eds.), *Exploring Transgenerational Entrepreneurship: The Role of Resources and Capabilities (Chapter 4)*. Cheltenham, UK, and Northampton, MA: Edward Elgar Publishing.

Chirico, F., & Salvato, C. (2008). Knowledge Integration and Dynamic Organizational Adaptation in Family Firms. *Family Business Review, XXI*(2), 169–181.

Colli, A. (2011). Business history in family business studies: from neglect to cooperation? *Journal of Family Business Management, 1*(1), 14–25.

Corbett, A. C. (2005). Experiential Learning within the Process of Opportunity Identification and Exploitation. *Entrepreneurship Theory and Practice, 29*(4), 473–491.

Davis, J. A. (2007). Business Family Dynamics. Industry and Background Note, Harvard Business School, Oct 1997, revised Sep 200712 p898058-PDF-ENG.

González, A., González, G., & Díaz, L. (2010). The Role of Tacit Knowledge in the Identification of Entrepreneurial Opportunities: A Qualitative Analysis in the Context of Family Businesses. Unpublished Chapter in Book, Bogotá: Universidad de los Andes.

Habbershon, T. G., Nordqvist, M., & Zellweger, T. (2010). Transgenerational entrepreneurship. *Transgenerational Entrepreneurship: Exploring Growth and Performance in Family Firms Across Generations*, 1–38.

Hamilton, E. (2013). *Entrepreneurship across Generations: Narrative, Gender and Learning in Family Business*. Cheltenham, UK and Northampton, MA: Edward Elgar Publishing.

Insch, G. S., McIntyre, N., & Dawley, D. (2008). Tacit Knowledge: A Refinement and Empirical Test of the Academic Tacit Knowledge Scale. *The Journal of Psychology, 142*(6), 561–579.

Jaskiewicz, P., Combs, J. G., & Ketchen Jr, D. J. (2019). Moving toward a generalizable theory of business-owning families' reference point shifts by embracing family differences. *Academy of Management Review, 44*(4), 916–918.

Konopaski, M., Jack, S., & Hamilton, E. (2015). How Family Business Members Learn about Continuity. *Academy of Management Learning & Education, 14*(3), 347–364.

Miller, D., & Le Breton-Miller, I. (2005). *Managing for the Long Run, Lessons in Competitive Advantage from Great Family Businesses*. Boston, MA: Harvard Business School Press. Chapter 1.

Minniti, M., & Bygrave, W. (2001). A dynamic model of entrepreneurial learning. *Entrepreneurship Theory and Practice, 25*(3), 5–16.

Nordqvist, M., & Zellweger, T. (Eds.). (2010). *Transgenerational entrepreneurship: Exploring growth and performance in family firms across generations*. Edward Elgar Publishing.

Olson, D. H. 1986. Circumplex model VII: Validation studies and FACES III. *Family Process, 25*, 337–351.

Olson, D. H. 2000. Circumplex model of marital and family systems. *Journal of Family Therapy, 22*, 144–167.

Olson, D. H., Russell, C. S., & Sprenkle, D. H. (1983). Circumplex model of marital and family systems: Vl. Theoretical update. *Family process, 22*(1), 69–83.

Polanyi, M. (1966). The Tacit Dimension. 1983. Gloucester, MA: Peter Smith.

Politis, D. (2005). The Process of Entrepreneurial Learning: A Conceptual Framework. *Entrepreneurship Theory and Practice, 29*(4), 399–424.

Reuber, A. R., & Fischer, E. (1999). Understanding the consequences of founders' experience. *Journal of Small Business Management, 37*(2), 30.

Rosa, P., Howorth, C., & Discua Cruz, A. (2014). Habitual and portfolio entrepreneurship and the family in business. *The Sage Handbook of Family Business*, 364–382.

Smith, B. R., Matthews, C. H., & Schenkel, M. (2009). Differences in Entrepreneurial Opportunities: The Role of Tacitness and Codification in Opportunity Identification. *Journal of Small Business Management, 47*(1), 38–57.

Wagner, R. K., & Sternberg, R. J. (1985). Practical Intelligence in Real-World Pursuits: The Role of Tacit Knowledge. *Journal of Personality and Social Psychology, 49*(2), 436–458.

Wenger, E. (1998). *Communities of Practice: Learning, Meaning, and Identity*. Cambridge: Cambridge University Press.

Zellweger, T., & Sieger, P. (2012). Entrepreneurial orientation in long-lived family firms. *Small Business Economics, 38*(1), 67-84.

Zellweger, T. M., Nason, R. S., & Nordqvist, M. (2012). From longevity of firms to transgenerational entrepreneurship of families: Introducing family entrepreneurial orientation. *Family Business Review, 25*(2), 136–155.

13

The Successor Conundrum: A Moral Dilemma

Miruna Radu-Lefebvre

Many family successions fail, even when both incumbents and successors are clearly committed to making succession happen. I remember a family business successor who enthusiastically engaged in an eight-year succession process only to abruptly abandon it after two years of unsuccessful attempts to introduce new ideas and new ways of doing business into his father's company. The succession was a failure due to the incumbent's resistance to his son's initiatives. The successor decided to launch his own business outside the family company. It was a successful new venture, and the family business of four generations was sold to external investors. As this example shows, incumbents often fail to preserve multigenerational family businesses because of their inability to help successors effectively deal with the moral dilemma of respecting the past versus building the future.

Indeed, successors of multigenerational family firms are lifelong prisoners of a persistent moral dilemma: how to preserve and honor the company's history and the business family's past without jeopardizing its future. From a strategic perspective, this moral dilemma has direct consequences when family business goals are prioritized over potential alternatives. Should family business successors primarily concentrate on ensuring continuity by preserving existing business models, clients, employees, and partners, or should they

M. Radu-Lefebvre (✉)
Department of Business & Society, Audencia Business School, Nantes, France
e-mail: mradu@audencia.com

© The Author(s), under exclusive license to Springer Nature Switzerland AG 2021 **173**
M. R. Allen, W. B. Gartner (eds.), *Family Entrepreneurship*,
https://doi.org/10.1007/978-3-030-66846-4_13

focus on increasing competitiveness by introducing change when necessary? This strategic challenge is not the exclusive appanage of successors; it is a common characteristic of CEO succession in general. But in family businesses, the duality between continuity and change is more intense than in any other organization. The struggle between continuity and change inherently affects family relations—especially those between incumbents and successors—and it also affects the willingness and the capacity of the business family to cultivate an entrepreneurial spirit and entrepreneurial initiatives over time.

From the perspective of the family, the successor's mission is shaped in relation to the past. Most successors feel—even as children and young adults—that it is expected that their priorities will be the preservation of *past* achievements and values. But we also know that from a business perspective, the mission of any CEO successor is shaped in relation to the *future*. Successors working in family firms quickly learn that their employees, customers, and other stakeholders expect them to primarily take responsibility for crafting the company's future. Within this context of contradictory expectations, successors find themselves confronted with a moral dilemma that is not only strategic but also emotional and related to who they are as individuals. Preserving the past versus building the future is, for them, not only a business choice but also a family decision. Moreover, this decision has implications regarding the successor's beliefs about who they are and who they want to be(come): a protector and a respectful family member or a reformer and a (potential) challenger of the family history? The risk of damaging relations with older generations and thus the risk of losing their trust and love may be seen as too dangerous. This is why successors may decide to postpone or abandon any intention to introduce change, even though this makes them feel frustrated and angry and even though it may lead to a loss for the company in terms of profitability or competitiveness. Incumbents, meanwhile, may encourage them to do so through their presence within the company and because of their tendency to value and acknowledge a continuity strategy instead of encouraging their successors to engage in entrepreneurship projects, such as those related to strategic renewal or the creation of new business units.

How do family business successors actually *live* with this moral dilemma? How do they manage the tensions between continuity and change in relation to incumbents? In our field studies conducted in France, we have discovered that successors experience ambivalent emotions—pride and anxiety, joy and frustration, and gratitude and deception—regarding the incumbent, their leadership role, and the family firm. This, of course, affects their personal and professional lives, causing high amounts of tension, stress, and constraint. When making decisions, we observed family business successors permanently juggling retrospective and prospective thinking, which is a highly challenging task that sometimes involves puzzling mental gymnastics. While doing this, successors know that making decisions anchored in past values and practices will most probably facilitate intergenerational relations and maintain family harmony and cohesion and that making decisions based on their unique vision of the future entails the risk of generating intergenerational conflicts and misunderstandings.

Family business academics frame this moral dilemma as a *tradition and innovation paradox* (Erdogan, Rondi, & De Massis, 2019) or as a *paradox of control and autonomy* (De Massis, Chua, & Chrisman, 2008; Ingram, Lewis, Barton, & Gartner, 2016). Studies show that successors successfully manage this moral dilemma by adopting various strategic and relational tactics. For instance, successors can manage the paradox of tradition and innovation by strategically anchoring innovation in the firm's past achievements, thus leveraging the past to promote an "innovation through tradition" solution (De Massis, Frattini, Kotlar, Petruzzelli, & Wright, 2016). Similarly, successors can manage the paradox of incumbent control and successor autonomy by deliberately engaging in "emotion management" when interacting with incumbents, by strategically displaying and hiding negative emotions, in particular (Radu-Lefebvre & Randerson, 2020). These strategies suggest that family business successors should live their life *within the limits* of the family business horizon. This is seen as normal and desirable, thus implicitly suggesting that successors must deal with their moral dilemma by acting as ambidextrous strategists or relational athletes, able to keep the right balance between the past and future at every moment and in every situation.

What about those successors who aim to get free from the burden of the past once in a leadership position? What about those successors who want to challenge the normative cage of the "good son" or that of the "good daughter" once designated as CEOs? What about those successors who intend to engage in entrepreneurial projects? What about those successors who want to explore what happens outside the limits of the family business? And what are the consequences of these different choices for the successor's identity as CEO and/or as an entrepreneur?

No Room for Rebels

Family firms often describe themselves as morally driven organizations. When interviewed by the media, family CEOs speak about themselves as "responsible leaders," dedicated to managing the company according to moral values, such as "honor, respect for people, fairness and persistence" (Chandler, Mosolygó-Kiss, & Heidrich, 2019, p. 144). This helps us understand why successor choice in these companies is shaped by lifelong commitment. The most desirable successor is a committed business family member (Richards, Kammerlander, & Zellweger, 2019). The successor's commitment is not always motivated by genuine attachment to the family business and may instead be triggered by purely calculative or normative reasoning (Sharma & Irving, 2005). Commitment, however, is still one of the most cherished moral values of business families; it originates in the social institution of the family (Creed, 2000). Selected based on their commitment, successors embrace a prearranged social role. A family business successor does not exist alone, but only in relation to a lineage. Drawing on the observation of 32 incumbent-successor dyads, Handler (1990, p. 43) noticed that the successors' "role in the business was shaped by the role of the predecessor." The family business successor's position is thus fundamentally relative and conditional: to be a family business successor is to accept a certain heritage and to commit to its preservation.

Several years ago, we conducted a qualitative study to identify family business successors' aspirations in relation to leadership (Radu-Lefebvre & Lefebvre, 2016). Our intention was to understand how successors envision their role as the head of their family business. We discovered that successors adopt four main leadership postures: the protector, the reformer, the opportunist, and the rebel. Protectors consider their core mission preserving continuity, whereas reformers feel responsible for transforming and developing the family business. Opportunists take on the leadership role because of its attached prestige and social benefits, whereas rebels initially refuse to enter the company but eventually take it over because of dramatic circumstances, such as the death of the former designated successor. The majority of the interviewed successors self-rated as being either a protector or a reformer. When successors were asked which of the four identified postures seemed most attractive to them, we were surprised to discover that, secretly, the rebel's profile appealed to them most. In parallel, when asked about which of these postures seemed the most desirable for them as family business owner-managers, incumbents chose the protector because of her commitment to honor the family and the business's past and to secure the company's DNA. These findings suggest that CEO succession in family business is not a place for rebels, at least not from the incumbents' perspective. The attractiveness of the rebel position in the successors' eyes, however, suggests how important it is for successors to have room to express their own ideas and initiatives. This reminds us of another family business where the successor, a dynamic and energetic young woman, arrived in the company with several ideas for strategic renewal, such as opening a new market for her father's painting and interior design company. Because the incumbent was open to listening to his daughter's proposal and encouraged her to test her ideas, the succession was effective, with both parent and daughter happy with their relationship, respectful of their experience and personalities, and engaged in further developing the second-generation family business. Incumbents should be aware that their natural tendency will be to try to make their successor act as they themselves would act in similar situations. Conformity and obedience come, however, with a cost. And sometimes this cost is too heavy for their successors. Our advice to incumbents is to be mindful of how much pressure they put on their successors' shoulders. Incumbents should try not to excessively downplay successors' strengths or encourage them to forget their aspirations and aims. The incumbent and the successor's respective expectations should be clearly stated from the beginning of the succession process, then renegotiated if necessary, so as to ensure that everyone is satisfied with the results of the trade-off between what must be preserved and what can be subject to change.

Impossible Emancipation?

Incumbents and successors are confronted with the challenge of transforming family businesses, which have been traditionally constructed as a moral place of deference and obedience over personal freedom. Framing succession through the lens of power can help us understand the successor's moral dilemma from the perspective of their relationship with the incumbent. We believe that there is a deeper power issue behind the apparent tensions between continuity and change and past and future. In multigenerational family businesses, successors are expected to accept the incumbent's *control* and the authority of family and business institutions and traditions. In most cases, successors are therefore granted only *limited autonomy*. How can effective leadership, however, be exerted without complete autonomy? The family business successor's moral dilemma cannot be resolved without addressing the surreptitious issue of succession: that of the successor's emancipation from the incumbent's power. Emancipation is the act of setting free from the power of another, and it may take various forms, from critique to resistance, rebellion, and even exit. The relationship between incumbent and successor is a power relationship, shaped by a double asymmetry: a child to her parent and an aspiring leader to the leader in command. As we all know, this power relationship may lead to successor obedience, compromise, or rebellion.

In family businesses, incumbents are rarely aware that they relate to their successors from a position of power. They generally describe their relationship with their successor as an apprenticeship relationship whereby an experienced leader shares her knowledge and network with a less experienced and younger family member. Succession is a time of transmission and learning as well as a time of performing, and successors are also expected to demonstrate expertise and managerial proficiency in order to be acknowledged as legitimate leaders (Dalpiaz, Tracey, & Phillips, 2014; Hytti, Alsos, Heinonen, & Ljunggren, 2017). Family business successors are, of course, indebted to incumbents, from whom they receive knowledge, contacts, and legitimacy. Moreover, as children, successors are indebted to their parents, to whom they owe lifetime respect. But it is also true that successors need to be emancipated from the incumbent in both the parental and the business relationship. They need to build their autonomy in order to be able to lead the company into the future by introducing necessary transformations. The tension between the successor's independence and dependence in relation to incumbents and the family business's past is highly difficult to deal with, however. Successors who actively try to reconcile the family business's past and future by engaging in open negotiation and confrontation with incumbents must accept the costs of disobedience. The moral dilemma originates within the successor's inner struggle between two forms of respect: the respect owed to their parents and to the legacy of the past and the respect owed to the company and its stakeholders outside the family sphere.

The consequences of this moral dilemma go even further, as evidence exists that the successor's lack of autonomy "constrains proactiveness and entrepreneurship in the future" (Brundin, Nordqvist, & Melin, 2011, p. 123).

What About Entrepreneurship?

Family entrepreneurship literature claims that life cycle models that conceptualize firms as inherently declining over time are challenged by those multigenerational family businesses that decide to "feed the entrepreneurial fire" (Rogoff & Heck, 2003). Some family firms are vibrant examples of transgenerational entrepreneurship, which means that they encourage the development of an entrepreneurial mindset in younger generations, and they are ready to commit resources to support the entrepreneurial projects and initiatives of younger generations. Engaging in transgenerational entrepreneurship leads business families to defy the "strategic status quo" (Randolph, Li, & Daspit, 2017, p. 532) and accept the necessity of strategic rejuvenation (Hoy,

2006) over the cultivation of a continuity mindset (Salvato, Chirico, & Sharma, 2010). The notion of "entrepreneurial succession" has been advanced in reference to these multigenerational family firms (Woodfield, 2007) to suggest an understanding of continuity as related to "the continuation of innovation and entrepreneurial behavior in the next generation" (Samei & Feyzbakhsh, 2015, p. 324).

These examples of family firms offer a different landscape for CEO succession. They enable the successor to manage their moral dilemma by anchoring past continuity not solely in family and family business legacies (Hammond, Pearson, & Holt, 2016) but also in the *entrepreneurial legacy* of the business family (Jaskiewicz, Combs, & Rau, 2015). Instead of maintaining and reifying the tension between continuity and change, entrepreneurial legacy—when acknowledged and cultivated—allows successors to engage in new business endeavors through corporate entrepreneurship initiatives (Brumana, Minola, Garrett, & Digan, 2017) by drawing on the entrepreneurial spirit transmitted over generations by the business family through socialization mechanisms (Sharma, Auletta, DeWitt, Parada, & Yusof, 2015). In these family firms, successors are free to explore other territories, both inside and outside the horizon of the family business. Entrepreneurship enables them to effectively build on the past without renouncing their own dreams about the future of the company. Conversely, in these companies, incumbents are happy to see continuity in the family's entrepreneurial spirit. As one incumbent told us recently in reference to his son, "He's an entrepreneur, like myself and my father. I know he wants to do things in his own way, but I'm not too afraid. I know that entrepreneurship will help our company survive for many years after I'll be gone."

Launching new entrepreneurial projects inside and outside the family business enables successors to embrace an entrepreneurial identity. By doing so, successors leverage available family business resources derived from past entrepreneurial achievements to (re)direct them toward new business opportunities, which secures "enduring entrepreneurship" (Jaskiewicz, Combs, Ketchen, & Ireland, 2016) in multigenerational family businesses. This process relates to the notion of "interpreneurship," introduced by Hoy and Verser (1994). Echoing the notion of organizational emergence (Gartner, 1993), the notion of interpreneurship refers to "the process of intergenerational emergence in which family members are interacting and creating new possibilities for themselves, their lives, their organizations whilst drawing upon past events, happenings, experiences and conversations that have gone before" (Fletcher, 2004, p. 38). Interpreneurship helps us understand that family business successors may reconcile past and future and continuity and change by courageously engaging in building new business paths while also avoiding intergenerational conflict. For this to be possible and effective, however, incumbents must secure a family and a business environment that encourages autonomy, initiative, and creativity. In this way, they can leverage entrepreneurship as a potential bridge between the past and future, thus offering the best answer to the successor's moral dilemma, that of entrepreneurship at the heart of the business family's history and future.

The unanimous celebration of entrepreneurship is, however, not without risks. This celebration is rooted in a public and media discourse that lauds those who take on entrepreneurial initiatives as heroes. Family business successors should be careful not to be trapped in the ideology of entrepreneurialism while trying to escape their moral dilemma.

References

Brumana, M., Minola, T., Garrett, R. P., & Digan, S. P. (2017). How do Family Firms Launch New Businesses? A Developmental Perspective on Internal Corporate Venturing in Family Business. *Journal of Small Business Management, 55*(4), 594–613.

Brundin, E., Nordqvist, M., & Melin, L. (2011). Entrepreneurial Orientation across Generations in Family Firms: The Role of Owner-Centric Culture for Proactiveness and Autonomy. In M. Nordqvist & T. Zellweger (Eds.), *Transgenerational Entrepreneurship: Exploring Growth and Performance in Family Firms Across Generations* (pp. 123–141). Cheltenham: Edward Elgar.

Chandler, N., Mosolygó-Kiss, Á., & Heidrich, B. (2019). Transferring Responsible Leadership: The Manifestation of Responsible Leadership Characteristics during Family Business Succession. *Academy of Management Global Proceedings*, 144.

Creed, G. W. (2000). 'Family Values' and Domestic Economies. *Annual Review of Anthropology, 29*(1), 329–355.

Dalpiaz, E., Tracey, P., & Phillips, N. (2014). Succession Narratives in Family Business: The Case of Alessi. *Entrepreneurship Theory and Practice, 38*(6), 1375–1394.

De Massis, A., Chua, J. H., & Chrisman, J. J. (2008). Factors Preventing Intrafamily Succession. *Family Business Review, 21*(2), 183–199.

De Massis, A., Frattini, F., Kotlar, J., Petruzzelli, A. M., & Wright, M. (2016). Innovation through Tradition: Lessons from Innovative Family Businesses and Directions for Future Research. *Academy of Management Perspectives, 30*(1), 93–116.

Erdogan, I., Rondi, E., & De Massis, A. (2019). Managing the Tradition and Innovation Paradox in Family Firms: A Family Imprinting Perspective. *Entrepreneurship Theory and Practice, 1042258719839712.*

Fletcher, D. (2004). 'Interpreneurship' Organisational (Re)emergence and Entrepreneurial Development in a Second-Generation Family Firm. *International Journal of Entrepreneurial Behavior & Research, 10*(1/2), 34–48.

Gartner, W. B. (1993). Words Lead to Deeds: Towards an Organizational Emergence Vocabulary. *Journal of Business Venturing, 8*(3), 231–239.

Hammond, N. L., Pearson, A. W., & Holt, D. T. (2016). The Quagmire of Legacy in Family Firms: Definition and Implications of Family and Family Firm Legacy Orientations. *Entrepreneurship Theory and Practice, 40*(6), 1209–1231.

Handler, W. C. (1990). Succession in Family Firms: A Mutual Role Adjustment between Entrepreneur and Next-Generation Family Members. *Entrepreneurship Theory and Practice, 15*(1), 37–52.

Hoy, F. (2006). The Complicating Factor of Life Cycles in Corporate Venturing. *Entrepreneurship Theory and Practice, 30*(6), 831–836.

Hoy, F., & Verser, T. G. (1994). Emerging Business, Emerging Field: Entrepreneurship and the Family Firm. *Entrepreneurship Theory and Practice, 19*(1), 9–23.

Hytti, U., Alsos, G. A., Heinonen, J., & Ljunggren, E. (2017). Navigating the Family Business: A Gendered Analysis of Identity Construction of Daughters. *International Small Business Journal, 35*(6), 665–686.

Ingram, A. E., Lewis, M. W., Barton, S., & Gartner, W. B. (2016). Paradoxes and Innovation in Family Firms: The Role of Paradoxical Thinking. *Entrepreneurship Theory and Practice, 40*(1), 161–176.

Jaskiewicz, P., Combs, J. G., & Rau, S. B. (2015). Entrepreneurial Legacy: Toward a Theory of How Some Family Firms Nurture Transgenerational Entrepreneurship. *Journal of Business Venturing, 30*(1), 29–49.

Jaskiewicz, P., Combs, J. G., Ketchen Jr., D. J., & Ireland, R. D. (2016). Enduring Entrepreneurship: Antecedents, Triggering Mechanisms, and Outcomes. *Strategic Entrepreneurship Journal, 10*(4), 337–345.

Radu-Lefebvre, M., & Lefebvre, V. (2016). Anticipating Intergenerational Management Transfer of Family Firms: A Typology of Next Generation's Future Leadership Projections. *Futures, 75*, 66–82.

Radu-Lefebvre, M., & Randerson, K. (2020). Successfully Navigating the Paradox of Control and Autonomy in Succession: The Role of Managing Ambivalent Emotions. *International Small Business Journal*.

Randolph, R. V., Li, Z., & Daspit, J. J. (2017). Toward a Typology of Family Firm Corporate Entrepreneurship. *Journal of Small Business Management, 55*(4), 530–546.

Richards, M., Kammerlander, N., & Zellweger, T. (2019). Listening to the Heart or the Head? Exploring the 'Willingness versus Ability' Succession Dilemma. *Family Business Review, 0894486519833511*.

Rogoff, E. G., & Heck, R. K. Z. (2003). Evolving Research in Entrepreneurship and Family Business: Recognizing Family as the Oxygen that Feeds the Fire of Entrepreneurship. *Journal of Business Venturing, 18*(5), 559–566.

Salvato, C., Chirico, F., & Sharma, P. (2010). A Farewell to the Business: Championing Exit and Continuity in Entrepreneurial Family Firms. *Entrepreneurship & Regional Development, 22*(3–4), 321–348.

Samei, H., & Feyzbakhsh, A. (2015). A Framework of Successor Competencies to Promote Corporate Entrepreneurship in Family Firms. *Journal of Enterprising Culture, 23*(03), 321–355.

Sharma, P., & Irving, P. G. (2005). Four bases of family business successor commitment: Antecedents and consequences. *Entrepreneurship theory and practice, 29*(1), 13–33.

Sharma, P., Auletta, N., DeWitt, R. L., Parada, M. J., & Yusof, M. (Eds.). (2015). *Developing Next Generation Leaders for Transgenerational Entrepreneurial Family Enterprises*. Edward Elgar Publishing.

Woodfield, P. J. (2007). *Entrepreneurial Succession: Intergenerational Entrepreneurship in Family Business*. IFERA Conference, European Business School, Oestrich-Winkel, Germany.

14

Family Entrepreneurship Education: Where Are We? Where Do We Need to Go from Here?

Kathleen Randerson and Alain Fayolle

In this chapter, we take stock of family entrepreneurship education (FEE), delving into its origins, exploring contents and practices to date, and more importantly dressing a roadmap of where we should go from here.

Introduction

The family is an important level of analysis for family entrepreneurship research (e.g., Nordqvist & Melin, 2010; Randerson, Bettinelli, Fayolle, & Anderson, 2015a; Uhlaner, Kellermanns, Eddleston, & Hoy, 2012). Recent research focuses on the intersection between the fields of family, family business, and entrepreneurship (e.g., Begin & Fayolle, 2014; Bettinelli, Fayolle, & Randerson, 2014; Fayolle & Begin, 2009; Randerson, Bettinelli, Fayolle, & Anderson, 2015a; Randerson, Bettinelli, Dossena, & Fayolle, 2015b) initiating the developing field of family entrepreneurship that has been defined as "the research field that studies entrepreneurial behaviors of family, family

K. Randerson (✉)
Audencia Business School, Nantes, France

A. Fayolle
Center for Innovation and Entrepreneurship Activities (CREA), University of Cagliari, Cagliari, Italy

© The Author(s), under exclusive license to Springer Nature Switzerland AG 2021
M. R. Allen, W. B. Gartner (eds.), *Family Entrepreneurship*,
https://doi.org/10.1007/978-3-030-66846-4_14

members and family businesses" (Bettinelli et al., 2014: 2). Similar to the fields of management, entrepreneurship, or family business, which already have their own academic programs and curricula in education, family entrepreneurship, as a developing field, should be at the heart of educational settings, courses, and programs for both initial and continuing education.

We define family entrepreneurship education as learning and teaching that take place in higher education institutions, in school-like environments, or in the world at large, aiming at transmitting and developing knowledge, values, and/or competencies related to developing the entrepreneurial behaviors of individuals, families, or family businesses. In order to do so, the scope of these initiatives should include theoretical and practice-based contents, values and skills stemming from the fields of entrepreneurship, family, and family business. It encompasses, yet goes beyond family business education in that family business programs focus on transmitting knowledge, values, and/or competencies related to developing the "next generation," educating family business owners or professional advisors of family enterprises.

Family entrepreneurship education is far from being as well documented as entrepreneurship education currently is (Fayolle, 2013). The field of entrepreneurship education research has already shed light on some key questions. Many educators and researchers have come to admit that entrepreneurship, or at least some facets of entrepreneurship, can be taught (Drucker, cited in Kuratko, 2005; Zahra, cited in Randerson, 2012). Nonetheless, there is a growing consensus that what entrepreneurs do is not what is taught in entrepreneurship courses (Edelman, Manolova & Brush, 2008; Honig, 2004). Entrepreneurship education needs to reflect the real-world environment more closely (Greene, Katz, & Johannisson, 2004). This can lead to questioning traditional practices (e.g., the focus on business planning, Honig, 2004), teaching different entrepreneurial decision-making processes (Sarasvathy, 2001), or taking into consideration previous exposure to entrepreneurship (the family environment, Bettinelli et al., 2014). Indeed, entrepreneurship education seems to have positive effects on students who are new to entrepreneurship (by increasing their entrepreneurial intention, attitudes, and self-efficacy: e.g., Sánchez, 2011; Wu & Wu, 2008), whereas for students who already have an entrepreneurial experience, an entrepreneurial family background, or high levels of entrepreneurial intention, the effects are found to be more negligible or even negative (Fayolle, Gailly, & Lassas-Clerc, 2006; Fayolle & Gailly, 2013; Von Graevenitz, Harhoff, & Weber, 2010).

Where We Are Now

Currently, *family business education* is mainly "practice-driven" (Sharma, Hoy, Astrachan, & Koiranen, 2007). Family business education was activated by the opening of the Center for Family Business, a national organization for business owners and their families, founded by Léon and Katy Danco in 1962 in Cleveland, Ohio. Extant literature focuses mainly on what programs should comprise in terms of services (McCann, DeMoss, Dascher, & Barnett, 2003) or what satisfaction criteria they should meet as perceived by member families (Kaplan, George, & Rimler, 2000). This model, referred to as the Kennesaw model (or "outreach model"), relates to executive programs for family business members who pay a yearly membership fee for programs and services (Sharma et al., 2007). Incorporating family business courses in initial education was pioneered by the Stetson University holistic model in 2000 (Sharma et al., 2007). The Stetson model, geared toward addressing the needs of students involved in degree programs, also includes outreach programs. Sharma et al. (2007) go on to illustrate (using the example of University of Alberta's School of Business) that the alignment of these models creates synergy supporting roles in teaching, research, and service. Steier and Ward (2006) propose a framework for family business education by classifying family business education offerings on a continuum according to the breadth and depth of scope. Collins, Seaman, Graham, and Stepek (2013) offer a stakeholder approach to family business education.

Family entrepreneurship education is practically inexistent. Indeed, there is a dearth paucity of programs including relevant theories, competencies, and soft skills from the three fields: family, entrepreneurship, and family business. This is problematic, especially when we consider that for students coming from an entrepreneurial family the effects of entrepreneurship education are lower or even negative (Fayolle et al., 2006; Fayolle & Gailly, 2013; Von Graevenitz et al., 2010). In order to unbundle how FEE could possibly be developed, we suggest pairing the category of stakeholders with their overarching learning goals.

Education programs respond to a variety of objectives set by various stakeholders: from the students themselves to their families, to family firms, institutions of higher education, public agencies, and governments (Byrne, Fayolle, & Toutain, 2014; Fayolle & Gailly, 2008; O'Connor, 2013). Broad categories of objectives have been identified: pedagogical, social, and/or economic (Fayolle & Gailly, 2008; Johannisson, 1991), or "bucket lists" going from very specific (student knowledge) to very broad (entrepreneurial success or career satisfaction; Alberti, Sciascia, & Poli, 2005). These objectives can schematically be presented as "soft" (linked to developing awareness, mindset, and culture) or "hard" (related to developing/transmitting techniques, skills, and decision-making tools to practice family entrepreneurship).

To illustrate how FEE can be mapped conceptually, we focus below on some overarching learning goals, drawing on the four objectives of entrepreneurship education identified by Liñán (2004; also see Hynes, 1996) that we summarize in Table 14.1. The goals are directly related to the target audiences of the program, enabling audiences to shift from one stage of entrepreneurship to another, and to the objectives set by stakeholders, for which we adopt Collins et al.'s approach (2013; see also Jones & Matlay, 2011).

Family entrepreneurship awareness education or teaching about family entrepreneurship (Kirby, 2007) aims to impart basic knowledge about family entrepreneurship for the learners to better understand the environment in which they operate and to act upon one of the elements that determine entrepreneurial intention (i.e., entrepreneurial knowledge, desirability, feasibility) (Liñán, 2004) or influence career choice. These initiatives convey mainly social objectives (Fayolle & Gailly, 2008) valued by internal, interface, or external stakeholders. Internal stakeholders such as faculty members may aspire to teach family entrepreneurship because it is also their research field or because it relates to their personal situation. Interface stakeholders such as family businesses, business families, or associations of family businesses can embrace this objective because it will ultimately increase the awareness of family entrepreneurship and its appeal. Boards of directors or governors may find an interest in awareness education in that it may contribute to facilitating and improving students' career choices, as well as increase the satisfaction of family businesses, business families, or associations in their communities, or for whom they operate family business centers. External stakeholders, such as Chambers of Commerce and Industry, economic development organizations, local, regional, and national governments, supra-national entities such as the EU or the OECD, may be more concerned about spreading information about how family entrepreneurship can influence economies and societies.

Education for family entrepreneurship (Fayolle & Gailly, 2008; Kirby, 2003; Liñán, 2004; Ray, 1997) is about developing the attributes of successful actors of family entrepreneurship among learners and weighing on individuals' perceptions of family entrepreneurship. These attributes can be related to entrepreneurship (e.g., firm start-up and related financial, legal and tax issues, and

Table 14.1 Learning goals, target audiences and impact of Family Entrepreneurship Education

Learning goals	Objective	Impact on stakeholders
Family entrepreneurship awareness education	Impart basic knowledge about family entrepreneurship Enable the learners to better understand the environment in which they operate Act upon one of the elements that determine entrepreneurial intention Influence career choice	For family businesses, business families, or associations of family businesses: Increase the awareness of family entrepreneurship and its appeal. For boards of directors or governors: Contribute to facilitating and improving students' career choices, increase the satisfaction of family businesses, business families, or associations in their communities, or for whom they operate family business centers. For external stakeholders[a]: The learners spread information about how family entrepreneurship can influence economies and societies.
Education for family entrepreneurship	Develop the attributes of successful actors of family entrepreneurship among learners and weigh on individuals' perceptions of family entrepreneurship. Acquire knowledge, techniques, and skills conducive to the entrepreneurial behavior of learners and that of families and family businesses	For external stakeholders: These learners will contribute directly to the economic development, for example, through succession, start-up within a family business group, or through improving the performance of existing businesses through consulting.
Education for family entrepreneurial dynamism	Develop entrepreneurial behaviors which can then be leveraged in a family firm	For external stakeholders: The learners will directly contribute to maintaining and developing existing organizations.

(continued)

Table 14.1 (continued)

Learning goals	Objective	Impact on stakeholders
Continuing education for individuals involved in family entrepreneurship	Refresh, develop, or update the skill set of the learner	Family entrepreneurs and their advisors: Improved performance of the family firm, family harmony, development of a family business group. External stakeholders: The learners will directly contribute to maintaining and developing existing organizations.

[a]Examples of external stakeholders: Chambers of Commerce and Industry, economic development organizations, local, regional, and national governments, supra-national entities such as the EU or the OECD

resource-marshaling), family business (e.g., succession, governance, and asset management), and family matters (conflict between generations, family dynamics). Education for family entrepreneurship conveys both social and economic objectives because it is about acquiring knowledge, techniques, and skills conducive to the entrepreneurial behavior of learners themselves but also that of families and family businesses. It is relevant to students in that it provides them with an extensive and adapted tool-box they will be able to use after completing the educational program, and it is also relevant to family businesses and business families because it gives them access to more and better-trained professionals of family entrepreneurship. Critical for boards of directors or governors of family business center, this is also of utmost importance to entities such as Chambers of Commerce and Industry, economic development organizations, local, regional, national governments, and supranational entities, such as the EU or the OECD, because these learners will contribute directly to economic development, for example, through succession, start-up within a family business group, or through improving the performance of existing businesses through consulting.

Education for family entrepreneurial dynamism promotes family entrepreneurship behaviors. Training individuals to develop entrepreneurial behaviors which can then be leveraged in a family firm (independently of the level, family status, or position held in the firm) is paramount for many family businesses today (Sciascia & Bettinelli, 2013) and directly influences firm performance and even survival. This objective is relevant to interface stakeholders such as boards of directors of higher education institutions who serve family businesses and business families either directly or through a family business center, as well as to external stakeholders. It is crucial to external stakeholders such as Chambers of Commerce and Industry, economic development organizations, local, regional, national governments, and supranational entities, such as the EU or the OECD, because the learners will directly contribute to maintaining and developing existing organizations.

Continuing education for individuals involved in family entrepreneurship aims at refreshing, developing, or updating the skill set of family entrepreneurs and their advisors, either directly or through a family business center. This responds to the needs of family business practitioners as learners and as external stakeholders (Sharma et al., 2007).

As we understand the link between each overarching goal and how it determines the objective of the educational activity or program, as well as how external stakeholders are impacted by the learners having accomplished the activity or program, we become aware of the extreme importance of family entrepreneurship education. Family business education focuses on the survival, transmission, and performance of the family firm; family entrepreneurship education impacts society.

If understanding how the objectives of the different stakeholders influence the goals and objectives of FEE and the purpose of each overarching goal, this is far from sufficient. Indeed, these models are not rooted in robust education science concepts, but focus mainly on identifying and satisfying the needs of family businesses and business families as a market and the possible means of addressing these needs while fulfilling the fundamental goals of a university (teaching, research, and service). The relative scarcity of research in family entrepreneurship education and the plethora of unstructured pedagogical practices could be attributed to the absence of an overarching framework and the insufficient grounding of research and teaching in the field of education (Fayolle, 2013). Selecting and using insightful concepts and theories from the field of education, for example, borrowing the concept of teaching model from education sciences and extending it to family entrepreneurship education could address these difficulties.

Where We Should Go from Here

Béchard and Grégoire (2005b: 107) define teaching models, as derived from Legendre (1993: 868): "representations of a certain type of organization (to address) a pedagogical situation in function of particular goals and objectives, and that integrate a theoretical framework that justifies this organization and gives it an exemplary character." "Theoretical" here is not to be taken in an academic sense, but "in the sense of a coherent ensemble of explanations and justifications offered by teachers for their classroom behavior" (Marland, 1995: 131). Therefore teaching models include both implicit and explicit elements and "form a bridge between educators' knowledge, conceptions and beliefs about teaching, and their teaching behavior per se" (Béchard & Grégoire, 2005b: 107).

Based on Dewey (1916), Joyce et al. (2009: 24) define teaching as "the design and creation of environments" and, for these authors, students "learn by interacting with those environments and they study how to learn." Consequently, a model of teaching is "a description of a learning environment, including the behavior of teachers when that model is used" (Joyce et al., 2009: 24). These authors have identified and validated several families of teaching models, backed by a number of research studies that test their theories and abilities to gain effects (Joyce et al., 2009). In a similar vein, Béchard and Grégoire (2005b: 108) suggest that "the relevance of teaching models is that the concept focuses on the link connecting the conceptions that scholars and educators have about teaching and their actual teaching behavior." In this light, the concept of teaching model incorporates key dimensions of the ontological and educational levels. The notion of learning theory is particularly important, as teaching models should identify the learning theories they are based on, from behaviorist to constructivist paradigms.

Fayolle and Gailly (2008) extended the work of Béchard and Grégoire (2005a, 2005b, 2007) by developing a generic teaching model for entrepreneurship education. We suggest developing a teaching model for FEE. Such a framework would encompass two levels—ontological and operational—and five dimensions—audiences and targets, teaching goals, contents, methods and pedagogies, and assessments (Béchard & Grvégoire, 2005b; Fayolle & Gailly, 2008)—and draw on the literature in education, entrepreneurship education, family business education, and family entrepreneurship.

Moreover, the learners would gain insights about family science, entrepreneurship, and family business. The vignette below showcases a course "Family, Entrepreneurship, and Society,"[1] an example *of education for family entrepreneurship* designed for a broad audience in order to help them develop competencies to be successful actors of family entrepreneurship and weigh on their

---

[1] The course "Family, Entrepreneurship, and Society" was designed by Kathleen Randerson and delivered during the 2016–2017 Summer School at the Uni Andes.

"Family, Entrepreneurship, and Society" (Education for Family Entrepreneurship)

Course description

If family businesses make up the overwhelming majority of all business enterprises, it is because family plays an important role in developing entrepreneurial behaviors of family members and family businesses. It is also well known that family businesses and business families are more prone to undertake corporate socially responsible activities and identify social entrepreneurship opportunities. But business schools have largely overlooked the unique, and often complex, interplay between family, entrepreneurship, and society.

Accordingly, this course seeks to provide students with an enlightened understanding of the special world of family entrepreneurship. The course will consider the key components that comprise the interface family—entrepreneurship—society with special attention on the aspects that are culturally specific.

The course will be of interest to all because family supports formally or informally nascent entrepreneurs. Also, considering the widespread nature of family businesses many students may work in a family firm as an employee. The course will be of special interest for students who come from families that own and/or manage one or more business enterprises.

Session 1: Introduction; the nature, importance, and uniqueness of families in business

Session 2: Who is family?

Session 3: Family dynamics

Session 4: Family—emotions and conflict

Session 5: Entrepreneurship—entrepreneurial processes: Effectuation and causation

Session 6: Entrepreneurship—founding a (family) firm, the young family business

Session 7: Entrepreneurship—Transgenerational entrepreneurship: STEP initiative; growing the family firm/family business group (innovation, internationalization)

Session 8: Society—families in business and CSR; context of institutional voids and emerging markets; stewardship

Session 9: Society working for a family firm/business family; key non-family management

Session 10: Wrap-up; "idea marketplace"

perceptions of family entrepreneurship. The course develops competencies in entrepreneurship, family matters, and family business.

Family entrepreneurship education would have an impact on society beyond that of performance, survival, and transmission of family firms. Indeed, members of business families would have a better understanding of the underlying dynamics, have access to paths of personal and professional development, and be better "citizens" of their family and community.

Stakeholders of family businesses (customers, suppliers, employees) would have a better understanding of the context in which they operate and would thus be better equipped to interact and participate in the business family ecosystem. The vignette below showcases a course "Introduction to Family Entrepreneurship," an example *of education for family entrepreneurship awareness* designed to introduce learners to the environment of family entrepreneurship, to trigger elements of entrepreneurial intention (entrepreneurial

---

"Introduction to Family Entrepreneurship" (Education About Family Entrepreneurship)

Course description

Considering that family businesses make up the overwhelming majority of all business enterprises, we are necessarily customer, supplier, employee or shareholder of a family business, or member of a business family at one moment or another in our lives. Family businesses are unique due to the influence the owning/managing family has on the values of the organization and the way they operate it. In order to navigate in this unique context, it is important to become aware of its specificities.

Accordingly, this course seeks to introduce students to the world of family entrepreneurship. The course will consider the key components that comprise the interface family—entrepreneurship—family business.

The course will be of interest to all because family supports formally or informally nascent entrepreneurs. Also, considering the widespread nature of family businesses many students may be a stakeholder of a family business. The course will be of special interest for students who come from families that own and/or manage one or more business enterprises.

Session 1: Introduction; the nature, importance, and uniqueness of families in business

Session 2: Types of family businesses and business families

Session 3: Family—family dynamics, emotions, and conflict

Session 4: Family growth and change, firm growth and change

Session 5: Entrepreneurship—entrepreneurial processes: effectuation and causation

Session 6: Entrepreneurship—starting an activity

Session 7: Entrepreneurship—growing the activity/family firm/family business group (innovation, internationalization)

Session 8: Society—economic and societal outcomes of family businesses and business families

Session 9: Working with or for a family firm/ business family; key non-family management

Session 10: Wrap-up

knowledge, desirability, feasibility) (Liñán, 2004) and to influence career choice.

Developing FEE raises two challenges. The first is related to the multidisciplinary aspect: teachers and researchers operate within silos, and covering entrepreneurship, family business, and family is a stretch that requires a lot of investment. A key challenge related to implementing a teaching model approach in family entrepreneurship education will be to create awareness among educators, instructors, and teachers as regards the impact that their individual characteristics and assumptions may have on their teaching behaviors. Teaching approaches, methods, and behaviors are influenced by gender, capabilities, attitudes, past experiences, the discipline one is educated in and the discipline one is teaching, and so on. How to find the right balance between codified knowledge and tacit knowledge based on personal experience?

Yet, developing family entrepreneurship by investing in bridging family, entrepreneurship, and family business and developing such a framework is important. Such work would also fill a gap for researchers in the fields of entrepreneurship, family business, family entrepreneurship, and education science and family entrepreneurship education (Fayolle, 2013) because scholars in these fields can find here a common framework in which research can be grounded. This should support the creation and development of cumulative knowledge at the crossroads of education and family entrepreneurship.

Conclusion

In this chapter, we traced the origins of family entrepreneurship education and differentiated it from family business education. We underscored the importance of targeting the family level, rather than the business level, in designing educational programs for actors of family entrepreneurship. In order to offer a first mapping on the conceptual level, we paired categories of stakeholders with the main learning goals of each category. We emphasized that the lack of research and a plethora of unstructured pedagogical practices can be remedied by choosing and mobilizing relevant concepts and theories from the field of education and extending them to family entrepreneurship education. More specifically, future research can borrow the construct of teaching model and extend it to family entrepreneurship education.

References

Alberti, F., Sciascia, S., & Poli, A. (2005). Entrepreneurship Education: Notes on an Ongoing Debate. *International Journal of Entrepreneurship Education, 2*(4), 453–482.

Béchard, J. P., & Grégoire, D. (2005a). Entrepreneurship Education Research Revisited: The Case of Higher Education. *Academy of Management Learning & Education, 4*(1), 22–43.

Béchard, J.P., & Grégoire, D. (2005b). Understanding Teaching Models in Entrepreneurship for Higher Education. In P. Kÿro & C. Carrier (Eds.), *The Dynamics of Learning Entrepreneurship in a Cross-cultural University Context* (pp. 104–134). Faculty of Education, Tampere: University of Tampere.

Béchard, J. P., & Grégoire, D. (2007). Archetypes of Pedagogical Innovation for Entrepreneurship Education: Model and Illustrations. In A. Fayolle (Ed.), *Handbook of Research in Entrepreneurship Education Volume 1* (pp. 261–284). Cheltenham (UK): Edward Elgar Publishing.

Begin, L., & Fayolle, A. (2014). Family Entrepreneurship: What We Know, What We Need to Know. In A. Fayolle (Ed.), *Handbook of Research on Entrepreneurship* (pp. 183–212). Cheltenham (UK): Edward Elgar Publishing.

Bettinelli, C., Fayolle, A., & Randerson, K. (2014). *Family Entrepreneurship: A Developing Field.* Now Publishers.

Byrne, J., Fayolle, A., & Toutain, O. (2014). Entrepreneurship Education: What We Know and What We Need to Know. In E. Chell & M. Karatas-Özkan (Eds.), *Handbook of Research on Small Business and Entrepreneurship* (pp. 261–288). Cheltenham (UK): Edward Elgar Publishing.

Collins, L., Seaman, C., Graham, S., & Stepek, M. (2013). The Future of Family Business Education in UK Business Schools. *Education + Training, 55*(4/5), 445–460.

Dewey, J. (1916). *Democracy and Education. An Introduction to the Philosophy of Education.* New York: The Macmillan Company.

Edelman, L., Manolova, T., & Brush, C. (2008). Entrepreneurship Education: Correspondence between Practices of Nascent Entrepreneurs and Textbook Prescriptions for Success. *Academy of Management Learning and Education, 7*(1), 56–70.

Fayolle, A. (2013). Personal Views on the Future of Entrepreneurship Education. *Entrepreneurship & Regional Development, 25*(7–8), 692–701.

Fayolle, A., & Begin, L. (2009). Entrepreneuriat Familial: Croisement de Deux Champs ou Nouveau Champ Issu d'un Double Croisement? *Management International/Gestion Internacional/International Management, 14*(1), 11–23.

Fayolle, A., & Gailly, B. (2008). Teaching Models and Learning Processes in Entrepreneurship Education. *Journal of European Industrial Training, 32*(7), 569–593.

Fayolle, A., & Gailly, B. (2013). The Impact of Entrepreneurship Education on Entrepreneurial Attitudes and Intention: Hysteresis and Persistence. *Journal of Small Business Management.* https://doi.org/10.1111/jsbm.12065

Fayolle, A., Gailly, B., & Lassas-Clerc, N. (2006). Effect and Counter-Effect of Entrepreneurship Education and Social Context on Student's Intentions. *Estudios de economía aplicada, 24*(2), 509–524.

Greene, P. G., Katz, J. A., & Johannisson, B. (2004). Entrepreneurship Education. *Academy of Management Learning and Education, 3*(3), 238–241.

Honig, B. (2004). Entrepreneurship Education: Toward a Model of Contingency-based Business Planning. *Academy of Management Learning and Education, 3*(3), 258–273.

Hynes, B. (1996). Entrepreneurship Education and Training—Introducing Entrepreneurship into Non-Business Disciplines. *Journal of European Industrial Training, 20*(8), 10–17.

Johannisson, B. (1991). University Training for Entrepreneurship: A Swedish Approach. *Entrepreneurship and Regional Development, 3*(1), 67–82.

Jones, C., & Matlay, H. (2011). Understanding the Heterogeneity of Entrepreneurship Education: Going Beyond Gartner. *Education + Training, 53*(8/9), 692–703.

Joyce, B. R., Weil, M., & Calhoun, E. (2009). *Models of Teaching* (8th ed.). Boston: Pearson.

Kaplan, T. E., George, G., & Rimler, G. W. (2000). University-Sponsored Family Business Programs: Program Characteristics, Perceived Quality and Member Satisfaction. *Entrepreneurship: Theory & Practice, 24*(3), 69–79.

Kirby, D. A. (2003). *Entrepreneurship.* Maidenhead: McGraw-Hill.

Kirby, D. A. (2007). Changing the Entrepreneurship Education Paradigm. In A. Fayolle (Ed.), *Handbook of Research in Entrepreneurship Education* (pp. 104–126). Aldershot: Edward Elgar Publishing.

Kuratko, D. F. (2005). The Emergence of Entrepreneurship Education: Development, Trends, and Challenges. *Entrepreneurship: Theory and Practice, 29*(5), 577–597.

Legendre, R. (1993). *Dictionnaire Actuel de l'Education* (2nd ed.). Montréal: Guérin.

Liñán, F. (2004). Intention-Based Models of Entrepreneurship Education. *Piccola Impresa/Small Business, 1*(3), 11–35.

Marland, P. W. (1995). Implicit Theories of Teaching. In L. W. Anderson (Ed.), *International Encyclopedia of Teaching and Teacher Education* (2nd ed., pp. 131–137). Oxford, UK: Pergamon Press.

McCann, G., DeMoss, M., Dascher, P., & Barnett, S. (2003). Educational Needs of Family Businesses: Perceptions of University Directors. *Family Business Review, 16*(4), 283–291.

Nordqvist, M., & Melin, L. (2010). Entrepreneurial Families and Family Firms. *Entrepreneurship & Regional Development, 22*(3/4), 211–239.

O'Connor, A. (2013). A Conceptual Framework for Entrepreneurship Education Policy: Meeting Government and Economic Purposes. *Journal of Business Venturing, 28*(4), 546–563.

Randerson, K. (2012). Shaker A. Zahra: L'entrepreneuriat comme Connaissance. *Revue de l'Entrepreneuriat, 2*(11), 53–62.

Randerson, K., Bettinelli, C., Fayolle, A., & Anderson, A. (2015a). Family Entrepreneurship as a Field of Research: Exploring Its Contours and Contents. *Journal of Family Business Strategy, 6*(3), 143–154.

Randerson, K., Bettinelli, C., Dossena, G., & Fayolle, A. (Eds.). (2015b). *Family Entrepreneurship: Rethinking the Research Agenda*. Routledge.

Ray, D. M. (1997). Teaching Entrepreneurship in Asia: Impact of a Pedagogical Innovation. *Entrepreneurship, Innovation and Change, 6*(3), 193–227.

Sánchez, J. C. (2011). University Training for Entrepreneurial Competencies: Its Impact on Intention of Venture Creation. *International Entrepreneurship and Management Journal, 7*(2), 239–254.

Sarasvathy, S. (2001). Causation and Effectuation: Toward a Theoretical Shift from Economic Inevitability to Entrepreneurial Contingency. *Academy of Management Review, 26*(2), 243–263.

Sciascia, S., & Bettinelli, C. (2013). Part III: Corporate Entrepreneurship in Context: 1. Corporate Entrepreneurship in Family Businesses: Past, Present and Future Research. *M@N@Gement, 16*(4), 422–432.

Sharma, P., Hoy, F., Astrachan, J. H., & Koiranen, M. (2007). The Practice-Driven Evolution of Family Business Education. *Journal of Business Research, 60*(10), 1012–1021.

Steier, L. P., & Ward, J. L. (2006). If Theories of Family Enterprise Really Do Matter, So Does Change in Management Education. *Entrepreneurship: Theory & Practice, 30*(6), 887–895.

Uhlaner, L. M., Kellermanns, F. W., Eddleston, K. A., & Hoy, F. (2012). The Entrepreneuring Family: A New Paradigm for Family Business Research. *Small Business Economics, 38*, 1–11.

Von Graevenitz, G., Harhoff, D., & Weber, R. (2010). The Effects of Entrepreneurship Education. *Journal of Economic Behavior & Organization, 76*(1), 90–112.

Wu, S., & Wu, L. (2008). The Impact of Higher Education on Entrepreneurial Intentions of University Students in China. *Journal of Small Business and Enterprise Development, 15*(4), 752–774.

Part V

Establishing the Entrepreneurial Family

15

Intrapreneurship: A New Lens on Developing Capability in the Rising Generation

Wendy Sage-Hayward

Introduction

Protecting all forms of family enterprise wealth across generations is increasingly challenging and complex, and yet vitally important, not only to the families who own enterprises but to the communities in which they operate and the broader global economy. Their health and growth have a large impact on every country's economic welfare. If enterprising families hope to maintain their relevance, they must anticipate change, innovate their enterprises, and ensure the rising generation is positioned to succeed, with the right skills and capabilities to collaborate and manage transitions effectively.

The core question, then, is how do enterprising families best transmit leadership capability and an entrepreneurial mindset to their successors?

Families need to foster a new form of *intrapreneurship* in their enterprises, one that includes a broad-based owner's mindset well beyond the typical "business-only" thinking. This chapter provides a comprehensive description of this type of intrapreneurship, identifies why being intentional about such development within the family enterprise matters, and offers practical suggestions for how families might go about developing intrapreneurial capability across generations.

To illustrate the ideas, the "Stevenson" family is utilized as an example. They are owners of a multi-generational business in eastern Canada who have

W. Sage-Hayward (✉)
The Family Business Consulting Group, Vancouver, BC, Canada

© The Author(s), under exclusive license to Springer Nature Switzerland AG 2021
M. R. Allen, W. B. Gartner (eds.), *Family Entrepreneurship*,
https://doi.org/10.1007/978-3-030-66846-4_15

holdings in a broad range of industries including manufacturing, real estate, media, and tourism. The parents founded the business decades ago and two of four siblings in the second generation work in the business. The younger two siblings are professionals in healthcare and secondary education, but have small ownership stakes equivalent to those of their older siblings. The business is highly successful, but there remain challenges around continuity, as the parents haven't yet delegated much leadership responsibility to the next generation despite being in their mid-60s. As we will discuss, the Stevensons have recently committed to taking a more intrapreneurial approach, with the help of outside resources.

Why Intrapreneurship Matters to Family Enterprises

Creating continuity across multiple generations is a highly complex process that requires the ability to juggle and coordinate many moving parts, including responding to market changes and disruptions; managing the needs and goals of diverse perspectives within the family; dealing with the challenges, overt and more subtle, of wealth; and navigating the political nature of a family environment among others. Indeed, business scholars agree that family firms face "even more heightened circumstances of ambiguity and intense dilemmas" than their non-family counterparts.[1]

Research by Williams and Preisser offers dramatic proof of this challenge, as an estimated 70% of family enterprises fail to transition to the rising generation, due largely to poor trust and communication and inadequate preparation of the successors.[2] In short, many families fail to promote a basic sense of collaboration, then struggle to understand why they're not making progress on a trust-based continuity process.

For enterprising families to succeed with continuity of every type, family members—especially the rising generation—need a sophisticated, diverse set of skills, knowledge, and capabilities to traverse the family enterprise landscape with greater agility and ease. That's where intrapreneurship comes in. Typically, intrapreneurial skills are thought of as being similar to entrepreneurial skills, but applied internally within the family enterprise rather than

---

[1] John Ward, "Managing Complexity: The Family Business Experience," in *Managing Complexity in Global Organizations*, Edited by Ulrich Steger, Wolfgang Amann, and Martha Maznevski, Wiley, 2012.

[2] Roy Williams and Vic Preisser, *Preparing Heirs: Five Steps to a Successful Transition of Family Wealth and Values*, Robert Reed, 2010.

externally to launching new ventures. That's a result of the broader definition of intrapreneurship or the idea of acting "like an innovative entrepreneur, but within the ecosystem of a larger, more traditional organization," which has also been considered "corporate innovation."[3]

Others have sought to define the components of intrapreneurship in a corporate setting. Antoncic and Hisrich, for example, suggest that the core dimensions include (1) a new business venturing dimension (pursuit of new products or markets); (2) an "innovativeness" component (creation of new offerings); (3) a self-renewal dimension (strategy reformulation, organizational modifications); and (4) a proactiveness component (initiative and risk-taking).[4]

While this traditional view of intrapreneurship is indeed relevant here, the definitions are too narrow when applied to family enterprise, due to the complexity of what the rising generation will inherit and must manage, as mentioned above. Thus, below a broader, more comprehensive definition of intrapreneurship is offered, one that encompasses capabilities more suitably fitted to promote the rising generation's future.

Intrapreneurial Capability in a Family Enterprise

This requires a set of wide-ranging knowledge, skills, and abilities across key areas including innovation and change, leadership, governance, family enterprise strategy, ownership, interpersonal relationships, and wealth and philanthropy, which together maximize a family's collective capacity for value creation across generations.

The diagram below depicts the core, interrelated skills related to intrapreneurship in a family enterprise (Fig. 15.1).

Focusing on this broad set of mutually reinforcing skills will equip rising family enterprise members with the best opportunity for continuity because it fosters talents and perspectives that specifically address the issues and challenges they will face in the family, business, and ownership systems through their transition to ownership and leadership, and beyond.

The Stevensons, our example family, faced multiple challenges in these areas, along with opportunities to take a more intrapreneurial approach. For

---

[3] Tomas Chomarro-Premuzic, "Why You Should Become an Intrapreneur," *Harvard Business Review*, March 26, 2020, https://hbr.org/2020/03/why-you-should-become-an-intrapreneur (accessed September 21, 2020).

[4] Bostjan Antoncic and Robert Hisrich, "Intrapreneurship: Construct Refinement and Cross-cultural Validation," *Journal of Business Venturing*, Volume 16, Issue 5, September 2001, Pages 495–527.

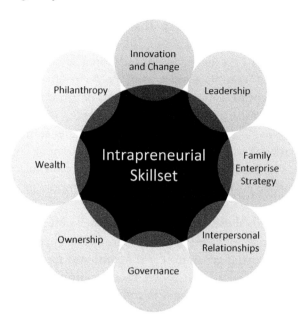

Fig. 15.1 Eight domains of intrapreneurial skills in a family enterprise

example, they had limited governance practices until recently, so there were no forums in which to communicate about issues related to expectations of family employee performance in the business or how they were trained, promoted, or compensated. There were also challenges around wealth and the family's relationship to money. "How do we want to use our wealth?" one rising generation family member asked her parents. There was great discomfort with the topic of money and thus no clear answer was offered. The family and business executives were struggling to make strategic decisions about how to deal with recent competition from a large national player in their real estate market of focus. This resulted in rental and pricing pressure on the properties they were developing or renting. The Stevenson family realized they would benefit from exploring new ways of managing their challenges which included building capacity in the rising generation to assume the responsibility for their enterprise when the time came for them to do so.

The Need for a Broad-Based View of Intrapreneurship

As mentioned above, managing and stewarding a family enterprise across generations require navigating a landscape that consists of multiple layers of complexity. The points below explain more specifically the challenges inherent to the family enterprise ecosystem, and why navigating these requires a broad-based skillset:

- *It's More Than Just a Business*: A given family enterprise can have any or all of these types of assets: operating businesses, financial assets, a real estate portfolio, philanthropic assets, heirloom assets (emotionally driven possessions such as the family beach cottage or art collection), deferred assets (such as insurance policies and trusts). Managing and sharing these assets within the family for the long term requires significant commitment, knowledge, and capability on the part of family owners.
- *All Owners Are Not Alike*: Within a multi-generational family enterprise, there might be a variety of ownership types including operating owners with day-to-day responsibilities, governing owners who sit on the board or family council, and active and passive owners who may have minimal involvement in the business but are a key part of the overall ecosystem of the family enterprise.
- *Multifaceted Family Dynamics*: Families are complex emotional systems. Every family has its own set of dynamics, whether around status needs, branch divisions, difficult interactions among specific members or factions, addictions and mental health issues, or other territory to navigate with regard to ownership, interests, visions for the future, or just plain getting along. This set of relationships and dynamics can be challenging enough to understand, much less to manage in service of continuity.
- *Integrated Governance*: Within a family enterprise, governance occurs at multiple levels, including those related to the business, family, ownership, and philanthropy. The systems and processes of each governance structure must be aligned and integrated with the other levels and types of governance. Roles, responsibilities, and relationships overlap, creating a complex web of interconnectedness among the governance bodies and their membership, which can again be challenging to navigate for enterprise members.
- *Continuous Change and Overlapping Transitions*: Transitions are occurring at the individual, family, ownership, business, and industry levels simultaneously and sequentially over time, which often creates ambiguity, conflicting needs, communication errors, and other emotion-laden challenges.

Family members, especially rising generation ones, need to be equipped with a comprehensive set of skills to thrive in this environment, to support the success of the family and its broader enterprise. Such development can also represent a challenging subject even to raise in a family, as discussed next.

The Importance of Development

Development in family enterprise matters. As mentioned earlier, family enterprises have large impact on the health and growth of *every* country's economy. Consider the numbers: together, even just the top 500 family firms are equivalent to the world's third-largest economy, employing about 25 million people, with total revenues of almost US$7 trillion.[5] The capabilities that enterprising owners bring to this role—including their individual leadership, collaborative ability, decision-making, and overall savvy—have a material impact on the outcomes for their enterprises, and by extension the lives and economies these businesses touch.

Yet most families pay little direct attention to development of skills in the rising generation. The Family Enterprise Foundation recently collected data from over 200 family members through their Family Forward Learning Assessment (familyenterprisefoundation.org). The information covered numerous aspects of family enterprise longevity, including families' learning and development activities. Less than 5% of the families reported that learning is a part of their overall strategy and 61% reported that they rarely or never learn together. Over 80% reported that their family's attitude toward learning was essentially indifferent.

That's unfortunate because development is critical for many reasons. For one, families have much at stake in their enterprises which goes beyond just their net worth. They must address a multitude of challenges such as those related to stakeholder relationships, reputation, and safety,[6] which again require development of specific capacities and capabilities. The greatest risk they need to manage and navigate is related to their family cohesion and connection.

The term "family business" is so ubiquitous we have forgotten to appreciate how complex this form of business actually is. The overlapping nature of the family, business, and ownership systems creates a highly sensitive and delicate environment to navigate.

Specifically, families seeking continuity need to align family members around a common vision and direction, decide how best to implement governance, welcome newcomers (i.e., in-laws), navigate different needs and interests of multiple generations, and foster family member engagement to name

---

[5] EY, The Global Family Business Index, St. Gallen University, http://familybusinessindex.com/ (accessed April 29, 2019).

[6] Fassler, M. & Sage-Hayward, W., Managing Risk in the Family Enterprise, Family Business Advisor (2016).

just a few. This needs to happen while maintaining strong relationships within and between generations.

Moreover, part of what makes development so challenging is that there's no "standardized" way to approach enhancement of intrapreneurial skills—compared to, say, an MBA program to gain business skills—and because many families don't take an active, intentional approach to this kind of development early enough.

Because of all this complexity and challenge, it's easy for enterprising families, even the best-meaning ones, to avoid discussing development, in some cases mistakenly believing that the rising generation's skills will develop naturally over time or be absorbed from senior family members through "osmosis." That's simply not true. Developing intrapreneurial skills in the rising generation, while not easy by any means, can be planned for and developed fully through education, experience, and other activities. Developing these skills doesn't happen by default; it requires preparation from a young age and is largely independent of whether a family member works for the family business or serves in a formal governance role. The concept of development and many of the foundational ideas here are rooted in human development theory, including as related to individual development over one's lifespan (such as the theories of psychologist Erik Erickson) and family systems work by a broad range of theorists and researchers.[7]

Here, the Stevensons, facing increasing complexity in their business, growth of generations (with an expanding third generation), and pressure from rising generation members, made a conscious effort to focus on development, specifically in the arena of intrapreneurship. They made a commitment to working proactively on this area and engaging all adult family members in an open, productive process.

How to Build an Intrapreneurial Skillset

A simple organizing structure to guide intrapreneurial development on multiple levels is listed below. This is followed by specific practical advice for gaining intrapreneurial skills. Together, the ideas here will help members avoid exclusive or disproportionate focus on the business domain, while illuminating the broad range of domains over which rising enterprise members should aim to gain capabilities:

---

[7] For an overview of family development theory and research, see Paul Mattessich and Reuben Hill, "Life Cycle and Family Development," in *Handbook of Marriage and the Family*, edited by Marvin B. Sussman and Suzanne K. Steinmetz, pp. 437–469, Springer, 2013.

- *Individual*: This dimension involves development of the successors' sense of self, as related to identity, resourcefulness, productivity, work ethic, and other areas that cut across modes of functioning.
- *Family*: This dimension is about the intertwined evolution of the individual and their family, or personal and collective growth. Intrapreneurial development here centers largely on one's ability to cultivate strong relationships with others, such that they may share responsibilities, work together, resolve conflicts constructively, and make sound decisions as a group.
- *Ownership*: The ownership dimension involves an understanding of complex issues surrounding collective ownership among a sibling or cousin group handling issues ranging from shareholders agreements to estate planning to voting rights to exiting the ownership system (hopefully without exiting the family system as well). Thus, ownership is far more than merely holding shares of a business, and requires developing a unique mindset, a positive character, and a set of knowledge and capabilities for success.
- *Business/Industry*: Development here centers early on promoting a positive attitude toward the business, along with basic understanding of business concepts, followed by more specialized business and industry knowledge. Over time, it becomes more about building specific capability based on roles(s) within the enterprise and across areas of innovation, change, creativity, and the like.

Next we'll consider several specific practical routes to promoting intrapreneurial development in a family enterprise based on the aforementioned categories. The core goal is for family members to learn continuously and contribute broadly to positive dynamics and decision-making within the enterprise. These development activities help rising generation family members "earn" the responsibilities and benefits of being part of the enterprise, by expressing their interest, capabilities, and enthusiasm for formal and informal roles within it.

Individual Dimension

The tips here center around two main ideas: building strong networks and creating feedback loops. With regard to networks, the idea is that families have social capital in addition to financial capital, and thus intrapreneurial development should be partly about creating a network of relationships related to the enterprise. With that in mind, find opportunities for younger family members to build connections with key stakeholders—from trusted longtime family advisors to key non-family leaders in the business and customers. These relationships will help them reap the rewards of mentoring, coaching, and other outcomes that profit the individual and the enterprise as a whole.

Feedback loops are critical drivers of growth and learning rarely happens without some kind of feedback.[8] And yet, asking for feedback is one of the more challenging tasks in a family enterprise—perhaps not surprisingly, as this can be difficult in many contexts. Families need to push past that natural barrier to search for and cultivate feedback loops in their system. Feedback will likely occur from within *and* outside of the family enterprise system, such as from family governance leaders, managers (whether working at or outside the family business), mentors, and others. The feedback may be formal, such as through performance evaluation in the business, or informal through channels, such as peer coaching or mentoring.

Family Dimension

The most central piece of advice here is to make working on family relational issues a priority. Families naturally accumulate emotional baggage and struggle to address it proactively. Too often, difficult relationships, emotional cut-offs, poor communication, and other resource-depleting issues get swept under the rug. To create a positive path to continuity, foster a willingness to work through these patterns and promote candid, frank conversation, openness to change, and forgiveness; this may include working through issues with an outside therapist or other advisors.

Ownership Dimension

One of the most challenging intersections in family enterprise is the one between family and money. Money and wealth is a taboo topic in many families, including who gets what when. Families who encourage a healthy and productive relationship to money are equipping their rising intrapreneurs with a key skill that specifically creates a clearer sense of accountability—it's not just about showing up but *earning* the rights and rewards of being part of the family enterprise. The goal, then, is to promote open, healthy communication about money, again relying on outside sources ranging from books to online materials to consultants, where appropriate.

---

[8] For more on feedback and leadership see James Kouzes and Barry Posner, *The Leadership Challenge*, Jossey-Bass, 2003.

Business/Industry Dimension

Fostering true innovation and change requires leaving your own backyard, expanding your horizons, and getting out of your comfort zone. To make that happen for family enterprise members, I recommend going on "learning expeditions," to new regions and territories to stimulate thinking and foster insight. This may mean traveling together to a conference or to listen to an industry speaker, or going as a group to a different country (or region) where you plan to expand your business to learn about the regional customs, build relationships, and gather market intelligence, among other activities. It is a process that involves the cycle of observing, doing, reflecting, and integrating new knowledge and information into your current way of doing business.

The Stevensons worked on multiple dimensions to improve intrapreneurship and future prospects. On the individual dimension, members agreed to engage in more regular provision of feedback for each other and to work toward relationship-building with an "everything on the table approach." Feedback loops were applied to both the business and family settings. The two siblings working in the business, for example, were provided more formal feedback on their performance from executives and board members—this had been avoided before—which helped them work on key leadership development areas. In the family, members spoke with unprecedented openness about their individual challenges and feedback for others, resulting in deeper understanding and, ultimately, harmony, after a series of tough conversations. For example, the younger siblings expressed feelings cut off from the business and noted that the parents and older siblings often talked about the business at the expense of everything else, which led to feelings of unfairness.

On the family dimension, one of their largest steps was more regular, facilitated discussion of challenging family issues, as suggested above. For example, the two younger siblings were concerned that they were being shut out of large financial opportunities—such as investing personally in portfolio firms—because they didn't work in the business. Through family meetings with outside consultants, the family developed a policy about sharing such investment opportunities with all the second-generation members.

This related directly to the ownership dimension, where the founding couple still controlled business decisions, including whether to reinvest or "harvest" proceeds from the ongoing business and sales of portfolio firms. For the first time, the family discussed individual member's needs and developed a policy that provided more flexibility for distributions where needed. The teacher, for example, wanted to use money from his share to help pay for his children's imminent college costs and was able to do that. In general, the family took a more proactive approach to learning about wealth and philanthropy and made collective decisions about causes to support, with input from all members.

The business dimension involved helping the siblings outside the business understand more fully in what markets the family played, and what current strategic risks they faced, including the large real estate competitor. The first- and second-generation members went on a joint "learning expedition" to visit properties and get a sense of "on-the-ground" market dynamics. This provided basic information and a surprising positive development, as the third sibling, a physician, helped family members understand new opportunities in health-technology businesses in which the family agreed to make small, promising investments, diversifying their holdings further and reducing risk.

Becoming an Intrapreneurial Learning Family

As the material so far suggests, intrapreneurship in a family enterprise requires broad-based development. It is a lifelong process that helps families assess their skills and capabilities, improve their awareness and identity, consider their role and responsibilities, and set goals in order to realize and maximize their value and potential for their family enterprise.

In this context, a wide range of activities and experiences contribute to the development of rising generation members and can occur at both the individual and collective family level, as suggested above. For example, family members take courses, attend conferences, perform on-the-job training and the like as individuals. Likewise, the family as a whole can develop their capacity together through focused discussions and workshops to expand their relationships and capability as a family. Rather than focusing only on the rising generation, we offer the notion of becoming an *intrapreneurial learning family*.

This concept is rooted in Peter Senge's definition of and work on "learning organizations," or "a group of people working together to transform and enhance their collective capacity with the aim of creating results they really care about."[9] This concept applies naturally to a family who is passionate about their jointly held (now or in the future) assets and who wishes to sustain ownership and related connectivity across generations.

---

[9] Peter Senge, *The Fifth Discipline Fieldbook: Strategies and Tools for Building a Learning Organization*, Crown Business, 1994.

The specific qualities of an intrapreneurial family include the following:

- *Focused and Proactive*: A learning family proactively designs learning opportunities with the intention of advancing both individual talent and the collective brain trust and establishes uninterrupted times and places to build capacity.
- *Growth-mindedness*: Family members grow, stretch, and enhance their capabilities continuously over time. All are encouraged to explore their purpose, passion, and interests.
- *Broadmindedness*: A learning family invites members to learn about *all* aspects of the family enterprise, so they understand their role and potential opportunities within it.
- *Responsiveness*: A learning family designs development activities in response to family members' needs and interests, in addition to specific family enterprise needs.
- *Prudent risk-taking*: In a learning family, mistakes are consider an integral part of development. Family members experiment, take risks, and try new ways of doing things without fear of reprisal or getting it wrong.
- *Emotional safety*: Family discussions are viewed as safe places to challenge assumptions, biases, and sacred cows. There are no undiscussables.
- *Feedback-oriented*: Family members give and receive feedback openly and constructively, as feedback is viewed as critical for growth and progress. Feedback loops are encouraged and expected.
- *Inclusive*: A learning family capitalizes on the diversity within the family by engaging all key stakeholders in key processes such as crafting the family's vision, purpose and value.
- *Practical*: A learning family develops a strategic plan for learning and development, including a budget and set of action steps including those built around the practical tips offered earlier here.

The Stevensons took the concept of a learning family to heart, working with outside consultants to embrace these characteristics, through their efforts on the four dimensions of intrapreneurship—individual, family, ownership, business—described earlier.

Where to Start

Suggestions on where to start your intrapreneurial development process should come as no surprise: *with communication*. Begin a conversation—about the need for development, about the benefits of intrapreneurship, and about family members' passion and appetite for the same. The level of interest in the topic should quickly become clear. The box below provides a practical exercise to stimulate this valuable group discussion.

How We Strengthened Intrapreneurialism in our Family

Imagine it is five years from now and we have created a family that is passionate about being the best, intrapreneurial, multi-generational family enterprise we can be. Let's describe what we think we would see and experience at that future time.

- What policies, events, and activities help us thrive?
- How do family members behave with each other in good times? In bad times?
- How do we interact with our key stakeholders?
- How do family members feel about the family and our enterprise?
- What do we care most about?
- What are we able to do that we can't or don't do today?
- What value are we creating for our family, our customers, and our community?
- How do we define and measure our success?
- How is all of the above different from how we operate today?
- What are the roadblocks we face to becoming a learning family?

After discussion and sharing of interests in your family, consider establishing a small, preferably multi-generational, committee to design a simple learning plan for the following year, including a small budget to get started on this process.

We recommend making the development process simple and personal to your family members. Consider starting with the exercise above, then pick one or two of the suggestions from earlier in this chapter—such as working on family relationships or building financial literacy—and start by relating it to family members' personal situations.

Given that most enterprising families are heavily focused on working in the business, it may be hard to pin down exactly what kind of learning is required. A needs assessment is a good first step to help rising generation members assess where they are today in terms of their knowledge, skills, and capability and where they want to be based on their vision, passion, and interests. Use the four dimensions presented earlier—individual, family, ownership, business/industry—as a way to structure the needs assessment.

Even when families recognize the importance of intrapreneurial development, it can be easy to get overwhelmed by its scope and potential time consumption. These tips can help facilitate a more proactive approach to it:

- *Don't get overwhelmed by complexity*: Instead, accept that complexity is an inevitable part of taking on worthwhile challenges which is why addressing them successfully is that much more rewarding.
- *Be intentional*: A conscious, proactive approach to intrapreneurial development will always lead to better outcomes and more lessons learned.
- *Recognize development occurs over time and stages of life*: Family enterprises are a true *gift* with large-scale potential for positive impact for oneself and others—it happens slowly over time and through continued focus and effort.

Again, the Stevensons, our example family, embraced these principles and took proactive steps to development, centered on commitment and communication. The intrapreneurship-focused efforts they made improved performance and satisfaction on every level, placing the family on a much clearer, more rewarding, collaborative path to continuity.

Remember: Hope is not a strategy, or at least not a good one. Use the ideas here to work actively on intrapreneurial development, navigating complexity on multiple dimensions comprehensively, with intention, thoughtfulness, and outside resources as needed. It's never too early to start or too late to benefit.

16

Gathering Multiple Generations at the Dining Room: The Secret Toward an Entrepreneurial Family Continuity

Fernando Sandoval-Arzaga, Geraldina Silveyra, and David S. Xotlanihua-González

More than 25 entrepreneurial families were graduating that day after a year of hard work and joint training, when a founder came up and said with emotion, "At first I was afraid to enter the Program, but now I am grateful for it. Thanks to it, my daughter got involved in the family business, has generated new projects and I have already decided to assign stock actions under her name and she hasn't even finished her university studies!"

A concern of every entrepreneurial family today is the engagement of the new generations, not only in the family business but also in their development as owners and entrepreneurs. Families usually have difficulties when new generations join the family-business system because they don't know how to work together.

In an effort to help entrepreneurial families, we have developed an educational and consulting program for family members to learn by doing how to work together. The program allows the entrepreneurial family to sit together multiple generations in the same classroom in order to increase the value of the family business.

F. Sandoval-Arzaga (✉) • G. Silveyra • D. S. Xotlanihua-González
Tecnologico de Monterrey, Business School, Monterrey, Mexico
e-mail: fsandoval@tec.mx; gsilveyra@tec.mx; xotlanihua@tec.mx

© The Author(s), under exclusive license to Springer Nature Switzerland AG 2021
M. R. Allen, W. B. Gartner (eds.), *Family Entrepreneurship*,
https://doi.org/10.1007/978-3-030-66846-4_16

The program is called "Strategic Value Creation for Entrepreneurial Families"; it has been taught for five years in a row and has impacted 109 entrepreneurial families already. Sitting multiple generations to work together has had positive effects: the involvement and commitment of the new generations, the development of the entrepreneurial family skills to work together, and the creation of entrepreneurial and /or innovation projects that increase the value of the family business or family wealth.

These results have contributed to the continuity of the entrepreneurial family through the generations. But what are the secrets that have allowed entrepreneurial families to achieve these results?

This chapter will help you as the leader or owner of your business family to find the keys (secrets) to potentiate entrepreneurship of the rising generations. These keys have been the result of the program that we have carried out at Tecnologico de Monterrey.

Secret 1: Identify Next Generation Intrinsic Motivation to Develop or Participate in Entrepreneurship Projects

In our experience, working with young family entrepreneurs when they are in the second and a half year of undergraduate program they have a *sincere desire* to get involved in entrepreneurship projects. We detected certain arguments which next generation used and showed authentic desire:

- *"I am interested in this program (entrepreneurial family project) because I want to help the family business in its growth and solve the problems it faces,"* or
- *"My mom or dad need help in running the family business,"* and, finally,
- *"I am interested in working in the company and I think the program is a good way to get involved."*

As we can see, the first two arguments are related to help the family business prevail over time, even if the student is not necessarily interested in working or permanently stay involved with it. The third argument relates to his/her interest to get involved in the company.

As the leader of the entrepreneurial family, when you talk with the next generations you should focus on promoting entrepreneurship and start-ups rather than, for example, on their involvement in the firm as employees, since this is much more attractive for the rising generations and could help them develop a sense of belonging to the family business.

Secret 2: Take Advantage of the Genuine Motivation of the Entrepreneurial Family Leader for the Firm Growth and Leave a Legacy

Taking advantage of the motivation of the enterprising family leaders promotes transgenerational entrepreneurship. They usually give arguments such as the following:

- "*I find it very interesting because my dream is to inherit the company to the next generations, I no longer want work all day long*";
- "*We need to improve and boost our position in the market, since we already have a lot of competition*"; or
- "*We must stop operating intuitively and incorporate professional methodologies.*"

Genuine desire usually has to do with leaving a legacy to the next generation or with the growth and professionalization of the company. Entrepreneurship satisfies this desire without a doubt. Not necessarily both parents or grandparents or uncles should be fully motivated, but if at least one of them is motivated (usually who is the actual leader of the entrepreneurial family), the motivation from the others arises during the entrepreneurship process and, particularly, when entrepreneurial projects are defined.

As a part of the next generation, especially if you want to get involved in the projects of the entrepreneurial family, you can open the conversation with the previous generation by proposing your ideas as your contribution to the growth and legacy of the entrepreneurial family, that is, appealing to this genuine motivation the leader has.

Secret 3: Change your Mindset as a Leader of the Entrepreneurial Family (from One Man Band Controller to Mentor Orchestra Director)

Many leaders of entrepreneurial families are born entrepreneurs since they have started the company from scratch, had to make it grow and had to make all the decisions in the company, from what kind of pencil to buy to a major investment of machinery. They often say:

- *"Why should I do things differently, if I've been having successful results for 30 years?"* And later, this same leader says, *"I would love to be able to leave the company, go on vacation or dedicate time to hobbies."*

That is, there is a paradox between *"leave the company"* versus *"it works."* They don't take the step because, deep down, their way of thinking is *"the company works because of me and I don't need to change because it has given me results."* This way of thinking in actual practice causes a learning barrier that prevents new generations from developing their entrepreneurial potential, leaving no space to the leader of the entrepreneurial family to implement new projects.

As the leader of the business family you must try to change your mindset focused on double-looped learning (Argyris, 1993), *that means, to realize that you must change the principles by which you are acting.* To achieve this, the first thing you must do is to be aware of the need to stop being *one man controller band,* which reflects not wanting to let go of control, and rather become an orchestra *director,* in which you open opportunities, guide the organization and the new generations, and do not lose control of the family business.

This change of mindset should involve a change of habit and routine of the leader. This is a process that takes time and as a leader you must put into practice day by day. You can do this by being mindful and aware of the way you act during meetings and ask for constant feedback. For example, in the program we designed, we accompany business families by holding monthly meetings to review entrepreneurial projects and the professor-consultant who participates in these meetings encourage and reinforce this change of habit in the leaders, giving them feedback when they are unconsciously controlling all decisions excessively.

Achieving this change in the mentality of the leader must also be supported by the decision-making mechanisms and the level of institutionalization of the family business, creating or strengthening the governing bodies and management practices that allow decisions to be delegated and systematized.

Secret 4: Empower the Rising Generation (Boost Your Self-Esteem and Show Results)

One dad told us, *"Before the program, I used to see my daughter as my little girl; now I see her as a professional who has a lot to contribute to the company's current and new projects."* The rising generations, in many cases, have only lived with their parents, grandparents, or uncles in the family sphere but very little in the business sphere. This has led to the show that, on both sides, the senior and the junior generations have not shown in practice their performance as professionals and entrepreneurs to each other.

We suggest to you to involve the next generations by assigning them entrepreneurial projects for which they are the leaders who must develop strategies to create value for the enterprising family and carry them out. Therefore, they must be in constant communication with the family leaders, follow up and promote concrete and effective measures to guarantee the advancement and transformation of the family business through these projects. Showing real progress is part of the rising generations' assessment. By design they must act as professionals to the senior generation, which empowers them.

We propose that continuous learning and feedback sessions be scheduled to promote the participation and listening of the rising generation (at least once a month). In the sessions you should prevent the conversation from being taken over by the senior generation, giving new generations a voice to joint decision-making of entrepreneurship projects.

These actions allow the new generation to increase their self-esteem and empower themselves, showing positive results (Sandoval-Arzaga, Ramirez-Pasillas, & Fonseca-Paredes, 2011). Examples of entrepreneurial projects that we have observed assigned to the rising generation are the creation of the online store, development of a new business unit (cinemas) not related to the original business (producing cookies), or exporting to new countries such as China or Germany.

Secret 5: Create a Space for Transfer Knowledge Among Generations

Creating an appropriate communication context (space) to foster family entrepreneurship learning is the most important feature of working together with multiple generations. Having a safe space for families to have difficult conversations, and get to agreements, allows the transfer of knowledge between generations to take place (Cabrera-Suarez, De Saá-Pérez, & García-Almeida, 2001). It generates confidence and opportunities for the experiences of senior generation and the new ideas of the next generation to get shared. A member of the rising generation commented, "*Now I can have conversations about the family business, come up with new ideas and even criticize my dad without us getting angry and leaving the room.*"

The first component to create a space for the transfer of knowledge among generations is the integration of family members around a *common project* that involves setting shared goals. Entrepreneurial families are the ones who decide, based on their needs, such project and its goals. The common project is established to determine the "locks" (bottle necks) which prevent them from moving from the current level of the family business to the next level and, in turn, to find the "keys" (value detonator projects) that will open those padlocks. We propose that the entrepreneurial family should have a strategic reflection in three fundamental components: its business approach (proposal and business model), the synergy of the business family (harmony and complementarity of family members), and the orchestration of the business (processes and business leadership).

The second component that has allowed the creation of this space is the formulation of a *shared vision* of the future and continuity of the business family. It is not about establishing or reviewing the vision and mission of the family business, but about sharing the dreams and future expectations of the members of the entrepreneurial family to build a shared vision.

It is important to mention that what has worked for us, when we accompany families, is to start by discussing the company and not the family itself; this has allowed the family to start sharing and developing a common language. Only after family has maintained this space of communication through their monthly meetings for six months, you can start to build the vision of the business family, that is, switch from discussing company issues to family issues.

Secret 6: Establish the Strategic Role of Facilitating and Accompanying

This role is key for achieving the entrepreneurial goals. It can be played by a family member or an outsider. The most important thing is that the profile of the person who should play this role is of a suitable mix between a professor and a business consultant.

The fundamental activity of this role of the "professor-consultant" is not of intervention but rather strategic. They should not teach classes or prescribe action, but facilitate, guide, and accompany the business family when defining its shared vision and the entrepreneurial projects. To achieve this, we suggest that their role must be based on the technique of generating powerful questions (Vogt, Brown, & Isaacs, 2003), which allow the entrepreneurial family to realize for itself what to do. This has involved a great deal of effort for the person who plays this role as they should talk less than the members of the entrepreneurial family, when a professor or a consultant is accustomed to doing the opposite. They must accompany the entrepreneurial family in their decision-making, guiding them only in the proposed methodology, but they should not intervene in the company nor solve the problems. The implementation of the projects is the responsibility and decision of the entrepreneurial family.

The "professor-consultant" role is to guide the rising generation as entrepreneurship project leaders. Sometimes they become mentors to next generations because they give them advice on how to deal, persuade, and communicate with their parents, siblings, or other members of the entrepreneurial family. We suggest that the person who assumes this role should have meetings every two weeks with the next generation in order to follow up on how they are doing both in personal life and with their entrepreneurial project.

Secret 7: Incorporate Innovative Learning Tools and Activities for the Creation of Entrepreneurial Family Value

Making learning truly experiential requires the use of innovative learning tools in order for entrepreneurial families to take action, learn collaboratively, and delve deeper into their reflections.

We recommend that when you work with the next generation you can use these learning tools or similar ones that we have usually tried in our family entrepreneurship programs:

(a) *Role Models and Teaching Cases.* You can invite leading family entrepreneurs from different generations who have already made entrepreneurial projects and can share their experiences, or family entrepreneurs who have developed a significant advancement in their company or in the harmony of their business family. We also use case studies prepared by academic instructors and appropriate to the reality and context of entrepreneurial families. These tools will allow you as a leader of the business family to look in a mirror and manage to change their mindset from one man band to mentor orchestra conductor.

(b) *Business Model Canvas, Competitive Matrix and Business and Processes Analysis.* These tools should be printed as large size posters and can be glued on a wall or blackboard and through post-its the entrepreneurial family can show their ideas on the canvases. This has been extremely useful for transferring and integrating knowledge among generations and making an external and internal strategic analysis of the family firm.

(c) *Lego Serious Play.* With Lego Serious Play (Trivium, 2013),[1] entrepreneurial families build their ideas, feelings, and thoughts from the individual to the group with their hands. The management of emotions, mediated by the Lego Serious Play, by the members of the entrepreneurial family has allowed the joint construction of the shared vision of the future of the entrepreneurial family.

(d) *Active Learning and Friendly Consulting.* These learning dynamics are based on the use of different types of questions to solve specific situations that concern entrepreneurial families. For example, in our programs, we create two groups, the senior generation group and the next generation group. We separate them and a member of the group raises their problems (e.g., I don't know how to get my cousins more involved in the business) and from there the dynamic runs. An open and constructive dialogue has been achieved in which the family members have learned from each other.

(e) *Orchestration Dynamic.* In this dynamic, we invite an orchestra director, we have musical instruments in the room and the dynamic is generated so that they understand—in a real way—what means the importance of being a good leader and the role they must play as owners. You can also observe the complementary skills and knowledge of members of the business family to make a melody together.

(f) *"Family Business Snapshot" Online Questionnaire.* This online questionnaire is discussed by different members of the entrepreneurial family, allowing them to be aware of their different individual perspectives. In addition, it allows to make a diagnosis of the family business by identifying the strong and weak areas.

Secret 8: Create or Participate in a Formal Transgenerational Entrepreneurship Learning Program for Your Business Family

We recommend that you create or participate in a formal transgenerational entrepreneurship program with which you invite the new generations and together build entrepreneurship projects. You should think that this program

---

[1] The intervention was designed according to the recommendations made in the manual: Trivium (2013) Facilitator's manual: designing and facilitating workshops with the Lego Serious Play Method. Not for publication. We also had the invaluable guidance of Jon Elejabeitia and Susanne Grimm of the Instituto Hune.

is an opportunity to value creation for the family business and the involvement of generations (rising generation) in the family business. In order to achieve this, the program could not be a traditional theoretical university course or a direct consulting program, but a combination of both that could allow the achievement of the two objectives.

Below we show the principles and characteristics from which we designed the "Strategic Value Creation for Entrepreneurial Families" program at Tecnologico de Monterrey so that you can use it as an example to create your own for your family or participate in a similar one.

For the design we ask ourselves, first of all, what was the true meaning of what we were doing, that is, on an ontological level (Fayolle & Gailly, 2012) before considering the educational level. To exemplify the above, we answered the following questions:

(a) What does entrepreneurship education mean in terms of family business? For us, it means the combination of two distinct but intrinsically related areas: the field of entrepreneurship and the field of the family business. In entrepreneurship, it consists not only of teaching the creation of new businesses but the formation of an entrepreneurial spirit based on autonomy, creativity, resilience, and risk-taking. In the business family, it means to understand the generational dynamics, expectations, and different desires from its members and its communication processes where the focus is not only the family business or the individual, but the *family team*, that is, to locate the entrepreneurial family in the center. The combination of the two fields led us to the conclusion not only of teaching techniques, models, and tools for entrepreneurship, but facilitating communication processes between family members and the transfer of knowledge between generations, orchestrated by a shared vision and leadership.

(b) What does education mean in the context of entrepreneurial families? The essence of Tecnológico de Monterrey relies on an entrepreneurial spirit. Therefore, we know that teaching entrepreneurship goes far beyond transmitting content, so we approach it through learning by doing and experiential methodologies which allow participants the development of entrepreneurial competencies (Ghina, Simatupang, & Gustomo, 2015; Pittaway & Cope, 2007). Family businesses are a fertile field for educating and enhancing entrepreneurship because they are entrepreneurs by nature, they grew up doing business, but they also have the laboratory: the company itself. We concluded that what we had to do was to create spaces for experiential learning (Kolb, 1984, p. 38) that would enhance the family business in different ways, from intra-entrepreneurship and innovation to the creation of new diversified businesses.

(c) What should be the role of students, business families, and educators? By answering these questions, we identified that in order to be successful we had to clearly and accurately establish the different roles. The program includes the following roles: (a) the entrepreneurial family—only owners and future owners responsible for creating value in the family business; (b) students, as leaders of value-creation projects; (c) teachers-consultants, responsible for being "educators" of students and strategic guide for the entrepreneurial family; and (d) instructors, entrepreneurship experts, and the family business who will transmit the contents and methodology of the program in modules (learning sessions).

With all this in mind, the premises for the design of the program would be as follows:

- Aimed at owners and future owners only (not employees, not external consultants).
- Students become the project leader for their own family business.
- Each entrepreneurial family is guided by teachers-consultants, who would guide the student in their learning process and would also be strategic consultants of the company.
- Applying an experiential learning methodology.
- Transmitting contents of entrepreneurship and family business.
- The entrepreneurial family is at the center of the training, so all family members should work together.

Table 16.1 shows the characteristics of the "Strategic Value Creation for Entrepreneurial Families" program.

In Practice

Pre-Hispanic Corporation

Pre-Hispanic Corporation has been in existence for 80 years. It was funded by Matías Benítez and it all started as an adventure, with an idea for selling pre-Hispanic handicrafts to the US market. To date, it has become an important and solid producer of handicraft and luxury gifts company, exporting to more than 28 countries.

Table 16.1 "Strategic Value Creation for Entrepreneurial Families" program

Program elements	Characteristics
Objectives	• To offer the business family an effective way to enhance the value creation of the family business, through correct and accurate strategic movements.
	• To allow natural communication, cohesion, and knowledge integration among generations.
Participants	• Leaders-owners of the family business (senior generation).
	• Students as coordinators of the strategic movements (rising generation).
	• Professors-consultants giving follow-up to each company.
	• Expert instructors in the methodology teaching the modules.
Activities and dynamic	1. Pre-diagnosis study.
	2. Four teaching modules (quarterly) of two days immersion—all business families together.
	3. Business meetings, student and professor-consultant (monthly)—at the company.
	4. Follow-up meetings, student and professor-consultant (weekly)

Source: Developed by the authors

Susana Benítez, 21, a member of the third generation, had the idea of developing an entrepreneurial project that would contribute to the growth of the company. Her interest arose after the company has lost value in the last two years, and she had seen her father, her two uncles, and her aunt very concerned about the financial situation in the company and their responsibility of maintaining the employment of more than 300 employees.

She had already tried to speak twice with Javier Benítez, her father and CEO, about her ideas, but her words had been blown away. She also tried one of her uncles but told her that those decisions should go through the family council coordinated by her aunt. Her aunt told her that according to her policies, she should present an executive summary of her project and the reasons she had for presenting it to decide if it was accepted.

Susana, a marketing student, used her knowledge to present her project of redesigning and creating new pieces of modern style for young people. Of the reasons, she wasn't sure what might impact her dad and her uncles. For this reason, she asked her mom what the family business means to her father, the answer was overwhelming: to leave a legacy for the benefit of the family and society for several generations. She took advantage of this idea and expressed her desire to work on the project to contribute to the continuity of the company and contribute to maintaining and increasing the legacy that her grandfather and the second generation had built. This led to a very positive reaction and the family council and the CEO (her father) accepted her proposal.

The problem was now that the business family did not know how they could articulate and incorporate the entrepreneurship project that Susana proposed to the company. They had policies and rules to incorporate family members as employees but not in new projects, they did not know if it should depend on the marketing area or even create a new area reported by the CEO. The decision they made was to enter the program for the strategic creation of value for the family business offered by the university. The initial surprise is that both generations should participate in the program or they would not be accepted. Reluctantly Javier agreed to participate. In the final presentation after one year of the program, Susana presented the following results and lessons learned for the company and the family:

- A new business model was created to export to Russia and China with three new products (sculptures and luxury gifts) and incorporating new materials. The key is contemporary designs with pre-Hispanic airs.
- The idea of exporting and the incorporation of new materials was a co-creation that took place in the initial sessions where all the owners participated and that allowed them to have a common project.
- They defined a new vision for the future of the business family that says: "To be a committed business family that works in an environment of trust, communication and harmony. To develop the next generations to start new businesses and thus give continuity to the legacy in a healthy, abundant and prosperous way."
- Learning for the business family was a change of vision and mentality in which the CEO made most of the decisions bearing the weight of the company and the family. It helped us to better lead the family-business system. Now there is a balance in leadership and greater openness.
- In a personal way, what impacted me the most was the experience of listening to the points of view of my father and my uncles, talking with them about the business, and thinking together for the good of the family.
- I also gained confidence to present myself to the company executives and promote projects. The guidance of the consulting teachers helped me to deal with the family and acquire knowledge.

Table 16.2 The unraveling of the eight secrets to potentiate transgenerational entrepreneurship

Secret	Description
1	Identify next generation intrinsic motivation to develop or participate in entrepreneurship projects.
2	Take advantage of the genuine motivation of the entrepreneurial family leader for the firm growth and leave a legacy.
3	Change your mindset as a leader of the entrepreneurial family (from one man band controller to mentor orchestra director).
4	Empower the rising generation (boost your self-esteem and show results).
5	Create a space for transferring knowledge among generations.
6	Establish the strategic role of facilitating and accompanying.
7	Incorporate innovative learning tools and activities for the creation of entrepreneurial family value.
8	Create or participate in a formal transgenerational entrepreneurship learning program for your business family.

Conclusions

We are sure that if you, as the leader of the entrepreneurial family, put into practice the key elements (secrets) and triggers that allow to *gather multiple generations at the dining table* to work together in transgenerational entrepreneurship projects, you will be contributing to achieve the continuity of your entrepreneurial family over time.

This chapter helps to understand, more clearly, the phenomenon of learning and education of entrepreneurial families and provides a number of practical examples for the enterprising family group (Salvato, Sharma, & Wright, 2015).

On the other hand, it is valuable for educators, consultants, and family councils as it allows them to generate ideas and reflections on how to generate robust programs to share knowledge and improve communication in transgenerational entrepreneurship. Table 16.2 synthetizes the eight secrets covered throughout this chapter:

References

Argyris, C. (1993). *Knowledge for Action: A Guide to Overcoming Barriers to Organizational Change*. San Francisco, CA: Jossey-Bass Inc.

Cabrera-Suarez, K., De Saá-Pérez, P., & García-Almeida, D. (2001). The Succession Process from a Resource- and Knowledge-based View of the Family Firm. *Family Business Review, 14*(1), 37–46.

Fayolle, A., & Gailly, B. (2012). *From Craft to Science: Teaching Models and Learning Processes in Entrepreneurship Education* (No. Halshs-00785011).

Ghina, A., Simatupang, T. M., & Gustomo, A. (2015). Building a Systematic Framework for Entrepreneurship Education. *Journal of Entrepreneurship Education, 18*(2), 73–98.

Kolb, D. A. (1984). *Experience as the Source of Learning and Development* (Vol. 1). Englewood Cliffs, NJ: Prentice-Hall.

Pittaway, L., & Cope, J. (2007). Entrepreneurship Education: A Systematic Review of the Evidence. *International Small Business Journal, 25*(5), 479–510.

Salvato, C., Sharma, P., & Wright, M. (2015). *From the Guest Editors: Learning Patterns and Approaches to Family Business Education Around the World—Issues, Insights, and Research Agenda*. Briarcliff Manor, NY: Academy of Management.

Sandoval-Arzaga, F., Ramirez-Pasillas, M., & Fonseca-Paredes, M. (2011). Knowledge Integration in Latin American Family Firms. In M. Nordqvist, G. Marzano, E. R. Brenes, G. Jiménez, & M. Fonseca (Eds.), *Understanding Entrepreneurial Family Businesses in Uncertain Environments: Opportunities and Resources in Latin America* (pp. 181–202). Cheltenham: Edward Elgar Publishing.

Vogt, E. E., Brown, J., & Isaacs, D. (2003). *The Art of Powerful Questions: Catalyzing, Insight, Innovation, and Action*. Mill Valley, CA: Whole Systems Associates.

17

Two Sides of the Same Coin—How Intra-Family Communication Affects Entrepreneurial Spirit over Generations in Family Businesses

Philipp Köhn, Miriam Lehmann-Hiepler, and Petra Moog

Introduction

Family businesses constitute the backbone of national economies and societies worldwide; they generate jobs, pay taxes, and contribute to the gross domestic product (Daspit, Chrisman, Sharma, Pearson, & Long, 2017; Dyer, 2003; Kraus, Craig, Dibrell, & Märk, 2012; Sharma, Chrisman, Pablo, & Chua, 2001). Thus, family businesses are, in many ways, important for economies (Astrachan & Shanker, 2003). However, they are essential not only for economic development but also for the families themselves, ensuring financial incomes and often sustainable wealth (Winter, Fitzgerald, Heck, Haynes, & Danes, 1998; Zachary, 2011). Besides the financial value, the business is often of high emotional relevance for the family (Astrachan & Jaskiewicz, 2008; Walker & Brown, 2004) as quotes from our previous qualitative research underline:

> *"Like any family business. Especially when it goes from the first to the second generation. [...] with five children our father always has a sixth and that's the company."*
> *"The business is like a third child for me and I treat it like that!"*

P. Köhn • M. Lehmann-Hiepler • P. Moog (✉)
Siegen University, Siegen, Germany
e-mail: Philipp.koehn@uni-siegen.de; Miriam.hiepler@uni-siegen.de;
Petra.moog@uni-siegen.de

© The Author(s), under exclusive license to Springer Nature Switzerland AG 2021
M. R. Allen, W. B. Gartner (eds.), *Family Entrepreneurship*,
https://doi.org/10.1007/978-3-030-66846-4_17

Thus, a unique emotional connection between the family and the family business exists (Bernhard, 2011; Bernhard & O'Driscoll, 2011; Björnberg & Nicholson, 2012). However, family business research revealed that intra-family succession decreases from generation to generation (McMullen & Warnick, 2015) and successors become more reluctant or even refuse to take over the family business. This is supported by one of our interviewed predecessors:

> It was important for us that things continue in an orderly way and a family business has certain demands on its successors. Nowadays, many family businesses are no longer able to regulate the succession because the next generation does not want to do that because there is no bed of roses here. That is really hard work and above all work when many other people have leisure time. We work on Sundays and holidays and in the evenings and at night and that is not so easy. There are a lot of problems to reconcile with the family and some of the successors say 'no, I don't want that'. Now with us, there is a little bit of this pressure perhaps behind the fact that it has been in the family for so long (over 300 years). Not direct pressure, the children wanted it on their own. That is otherwise forcing. And fortunately, the eldest daughter has found a partner who is from the same industry, so that they are on the same wavelength. Because if he would have a different profession, then this place would not be a good place to work.

This is due to different reasons, for example, low relatedness and commitment toward the firm, no interest in the business or industry, or to stay in the region where the family business is located (Björnberg & Nicholson, 2012; De Massis, Chua, & Chrisman, 2008; McMullen & Warnick, 2015). However, in other cases, potential successors and even formerly reluctant successors take over the business happily or in the case of tender of last resort. This raises the question, why some families are able to raise successors with an intention to take over the business and develop an entrepreneurial spirit and others do not?

Considering the financial and the emotional value of the business for the family the main obligation for families owning a business, is to secure its transgenerational and long-term survival. One crucial aspect for achieving this goal is the preservation of the entrepreneurial spirit over generations within the family and the firm (Cruz & Nordqvist, 2012; Schulze, Lubatkin, & Dino, 2002; Smith, 2009). Entrepreneurship literature shows that the family, especially parents and grandparents, affects the entrepreneurial behavior and therefore the entrepreneurial spirit of their (grand)children (Kirkwood, 2012; Laspita, Breugst, Heblich, & Patzelt, 2012). Based on several studies

(Kindermann & Valsiner, 2013; Kroger, 2004; Valsiner & Connolly, 2005), we suggest that the impact of the elder generation is mainly exerted by intra-family communication among the different generations. Hence, intra-family communication, particularly when concerning the family business, might be a crucial determinant to keep and even to foster the entrepreneurial spirit of the next generation at an early age. Through the omnipresence of the family business within a family's conversations, children perceive manifold facets of it while growing up. This perception, formed through the intra-family communication, may have both positive and negative effects on their entrepreneurial spirit (Murphy & Lambrechts, 2015; Pieper, 2010). Since we believe that this spirit affects the decision of a potential successor to take over a family business, which is a pillar of its sustainable continuation, we aim to answer the following research question:

> How does intra-family communication influence entrepreneurial spirit over generations even before the succession of the family business starts?

To answer this question, we refer to the current literature on family businesses, entrepreneurial communication, and intra-family communication. We also consider our previous research results on family business and our consultancy experiences with them.

Intra-Family Communication Behind the Business—Two Sides of the Same Coin

The family has been, still is and probably will always be a central element of our society. This initiated a huge amount of studies about the family phenomenon and related aspects (Kindermann & Valsiner, 2013; Valsiner & Connolly, 2005). The research interest in families has gained importance for the management and business research; and although the body of knowledge in family business research is constantly growing, there is still a need for a more pronounced understanding of this topic and especially for the family behind the business (Dyer, 2003). From literature, we know that the borders between the family and family business are often fluent, which can be traced back to their overlapping and complementing resources (Olson et al., 2003; Tagiuri & Davis, 1996). This unique interrelation between the family and the firm implies that young children of family business owners can unintentionally become a part of the firm long before they officially enter it through succession.

This assumption is supported by some other research provided by us, indicating that the unintentional entrance of the follow-up generation into the family business is evoked by early non-professional experiences within the firm itself and by business-related conversations with family members at home:

> "We have a family business here. You grew up with the company. The company has always been a topic of conversation. When we were children, this was our big adventure playground, when our father was down here on Sundays and worked here, we were with him. [...] So, we were always here, we did holiday work from an early age, not from 15, but from 8 or 9."
> "Was the family influenced by what happened in the company?" "Yes, there was much conversation. We used to sit and sit and sit and talk about it."
> "Where are private matters and where are business matters discussed? Is there a separation?" "There is no separation. Very rare in a family business."

Looking at the aforementioned quotes it becomes obvious that family business owners are aware that business issues are carried at home and discussed within the family. This might imply not only positive and pleasant topics but also burdensome aspects. Especially in the case of these latter ones, the family—and the communication within it—can be an important support for the business owner.

> Of course I often talked with my wife, because there is always a small residual risk in the whole thing (owning a family business). And of course, you had to clarify everything, to what extent the support of the family at home is given.

We strongly agree with these statements knowing that business-related issues—regardless of whether they are positive or negative—are discussed at home and are a central topic of conversation (Stavrou, 1999; Stavrou & Swiercz, 1998). Whereas positive incidents like success are often just briefly mentioned and not sufficiently celebrated, negative events, for example, bad news, challenges, or problems, are emphasized and thus last stronger and longer in families' memories (Baumeister, Bratslavsky, Finkenauer, & Vohs, 2001). In terms of family businesses, this unbalanced handling of negative business-related issues could, for example, lead to a biased perception and negatively afflicted connotation with the family business. We propose that this negative association with the family business might paralyze the next generation, prevent them from taking certain risks, and therefore reduce the entrepreneurial spirit of potential successors.

"Well, I am often with customers at night [mentally]. [...] For me it's already present and my husband can soften it up a bit, but I also know that if there are problems, he's a bit quieter here in the evening. So, I think you can't leave that out."

"My wife, she never wanted a painter. Because she lived through all this. My father-in-law, he never kept it away from the family. All they talked about was the challenges and problems. She was tired of all this talk. And I always tried to avoid it—to keep business away from the family."

"The disadvantage [of a family business] is that the family is under a lot of stress. [...]. Of course, you take a lot with you in your private life. Usually, the whole family is involved. The family and also financial stories, and I think financial stories can shake family relationships very much. I think that I find it difficult to reconcile all this. You can never switch off completely. [...] You always take everything home with you."

On the other hand, involving the children in business-related discussions provides a first contact with the business and its inherent tasks and challenges. By openly talking about such tasks and challenges, they get a realistic impression of the daily routines within the business, which is characterized by both throwbacks and successes.

First of all, the children experienced it (family business) in the family. I often took them with me, even abroad. When I had my suppliers here, I invited the children to join me. What I also did, which is quite unusual, I took my suppliers for coffee or dinner in the evening home with me after the business-related part of meetings. And I took my sons with me. So that they could experience what happened. How does the father do it? And that also with customers, even if the father says "no", so that they learn to say "no". That's not always easy.

Through integration into conversations and contact with business matters, children might learn how to cope with certain business-related problems and, beyond this, they even might learn how to solve them. This may be an important lesson for their personalities and their entrepreneurial spirit (Belausteguigoitia Rius & Rocha Martínez, 2012). In addition, anxieties and doubts toward family business-related topics are reduced and a connection already at an early age between the potential succeeding generation and the business is established. This connection may lead to the offspring's strong commitment to the family business (Sharma & Irving, 2005) and contribute to the firm's long-term survival and its sustainable success (Björnberg & Nicholson, 2012).

But it is then also the family members in the business, who have also noticed everything from the beginning, who have this family connection.

Knowing that the family business seems to be omnipresent within a family's conversations (Dyer, 2003) and that the family is the first communication context of children in which they learn how to interact with others and in which their personality is formed (Booth-Butterfield & Sidelinger, 1997), we argue that the intra-family communication is part of a general socialization process. Particularly we think this is about business-related topics and that this is a crucial determinant promoting or weakening the family's entrepreneurial spirit over generations. Different analyses show that an aggressive communication style has a destructive power on children's communication as it suppresses the sharing of opinions and the expression of emotions, whereas a communication characterized by awareness of and dealing with emotions fosters an open and equal communication (Booth-Butterfield & Sidelinger, 1997). The way the family communicates with each other also affects the relationships among family members. Particularly in the context of families owning a business, the ties between the parents and their children shape children's attitude toward the firm resulting either in strong commitment or in deviant behavior (Eddleston & Kidwell, 2012). This affects the decision of a potential succession (Lansberg & Astrachan, 1994) and finally boosts or kills the entrepreneurial spirit of the follow-up generation. However, family firms depend on sustaining such a spirit of *"entrepreneurial legacy"* (Jaskiewicz, Combs, & Rau, 2015, p. 29) as a driver of innovation (Lumpkin, Brigham, & Moss, 2010), finally ensuring long-term survival of the business (Kraus et al., 2012; Littunen & Hyrsky, 2000) and families' well-being. Thus, *"good intra-family communication is good for the business and for the family"* (Lundberg, 1994, p. 36).

To show how intra-family communication can influence the entrepreneurial spirit within the family and the firm in both positive and negative directions, we refer again to some exemplary quotes of our former research. In our opinion, intra-organizational and intra-family communication are not the same; however, certain communication patterns promoting entrepreneurial spirit within a firm may strengthen as well the entrepreneurial spirit within the family.

According to our sample, good communication enhancing entrepreneurial spirit is reflected in a direct and emotional speech inspiring and integrating various perspectives and opinions.

"… but getting the team to go there as well is often better in family business because the proximity is much stronger. So, if I can reach someone emotionally if I can reach someone directly in a speech … this helps …"

"Good communication. So, if you have good ideas and can communicate them well, then you inspire people and then they are carried along. If you say I think that's right and I'm not interested in your opinion and now this is how it is done, then you don't get anyone to follow you."

In addition, the entrepreneurial spirit can be maintained by constantly emphasizing the vision and the related strategy for the firm, as indicated by Smith (2009).

Well, I think that only works if you show rigour—if you preach the same thing every day. But we have to go there now, we have to go there and do it repeatedly and above all build up a vision and say: "That's where we want to go!" And this is the strategy!

Complementing to the findings of Booth-Butterfield and Sidelinger (1997), our data revealed that aggressive communication does not motivate employees to engage entrepreneurially. Instead, they prefer open and equal discussions.

I don't think that there is a great deal of yelling or anything else in our company. Of course, in the heat of the moment, a voice can get louder, but basically, the head of the department is not the one who is constantly running around the factory floor shouting, but rather the one who is discussing things with the employees.

Finally, a negative narrative and destructive criticism does not help achieving the goals set and harms the entrepreneurial spirit within organizations.

It depends on whether it's destructive or constructive behavior. If I always say things badly, it doesn't help anyone. If I don't like ideas at first but say that you have to give it another try, then that is very valuable because nobody has the golden idea alone […] that constructive criticism is very helpful, destructive behavior is of no use to anyone.

Thus, open and respectful communication helps in a business environment and we think this is the same in regards to family members and potential successors.

Practical Implications

Considering the previous discussion on literature, interview quotes, previous research, and consultancy experiences, the practical contributions of this chapter here are manifold. First, families owning a business who want to keep or even promote the entrepreneurial spirit within their family over generations should be aware that intra-family communication could influence this spirit in both positive and negative ways. Thus, they should establish a positive and constructive intra-family communication, allowing every family member to share opinions in a respectful way, to contribute to discussions, and to express emotions instead of banning and suppressing them. Involving all family members and especially the children in the whole process of solving the current firm's challenges might help to prevent emerging anxieties toward business-related issues and teach the offspring how to cope with problems or throwbacks. This is an essential entrepreneurial lesson for any personal and professional development. Families should not overemphasize the negative aspects, sorrows, and challenges but instead focus on the problems solved, on benefits and success. Moreover, we advise communicating and celebrating positive events of the daily business as well as remarkable moments of success within the family, which may create a positive perception of the firm and the related entrepreneurial actions to improve the firm's current situation. As our interviews revealed, the owning family organizes business events for celebrating special milestones in the firm's history.

> "Due to the opening event we had, where of course the colleagues were invited, the new starts in the network were of course also made easier. I was welcomed there with very open arms and was immediately given confidence so that this integration was very pleasant and easy."
>
> "Events are also very popular. For example, in the evenings I lock my customers in, (laughs) who then celebrate great events and parties. So they arrange to meet friends, neighbors, relatives, work colleagues and have great evenings here. That is just incredibly moving on. That is very successful."
>
> "… that you really get the most important customers and suppliers on board and then sit down at a table again and then maybe have a celebration. That's already planned."

It could be assumed that such events might be adapted into the family context to promote the entrepreneurial spirit of the next generation and thus family as well as firm performance can be improved. The narrative and celebration of special moments may create a positive and fulfilling image of running a family firm.

Practical Takeaways for Business Families

For business families that want to keep or even promote the entrepreneurial spirit within their family across generations, our practical implications include various aspects that enhance such families to achieve this aim. Therefore, we derived an action plan from these practical implications and summed them up as follows:

1. Be aware of the impact of intra-family communication on the entrepreneurial spirit of your children.
2. Establish a positive, constructive, and respectful intra-family communication.
3. Allow every family member to participate in the intra-family communication.
4. Do not suppress any opinions or emotions of family members.
5. Integrate all family members and especially your children in the process of solving firm's challenges and problems.
6. Do not overemphasize negative aspects, sorrows, and challenges; rather focus on solved problems or successful moments and use a positive narrative regarding your business.
7. Instead, communicate and celebrate successful and remarkable moments of your business with your family.

By following our recommendations for actions, the benefits for business families can be manifold:

1. The entrepreneurial spirit can be promoted over generations within your family.
2. The probability that your children and other family members will develop business-related anxieties decreases leading to less subliminal worries and thus to a more relaxed atmosphere within your family.
3. The interest of your family in the family business can increase resulting in multiple sources of ideas and a stronger family cohesion.
4. Your children learn how to cope with problems or throwbacks, which is an important lesson for their life.
5. A positive perception of the family firm can be created.

Conclusion

This chapter aimed to investigate how intra-family communication influences the entrepreneurial spirit over generations even before the succession of the family business starts. Working with mixed data from current literature, our research on family business, and interviews as well as consulting family firms, we draw the conclusion that the narratives in this communication should create a positive image of running a family firm. The intra-family communication of business-related topics may influence the perception of the family business and thus the entrepreneurial spirit with regard to the family business at a very early age of the next generation in both positive and negative directions. Therefore, we propose that *"good intra-family communication is good for the business and for the family"* (Lundberg, 1994, p. 36) as it creates a positive association with the family business. It increases the probability that children with a family business background act more entrepreneurially and like to take over a family business and all the inherent responsibilities. This might result in taking over the business to keep the family's and business's heritage alive over generations with an entrepreneurial spirit to further develop the family business.

References

Astrachan, J. H., & Jaskiewicz, P. (2008). Emotional Returns and Emotional Costs in Privately Held Family Businesses: Advancing Traditional Business Valuation. *Family Business Review, 21*(2), 139–149.

Astrachan, J. H., & Shanker, M. C. (2003). Family Businesses' Contribution to the U.S. Economy: A Closer Look. *Family Business Review, 16*(3), 211–219.

Baumeister, R. F., Bratslavsky, E., Finkenauer, C., & Vohs, K. D. (2001). Bad is stronger than good. *Review of General Psychology, 5*(4), 323–370.

Belausteguigoitia Rius, I., & Rocha Martínez, M. (2012). *Empresas familiares: Dinámica, equilibrio y consolidación.* México: McGraw Hill.

Bernhard, F. (2011). *Psychological Ownership in Family Businesses: Three Essays on Antecedents and Consequences* (1. Aufl). Lohmar: Eul.

Bernhard, F., & O'Driscoll, M. P. (2011). Psychological Ownership in Small Family-Owned Businesses: Leadership Style and Nonfamily-Employees' Work Attitudes and Behaviors. *Group & Organization Management, 36*(3), 345–384.

Björnberg, Å., & Nicholson, N. (2012). Emotional Ownership: The Next Generation's Relationship With the Family Firm. *Family Business Review, 25*(4), 374–390.

Booth-Butterfield, M., & Sidelinger, R. J. (1997). The Relationship Between Parental Traits and Open Family Communication: Affective Orientation and Verbal Aggression. *Communication Research Reports, 14*(4), 408–417.

Cruz, C., & Nordqvist, M. (2012). Entrepreneurial Orientation in Family Firms: A Generational Perspective. *Small Business Economics, 38*(1), 33–49.

Daspit, J. J., Chrisman, J. J., Sharma, P., Pearson, A. W., & Long, R. G. (2017). A Strategic Management Perspective of the Family Firm: Past Trends, New Insights, and Future Directions. *Journal of Managerial Issues, 29*(1), 6–29.

De Massis, A., Chua, J. H., & Chrisman, J. J. (2008). Factors Preventing Intra-Family Succession. *Family Business Review, 21*(2), 183–199.

Dyer, W. G. (2003). The Family: The Missing Variable in Organizational Research. *Entrepreneurship Theory and Practice, 27*(4), 401–416.

Eddleston, K. A., & Kidwell, R. E. (2012). Parent–Child Relationships: Planting the Seeds of Deviant Behavior in the Family Firm. *Entrepreneurship Theory and Practice, 36*(2), 369–386.

Jaskiewicz, P., Combs, J. G., & Rau, S. B. (2015). Entrepreneurial Legacy: Toward a Theory of How Some Family Firms Nurture Transgenerational Entrepreneurship. *Journal of Business Venturing, 30*(1), 29–49.

Kindermann, T. A., & Valsiner, J. (Eds.). (2013). *Development of Person-Context Relations*. Psychology Press.

Kirkwood, J. (2012). Family Matters: Exploring the Role of Family in the New Venture Creation Decision. *Journal of Small Business & Entrepreneurship, 25*(2), 141–154.

Kraus, S., Craig, J. B., Dibrell, C., & Märk, S. (2012). Family Firms and Entrepreneurship: Contradiction or Synonym? *Journal of Small Business & Entrepreneurship, 25*(2), 135–139.

Kroger, J. (2004). *Identity In Adolescence* (1st ed.). Routledge; London/New York.

Lansberg, I., & Astrachan, J. H. (1994). Influence of Family Relationships on Succession Planning and Training: The Importance of Mediating Factors. *Family Business Review, 7*(1), 39–59.

Laspita, S., Breugst, N., Heblich, S., & Patzelt, H. (2012). Intergenerational Transmission of Entrepreneurial Intentions. *Journal of Business Venturing, 27*(4), 414–435.

Littunen, H., & Hyrsky, K. (2000). The Early Entrepreneurial Stage in Finnish Family and Nonfamily Firms. *Family Business Review, 13*(1), 41–53.

Lumpkin, G. T., Brigham, K. H., & Moss, T. W. (2010). Long-Term Orientation: Implications for the Entrepreneurial Orientation and Performance of Family Businesses. *Entrepreneurship & Regional Development, 22*(3–4), 241–264.

Lundberg, C. C. (1994). Unraveling Communications Among Family Members. *Family Business Review, 7*(1), 29–37.

McMullen, J. S., & Warnick, B. J. (2015). To Nurture or Groom? The Parent-Founder Succession Dilemma. *Entrepreneurship Theory and Practice, 39*(6), 1379–1412.

Murphy, L., & Lambrechts, F. (2015). Investigating the Actual Career Decisions of the Next Generation: The Impact of Family Business Involvement. *Journal of Family Business Strategy, 6*(1), 33–44.

Olson, P. D., Zuiker, V. S., Danes, S. M., Stafford, K., Heck, R. K. Z., & Duncan, K. A. (2003). The Impact of the Family and the Business on Family Business Sustainability. *Journal of Business Venturing, 18*(5), 639–666.

Pieper, T. M. (2010). Non Solus: Toward a Psychology of Family Business. *Journal of Family Business Strategy, 1*(1), 26–39.

Schulze, W. S., Lubatkin, M. H., & Dino, R. N. (2002). Altruism, Agency, and the Competitiveness of Family Firms. *Managerial and Decision Economics, 23*(4–5), 247–259.

Sharma, P., Chrisman, J. J., Pablo, A. L., & Chua, J. H. (2001). Determinants of Initial Satisfaction with the Succession Process in Family Firms: A Conceptual Model. *Entrepreneurship Theory and Practice, 25*(3), 17–36.

Sharma, P., & Irving, P. G. (2005). Four Bases of Family Business Successor Commitment: Antecedents and Consequences. *Entrepreneurship Theory and Practice, 29*(1), 13–33.

Smith, R. (2009). Mentoring and Perpetuating the Entrepreneurial Spirit Within Family Business by Telling Contingent Stories. *New England Journal of Entrepreneurship, 12*(2), 27–40.

Stavrou, E. T., & Swiercz, P. M. (1998). Securing the Future of the Family Enterprise: A Model of Offspring Intentions to Join the Business. *Entrepreneurship Theory and Practice, 23*(2), 19–40.

Stavrou, E. T. (1999). Succession in Family Businesses: Exploring the Effects of Demographic Factors on Offspring Intentions to Join and Take Over the Business. *Journal of Small Business Management, 37*(3), 43–61.

Tagiuri, R., & Davis, J. (1996). Bivalent Attributes of the Family Firm. *Family Business Review, 9*(2), 199–208.

Valsiner, J., & Connolly, K. J. (2005). *Handbook of Developmental Psychology.* Abgerufen von http://sk.sagepub.com/reference/handbook-of-developmental-psychology

Walker, E., & Brown, A. (2004). What Success Factors Are Important to Small Business Owners? *International Small Business Journal, 22*(6), 577–594.

Winter, M., Fitzgerald, M. A., Heck, R. K. Z., Haynes, G. W., & Danes, S. M. (1998). Revisiting the Study of Family Businesses: Methodological Challenges, Dilemmas, and Alternative Approaches. *Family Business Review, 11*(3), 239–252.

Zachary, R. K. (2011). The Importance of the Family System in Family Business. *Journal of Family Business Management, 1*(1), 26–36.

18

The Family Business University: How to Live, Create and Tell Your Family Business Story

Maura McAdam and Dalal Alrubaishi

Introduction

Within both academic and practitioner spheres, there has been increasingly attention paid to the passing on of values within family businesses from one generation to the next. Values such as loyalty, trust, respect, honesty and entrepreneurial know-how not only define the family business's culture but also enhance its longevity and prosperity. However, we know little about *how* these values are passed on. This chapter explores role modelling and storytelling in the transmission and embedding of values across generations. In so doing, the chapter underscores ways in which the family business can promote entrepreneurial behaviour through the concepts of the family business university and imprinting.

M. McAdam (✉)
DCU Business School, Dublin City University, Dublin, Ireland
e-mail: maura.mcadam@dcu.ie

D. Alrubaishi
College of Business Administration (CBA), Princess Nourah bint Abdulrahman University (PNU), Riyadh, Saudi Arabia
e-mail: daalrubaishi@pnu.edu.sa

© The Author(s), under exclusive license to Springer Nature Switzerland AG 2021
M. R. Allen, W. B. Gartner (eds.), *Family Entrepreneurship*,
https://doi.org/10.1007/978-3-030-66846-4_18

Putting the *Family* in Family Business

Given the dominance of family businesses in economies on a worldwide basis, the rapidly growing interest in family business research may not be surprising. However, what is surprising is that most family business research tends to focus on the *business* in family businesses and less on the *family*. Family is the first institution of moral education and indoctrination and the most dominant when it comes to the transference of values, norms and attitudes to its group members (Berger & Luckmann, 1967). Indeed, family is the first group that has a significant imprinting influence on children's values, attitudes, beliefs and behaviours (Giddens, 1984). It is now commonly accepted among anthropologists that families can vary in fundamental ways based on the values they regard as foundational. Unconsciously but inevitably, each generation absorbs parental values which define elementary human relationships. This intergenerational reproduction of people and values is echoed by Bourdieu's (1996) who argues that the family is central to understanding and making sense of how broader structures of social and cultural domination are lived, reproduced and transformed in everyday life (Atkinson, 2014).

Over the years scholars have left us compelling reminders that differences in family structure among families shape family business goals, behaviours and outcomes (Olson et al., 2003; Rogoff & Heck, 2003). Family structure refers to a group of individuals who share family ties, consider themselves as part of a family and interact with each other. Traditional family structures include the nuclear family (i.e. a married couple with children) and the extended family (i.e. a nuclear family plus other adult(s), e.g. grandparents). Acknowledgement of non-traditional family structures are important as often "what is meant by the family is taken to be both uncontentious and unchanging" (Holt & Popp, 2013, p. 9). However, few family business researchers distinguish between family structures, implicitly assuming the prevalence of particular family structures such as the western nuclear family. However, in Saudi Arabia for example (a geographical context which will be used to provide practical examples in this chapter), family refers to relationships beyond that of just parents and children living together but rather includes relatives of both affine and kin (Stewart, 2003). Thus, if we are to really put *family* into family businesses we need to be cognizant of important differences in family structure within and across cultures.

Research Box

"We have strong relations between all of us as a family, we are brothers from different mothers, you never feel that this is my sister from my dad's side or this is my brother from my father's side, we share all the sadness and happiness moments together."
Source: Saudi Entrepreneurial Family Business Study

Key Actionables

Family size differs significantly across countries with the average household size ranging from 1.8 in Sweden to 4 in Mexico according to the OECD family database. However, it is important to think of "family" in broader terms to incorporate in-laws, divorce and stepfamily relationships as more and more family businesses are made up of blended families. It is also important to think of and treat employees as part of the family and include them in important decision making.

The Family Business Incubator

Family businesses are considered to have unique values compared to their nonfamily business counterparts, which are often attributed to their family orientation, and to a strong sense of belonging and loyalty to the birth family (Ellingsen et al., 2012). Family firms are regarded as being value oriented with the founding family creating and reinforcing such values (Distelberg & Sorenson, 2009). Values such as loyalty, trust, respect and honesty (Haugh & McKee, 2003) not only define the family business's culture but also guide decision making. Founders socialise values in the family business by making evident the values that they want to convey to the next generation (Sorenson, 2013). These enduring values often transcend differing political or social beliefs. Frequently, religious beliefs underpin these values and indeed there is increasing evidence illustrating that family businesses often adhere to religious beliefs as a rationale for their business actions (Tracey, 2012). As such, family businesses act as *incubators* that can promote moral and social values for the next generation (Neal & Vallejo, 2008). The *passing on values* results in founder prioritising his/her important life lessons including entrepreneurial know-how. Families who transfer entrepreneurial know-how across generations have an intuitive understanding that family values are the glue that binds family members together across multiple generations. Entrepreneurship know-how as a value can be transmitted, fuelled and enriched through a process of nurturing; it can be transferred through example (*as values are lived*), explanation (*as values are explained*) and codified by the older generation.

Families cannot assume that the values of previous generations will be shared by subsequent generations. For entrepreneurial family businesses, as future generations enter (i.e. Generation X, Generation Y, Generation Z or the Millennial Generation), one can expect changes in their value orientation. For example, Generation X professionals are characterised as valuing work/life balance, individualistic, flexible, technology orientated, while their Generation

Y counterparts are considered to be achievement orientated, family centric, feedback pursuing and team orientated (Krahn & Galambos, 2014). For many of the current generation (e.g. Baby Boomers), their values are considered to founded on a strong work ethic and are competitive, goal orientated and disciplined (Gibson et al., 2009). To ensure longevity, entrepreneurial families will need to embrace this diversity and divergence in value orientation by aligning the personal interests and skills of family members with the need for future leadership. In order to achieve this, they will need to create educational, experiential and mentoring opportunities that allow the next generation to make informed choices about diverse career paths while grooming future family leaders.

Research Note

"I changed a lot in him! I am his source of information, I gave him my experience, as if he was drinking tea or water, I put it in his mind and filled his body with it, and it became a base for him to build his future on."
   Source: Saudi Entrepreneurial Family Business Study

Key Actionables

- How have the values that are driving your family business changed over the years?
- Are the same values prioritised by the different generations in your family business?
- What are the formal and informal ways in which your values can be embedded across generations?

Also …. Family businesses should think about the most important values they want to keep in the business for generations to come. Such values originate usually from the business founder and are embedded in the business both formally and informally. One formal way is by incorporating family values in the Family Business Charter. For example, one Muslim family identified their family values based on Islamic values when it comes to investment opportunities, such as prohibiting dealing with harmful products such as tobacco and engaging in Riba (interest). The informal ways of embedding values in the family business include role modelling and storytelling.

Storytelling

"The greatest art in the world is the art of storytelling." Cecil B. DeMille

According to Charles Collier, author of *Wealth in Families* (2006), a key ingredient of successful family businesses is the telling and retelling of the family's important stories. As discussed, family is a dominant institution when it comes to the transference of values and norms. Once a family business has created their list of core values and behaviours that are meant to guide the next generation in making decisions, the next stage is to figure out how to pass these values on. We concur with Sole and Wilson of Harvard University that stories can "powerfully convey norms and values across generations within the organization and are an effective way in which to pass on values, advice and lessons and onto the next generation". Storytelling is part of the human condition—from cave paintings to the Mahabharata in the East, the Iliad in the West and onward to the present. Given that families are social groups that share "emotional kinship" because of their history and shared memories, family values will be reinforced by the telling of stories to the children of the family. **Such stories** have entrepreneurial legacy that is passed from each generation to the next. For example, a narrative about the family's achievements and how it survived tough times. Stories are therefore mechanisms by which values (both familial and entrepreneurial) can be transmitted across to the rest of the tribe and within a family business a lot of these stories are transmitted across the kitchen table. Stories can also have a mentoring role and can act as inspirational tales and catalysts in the perpetuation of these behaviours, as "surrogate mentors". The next generation will therefore be surrounded by a reinforcing circle of inspirational stories—as "entrepreneurial behaviour … is a portable wisdom in stories that can passed onto others as we walk and talk through life" (Smith, 2009, p. 10). Stories should contain both information and experiences; while informative content is important with regard to conveying the essence of the story, the emotional experience connected to the story will generate bonding through emotional kinship. Consequently, when the family leader departs, it is important that family members still recall the stories of the founder's behaviour and decision making, so that the founder's values remain a reference point embedded in the family firm (Zwack, Kraiczy, von Schlippe & Hack, 2016).

The telling of stories anecdotally is considered the secret ingredient with regard to success beyond the first generation. This secret ingredient is worth exploring as approximately 70% of family businesses want their business to transition to the next generation, 43% do not have a succession plan and only 30% will actually be successful in this regard. Less than 12% of these family businesses survive to the third generation (Bjuggren & Sund, 2001), which provides the premise to the old English saying, "clogs to clogs in three generations".

Research Note

"I have stories about how things were tough back then, my father in the late 1960s went bankrupt again. So, he has always taught us that when the going goes tough fasten your belt, take it easy, no need to spend more than you have to. I believe this is something we still adhere to today. I mean I've been very consistent in terms of dividends, even in the good years, I will not increase the dividends, we have always kept a steady dividends policy."

Key Actionables

1. Share: Share stories about the family business's founding. What were the reasons behind critical decisions? Recount achievements and failures.
2. Record: Recording can be in written in different forms such as in cases or books, voice recorders and video cameras.
3. Keep: Someone should be responsible as the "legacy keeper". Look out for supplementary material to enrich the storytelling. These can include photos, memorabilia, old films and videos.

Also ....

While recording and the keeping of stories are formal ways of storytelling and important means to preserve stories for generations to come, is the informal verbal sharing of stories to children. Indeed, family stories create bonds with the business and in so doing pass on values to youngsters helping them form powerful memories for a lifetime. Moreover, psychological studies have shown that kids who know more about their family's history develop higher self-esteem and a strong sense of control over their lives. Family business leaders are usually busy running the business, but it is important to maintain a ritual of quality time with kids talking about the family and the business. This could be over meals, while driving them to school or as a bedtime story.

Learning Business

Prior to joining the family business, it is not uncommon for incumbent to insist on the next generation not only going to college but also taking up paid employment somewhere else to "learn business". In fact, García-Álvarez, López-Sintas and Saldaña Gonzalvo (2002) argue that formal education and training are key components of a family socialisation process experienced by the next generation. They suggest that this formal period of education and training (e.g. third-level education and international work experience) is coupled with entrepreneurial learning and training (e.g. attendance at trade fairs, business trips) which together facilitate "strong emotional aspects and cognitive learning that are the basis for a descendant's identification with his or her own family". As a result, they are exposed to new trends and also different ways of doing business; with this affording them "a greater ability to engage in analysing markets and competitors in order to find room for new entrepreneurial activities" (Cruz & Nordqvist, 2012, p. 37). Interestingly, on their re-entry to the family business, the next-generation members typically impart learnings to the incumbent generation regarding best practices obtained from international work experience as well as unlearning in relation to outdated practices. This is significant as in order to remain entrepreneurial often requires engaging in a process of unlearning whereby obsolete practices are discarded. According to Clinton, McAdam, Brophy, and Gamble (2020) learning processes in entrepreneurial families are bi-directional and multi-generational, involving multiple forms of co-participation from members of the family ownership group.

Research Note

"After graduation, I worked as an accountant in a company for three years and then I moved to internal auditing. Internal auditing gave me exposure to the operations, project management, purchasing, human resource management, marketing, logistics, and sales, and that helped me to work with my father in an indirect way. So I thought instead of working with my father full time, I will exhaust myself and gain knowledge elsewhere until I reach a point where I can't learn more; whatever I learn, I then share and transfer the knowledge to my family business."

Source: Saudi Entrepreneurial Family Business Study

Key Actionables

- What are important ways in which the next generation can learn "business", for example, college degree or working for a certain number of years for a large corporate (within or outside your industrial sector)?
- Should this become a "rule" in your family business? If so, would you include it in the bylaws?
- Will the family have a say on the university degree, company choice and/or type of job?

Also ....

Sometimes when the next generation work for other organisations, they get exposed to different situations where they have found that their future career path does not belong to the family business. Thus, they may decide to stay where they are and support the family business from a distance. When sending the next generation to gain work experience, families should take into consideration that they might not return to the family business. This is especially true in professions such as accounting and law. In fact, families cannot always guide the next generation to study a university degree related to the family business. In fact some next-generation members may decide early on in life that they want to pursue a career away from their family business such as being a medical practitioner.

The Imprinting of Entrepreneurship

The concept of imprinting originally emerged from studies by animal biologists at the end of the nineteenth century, whereby the early behavioural traits of birds that leave the nest early were studied. It emerged that they formed an instinctive bond with the first moving object they saw within hours of hatching, with the learning stamped during their early life being engrained and persisting throughout their life (Lorenz, 1937). Accordingly, in the parent-child relationship, certain values, behaviours and family attitudes are imprinted, transferred and interpreted between and amongst generations through the family culture (Pieper et al., 2015). The early exposure of the next generation to the businesses is an important factor in the development of the next generation and in the transfer of values, including entrepreneurial know-how. In fact, imprinting is found to have a role in entrepreneurial actions with this imprinting coming from family, friends and partners and takes place early on in life (Mathias, Williams, & Smith, 2015).

The literature has noted the influential role that family business founders play in forming family business values and in fact founders leave the original array of imprints. The founder's value systems not only guide the founder's behaviour and decision making but also is a legacy to be transmitted to the next generation (Koiranen, 2002; Flory, Iglesias, Parada, & Viladás, 2010). The founder socialises values in the family business, by making evident the values that he or she wants to convey to the next generation, and in so doing builds an organisational culture around his/her values (Sorenson, 2013). The values espoused in the family firm are imprinted onto the next-generation leaders as a result of early exposure to the family business and facilitated by mentoring, role modelling and job shadowing. Indeed, children raised in the family business are exposed to the challenges and opportunities of the business, which play a major role in articulating the significance of particular values (Zellweger et al., 2011). These mechanisms have an enduring imprinting effect and in doing so provide and establish powerful behaviour guidelines as to what is deemed appropriate behaviour. Thus, imprinting in family firms is an agent-driven process, which can be found in the everydayness of family businesses.

Research Note

"We built a family value model, it's a model that we built that was translated into a risk assessment, risk appetite let's say. We had values in terms of what is a big NO … what to invest in, and what is ok, and what is not …. which all came from my father. Our understanding of our values all came from him."
Source: 2019 STEP Entrepreneurial Project

> **Key Actionables**
>
> - What are ways in which the next generation can learn your family business?
> - Think about informal ways in which the way you do business is imprinted?
> - What age does this typically start?
> - Is working in the family part of growing up and where does this imprinting typically take place?

Learning Your Family Business—The Family Business University

Apple University is a training facility of Apple Inc. located in Cupertino, California. This corporate university was designed to instruct personnel employed by Apple in the various aspects of Apple's technology and corporate culture. Founding conditions, or the environmental characteristics, at the time of the birth of the firm have been shown to have a significant bearing on the values, attitudes and actions of the firm, long after the founder has departed (Marquis & Tilcsik, 2013). Therefore, Apple University is a training facility aimed at equipping new employees with the values of the founder who is no longer alive. This is an interesting conceptualisation that ensures that the values of the founder have an enduring effect across generations. Given the previous discussion on storytelling, mentoring and imprinting, it is evident that entrepreneurial family businesses already have their own built-in university, with family business members who are committed, imprinted emotionally with the same core values in attendance. **Early exposure** to business and formation of emotional attachment to the business from an early age is a key characteristic of this university, with learning about the business via daily conversations and experiential learning (e.g. learning by doing) core elements of the curriculum. In addition to learning by doing and value transmission, the family business university equips family members with powerful social capital. Indeed, social capital is found to be an important driver of value creation across generations (Salvato & Melin, 2008). Networks and relationships built by the founder are introduced and connected to family members early in their professional career. Such social networks keep the family business informed about the market and are considered as an essential means of opportunity recognition and resource accumulation. Therefore, the next generation are exposed to a wide network of stakeholders and key relationships in the family business university from which they can base their entrepreneurial endeavours. There could even be a fast-track option for in-laws as truly entrepreneurial families actively integrate future in-laws into the family and the family business, whereby such individuals are not only human capital but also play an important role in the cultivation of the next generation of entrepreneurs.

Key Actionables
- What would be the key courses (e.g. lessons, values) taught at this university?
- What would be your Family Business University Motto?

Concluding Remarks

This chapter explores some of the ways as to how values are imprinted and entrepreneurial behaviour is learned within family business. Entrepreneurial knowledge is shared between generations, with learning from the past deeply embedded within everyday social practices in the family and the business (McAdam, Clinton & Dibrell, 2020). An important aspect of social practices is where they take place, and for family business, it is learning on the job and oftentimes across the kitchen table. Furthermore, it important to consider how these social practices are passed on and this chapter underscores the importance of storytelling. Storytelling is an effective way in which to pass on values, advice and lessons onto the next generation and in so doing build resilience and entrepreneurial legacy.

References

Atkinson, W. (2014). A Study of 'Family' as a Field: from Realized Category to Space of Struggle. *Acta Sociologica, 57*, 223–235.

Berger, P., & Luckmann, T. (1967). La construcción social. *Xa Realidad. Buenos Aires.*

Bjuggren, P. O., & Sund, L. G. (2001). Strategic Decision Making in Intergenerational Successions of Small-and Medium-Size Family-Owned Businesses. *Family Business Review, 14*(1), 11–23.

Bourdieu, P. (1996). On the Family as a Realized Category. *Theory, Culture and Society, 13*, 19–26.

Clinton, E., McAdam, M., Gamble, J. R., & Brophy, M. (2020). Entrepreneurial Learning: the Transmitting and Embedding of Entrepreneurial Behaviours within the Transgenerational Entrepreneurial Family. *Entrepreneurship & Regional Development*, 1–22.

Collier, C. W. (2006). *Wealth in Families.* Harvard University.

Cruz, C., & Nordqvist, M. (2012). Entrepreneurial Orientation in Family Firms: A Generational Perspective. *Small Business Economics, 38*(1), 33–49.

Distelberg, B., & Sorenson, R. L. (2009). Updating Systems Concepts in Family Businesses: A Focus on Values, Resource Flows, and Adaptability. *Family Business Review, 22*(1), 65–81.

Ellingsen, I. T., Stephens, P., & Størksen, I. (2012). Congruence and Incongruence in the Perception of 'Family' among Foster Parents, Birth Parents and their Adolescent (Foster) children. *Child & Family Social Work, 17*(4), 427–437.

Flory, M., Iglesias, O., Parada, M. J., & Viladás, H. (2010). Narratives: A Powerful Device for Values Transmission in Family Businesses. *Journal of Organizational Change Management, 23*(2), 166–172.

García-Álvarez, E., López-Sintas, J., & Saldaña Gonzalvo, P. (2002). Socialization Patterns of Successors in First-to Second-Generation Family Businesses. *Family Business Review, 15*(3), 189–203.

Gibson, J. W., Greenwood, R. A., & Murphy Jr, E. F. (2009). Generational Differences in the Workplace: Personal Values, Behaviors, and Popular Beliefs. *Journal of Diversity Management (JDM), 4*(3), 1–8.

Giddens, A. (1984). *The Construction of Society*. Cambridge: Polity.

Haugh, H. M., & McKee, L. (2003). 'It's just like a Family'—Shared Values in the Family Firm. *Community, Work & Family, 6*(2), 141–158.

Holt, R., & Popp, A. (2013). Emotion, Succession, and the Family Firm: Josiah Wedgwood & Sons. *Business History, 55*(6), 892–909.

Koiranen, M. (2002). Over 100 Years of Age but Still Entrepreneurially Active in Business: Exploring the Values and Family Characteristics of Old Finnish Family Firms. *Family Business Review, 15*(3), 175–187.

Krahn, H. J., & Galambos, N. L. (2014). Work Values and Beliefs of 'Generation X' and 'Generation Y'. *Journal of Youth Studies, 17*(1), 92–112.

Lorenz, K. Z. (1937). The Companion in the Bird's World. *The Auk, 54*(3), 245–273.

Marquis, C., & Tilcsik, A. (2013). Imprinting: Toward a Multilevel Theory. *Academy of Management Annals, 7*(1), 195–245.

Mathias, B. D., Williams, D. W., & Smith, A. R. (2015). Entrepreneurial Inception: The Role of Imprinting in Entrepreneurial Action. *Journal of Business Venturing, 30*(1), 11–28.

McAdam, M., Clinton, E., & Dibrell, C. (2020). Navigation of the Paradoxical Landscape of the Family Business. *International Small Business Journal, 38*(3), 139–153.

Neal, J., & Vallejo, M. C. (2008). Family Firms as Incubators for Spirituality in the Workplace: Factors that Nurture Spiritual Businesses. *Journal of Management, Spirituality & Religion, 5*(2), 115–159.

Olson, P. D., Zuiker, V. S., Danes, S. M., Stafford, K., Heck, R. K., & Duncan, K. A. (2003). The Impact of the Family and the Business on Family Business Sustainability. *Journal of Business Venturing, 18*(5), 639–666.

Pieper, T. M., Smith, A. D., Kudlats, J., & Astrachan, J. H. (2015). Article Commentary: The Persistence of Multifamily Firms: Founder Imprinting, Simple Rules, and Monitoring Processes. *Entrepreneurship Theory and Practice, 39*(6), 1313–1337.

Rogoff, E. G., & Heck, R. K. Z. (2003). Evolving Research in Entrepreneurship and Family Business: Recognizing Family as the Oxygen That Feeds the Fire of Entrepreneurship. *Journal of Business Venturing, 18*(5), 559–566.

Salvato, C., & Melin, L. (2008). Creating Value Across Generations in Family-Controlled Businesses: The Role of Family Social Capital. *Family Business Review, 21*(3), 259–276.

Smith, R. (2009). Mentoring and Perpetuating the Entrepreneurial Spirit Within Family Business by Telling Contingent Stories. *New England Journal of Entrepreneurship, 12*(2), 27–40.

Sorenson, R. L. (2013). How Moral and Social Values Become Embedded in Family Firms. *Journal of Management, Spirituality & Religion, 10*(2), 116–137.

Stewart, A. (2003). Help One Another, use One Another: Toward an Anthropology of Family Business. *Entrepreneurship Theory and Practice, 27*(4), 383–396.

Tracey, P. (2012). Religion and Organization: A Critical Review of Current Trends and Future Directions. *Academy of Management Annals, 6*(1), 87–134.

Zellweger, T., Sieger, P., & Halter, F. (2011). Should I Stay or Should I go? Career Choice Intentions of Students with Family Business Background. *Journal of Business Venturing, 26*(5), 521–536.

Zwack, M., Kraiczy, N. D., von Schlippe, A., & Hack, A. (2016). Storytelling and Cultural Family Value Transmission: Value Perception of Stories in Family Firms. *Management Learning, 47*(5), 590–614.

Part VI

Fostering Family Entrepreneurs

19

Nurturing the Next-Generation Family Entrepreneurs in the Business Family

Jia Bao, Saisai Wu, and Jess Chua

While helping prepare a business family for their transitions of ownership and leadership to the next generation, we interviewed all the family members. This was to understand their different visions for the family and the enterprises, their values, and, most importantly, their respect for, and willingness to accommodate, the differences among them in personal interests and priorities. The last two were sisters, eight and six years old. In the middle of the interview, the eight-year-old asked: "When I grow up and start my business, does it have to be related to our current family businesses? Will I have to share the business with the rest of the family?" The six-year-old then said that they had discussed

J. Bao
School of Management, Zhejiang University, Hangzhou, Zhejiang, China

Department of Industrial Systems Engineering & Management, Faculty of Engineering, National University of Singapore, Singapore, Singapore

S. Wu
School of Management, Zhejiang University, Hangzhou, Zhejiang, China

J. Chua (✉)
School of Management, Zhejiang University, Hangzhou, Zhejiang, China

Haskayne School of Business, University of Calgary, Calgary, AB, Canada

Lancaster University Management School, University of Lancaster, Lancaster, UK
e-mail: chua@ucalgary.ca

© The Author(s), under exclusive license to Springer Nature Switzerland AG 2021   **253**
M. R. Allen, W. B. Gartner (eds.), *Family Entrepreneurship*,
https://doi.org/10.1007/978-3-030-66846-4_19

it and she would be her sister's partner. How could an eight-year-old and a six-year-old be thinking about starting a business already?

The Theory of Planned Behavior (TPB) has been used extensively by management and social psychology scholars to explain intentional behavior. Related to the topic here, TPB was first applied by Krueger and Carsrud (1993) to study entrepreneurship and by Stavrou (1999) to study successors' intention to take over leadership of an organization. TPB proposes that the probability of a person engaging in a particular behavior is closely related to the intention to engage in that behavior. In turn, intention is determined largely by the actor's attitude toward the behavior; her/his positive subjective view about the social norms surrounding the behavior; and her/his perceived personal control over the behavior (Ajzen, 1991). Attitude is whether the actor perceives the behavior to be desirable or, in other words, good or bad while subjective view about social norms is whether the actor believes her/his social reference group would approve of her/his engaging in the behavior. Within TPB, perceived behavioral control refers to the actor's perception of the ease or difficulty in performing the behavior and has two parts. One is the locus of control, that is, that the decision is up to the actor; if she/he decides to do it, others will not or will not be able to stop her/him. The other is efficacy, that is, that the actor believes she/he knows how to do it and can overcome the difficulties involved. Recently, more focus has been placed on efficacy, which is related to sense of competence, than on locus of control.

Putting the eight-year-old in the TPB context, the enthusiasm she conveyed reflects not just a positive but in fact passionate attitude toward entrepreneurship. That she thought she would be starting a business when she grew up suggests a belief that her family—her social reference group—would approve the behavior. In other words, two of the three conditions that TPB prescribes for intention to engage in entrepreneurship appear to be satisfied. But at eight years old!

In the previous case, intention was already there. What if it was not? The scion of another business family told a story about how he decided on entrepreneurship as his lifework. He said that his father, an electrical engineer who became a serial entrepreneur, insisted that he go to engineering school to develop a strong technical background and, especially, ability to solve out-of-the-box problems. After completing his engineering education, about which he was disinterested and he thus found to be an agonizing experience, he knew he did not want engineering work and was without a calling. An uncle who was another entrepreneur then suggested that he take a course in entrepreneurship. He found the material more interesting than engineering; the classmates had exciting and contagious big dreams; and the class atmosphere very invigorating. Comparing himself with the classmates, he thought that he was smarter based on his top performance in the class and would have more financial backing from the family. That made him start to think about entrepreneurial opportunities. Once he made the decision, he never doubted that he would receive the family's approval and support.

In these two cases, it appears that the first two conditions specified by TPB were satisfied. But the third condition specified by TPB in terms of perceived behavioral control, especially efficacy or sense of competence, is unlikely to have been realistically satisfied in the case of the eight and six years old. However, the business family may develop these perceptions through mentoring and nurturing.

TPB and Business Family Entrepreneurship

As Steier, Chrisman, and Chua (2015) pointed out, most of the academic family business literature implicitly assumes that the family has only one business; but most large family enterprises consist of portfolios of businesses. Thus, there is a difference between the family in business that perceives itself as a family business or as a business family. The family that thinks in terms of a family business focuses on the single business that it owns and operates while the family that identifies itself as a business family thinks of its family enterprise as a business portfolio that will be dynamically optimized continuously over time. Existing businesses to which the family can no longer make unique contributions and that no longer contribute to the family's vision will be changed, shut down, sold, or replaced by new ones that do (Steier et al., 2015).

There are many reasons why business families add new businesses to their portfolios. Business families, if they want to continue to work together generation after generation, face a "growth imperative." This is because families grow exponentially and the families' enterprises must grow to accommodate all the willing and able family members while providing improving standards of living for everybody. But all businesses have their limits in scale and scope. Besides, once the businesses become professionalized, in the sense of having formalized and enforceable rules of competition between family and nonfamily members for positions, the positions available within these existing businesses to the exponentially growing number of family members will be limited. These are important reasons why many business families end up pursuing portfolio entrepreneurship (Sieger, Zellweger, Nason, & Clinton, 2011). It would allow the family enterprise to continue growing despite the scale and scope limitations of existing businesses and the extent to which the family can continue to make unique contributions to existing businesses. It could also provide lifework for able and committed family members plus diversify the risk to which the family wealth is exposed. Successfully creating new businesses for the family will require both an "interpreneurial" environment (Poza, 1988) and next-generation family entrepreneurs (NGFEs) who want and intend to lead a life of venture creation. We focus here on the NGFE.

The persons in the two cases described above grew up in two different business families that owned multiple lines of business. They were both members of the third generation whose grandparents started the business. Their family enterprises which originally consisted of a single line of business grew organically until the second-generation members graduated from university and joined the firm. These second-generation members were educated in science, engineering, accounting, and finance but none of them practiced in the professions for which they were educated. With better education; networks of the elder generation and of their own friends and classmates from top universities; plus access to the family's own capital as well as bank financing, the team of second-generation family members expanded the family's business enterprise at an exponential rate through organic growth and by adding many new lines of businesses.

That their parents launched successful new businesses could explain why the third-generation family members, at their early ages, would think of entrepreneurship as desirable and believe that their social reference group would approve if that is what they decide to do. As observed by family business scholars (e.g., Morris, 1998), family members becoming entrepreneurs may not be so much the result of innate conditions as the outcome of learning from the experiences of other family members. Thus, these aspects of the business family culture and environment naturally help satisfy TPB's two conditions for developing the NGFE's positive attitude and positive subjective perception about social norms toward entrepreneurship. What will not develop readily and requires the family's deliberate policy and action is satisfying the third condition of efficacy.

Most new ventures fail. If the new venture is started by the NGFE with the family's money, she/he will not be the one to lose the major portion of the financial capital. Instead, she/he will suffer a two-fold loss in reputation and credibility within the family's businesses and, arguably even more importantly, within the family. To prevent a family entrepreneur, especially one with the inclination, drive, capabilities, and commitment, from being discouraged or from suffering long-term loss of credibility within the family and the family enterprise because early ventures attempted failed, potential family entrepreneurs should be carefully prepared. Therefore, a most important task of the business family is to mentor the NGFE such that the chances of failure or, at least the justifiable blame for failure, is minimized. In other words, the NGFE's efficacy must be developed through proper mentoring.

Developing Efficacy Through Mentoring

Mullen (1998) defined mentoring as a relationship in which an experienced person provides development functions to a less experienced person. Many people equate mentoring with coaching. But as recommended by Kram (1983), career-related mentoring should not only develop in the NGFE increased knowledge, skills, and competencies needed to prepare the NGFE for entrepreneurial opportunities as they arise. It should also include sponsorship, protection, exposure and visibility, and increasingly challenging work assignments. To these, we add the development of the NGFE's network and someone with whom the NGFE may discuss personal, emotional, and psychological issues. Thus, we believe that the mentor must play five roles: coach, cheerleader, bodyguard, matchmaker, and confidant.

As a *coach*, the mentor's responsibility is to help the NGFE develop the entrepreneurial and managerial capabilities and skills. These include technical skills and knowledge such as strategic thinking, understanding of accounting numbers; operation planning; project management; time management; reading contracts, among others. Some of these are better and more efficiently learned through formal education or training courses while others must come from experience.

As the *cheerleader*, the mentor's responsibility is to find opportunities for the NGFE to shine—what Kram (1983) calls sponsorship, visibility-exposure, and increasingly challenging work assignments. Starting with low-hanging fruits, the mentor should identify projects with escalating challenges for the family member. By overcoming a series of progressively challenging projects, the next-generation family member will not only build a reputation for competence but also self-confidence—the perception of efficacy or sense of competence.

New ventures are very risky and most of them fail. So, the family must expect the NGFE to fail through bad luck or mistakes. Assigning blame for the failure is often a fruitless exercise causing family disharmony. Unless it is a case of dishonesty or fraud, the NGFE must be protected (Kram, 1983). The mentor as *bodyguard* should first analyze the causes of failure of the venture;

get the NGFE to accept responsibility for and learn from mistakes; plus help to minimize any trustworthiness, credibility, and reputational damages.

Social capital is indispensable for success in life and entrepreneurship. The mentor's job as *matchmaker* may be simply stated as getting the NGFE to know all the people she/he needs to know and to have the people who should know the NGFE know her/him. The entrepreneur's network will include strong and weak ties (Granovetter, 1973). Weak ties help the NGFE acquire public information and may be developed by choosing, with the help of the mentor, the professional and social clubs that the NGFE should join. The strong ties are with those people inside and outside the family from whom the NGFE may acquire resources. From some, it will be private information; from bankers borrowed capital; from government officials, especially in economies with underdeveloped institutions, ways of navigating through government bureaucracy; from the investor community potential future business partners; and from friends introductions to the people from whom the NGFE needs cooperation for ventures to succeed.

The NGFE will encounter business and especially personal, emotional, and psychological issues that cannot be discussed with even the spouse, siblings, or parents. These will build up into dysfunctional stresses with deleterious effects on the short- and long-term productivity and psychological state of the NGFE. Having a trusted, empathetic, and sympathetic mentor as *confidant* with whom the NGFE can discuss these issues, even if just as a release and not to seek solutions, will greatly help the NGFE navigate more smoothly through the entrepreneurial process.

The Who of Mentoring the NGFE

Cull (2006) argued that mentoring will fail when there is a mismatch of values between the mentor and the mentee, while Kram (1983) pointed out that mutual trust is a vital component of the mentoring relationship and the outcomes of the functions are heavily dependent on it (Ragins, 1997; Ragins, Cotton, & Miller, 2000). To trust, Cull (2006) adds mutual respect and a relationship that allows mutual freedom of expression while Sullivan (2000) stresses the mentor's empathy and ability to listen. Ragins and Cotton (1999) point out that frequency of contact is very important, especially at the early stage, and argued for physical proximity which would also promote closeness.

It is best if mentors can serve as role models or as sources of inspiration. Clearly, to be a role model for entrepreneurship, the mentor must ideally be or has been a successful entrepreneur. This is because the more the mentors enjoy and are full of passion about entrepreneurship the more convincing and attractive they will be to the NGFEs. Having been entrepreneurs, mentors are likely to understand better the needs of the NGFE if the latter is to develop a self-image of what she/he is or will be as an entrepreneur (Lockwood, Jordan, & Kunda, 2002).

The How of Mentoring the NGFE

Mentors' role is to help the mentees find the answers and solutions by themselves. That is why St-Jean and Audet (2013) recommend a "maieutic" approach—questioning that aims to give birth to spirits—thereby enabling individuals to become aware of the knowledge buried within them. In other words, it is important to get the NGFE to talk and for the mentor to lend an attentive ear. Pollock (1995) suggests that the psychosocial function is more important than the career-related function in the early stage of mentoring. At this time, mentors must pay special attention to the way they present things in order not to hurt feelings and push the NGFE away or out.

The mentoring in the business family will not proceed in a vacuum because, inside the business family, the mentee will be interacting with other family members who are also conducting entrepreneurial activities. These interactions, including information sharing, career strategizing, confirmation, and emotional support (Kram & Isabella, 1985), could easily become a parallel, mutual, and informal mentoring due to the even closer physical proximity and more frequent exchanges. The mentor should be critically aware of this happening and ensure that it is reinforcing and not undermining.

Beyond Mentoring

As discussed previously, the business family that wishes to stay together needs a continuing stream of new businesses to meet its growth and strategic goals. Thus, it will be tempting for the family to focus exclusively on developing the NGFE's competence and effectiveness through mentoring in order to meet these goals. That would neglect the family's responsibility toward the psychological well-being of its next-generation member which, in this context and especially in the long run, is related to congruence between entrepreneurship and her/his personal goals and identity.

Self-Determination Theory (SDT) proposes that three psychological needs of the NGFE must be satisfied if she/he is to achieve that congruence (Ryan

& Deci, 2000). These are the needs for autonomy, competence, and relatedness. The need for autonomy is the psychological need to have volition as well as a significant say in making decision. The need for competence is the psychological need for feeling that one has the competence to deliver results. This need overlaps TPB's concept of efficacy or sense of competence. And the need for relatedness is the psychological need to feel accepted and connected to one's community.

The need for competence should have been satisfied through mentoring. Thus, going beyond mentoring means satisfying the needs for autonomy and relatedness. The key to satisfying these two needs is to distinguish between the business family's needs and the NGFE's personal needs. Congruence between the two must come from integration of the two needs by the NGFE's own choice.

The most autonomy that the NGFE is likely to have is to pursue a career or venture independent of the family and without using any of the family's resources while the least autonomy will be working within the structures, policies, and systems of one of the family's existing businesses. Autonomy when starting a venture as a part of the business family's portfolio would be in-between. In this context, the business family must emphasize choice rather than control such that pursuance of entrepreneurship as lifework is accepted by the NGFE as her/his own decision.

The NGFE in the business family who starts a new venture for the family will naturally be accepted and, from the acceptance, feel related to the rest of the family. The NGFE's own feeling is insufficient, however, because satisfying the psychological need for relatedness must also be achieved through interactions with the rest of the family. Family harmony and inclusion in deliberations about the strategic directions for the family's business portfolio will contribute importantly to satisfying this need (McMullen & Warnick, 2015).

Epilogue

The eight-year-old graduated from university with a business degree. It took her a year to do the research and write a business plan that was funded by the family. With an uncle as a mentor, the venture was generating sales of around $10 million after three years. The six-year-old graduated from medical school and passed the certification examinations. But, following the footsteps of her elders who did not work in the professions for which they were educated, she decided not to practice medicine and, instead, went back to school to get an

MBA. She has now launched a software venture in partnership with an elder cousin who had previous experience in software entrepreneurship. The scion's first venture, despite close supervision and mentorship by the father, failed for reasons beyond his control. But his second new venture in solar energy is successful. Currently, he is negotiating for the financing to build his second solar energy plant. His education in engineering has come into use after all.

Implications for the Business Family

A large part of the family business literature, both academic and professional, deals with leadership and ownership succession for the implicitly assumed single business. But many large family enterprises consist of multiple businesses. These families think of themselves as business families that hold a business portfolio which is dynamically adapted to the evolving family and to the changing economic, technological, social, and political environment. They change, sell, or shut down businesses that no longer fit the strategic direction envisioned by the families while adding new ones that do. Succession in these families is about more than taking over an existing business; instead, it is about meeting the families' needs for growth, to a large extent through new businesses (Steier et al., 2015). Thus, in terms of promoting entrepreneurship among next-generation family members, the environment within these family enterprises is very different from that of single business families. The environment here would already be very conducive to the launching of new ventures by strongly committed and able family members. This is because ensuing generations will have observed their elder generations launch successful new businesses and receive the accolades accompanying such successes, thus satisfying TPB's two conditions of positive attitude and perceptions about social norms.

On the financial side, getting strangers to write a check for pursuance of the entrepreneur's vision is, in our opinion, one of the most if not the most difficult part of launching a new venture. This is much less difficult in the business family because family members would derive benefits in addition to financial ones from the investment (Chua, Chrisman, Kellermanns, & Wu, 2011; Wu, Chua, & Chrisman, 2007). Thus, we believe that business families should encourage their members who aspire to entrepreneurship to look first at the strategic needs of the business family's portfolio. The NGFEs will, indeed, find it much easier to secure the resources needed to pursue their entrepreneurial goals if their new ventures fit the family's strategic needs.

While it is much easier for a business family member to secure the approval and resources to engage in entrepreneurship, there cannot be a string of failures. Therefore, we emphasize the need for proper mentoring of family members who are prepared to assume this responsibility for the business family. This is because she/he needs entrepreneurial and management skills; self-confidence; reputation for trustworthiness and competence within and outside the family; protection when she/he makes mistakes; social capital; and the ear of someone who is trusted and non-threatening to listen to frustrations, stress, and doubts plus seek advice for personal issues. We have characterized the roles of the mentor with respect to these developmental needs of the NGFE as being the *coach* to help develop the knowledge and abilities; *cheerleader* to help promote visibility and find increasingly challenging opportunities; *bodyguard* to provide protection from long-term loss of credibility and trust when the mentee makes mistakes; *matchmaker* to assist in developing the NGFE's network; and *confidant* to facilitate the mentee's navigation through emotional and psychological issues. This would then satisfy TPB's third condition of efficacy.

Ultimately, the family's responsibility toward its members is to help them live a useful and satisfying life which requires the family to nurture by going beyond mentoring. Self-determination theory proposes that nurturing requires satisfaction of the NGFE's psychological needs for autonomy, competence, and relatedness. Proper mentoring should help meet the need for competence. To meet the need for autonomy the family must ensure that pursuing entrepreneurship as one's lifework is the NGFE's choice rather than that of or through control by the family. Finally, meeting the need for relatedness means the family must include the NGFE in the family's deliberations about the family's vision and strategic directions for the family's enterprises.

This has been a meandering discussion about how the next-generation family member of a business family who has the intention, capability, energy, persistence, and emotional maturity may be mentored and nurtured for a lifework in entrepreneurship. It is not written for an academic audience. Therefore, we have taken liberty with respect to rigor. Instead, we have used anecdotes and even conjectures to illustrate our thoughts. Our hope is that this article will stimulate more thinking about the subject on the part of the reader and, maybe, even motivate family business researchers to develop more rigorous theories and empirically test the hypotheses that they generate.

References

Ajzen, I. (1991). The Theory of Planned Behavior. *Organizational Behavior and Human Decision Processes, 50*(2), 179–211.

Chua, J. H., Chrisman, J. J., Kellermanns, F., & Wu, Z. (2011). Family Involvement and New Venture Debt Financing. *Journal of Business Venturing, 26*(4), 472–488.

Cull, J. (2006). Mentoring Young Entrepreneurs: What Leads to Success? *International Journal of Evidence-Based Coaching and Mentoring, 4*(2), 8–18.

Granovetter, M. S. (1973). The Strength of Weak Ties. *American Journal of Sociology*, 1360–1380.

Kram, K. E. (1983). Phases of the Mentor Relationship. *Academy of Management Journal, 26*(4), 608–625.

Kram, K. E., & Isabella, L. A. (1985). Mentoring Alternatives: The Role of Peer Relationships in Career Development. *Academy of Management Journal, 28*(1), 110–132.

Krueger, N. F., & Carsrud, A. L. (1993). Entrepreneurial Intentions: Applying the Theory of Planned Behaviour. *Entrepreneurship & Regional Development, 5*(4), 315–330.

Lockwood, P., Jordan, C. H., & Kunda, Z. (2002). Motivation by Positive or Negative Role Models: Regulatory Focus Determines Who Will Best Inspire Us. *Journal of Personality and Social Psychology, 83*(4), 854–864.

McMullen, J. S., & Warnick, B. J. (2015). To Nurture or Groom: The Parent-Founder Succession Dilemma. *Entrepreneurship Theory & Practice, 39*(6), 1379–1412.

Morris, M. H. (1998). *Entrepreneurial Intensity: Sustainable Advantages for Individuals, Organizations, and Societies*. Verenigde Staten: Greenwood Publishing Group.

Mullen, E. J. (1998). Vocational and Psychosocial Mentoring Functions: Identifying Mentors Who Serve Both. *Human Resource Development Quarterly, 9*(4), 319–331.

Pollock, R. (1995). A Test of Conceptual Models Depicting the Developmental Course of Informal Mentor-Protégé Relationships in the Workplace. *Journal of Vocational Behavior, 46*(2), 144–162.

Poza, E. J. (1988). Managerial Practices That Support Interpreneurship and Continued Growth. *Family Business Review, 1*(4), 339–359.

Ragins, B. R. (1997). Diversified Mentoring Relationships in Organizations: A Power Perspective. *Academy of Management Review, 22*(2), 482–521.

Ragins, B. R., & Cotton, J. L. (1999). Mentor Functions and Outcomes: A Comparison of Men and Women in Formal and Informal Mentoring Relationships. *Journal of Applied Psychology, 84*(4), 529–550.

Ragins, B. R., Cotton, J. L., & Miller, J. S. (2000). Marginal Mentoring: The Effects of Type of Mentor, Quality of Relationship, and Program Design on Work and Career Attitudes. *Academy of Management Journal, 43*(6), 1177–1194.

Ryan, R. M., & Deci, E. L. (2000). Self-Determination Theory and the Facilitation of Intrinsic Motivation, Social Development, and Well-Being. *American Psychologist, 55*(1), 68–78.

Sieger, P., Zellweger, T., Nason, R. S., & Clinton, E. (2011). Portfolio Entrepreneurship in Family Firms: A Resource-Based Perspective. *Strategic Entrepreneurship Journal, 5*(4), 327–351.

Stavrou, E. T. (1999). Succession in Family Businesses: Exploring the Effects of Demographic Factors on Offspring Intentions to Join and Take Over the Business. *Journal of Small Business Management, 37*(3), 43–61.

Steier, L. P., Chrisman, J. J., & Chua, J. H. (2015). Governance Challenges in Family Businesses and Business Families. *Entrepreneurship Theory & Practice, 39*(6), 1265–1280.

St-Jean, E., & Audet, J. (2013). The Effect of Mentor Intervention Style in Novice Entrepreneur Mentoring Relationships. *Mentoring & Tutoring: Partnership in Learning, 21*(1), 96–119.

Sullivan, R. (2000). Entrepreneurial Learning and Mentoring. *International Journal of Entrepreneurial Behavior & Research, 6*(3), 160–175.

Wu, Z., Chua, J. H., & Chrisman, J. J. (2007). Effects of Family Ownership and Management on Small Business Equity Financing. *Journal of Business Venturing, 22*(6), 875–895.

20

Upping Your Family's Entrepreneurial Game

Judy Lin Walsh, Sam Bruehl, and Nick Di Loreto

Business families who achieve great wealth and hold onto it for generations know the secret is not to rest on your laurels, but to continually promote the entrepreneurial spirit that led to their initial success. For business families who hope to continue for generations to come, inculcating that entrepreneurial drive not only helps the younger generation grow and develop as individuals, it can also help ensure that the collective family business continues to flourish.

Instilling entrepreneurial drive in general isn't easy. But doing it successfully in a family business can be even more challenging. It's easy to get lost in a sea of questions about how to develop this drive without creating unnecessary conflict and complexity—or even to ignore the effort altogether, as if somehow entrepreneurship is in your family's genes and will emerge through serendipity. The truth is, talent alone is not enough to turn a great idea into an enterprising business. The innate drive has to be there and the right foundations have to be in place for the spark to catch.

When it comes to promoting entrepreneurialism in the next generation, families tend to veer to two extremes: "if you build it, they will come" or "you figure it out." There are flaws with each approach.

J. L. Walsh (✉) • S. Bruehl • N. Di Loreto
BanyanGlobal, Wellesley, MA, USA
e-mail: jwalsh@banyan.global; sbruehl@banyan.global; ndiloreto@banyan.global

M. R. Allen, W. B. Gartner (eds.), *Family Entrepreneurship*,
https://doi.org/10.1007/978-3-030-66846-4_20

With the first, there is a disconnect between what one generation perceives as the right approach and what will actually work for the next. Many in the senior generation struggle to distinguish the fine line between nurturing entrepreneurial talent and coddling. Some worry whether younger generation family members have real entrepreneurial ambition and a valid business idea—or if they are just pursuing pet projects and expensive hobbies. Others may be concerned about the perception of fairness throughout the family— whose projects do you support and how much? As a result, the plans they design tend to be skewed based on what they're trying to protect *against*, rather than what will work *for* the next generation. The disconnect can be stark and result in elaborate development programs or venture funds that no one signs up for, leading the senior generation to wonder, "What do we have to do to motivate them?" And so, even with the best of intentions, they inadvertently widen the rift across generations.

The second approach, "you figure it out," is equally flawed because it expects the next generation to become entrepreneurs by osmosis, without any guidance or shared expectations. This is problematic at best if you have just one son or daughter who is trying to make it on his own, but it is almost impossible if you have multiple next-generation members who are trying to find their path (for themselves, and vis-à-vis each other). Aspiring next-generation entrepreneurs have their worries, too. What is the right life path to take—start a business of my own, join the legacy family business, or pursue a career elsewhere? How do I know if I have a "good enough" idea to make it? What happens if I don't—am I unwittingly giving my family a front row seat to witness my failure? What family resources, if any, might be available to me—connections, mentorship, financial support, and so on? And if I do accept family funding or resources, how do I establish boundaries between the family, the family business, and my pursuits so that I don't lose my identity or independence? The list goes on. Without adequate guidance, the next generation are often left paralyzed, wondering not "if" they should take the entrepreneurial leap, but "how" to do it without being overwhelmed by the prospect.

What these two approaches fail to consider is that the family as a whole needs to come together to build a foundation to develop and sustain entrepreneurial drive across generations. Focusing on either extreme—extraordinary structure without room for individual growth or a "free range" approach without any guidance—is often a recipe for disaster. But the good news is it is possible to get this right. We've seen many successful family business members build their own entrepreneurial ventures. Sometimes within the legacy business, other times outside of it. Sometimes supported by their families, sometimes entirely on their own. Sometimes launched earlier in life, and other times much later. We've learned there is no one right formula to stoke entrepreneurial ambition in the next generation, but the winning approach is somewhere in the middle of the two extremes.

What successful families have in common is they recognize the value of entrepreneurial drive and they balance across four core elements to cultivate it. Like a professional tennis player, they develop their groundstrokes, their serve, their net game, and their conditioning together—so that when the big match comes, they're fully prepared.

So what are the four foundations to balance across for entrepreneurial families?

- Foundation 1: Communicate appropriate **stories** to frame reality and set expectations.
- Foundation 2: Create **structures** to clarify the rules of the game, before they are needed.
- Foundation 3: Carefully calibrate what it means to **support** entrepreneurs.
- Foundation 4: Give enough **space** for entrepreneurs to try, create, stumble, and learn.

By knowing and developing these foundations, you can avoid unintentionally triggering landmines and create a healthy sense of entrepreneurial ambition within your business family. Here's how to build and strengthen your family's entrepreneurial game.

Communicate Your **Stories** Well

Many family businesses are built around the legend of the entrepreneurial founder who persevered in the face of adversity. These stories play an important role in inspiring future generations. They're often what first sparks the next generation's entrepreneurial flame. For example, Thierry Hermès, founder of the now-iconic luxury empire, was the sixth child of an innkeeper. Orphaned by disease and war, he went to Paris to learn the leather business, founding his own shop in 1837 making horse harnesses. His clientele grew to include French emperor, Napoléon III. Today, the sixth generation of Hermès family leaders owns a business approximately worth $50 billion. How inspiring is that? But the key in this rags-to-riches story (and many others) is *not* the successful outcome—it's the fact that the story includes the hardships, struggles, and failures that came *before* the glory. There's little benefit in sharing the founder's story if you gloss over the gritty truth. Rather than raising the founder's legacy to mythical proportions, humanize him or her so that your family can relate to and learn from their experience.

In one third-generation winemaking family, the founder made it a point to tell his children how he almost went bankrupt multiple times.[1] "We always had to stay one step ahead so the banks wouldn't foreclose. Every season, one bad frost could be the difference between whether the business could survive or not." To him, cash was king—he always made sure to have at least one year's worth of cash on hand to weather any down cycles. Now, his children and grandchildren know the stories of the boom-and-bust years as well as he does. They're proud of the family success but know it wasn't always glamorous. Each is driven to make their own mark on the business and constantly look for new business opportunities to increase the family's proverbial lead on the banks.

Establish <u>Structures</u> Before You Need Them

Once the entrepreneurial spark is lit, the next step is to grow it and sustain it. Being a part of a business family can be an advantage here. Whether you elect to set aside a financial fund to support family entrepreneurial dreams or just provide access to family resources, it's critical to establish clear objectives for what support (if any) will be provided. Have a cross-generational dialogue about what you want the purpose of a fund to be, what the ground rules are for access and usage, and how the family and the entrepreneur will interact (e.g., what influence will the family expect to have in the process, when and how much information will be shared). Any type of family support requires clarity up front to maintain fairness and keep the peace down the line.

One family almost came to blows when the "golden son" seemed to get preferential treatment in his new ventures. "Dad was the mastermind behind his business—he fed him the idea, let him use family resources to develop the business on family property—and then my baby brother got all the credit AND all the profits." Listen, it's always tough to keep family emotions separate from family business. Setting clear expectations up front will go a long way— who has access to family funding, what other family resources may be provided, whether you need to offer your family members an opportunity to invest, and how ownership will be divvied up. There's no one way to do it, but

---

[1] All identifying details have been disguised to protect confidentiality.

a good practice is to have an open, intergenerational dialogue to develop policies together, before they are needed, so that everything is transparent and follows the ground rules described above.

Calibrate Your Support

Great entrepreneurial families calibrate their support by leveraging external markets to test for viability, by offering benefits beyond money, and by offering boosts without micromanaging. But what does that mean in practice?

Test for Viability

Financial support is not always a positive for a young entrepreneur, especially if it's readily available from family coffers. Indulging every half-baked idea that a budding entrepreneur has will not help him in the long run. Instead, offer him the benefit of the family's collective wisdom and experience. Ask smart questions and require well-thought-out answers. Hold ideas up to a "public standard" to see if they *could* withstand investors' scrutiny and attract outside interest. And if appropriate, have them pitch to outside capital—for the experience, if nothing else. If it's business idea only a mother could love, then ask the entrepreneur to further develop it before pulling out the family checkbook. If it has merit, then, by all means, proceed.

One family prized entrepreneurship so much that every new idea was immediately approved after a quick pitch to the patriarch. He had made his fortune in variety of pursuits ranging from real estate to pharmaceuticals to restaurants. No idea was too wild or aspirational. What mattered most was that his six children follow his footsteps and dream big. Some did, with great success. Others realized that they were just trying to "be an entrepreneur for entrepreneur's sake," without having any real passion for the underlying business ideas. After the third yoga/wellness studio/juice bar idea tanked, the family realized they needed to raise the bar and develop real business concepts instead of just spinning their wheels. They set up a New Ventures Committee that would formally review and respond to every new business idea (which required a complete business case with market analysis and financial projections to be eligible for submission). The patriarch was on the committee, but so were other trusted family and non-family members who could help test for viability. The approval rate for new ventures dropped significantly, but the success rate of those who made the cut increased substantially.

Offer Benefits Beyond Money

Instead of freely throwing money at an idea, consider what "extra benefits" your family can offer that your rising entrepreneur may not be able to get externally. Money can come from multiple sources. If an idea is good enough, there will be no shortage of financial backers trying to stake a claim. As a business family, you're in a unique position to offer *more* than just money. Could your head of strategy act as a mentor as your entrepreneur develops his business plan? Could you offer connections to help with marketing, supply, or distribution? Could you structure financing as a loan so that the entrepreneur doesn't have to surrender a large chunk of shares?

One-fourth generation family in business was surprised when none of their highly entrepreneurial G5 took them up on their offer to invest family money in new ventures. Although they had set aside a dedicated fund, none of the twenty- and thirty-year-olds in G5 were interested. One senior generation member lamented, "I just don't understand Millennials. I would've leapt at the opportunity to have someone provide seed money when I was their age." In contrast, his niece explained, "It's a generous offer, but if I'm going to give up equity in my idea, I might as well go to Silicon Valley, where they can help me navigate the start-up challenges. At least then I'll know I've made it on my own." The two perspectives were both valid. Shared openly, they might have found there was an opportunity to work together. A simple loan instead of a typical venture capital structure might have allowed the next generation to preserve their "ownership" of the idea, while allowing the senior generation to contribute meaningfully to the next generation's aspirations.

Give "Boosts" Without Micromanaging

One of the biggest challenges for successful entrepreneurs who have built tremendous businesses is how to mentor their next generation without taking over. How do you balance giving the next generation enough guidance so that they can learn from your mistakes—but not too much that they dismiss all advice outright? Done effectively, a transfer of knowledge can carve years off of a new business's development time and increase its likelihood of success. Done poorly, it can damage family relations if both sides are not clear on what would be valued and well-received.

One set of siblings navigated this by setting boundaries around when they would talk about new business ventures with their über-successful parent. "We knew Dad wouldn't be able to resist giving us advice all the time if we let him. We really wanted his guidance, but we also wanted to be in control of our own businesses." The family agreed to limit shop talk to their semi-annual camping trips, which became highly anticipated by both generations. Each sibling was eager for special time with each other and their parent. They brought only big issues forward for input. It was enough to give their parent a snapshot of what was happening so that he could give them prized tips, but not so much that they couldn't stumble and learn on their own.

Give Space

And finally, business families provide space to their next generation by supporting those who want to flourish on their own, by giving creative space to those who choose to work in the business, and most importantly, by allowing them to fail.

Support Aspiring Entrepreneurs Who Want to Flourish on Their Own

Don't be afraid to let promising talent venture outside the family business. For one, they could learn skills and lessons on the outside that they can later apply within the legacy business—either in an operational role, as a board director, or as an active shareholder. And two, the potential upside for a revolutionary new idea or business (and the personal satisfaction and fulfillment your son/daughter will have doing it) is limitless. Consider the next generation striking out on their own as a sign that you have *succeeded* in instilling entrepreneurial drive.

When one second-generation patriarch laid down his expectations for his son ("Your grandfather was in the radio business, I was in the radio business, therefore, you will be in the radio business!"), you can imagine the reaction he received. Beyond objections about the future of the industry, the radio business was simply not G3's interest or passion. When his father grumbled that he had experienced the same pressure from his father, his son asked, "Why? What did you want to do back then?" This led to a breakthrough talk between father and son that had both realizing they weren't so different after all. Entrepreneurship—the drive to take risks and succeed—was in their blood. And each had to choose his own path. The father did so in the legacy business by growing it from a few local stations to syndicated shows and expanded presence. The son applied the entrepreneurial spirit in a different media forum, streaming. In time, the father became the biggest champion for his son's new business venture.

Allow an Intrapreneur Breathing Room

Some of the best visionaries we know made their mark *within* an existing family business. Because they have the benefit of learning the lessons from the generation before them, they're able to capitalize on that advantage by applying it to evolving market trends—putting the business at the forefront of a new market. The Hermès family innovated multiple times, expanding their business lines from horse saddles in the 1800s, to silk scarves and neckties in the 1930s, to leather belts and the infamous Birkin bag in the 1980s. Each generation re-invented the business to grow and maintain its standing in the global luxury goods market. Sixth-generation artistic director, Pierre-Alexis Dumas, once said, "My job is to keep the strong creativity of Hermès alive. To nourish the rigor and the vision to make these values vibrate."[2] Notably, it was *not* to ensure the family business kept making horse saddles, generation after generation.

If you have a promising intrapreneur, make sure to give them room to test out their ideas, to learn, and to grow—even if it's not exactly how you would do it personally. Next-generation intrapreneurs are often reacting to different market cues than what worked in prior generations. Stoke their talent and interests. It will ultimately be a boon to the family business if the next generation are engaged, driven, hungry, and enabled to create something of their own.

One patriarch dominated his niche in the entertainment industry for decades, but viewership had recently dropped as his core demographic aged up. The next-generation leader, identifying a trend in the market to go behind the scenes, created a gritty, reality TV version of the core product, and captured a whole new demographic. "I couldn't do what my dad did— it would have felt like I was playing a part instead of being me. I loved the family business, but I had to put my own spin on things." The family was able to keep family talent under the family business umbrella, all because they allowed room to innovate and didn't force the next gen into their father's shoes.

---

[2] https://www.wsj.com/articles/SB10001424053111903596904576517151602728260. Earlier quotations on Hermes: https://www.vanityfair.com/news/2007/09/hermes200709; https://www.bloomberg.com/features/2018-richest-families/

Allow Them to Fail

Failure is only a tragedy if it's a destination rather than a step along the journey. As tempting as it may be to have a safety net always in place, it can be more of a hindrance to individual development and entrepreneurial drive in the long-term than a benefit. Allow your next generation the space to take risks, to fall down, to fail. And if failure does occur, encourage them to learn from their mistakes, recover, and chart a new course.

For another seasoned entrepreneur we know, the idea of failure was as prized as the idea of success. He put $8 million in a collective fund for his six children to invest in entrepreneurial pursuits with no rules or strings— just "live ammo." The next generation was astonished by the degree of trust he had in them. They promptly divvied up the fund into equal $1 million shares, one for each of the six, and set aside the remaining $2 million for a joint venture later. Absent any structure or guidance, each stumbled in their own entrepreneurial attempt, all of which differed wildly (space rockets, surgical robots, a brew pub, and commercial real estate, to name a few). When they sheepishly reported back the loss of the first $6 million to their father, instead of getting mad, he hooted and asked them what they learned in the process. Once they peeled apart the lessons they learned individually, their combined experience led them to invest the final $2 million in an innovative medical device, which became a sensational success. They all agreed, "That first $6 million was a spectacular failure, but it was also the best investment we ever made in ourselves."

Conclusion

Each of these foundations highlights how important it is to find the balance between offering expertise and dictating how something must be done so that you stoke the next generation's entrepreneurial fire. No matter how great the founding idea or business is, it cannot last indefinitely. Business families need fresh infusions of entrepreneurial drive and passion to be able to adapt to changing environments and continue to thrive. And individuals need to test their own mettle and be driven to succeed on their own for their own sense of self-worth.

Remember, nothing about entrepreneurship is straightforward. There is no prescribed formula or established way for developing something revolutionary. Your own family business legend will attest to that. Even if you have all the guidance in the world and pledge to follow all the principles in this book, things can—and will—still go awry. But making mistakes, learning, and course correcting is part of being an entrepreneur. Rather than sweat the small stuff, focus on elevating the foundations of your family's entrepreneurial game. Just as was true for your family business, success won't come overnight. But laying the right groundwork over time will help, whether you're a senior generation or next-generation family member. The key is to make sure your family's overall entrepreneurial game is strong so that you can handle whatever inevitable challenges get thrown your way and come out on top.

Case Study: A "Pot of Gold" with Rules and Communication

The Story

Akhil was orphaned as a child and grew up in the slums of Bombay (now Mumbai). He never received a traditional education and was illiterate. Despite these great personal challenges, Akhil had a natural instinct for business and ended up being a highly successful entrepreneur.

As a teenager, he landed a job with a local currency trader who worked at the port servicing seafarers coming into the city. Eventually, he saved enough money to open his own currency trading business. Over time, he established a strong customer base and through a series of calculated but risky "big moves" transformed his trading business into a major private bank serving the shipping industry in the fast-growing financial hub of Mumbai. Having heard all of Akhil's wild childhood **stories** growing up, his children understood that Akhil's entrepreneurial success came from working long hours, being financially savvy, taking risks, and treating people fairly. Later in life, they made sure to never forget their father's humble beginnings or how his need for survival drove his entrepreneurial spirit.

Akhil passed away in 2004 and left his business portfolio to his six children as well as approximately $10 million in cash that G2 called the "pot of gold." An important part of their father's legacy that G2 wanted to pass to their children was his entrepreneurial spirit. But beyond sharing his story, they were unsure how to inspire their children to be entrepreneurial.

What They Did

They decided that **structure** would be necessary, as each G2 had many children of their own, resulting in 35+ members in G3. As a group, G2 agreed to use their pot of gold as a family investment fund to support the next generation with their entrepreneurial aspirations. They wanted the fund to allow the next generation to have the freedom to form their own professional identities outside the family business if they chose not want to work within it. However, they did not want to just give them "free money" to spend on frivolous or ill-conceived ideas. They agreed clear rules needed to be put in place to protect their pot of gold.

The six G2 spent two days together, hammering out a policy for access to the investment fund. At the end of their time, they applauded themselves for developing a world-class next-generation investment fund policy. Requirements included: a professionally developed business case, an expected return on investment within one-, three-, and five-year periods, and an equity share of 50% in the new venture in exchange for their initial capital investment. They sent the policy to the next generation with a flourish. (But notably, they did not engage G3 in a cross-generational dialogue to develop the structure for the fund.)

Months later, they wondered why no G3 submitted an application for funds. Did no one have an idea they wanted to pursue? They were further stymied when they heard one of the most promising next-generation members, Nitin, was pitching ideas to an outside investment firm for funding. Why didn't he approach the family investment fund first? Baffled, they asked an advisor to talk to Nitin to understand the disconnect.

What They Learned

They discovered the consensus among G3 was that the policy was too restrictive. Despite their best intentions, G2 had miscalibrated what **support** would be helpful to G3. Some G3 had great ideas, but they needed help developing those ideas into a business case. Others worried that they would not be able to meet the return requirements within such short timeframes, as ideas needed more time to incubate. As a result, many were too afraid to even try to approach the family fund. Those who did have well-developed ideas, like Nitin, were deterred by the funding model. Giving up 50% equity seemed like too much. He preferred to take his chances with external investors to retain more control of his idea. At least then, he would feel confident that any success achieved would be by his own merit. His desire for **space**—an identity separate from the family's legacy—led him away from the family investment fund.

What We Advised

It was clear to us that G2 was on the right track, but they made a few critical foundational mistakes in the development of their policy. They told the right **stories** and established some preliminary **structure**, but by not including the next generation in the creation process, they misunderstood what kind of **support** the next generation truly needed. It wasn't the money—that was a secondary benefit. The primary value of a shared fund was to provide resources to support the next generation's development and to foster the teamwork needed to turn a promising idea into a legitimate business.

To break this divide, the G2 and G3 met together to talk about whether they all believed in the spirit of the investment fund, and if so, what they would need to make it take flight. Through much dialogue, they collectively designed a new family fund **structure** that both generations felt proud to have developed and be a part of. Namely, they agreed to pivot the idea from an "investment fund" to an "entrepreneur fund" which would still require a business case to be brought forth, but that would offer resources from within their banking business to help with financial modeling and strategy. They kept the same return on investment expectations but extended the timeframes out to three and five years. And notably, they agreed that the funding should be provided as a loan, to be repaid if the venture was successful, but with no equity required in exchange. This would allow individual family entrepreneurs to retain the sense of identity and ownership that all entrepreneurs strive for. This was the "gift" the family would give the next generation from their pot of gold, so that they could build on Akhil's legacy and use his success to develop their own.

Questions for You to Consider

This family got a lot of things right, but there was room for improvement.

- What did the G2 do well in fostering entrepreneurial drive in the G3?
- What more could G2 (or G1) have done to cultivate entrepreneurship?
- What could G2 and G3 have done differently to balance across the four S's?

Reflect on what this family did well (and what they could have done better) and compare it to your own family's situation. Consider the state of your four S's—stories, structures, support, and space. How will you find the right balance to improve your family's entrepreneurial game?

Part VII

The Future of Family Entrepreneurship

21

Fostering Entrepreneurialism and Intrapreneurialism Within the Family Enterprise System

Peter Vogel and Marta Widz

Enterprising Families in Times of Change and Disruption

We live in times of unprecedented change and transformation with the speed of disruption exceeding anything seen before. New entrants are pushing innovative products and services into the market, leveraging novel business models that are disrupting entire industries and businesses. This affects both family and non-family businesses alike.

Despite their significant market dominance and availability of resources, many incumbent businesses are increasingly uncertain about the future. In particular, family businesses have realized that if they want to stay alive and ahead of the game for generations to come, they need to anticipate disruption. In particular, enterprising families have to be strategic about embracing entrepreneurialism within its internal (i.e., within the family and the business) and in the external entrepreneurial ecosystems, capitalizing on the strengths which family businesses bring with them, such as well-established industry connections, prudent and long-term investment strategy, financial strength and independence as a result of less debt, loyalty and trust of their

P. Vogel (✉) • M. Widz
IMD Business School, Lausanne, Switzerland
e-mail: peter.vogel@imd.org; marta.widz@imd.org

© The Author(s), under exclusive license to Springer Nature Switzerland AG 2021
M. R. Allen, W. B. Gartner (eds.), *Family Entrepreneurship*,
https://doi.org/10.1007/978-3-030-66846-4_21

281

workforce, a commitment of the family shareholders, a legacy of entrepreneurialism, a high degree of tacit knowledge, and quick decision-making processes.

Core aspects of this strategy are to (a) develop a wide spectrum of mechanisms that foster entrepreneurialism and intrapreneurialism (i.e., *applying methods of entrepreneurialism within an existing organization*) of both family members and employees, and (b) engage with the external start-up and innovation ecosystems. The purpose of this chapter is, therefore, to explore how enterprising families embrace the desire to become more entrepreneurial by fostering both *entrepreneurialism* and *intrapreneurialism*, and staying close to the *external* entrepreneurial ecosystem, capitalizing on the family and corporate resources.

Growing Desire of Enterprising Families to Foster Entrepreneurialism

Even though family businesses are traditionally not viewed as being particularly innovative, they have an inherited intuition for entrepreneurialism, stemming from the innovative and entrepreneurial thinking and acting of their founding fathers. Long-lasting family businesses, which achieved a significant global presence, went through a journey of converting themselves from *families in a single business* toward a *family enterprise system* with multiple activities, multiple businesses, investment vehicles, private equity activities, start-up investment vehicles, and family offices.

As business families grow and transform into family enterprises, we observe a growing desire—partially triggered by market shifts, disruptive trends, a decreasing interest of the next generation to "just" take over the legacy business and do business as usual or the next generation being increasingly interested in entrepreneurship—to be more entrepreneurial (either by venturing into completely new areas or by transforming the business model of their existing businesses) and become true *enterprising families*.

Building on that desire, we observe two main emerging trends of enterprising families fostering entrepreneurialism within their *internal* family and corporate ecosystems as well as in engaging with the *external* entrepreneurial ecosystem (Fig. 21.1).

In the *internal* family and business ecosystem, enterprising families are increasingly interested in bringing entrepreneurial thinking and acting inside their core business(es) (*intrapreneurialism*) in order to innovate and renew the

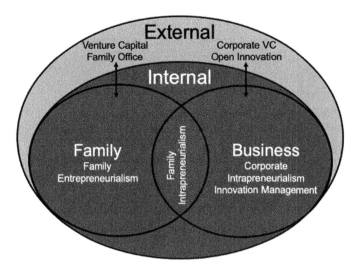

Fig. 21.1 Different forms of entrepreneurialism and intrapreneurialism within the family enterprise system and engagement with the external ecosystems

business models and consequently ensure competitiveness. Additionally, they experiment with the creation of new ventures outside their core business(es) (*entrepreneurialism*).

Besides these efforts of *intrapreneurialism* and *entrepreneurialism*, we observe an increasing interest of enterprising families to actively engage with the *external* entrepreneurial ecosystem using the family and/or corporate resources, such as human capital and financial capital. On the one side, there is an increasing interest of businesses (both family businesses and non-family businesses) to directly invest into start-ups (e.g., via corporate venture capital) and to engage in open innovation activities. On the other side, enterprising families are also increasingly active in direct investments into start-ups (e.g., via venture capital or directly through their family offices), both early-stage as well as later-stage (including pre-IPO).

Fostering the *entrepreneurialism* and *intrapreneurialism* as well as engaging with the *external* entrepreneurial ecosystem leads to multiple benefits on both family and business sides. It:

- nurtures the entrepreneurial behavior and acting of the family members
- builds emotional ownership of family members
- creates an opportunity for generations to work collaboratively
- creates a bond among family members

- constitutes the platform for the next generation to test themselves and thus shapes more confident successors, rather than fearful, passive heirs
- ensures continued innovativeness and competitiveness of the business
- triggers employee engagement
- contributes to the longevity of the business
- contributes to the agility of the business
- leads to the evolution of the portfolio, especially if the new ventures are integrated into the core business

Trend 1: Fostering Entrepreneurialism and Intrapreneurialism Within the Family Enterprise System

The first trend is to foster *entrepreneurialism* and *intrapreneurialism* within the family enterprise system (i.e., inside the family and the business). Organizations around the world (family-controlled or not) are increasingly interested in creating a start-up ecosystem inside their businesses as a mechanism to respond to various external trends, trying to tap into the creativity and innovativeness of their workforce.[1] Similarly, enterprising families, especially the larger ones, are replicating such mechanisms within their families.

Never before has there been such a push for family members and employees to embrace entrepreneurialism, which may take the form of (1) family entrepreneurship, (2) family intrapreneurship, and (3) corporate intrapreneurship. Table 21.1 looks at these three options in more detail, analyzing them alongside a range of dimensions such as:

1. Who "owns" the activity (from idea to execution)?
2. Who provides the resources and the capital?
3. Where is the activity positioned within the family enterprise system?
4. Who bears the risks and carries the returns?

In order to ensure the multigenerational success of the enterprising family and their respective businesses, it is of critical importance that they embrace at least one of the listed approaches of *entrepreneurialism* and *intrapreneurialism*. This is vital because the majority of businesses have a natural lifecycle and if the owning family wants to ensure that their wealth is preserved (or even

---

[1] Vogel & Fischler-Strasak, 2014. Fostering Sustainable Innovation Within Organizations. In Weidinger, Christina; Fischler, Franz & Schmidpeter, René (ed.): Sustainable Entrepreneurship: A New Business Concept for Sustainability. Berlin: Springer, 2014, S. 191–205.

Table 21.1 Forms of entrepreneurship and intrapreneurship of enterprising families

	Family entrepreneurship	Family intrapreneurship	Corporate intrapreneurship
Ownership & leadership of activity	Family entrepreneur	Family (and employees of the business)	Employees of the business
Resources & capital	Family (sometimes also outside investors)	Business	Business
Positioning within family enterprise system	Outside the core business	Predominantly inside the core business	Predominantly inside the core business
Risks & gains	Family entrepreneur(s) & family	Business (indirectly: Family)	Business (possibly bonus / Stocks for intrapreneur)

better grows) over time, they need to constantly innovate and develop new ventures or reinvent, transform, or redesign the existing business model.

Those families who master these approaches know how to stimulate entrepreneurial thinking and acting inside the family so that the next generation and the incumbent generation can develop new venture projects (*family entrepreneurship*). Further, enterprising families often create a platform for the family members (and especially the next-generation members) to bring their entrepreneurialism inside the scope of the current business portfolio (*family intrapreneurship*). Finally, enterprising families also foster entrepreneurialism of the employees, which is often triggered by the entrepreneurial legacy and values of the owning family (*corporate intrapreneurship*).

Trend 2: Engaging with the External Entrepreneurial Ecosystem

The second trend builds on an increasing desire of enterprising families to directly engage with the *external* entrepreneurial ecosystem, either by investing their resources alongside established PE (Private Equity) or VC (Venture Capital) firms or by (more and more often) directly investing into start-ups, both as individuals and via their family offices. Direct investments into start-ups (both early-stage and later-stage) have gained traction over the past years as a result of several trends and developments:

- Disruptive players are transforming industries and enterprising families are concerned about the future of their legacy businesses, pushing them to seek alternative investments in order to create a diversified portfolio of assets.
- Families of wealth are increasingly uncertain about the quality of service of investment companies and banks and are hesitant to continue paying the managerial fees, thus they are looking at more direct opportunities.
- An abundance of capital in the markets, paired with a lack of alternative investment opportunities (low-yield environment) leads families to take up more risky investment opportunities.
- The next generation of wealth owners has a growing desire to think and act entrepreneurially or to be close to the world of entrepreneurship, thus redefining the investment agenda of their family wealth.
- There is an increasing proportion of "first-generation wealth owners" worldwide, that is wealth owners who have created the majority of their wealth on their own (vis-à-vis those who have inherited the majority of their wealth). These are, by characteristics, more entrepreneurial, and wish to stay close to the world of entrepreneurship.
- Over the past two decades (since the dot com crash), technology-driven ventures have reached massive valuations in relatively short periods. While in 2015 there were less than 100 unicorns (start-ups with at least 1 billion USD valuation), there were over 400 at the end of 2019. These sky-high valuations, paired with a growing desire of these tech ventures to do an IPO, has lured many wealthy investors into this market, hoping to get access to a part of the cake.

Table 21.2 describes the family and corporate engagement with the entrepreneurial ecosystem in more detail, analyzing these two options alongside a range of dimensions such as:

Table 21.2 Family and corporate engagement with the external ecosystem

	Family engagement with the entrepreneurial ecosystem	Corporate engagement with the entrepreneurial ecosystem
Vehicle	Direct investments via the family office Indirect Investments via VC firms	Investments via corporate venture capital
	Direct investments of family members	Open innovation projects
Resources & capital	Family	Business
Positioning within family enterprise system	Usually not aligned with the core business	Usually aligned with the core business
Risks & gains	Family	Business

1. What's the vehicle leveraged for engaging with the entrepreneurial ecosystem?
2. Who provides the resources and the capital?
3. Where is the activity positioned within the family enterprise system?
4. Who bears the risks and carries the returns?

It must be mentioned that, depending on the governance structure of the family, business, or family office, there might also exist mixed forms of investments between the family and the corporate side. For example, it is possible that the family office (and its investment expertise) is being leveraged to manage the corporate's investment activities, and vice-versa.

Reaching out to the external entrepreneurial ecosystem by investing with family resources and corporate resources is a particularly interesting opportunity for families to diversify their portfolio, hedge their risks, and foster entrepreneurialism among the family members.

Five Mechanisms of Fostering Entrepreneurialism and Intrapreneurialism Within the Family Enterprise System

If enterprising families want to stay competitive in the future and ensure that their wealth is not only preserved but grows over time, they must foster *entrepreneurialism* and *intrapreneurialism* within the family and the business and, at the same time, figure out best ways to closely interact with the *external* start-up ecosystem and a broader innovation ecosystem outside their core domain, capitalizing on the family and corporate resources.

More specifically, family businesses shall develop a spectrum of mechanisms to embrace all domains of entrepreneurialism (Fig. 21.2). In particular,

1. Family Entrepreneurialism—embracing entrepreneurialism (outside of the core business) with the family resources.
2. Family Intrapreneurialism—embracing intrapreneurialism (mostly within the core business) with predominantly corporate resources.
3. Family Investments in the external ecosystem—family direct and indirect investments into start-ups and more mature business entities either via VC firm or via a family office.
4. Corporate Intrapreneurialism and innovation management—embracing intrapreneurialism (within the core business) with corporate resources.

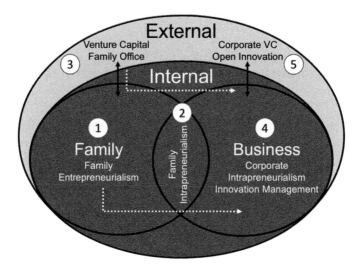

Fig. 21.2 Five mechanisms (1–5) of embracing entrepreneurialism and intrapreneurialism and reaching out to the external entrepreneurial ecosystem, capitalizing on the family and corporate resources within enterprising families; and three strategic connections (I–III) between these mechanisms

5. Corporate Engagement in the external entrepreneurial ecosystem (via corporate venture capital or open innovation).

While these five different mechanisms can, in principle, happen in isolation we do see quite frequently a closely knit connection between them, in particular, if there are an overarching and holistic vision and innovation strategy in place for the family enterprise system. More concretely, we see the following frequent connections:

I. <u>Between 1 and 4</u>: While family entrepreneurialism (mechanism 1) is oftentimes positioned outside the core family business(es), we have seen cases where there is a strategic link to the legacy business. For example, by fostering family entrepreneurship in domains and industries which are strategically close with the legacy family business and considering strategic alliances between the two activities. Furthermore, if successful, the entrepreneurial ventures founded by the family can be integrated into the core business or within the portfolio of businesses (e.g., if the family operates multiple businesses).

II. <u>Between 3 and 5</u>: There are numerous opportunities for strategic alliances between the family's private investment activities and business investment activities. For example, in some cases, the family office also serves as the investment body (scouting, investment committee, etc.) for the business, or vice-versa, depending on which of the two is more advanced and how strategic investments are for the respective entity.

III. <u>Between 5 and 4 and between 3 and 4</u>: While there is a very apparent connection between 5 and 4—that is, a *business* invests in a new venture in the external ecosystem with the intention to integrate their knowledge, expertise, client database, revenues, product portfolio, or other resources back into the core business—there can also be a connection between 3 and 4, in case the enterprising *family* decides to invest into a new venture out on the market that can then later be integrated with, or combined with, the core business(es). This route can be interesting in case the family invests into a venture that they might find interesting, but that might not (yet) be of strategic relevance to the core business. Alternatively, the family may decide to diversify their business activities into other fields with the intention to integrate them under the revisited governance structure, such as under the umbrella of a holding, in the future.

In the following we will particularly elaborate—and illustrate with case studies—the following mechanisms: (1) family entrepreneurialism, (2) family intrapreneurialism, and (3) family investments in the external ecosystem. The mechanisms of (4) corporate intrapreneurialism and innovation management and (5) corporate investments in the external ecosystem and innovation management are not specific to family businesses and apply to any business and thus covered in the wider innovation literature.

Illustrating Family Entrepreneurialism, Family Intrapreneurialism, and Engaging with the *External* Entrepreneurial Ecosystem: Case Studies

Mechanism 1: Family Entrepreneurialism. Association Familiale Mulliez (AFM)

The Mulliez, originally from Roubaix, in the north of France, where wool textiles in the later nineteenth century was a specialty and the starting point for the Mulliez business empire. While many of the other textile-based businesses from the region did not manage to flourish, the Mulliez family has managed to not only remain successful across generations but to become one of the most influential and successful business families in France. Their family unity has repeatedly been recognized as one of the main drivers of their continued success. Besides, their entrepreneurial spirit and energy have contributed to continuous renewal and adaptation to new market environments.

Founder Louis Mulliez and his wife Marguerite Lestienne raised 11 children. Their sons worked in the family business. A family solidarity "pact" was signed in 1955 to ensure long-term success as well as family unity across generations. Under the leadership of two of the brothers, Louis and Gérard, the family created the family association called Association Familiale Mulliez (AFM), which was based on the principle of "everyone in everything" (*Tous dans tout*). That meant that family members would invest in and benefit from all family-owned companies, which brought many advantages to the businesses controlled by the descendants of Louis Mulliez and Marguerite Lestienne. AFM is a holding through which the family controls its businesses.

Today, the Mulliez family controls one of the largest retail empires in the world, with major brands such as Auchan (supermarkets), Decathlon (sports), and Phildar (hosiery and yarn) under their control (refer to Exhibit 21.1).

None of the Mulliez businesses are listed on the stock market and the family patient-capital, together with the scrutiny from the family, often pays out.

Association Familiale Mulliez

Auchan	Decathlon	Leroy Merlin
Picwic	Sonepar	Macopharma
Oxylane	Phildar	Atak
Pimkie	Top Office	Midas
Weldom	Bricoman	Saint Maclou
Auto 5	Norauto	Grossbill.com
Flunch	Amarine	Pizza Pai
Kiabi	3 Suisses.fr	Cultura

Exhibit 21.1   Main businesses of Association Familiale Mulliez (AFM)

For example, Auchan supermarkets—started in 1961 and originally named Ochan—were not an overnight success. It took Gérard many years to find out the right business model for long-term success, which was based on a high volume and a low margin in order to address the mass market.

With over 700 shareholders, the Mulliez family has managed to create a unique entrepreneurial ecosystem within the family and shareholder group, offering in-house education as well as seed funding for any aspiring family entrepreneur. This is based on the time-proven family philosophy, which dictates that the family must not solely rely on the achievements of earlier generations but, most importantly, think about new ways of wealth creation in each of the generations to follow.

The ability of the family to instill an entrepreneurial spirit in the next generation is a key value and driver of the continued family success. Over the years, the Mulliez families have created a multitude of activities to foster entrepreneurial thinking and acting among family members and to be close to the world of entrepreneurship outside of the family. In 2002, the Mulliez family created Creadev as an evergreen investment company, focusing on five core areas: sustainability, food, care, skills, and customer experience. To date, over €1 billion have been invested into ventures in various stages, from venture capital to growth equity to buyout.

Besides investing in start-ups, many Mulliez family members founded their own ventures. Dimogestion (software editor), Cadréa (framing and wall decoration specialist), and Olivarius (apartment hotel) are among the many companies launched by family members. A few years after the formation of Creadev, the family created a dedicated family internal venture incubator, helping family members launch and scale up their ventures, offering funding, mentoring, among other things. There exists a structured process for family members to pitch their business plans to the family investment committee. One example is Epi Breads, which was initially started by a family member, Nicolas Mulliez, and a non-family external business partner. In 1991, AFM, as well as several family members, provided equity financing to scale up this business.

Mechanism 2: Family Intrapreneurialism. De Agostini[2]

The De Agostini group, headquartered in Novara and Milan, Italy, employs over 13,000 people worldwide and generates a turnover of about €4.8 billion.

---

[2] Leleux, B. & Widz, M. (2019) De Agostini: Repurposing the Business & the Family. IMD-7-2072.

Established in 1901 by cartographer Giovanni De Agostini, the company was acquired almost 20 years later by partners Marco Adolfo Boroli and Cesare Angelo Rossi. In 1946, Marco Adolfo Boroli's two sons consolidated De Agostini in the Boroli family's hands.

For over 80 years, De Agostini operated in its original cartography, publishing, graphics, and printing industries. From the late 1980s, third-generation chairman and family leader Marco Drago took the company on a global expansion, which began with the international expansion of the legacy publishing business.

An important milestone for De Agostini came in 1997 with its participation in the privatization of Seat Pagine Gialle (Yellow Pages). After a successful turnaround, it was sold to Telecom Italia in 2000 for a more than seven times multiple. This liquidity event marked the beginning of the group's rapid diversification. Within just two decades, De Agostini transformed itself from a traditional business, active predominantly in publishing and printing, into a diversified holding company, with assets in four business areas (refer to Exhibit 21.2). Many new ventures were established—for example, Dea Capital, which with time was also listed on the Milan Stock Exchange.

Marco Drago proved to be a true family intrapreneur and fostered the desire of the next generation to experiment with family intrapreneurialism. He established the Strategic Lab—part think-tank and part assessment tool for the next-generation talent of the Drago-Boroli family—which was a safe "playground" for the talented family members to tackle real challenges of the family business (refer to Exhibit 21.3):

A recent challenge the family faced was related to the legacy publishing business. Over the last 20 years, as a result of intense diversification, the legacy

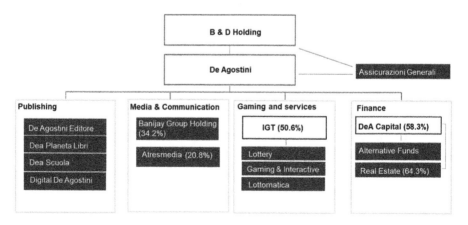

Exhibit 21.2   De Agostini portfolio

> **Strategic Lab**
>
> Simulation of strategic decisions
>
> Members:
> - Chairman (family)
> - CEO (non-family)
> - independent members (top managers from other companies)
> - selected Next Gen members

Exhibit 21.3 De Agostini's Strategic Lab: a tool to foster next-generation family intrapreneurship

publishing business was reduced to about 3% in the overall portfolio in terms of net asset value and was suffering from a recurrent lack of profitability. However, no one in the family was ready to give it up. As Marco Drago put it, "Our approach towards the legacy publishing business is romantic and emotional." In an attempt to revitalize it, the family board appointed Nicola Drago, the son of Marco Drago, as CEO of the publishing business. Nicola recounted his journey into the publishing business:

> I got exposed to the legacy business in a spontaneous and natural way. De Agostini Editore has many books for children, so I knew its products. After graduate studies, I worked in investment banking and consulting. Then I did my MBA and joined De Agostini Group at the age of 27 in the digital arm of the television business.

In summer 2016, when Nicola took on the position of CEO, he looked at the publishing business through the lens of his accumulated experience:

> I saw lots of assets and a half-baked business model that shareholders may not be fully aware of. I also saw lots of legacy and emotions, which give me the motivation to re-shape the business. I want to bring that publishing house to the good shape I remember from my childhood.

Plans for the legacy business included two options. The first was to keep it in the portfolio as a "legacy flag." It seemed possible to implement some operational measures to overcome the profitability problem and achieve reasonable business results in Italian operations. The rest could be disposed of when appropriate. A second, more exciting option was to reinvent the business for the new digital age and give it the means to capture global opportunities. It was the assignment of the strategic lab to analyze the situation and present the strategic plan.

Nicola and four other fourth-generation family members, assisted by top executives from De Agostini, family chairman as well as three top external executives, worked on a plan. In the attempt to rejuvenate the publishing business, Nicola Drago launched a new venture called Betterly—a box series, delivered by post, which includes various products to "discover a new, better part of you." The "Me Time" series, for example, include products such as "Paint and Colour," "The Power of Divination," "The Energy of Crystals," and "They Got Blues" and have percentages assigned to Discover, Play, Feel, Create, Inspire to help customers navigate among various boxes.

Betterly, which started as a result of an internal seed fund, is positioned as an innovation, which is built on the tradition with slogans such as "a 119-year-old start-up" and "a start-up with a solid foundation." What started off as a declining legacy business in a troubled industry has the potential to become a new and exciting business fit for the twenty-first century, led by the visionary family intrapreneur Nicola Drago.

Mechanism 3: Family Investments in the External Ecosystem. Pentland Group[3]

Pentland Group plc, the global brand management company is headquartered in London, UK. Owned by just six family members from the second and third generation, it employs more than 20,500 people worldwide and generates about £2.9 billion in sales.

Pentland Group's roots can be traced back to 1932, when Berko and Minnie Rubin—immigrants from Eastern Europe—set up the Liverpool Shoe Company, a small fashion footwear business, with just over £100 as a capital base raised from family and friends.

In 1969 Stephen, the only child of the firm founders, took over the business when his father passed away. He immediately started with diversification

---

[3] Leleux, B. & Widz, M. (2018) Pentland Group: A Family of Brands. IMD-7-1937.

investments and pioneered the outsourcing of footwear manufacturing to Asia in the early 1970s. Stephen's natural flair for entrepreneurship allowed him to strike some spectacular deals. In 1981, Pentland invested US$77,500 for a majority stake in a struggling American sports brand called **Reebok**. This investment was sold 10 years later for $770 million, a 10,000+ multiple and the stuff of legends.

With the sale of the Reebok stake, Pentland was flush with cash and used it to finance a series of acquisitions to build a family of prestige sporting goods labels, such as **Speedo**, **Berghaus**, **Canterbury**, **Mitre**, and **KangaROOS**— all operated from within the legacy business, Pentland Brands. Next to it, the Pentland group also holds a 57% ownership stake in **JD Sports Fashion**, a chain of retail shops. As the third pillar of their activities, the Pentland Group operates an **Investment Division**, which supports group diversification by investing in new ventures or partnering with start-ups with a mandate to learn from entrepreneurs and innovate (refer to Exhibit 21.4).

Pentland's Investment Division is a quasi-family office, collating financial information about the group operations, taking on financial risk-management duties, and managing tasks such as taxes, insurances, and estate planning. Its main role, however, is to act as the investment arm of the family with the primary goal to diversify the family's wealth and generate strong returns. At any given moment the Investment Division has dozens of fund-type investments and dozens of investments in businesses. Venturing with family capital has a broadly defined scope with most of the investment being clear

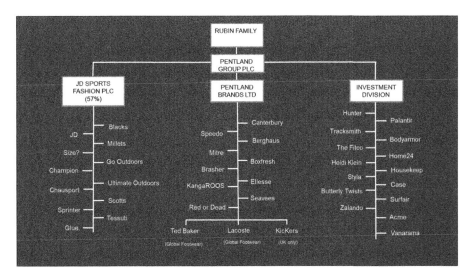

Exhibit 21.4   Pentland Group Structure in 2018

diversification investments—in non-core activities—such as the recent investment in Body Armor, as explained by Pentland:

> We invested in Body Armor, an American soft-drinks business. The drink is based on coconut water, a healthy alternative to many other incumbent drinks, with endorsements from multiple American athletes. Body Armor is probably the only strongly growing brand in the sports drinks category in the US. It has shown over 100% revenue growth every year for the past three years and we are very happy with its performance.

All investments are done with the goal of contributing to the entrepreneurial venture but not controlling them. And Stephen receives two or three phone calls a day about expansion opportunities. "We have taken about 10% of these to our investment side," he says, "And all of them came to us because of our reputation." Pentland is proud to have a "management-friendly" approach, rooted in Stephen's belief that "hostile takeovers are highly immoral":

> One of the major attractions to entrepreneurs is not just expertise but the fact that we are considered long-term patient capital. Unlike private equity, we are not pushing for the exit within three to five years. We can hold investments for a long time, 20 to 30 years, or potentially forever. We partner with entrepreneurs who want some backing but who don't want to sell out and don't want to be employees.

Indeed, entrepreneurs do not go to Pentland just for the money. Heidi Klein, a boutique beachwear brand founded by friends Heidi Gosman and Penny Klein, was introduced to Pentland by a banker. Pentland did a seed investment and offered Heidi Klein the platform it needed to grow. One of the Rubin family members joined as a company director and Pentland's ownership share increased to 60%. The two founders are still equal minority shareholders and directors of the company, with Heidi as creative director and Penny as commercial director.

Brands do not usually transfer from the Investment Division to Pentland Brands because that would require fitting in the strategy of that particular brand to Pentland Brands' strategy, and because the investments by the Investment Division are usually limited to minority stakes. A good example is the iconic rubber boots brand, Hunter, with roots going as far back as 1856, in which Pentland bought a 49% stake, as Stephen recalled:

The Hunter brand was terrific, especially in hunting, shooting, and fishing. I thought we could use the brand in fashion, so we tried to buy it, but the other three shareholders were already involved.

Hunter profited from Pentland's sourcing experience for some six years, and when a very good opportunity to realize significant returns arose in 2012, Pentland sold down its stake to the private equity investor Searchlight Capital Partners, retaining a small stake in the business.

The venturing and investment life cycle of any investment is closely monitored by the Investment Committee, which reports directly to Pentland Group's board and includes key non-family stakeholders such as the non-family CEO of Pentland Brands.

Lessons Learned

As enterprising families try to navigate a rapidly changing and highly dynamic VUCA (volatile, uncertain, complex, and ambiguous) world, they need to understand that their survival and longevity can only be ensured if they fully embrace the concept of entrepreneurial renewal and adaptation. While family businesses are among the oldest institutions in the world, it becomes apparent that those family businesses with a significant global impact are all, comparatively young. The roots of a great majority of them can be traced to the second and even more so the third industrial revolution.

It is not surprising that none of the oldest family businesses are among the biggest ones. There is a simple explanation for this: In times of change, transformation, and crisis, it is the entrepreneurially minded (and oftentimes smaller and nimbler) businesses that manage to adapt to the new reality.

History has clearly shown that the long-lasting family businesses made the re-occurring experience of adapting to dramatic changes in the external environment (such as industrial revolutions, economic depressions, and world wars). Through those experiences, they learned how to constantly adjust and renew themselves by building on their entrepreneurial legacy. Thus, family businesses and enterprising families who will thrive in the VUCA world are those who:

- Foster entrepreneurial and intrapreneurial *adaptation*: Understand what is coming and what challenges their industry and business may face, as well as embrace the inevitable developments in the external environment, including social, technological, economic, environmental, and political forces (STEEP framework),

- Foster entrepreneurial and intrapreneurial *renewal* within the *internal* and *external* entrepreneurial ecosystems: Consider one or more of the *five mechanisms* of (i) family entrepreneurialism, (ii) family intrapreneurialism, (iii) family investments in the external ecosystem, (iv) corporate intrapreneurialism and innovation management, and (v) corporate investments in the external ecosystem,
- Embrace the notion of VUCA leadership (visionary, understanding, clarity, and agility), take entrepreneurial risks, and cultivate their entrepreneurial legacy with the support of ideas, talents, capital, and governance structures.

22

From Allocators to Acquirers: The Family Investing Model and Transgenerational Entrepreneurship

Jennifer Pendergast and Sachin Waikar

A recent survey shows that 66% of family offices surveyed plan to increase their direct investments in the near future (Zhou, 2017). About 25% of responding families were already investing in companies in a private-equity-style model.

This is one of the latest developments in the broader trend of transgenerational entrepreneurship in family enterprise. Indeed, the ability to pass along entrepreneurial spirit and related skills has been the linchpin of success for generations of family firms. Habbershon, Nordqvist, and Zellweger (2010) define transgenerational entrepreneurship as "the processes through which a family uses and develops entrepreneurial mindsets and family influenced resources and capabilities to create new streams of entrepreneurial, financial and social value across generations."

Historically, this has been achieved by moving in and out of sectors and businesses to capitalize on opportunities to harvest capital and to ensure the business portfolio remains profitable and competitive. Families who are successful have also accumulated liquid wealth along their journey and have often created a separate entity to manage that money: the family office. Since the early industrialists—Vanderbilts, Rockefellers, and the like—took public or

J. Pendergast (✉) • S. Waikar
Kellogg School of Management, Northwestern University, Evanston, IL, USA
e-mail: Jennifer.pendergast@kellogg.northwestern.edu

© The Author(s), under exclusive license to Springer Nature Switzerland AG 2021
M. R. Allen, W. B. Gartner (eds.), *Family Entrepreneurship*,
https://doi.org/10.1007/978-3-030-66846-4_22

sold their companies, the family office has been an entity that housed family wealth and supported its protection and transmission across generations.

Today we are witnessing a large movement from the family office toward a *family investment company* approach. In the words of one family investor, "Families are moving from allocators to acquirers," deploying their capital directly into operating entities rather than allocating it across a range of asset managers or investment funds. This means that families are seeking transgenerational entrepreneurship through their investing ventures, not just their operating ventures.

This increasingly popular investment approach provides distinct advantages, including the ability to leverage the family's history and expertise in operating entities, a strategic path to leverage capabilities to move away from legacy industries with diminishing returns, and an enticement for next-generation family members to get involved in interesting new businesses. Put more simply, these investing activities present a new way to address the dual challenge of business and family.

This chapter introduces a new model for how families achieve transgenerational entrepreneurship, through a broader-scope investing model focused on direct investment. We will describe the motivation behind the Family Investing Model, explain its related dimensions and challenges, and illustrate it with stories from multiple families that have proceeded down this path, reaping the benefits of family investing while managing associated risks.

The Dual Challenge of Business and Family

Families that use investing as a way of promoting transgenerational entrepreneurship do so in the context of and as a response to unprecedented challenge and complexity in both of the domains that they simultaneously occupy: business and family. Broadly, those who are most successful find ways to address the challenges head on, in many cases by effectively reinventing the business and broader enterprise, along with the family's approach to these.

In the *business* domain, for example, mounting challenges revolve around the rapidly changing marketplace, with disruption of established business models based on technology, new competitors, and other factors. This is embodied in the Amazon effect across the retail industry, and the impact of disruptors like Uber and Lyft on transportation and Airbnb and Sonder on hospitality. The traditional industries family firms occupy—distribution, retail, hospitality, real estate, and media—are all undergoing dramatic change. These fast-moving trends require families to rethink whether and how the enterprise in its current form and with its current capital structure (predominantly private with limited debt) can thrive. The resource-based view of the firm argues that sustainable competitive advantage derives from developing superior capabilities and resources (Barney, 1991). To generate a competitive advantage, resources must be valuable, rare, imperfectly imitable, and not substitutable. However, in our increasingly digital and global world, resources are more easily imitated or substituted, causing obsolesce of products, services and even business models. Thus, families who aspire to be in business for generations must rethink how they can deploy their resources differently to derive value.

Meanwhile, the concept and nature of *family* itself is also changing, with greater global dispersion of family members, fewer entering or planning to enter the business, and Millennial and more recent generations driven largely by different interests and expectations than prior generations have been, with emphasis on living out their values and bringing their "authentic selves" to work (e.g., Peart, 2019). The families striving to get ahead of these trends recognize they can't assume "family business as usual" in terms of the future or even the present, and are thinking proactively and strategically about the best short- and long-term approaches.

A central theme for enterprising families in this context is the critical question of what business they are in. Families grappling actively with the dual challenges noted above have let go of the assumption that they either own and operate legacy businesses or sell their business(es) and focus on wealth preservation as allocators of capital. Instead of making that assumption, they think more broadly about their business portfolio, especially with regard to rethinking their approach to passive investing, and in its place actively seeking investments where they are more engaged and can add value. Or put another way, families are thinking about how they can deploy their valuable resources and capabilities, honed through their legacy operations, to develop a sustainable competitive advantage in different arenas.

The Family Investing Model presented in the next section captures how many families have begun to approach investing, as a new channel/approach to achieving transgenerational entrepreneurship, in the broader context of addressing business and family trends/challenges and evolving the family enterprise on multiple dimensions.

The Family Investing Model

An emergent model of family investing integrates the two approaches noted above, which most families held previously as mutually exclusive: focus on one or more operating companies, and maintenance of a passively invested portfolio. Families embracing this model may continue to operate one or more businesses, but they also invest actively in new businesses that fit their purpose (see below), whether buying these outright or owning minority or majority share in them, thus following more of a private equity-type model. As such, the new model requires clear understanding and buy-in regarding the approach and related opportunities/risks among family owners, along with the actions required to make it successful, including development of new management capabilities, governance structure, family education mechanisms and, in many cases, broader family involvement.

As shown in the figure, the model proposes that *family purpose* is the core driver of investing choices, and thus families need to understand and make decisions around their purpose, or what impact they want their wealth to have on the family, their communities, and the broader world. Often, the purpose is not well-defined; it may be implicit, but hasn't been discussed, affirmed, and articulated by the family. Moreover, the core purpose the founder had in creating the legacy business may no longer be relevant to the family. For example, the founding objective may have been to create jobs for the family, as a way to provide for the family financially; but later generations may not rely on the family business in this way, forging their own paths outside the firm.

So, when families get into later stages of enterprise ownership, they really need to think about why they wish to stay together as a wealth-holding family and what they want to achieve through their wealth. In many cases, a family's core purpose reflects the desire to have positive impact on the world. For example, the Herschend family which owns multiple theme parks and other entertainment assets including Dollywood and the Harlem Globetrotters has always prided itself on treating employees well; so an element of their core purpose has been investing in businesses that employ many people. In 2019, Herschend-owned businesses employed about 12,000 year-round and seasonal employees. In doing so, they espouse stakeholder theory, which stresses the interconnected relationships between a business and its customers, suppliers, employees, investors, communities and others who have a stake in the organization. The theory argues that a firm should create value for all stakeholders, not just shareholders. (Freeman, 1984) While stakeholder theory has become more popular recently in the publicly held company realm, family enterprises have long understood the multiple benefits of focusing on a broader stakeholder group.

The Chicago-based Steans family, which started in financial services and expanded to other business holdings, sees their wealth as enabling every family member, of both current and future generations, to be the most impactful and beneficial member of society they can be by pursuing their individual passions toward professional and personal goals. Thus, their purpose of creating wealth—through investment in wide-ranging businesses through the family's Financial Investments Corporation—is to endow family members with the freedom to pursue paths that may not be as lucrative as others but still create meaningful impact. More broadly, the Steans's investment in entrepreneurial ventures drives additional impact by helping those founder-entrepreneurs and others create ripples of stewardship and community-focused value where they operate.

These and other examples reflect the growing reality that family investors "are not all just groups of wealthy investors solely seeking to maximize their return on investments; instead, many are writing a new narrative, one intended to shift the investment paradigm," as one family enterprise advisor suggests (Rosplock, as cited in Jaffe, 2019). They are seeking to fulfill an investing purpose beyond returns alone, as informed by their broader family purpose.

In any investing context, family or otherwise, investment choices are guided by an investment philosophy or thesis targeted to meet a set of financial expectations around growth, return, liquidity, and risk—again as shown in the model. An individual investor, for example, would select a mutual fund or stock with an investment advisor by answering questions around their financial desires, goals, and expectations. For a mutual fund manager, an investment thesis guides investment selection based on thesis criteria around desired risk/return parameters and, increasingly, as related to the values of institutional and individual investors, such as investing in companies that attend carefully to environmental, social, and governance (ESG) issues. That thesis is informed by the strategic expertise, experience, and capabilities that the investment team brings to the table.

In the family investing case, the resources the family brings to bear to add value to its investment selection and management include the family's legacy, reputation, and industry knowledge/experience, along with the expertise, capabilities, and relationships of their investment management team. Financial Investments Corporation, owned by the Steans family, for example, invests in business services because Ken Hooten, a Partner in their direct investment arm, was previously an executive at ServiceMaster, and knows that domain well. Similarly, the Schurz family targeted industries where close intimate relationships with customers, employees, and/or communities can provide strategic advantage, a hallmark of their experience in small-market media. The premise is that good investors improve their investments, not by just doing good due diligence to buy value but also by *adding* value through the relationships, expertise, and other resources they bring to the business. As they evolved from a traditional family media company, owning publishing and TV and radio stations, the Schurz family espoused a purpose beyond its roots. According to CEO Todd Schurz, "Entrepreneurial stewardship means owners have a responsibility first to future generations as well as a debt of gratitude and honor to prior generations. Our sacred cow is not a specific asset; it's to be in this together."

While the investment thesis and strategic resources are important, in the family context an additional set of unique drivers impacts investment choices: family values and preferences. These may result in the family seeking out or avoiding certain kinds of investments or partnerships, as guided by spoken or unspoken "rules" and guidelines. As an example of values-driven investment decisions, descendants of the Rockefeller family urged their foundation to divest itself of fossil fuel investments, even though that sector had generated the family's wealth. On the preferences side, a given family may wish not to enter into partnerships in general, or may want to avoid taking on what they see as excessive debt.

Of course, values and preferences may be related, as a family value of thriftiness may result in avoiding investments of a certain size or multiple (ratio of purchase price to revenue). Families that value entrepreneurship may prefer to make capital available to invest in family members' ideas (i.e., the family bank concept). Families may also encourage participation in investment decisions to help individuals gain a sense of personal responsibility: that is, members have to learn to live with the outcomes of their investment choices. On the flip slide, some families may discourage participation in investment selection, to protect accumulated wealth by leaving the decisions exclusively to trained professionals.

Finally, related to the last points above, families often pursue active investing as a way to support the broad goal of family cohesion and engagement, which is crucial to continuity of wealth. Without a genuine desire to stick together among family members, entropy sets in, as the family is likely to become more geographically dispersed and lose familiarity among members in later generations, with a lack of appreciation for and interest in continuing the family legacy. As such, investing can be a lever to pull the family together, by getting them excited about what the family is doing and engendering pride in what the family is accomplishing through its investments, as well as by creating opportunities for family members to meet and connect around decision-making or education about their investments.

How Families Are Getting It Right

Investing in any form has inherent risk. This is especially true in family enterprise, where owners pursuing broader investments are getting into a new business where:

- They likely have limited expertise
- They will need to build or acquire new skills sets beyond those of the existing professional staff and board, in many cases
- They will need to invest additional capital to build an investing infrastructure
- They will need strong alignment of the broader shareholder group to make the shift
- They will need solid guardrails to protect the family from losses

The following sections cover how families have taken specific steps to mitigate the risks involved in broader investment activities, thus reaping greater rewards. The examples illustrate how families are successfully implementing key features of the family investing model presented earlier, as reflective of their purposes, values, and preferences.

Alignment Around Purpose and Process

Earlier we presented examples of the sense of purpose with which several families approach investing. But aligning members around that purpose and how to carry it out is itself a challenge for many families, requiring commitment and a process to get there. According to family business expert Dennis Jaffe (2019), "relatively little is known about how family investors work together as a family." Unlike in typical reinvention driven by management, for a business to stay relevant, in the family business context there will be a complex set of stakeholders engaged in such evolution, including management, owners, board, family members. Reinvention in full or in part as an investing entity could be instigated by any stakeholder group, and requires coordination and alignment across them, informed and aligned by a clear sense of purpose: What are we trying to achieve for individual family members, the family as a group, and other stakeholders?

Here, too, examples from families committed to large-scale investing activities shed light on how to achieve alignment in this domain. For instance, Craig Duchossois, Chair and CEO of the Duchossois Group and Chairman of the family's investment arm Duchossois Capital Management (DCM), engaged consultants to interview all family members to understand their interests and preferences as related to investment approaches, and to gain approval for DCM's structure. Family members were pleased to be involved in the process, which resulted in fewer "unilateral" investment decisions.

In another example, the family leadership team and board of E Ritter, & Company, a 130 year old agribusiness and communications concern determined that selling some land, at all-time-high prices, would create an opportunity to diversify the family's holdings. To convince the family, the CEO and board chair went on a roadshow, visiting all key shareholders to explain the investment thesis and to make the case for creating an investment fund. They then hired a consultant to identify areas for investment, and ultimately changed the board's structure to incorporate investing expertise. In all, the effort took several years, due to the need to bring all stakeholders on board with the decision.

As these examples suggest, families can and should do their "homework" about how to develop strong investing capabilities, understand potential risks and returns, and bring as many members as possible up the related learning curve. One of the best sources of such learning is other families who are further along this path. For example, the Carlson family, owners of Carlson, Inc., talked to several other families to secure advice about how to set up their direct investing arm, Carlson Private Capital Partners (CPC), to benefit from their experience and knowledge. Says Carlson Inc. board member and family owner Wendy Nelson, "We benefited from the generosity of knowledge from other families who are further down the path on their direct investing journey."

Investment Focus

"The best form of philanthropy is giving someone a job." That's what Curt Carlson, late founder of Carlson, Inc., always told his family. That philosophy is reflected in the family's direct investment subsidiary CPC, as described Wendy Nelson. She notes the purpose-driven goal for each investment company to carry on the legacies of the original founders with a shared view of success focusing on customers, employees, community and shareholders. To do that, CPC leverages the expertise and experience of its dedicated direct investing team.

As mentioned earlier, the Chicago-based Steans family, through their Family Investments Corporation (FIC), invests in entrepreneurs and works closely with them to grow their businesses through organic strategies, acquisitions, and add-on investments. According to the website, FIC partners with "leading middle market companies by providing capital and strategic advisory to accelerate long term value creation … to achieve extraordinary results" (Concentric Equity Partners, 2020).

To determine their investment focus, the Schurz family spent over a year developing specific, codified primary and secondary investment criteria including the presence of recurring revenue with a "diverse, sticky customer base"; an understanding of skills sets needed to be a "differentiator" for successful competition in the industry; and a business sharing common characteristics with at least one existing Schurz-owned business, thus providing opportunity to leverage existing core skill sets or assets.

Cavallo Ventures, the investing arm of nearly 100-year old family business Wilbur-Ellis, states that it seeks "pioneering entrepreneurs that insist upon building successful companies without taking shortcuts" (Cavallo, 2020). Similarly, the Duchossois family looks to invest in operators "doing things the right way" from a values perspective. In line with this, the leaders of DCM have "walked away" from promising investment deals if they felt the leadership teams involved didn't share their values, especially on the dimension of integrity.

Governance & Operations

Families also pay close attention to the governance and operations of their investment arms, to create structures and processes that yield multiple kinds of business and family-related value.

At Duchossois Capital Management, smaller investments require only management or investment committee approval, while larger ones must be approved by the entire shareholder group, as part of their "levels of authority" governance approach. The Steans family, too, asks members to opt in on investments recommended by FIC. Duchossois family members also maintain some of their own investments beyond those of DCM, to have personal responsibility for and control over a portion of their wealth.

Families must also decide whether to house investment and entrepreneurial activities within or outside of the core operating business. The Carlson Family recognized the benefit of housing Carlson Private Capital Partners within Carlson, Inc., given the governance structure which includes both family and independent directors as well as the opportunity to leverage their 80 years of expertise operating global businesses.

The family owners of Wilbur-Ellis launched Cavallo Ventures with a separate board. But they consider the company and venture division affiliated, and the website highlights the value of this relationship: "Beyond capital, we provide our deep expertise and market knowledge. We enable founders to launch new products and services, run trials, expand and recruit new talent" (Cavallo, 2020).

Operating decisions include those related to staffing and compensation, as well. The Steans, Duchossois, and Carlson families, for example, all realized they had to make compensation for their investment professionals competitive with the private equity market to attract strong talent. Similarly, DCM allows management to buy in to deals where the family makes minority investments, to share the upside.

Staffing decisions include which *investment professionals* to maintain in-house or outsource. Steans, Duchossois, and Carlson employ in-house investment teams to lead their investment divisions. Steans also houses personal investment advisors in their family office; these advisors meet with family members quarterly, providing investment-related education and improving the family's connection to the enterprise.

Another way families engage members and their interests through the investing process is by making funds or other support available to family members to pursue related entrepreneurial ventures outside of the family business's corporate structure. Consider the example of Zach Richner, a third-generation member of a family that owns 60 local media publications in the New York state area. Zach helped out at the business in his youth, but was never formally employed there. After college, he worked for the Obama campaigns and administration and, later, led large infrastructure projects for New York governor Andrew Cuomo's administration, before attending business school.

Post-MBA, Richner decided to pursue entrepreneurship, but in a space related closely to his family firm. "Hyperlocal content and advertising is in high demand," he says. "So I built a business where we invest in startups in exchange for equity then help them gain customers through our network of local media outlets, and take additional equity for growth we help drive." Arrandale Ventures, his fledgling investment fund, now has a nationwide network of nearly 600 local media partners, and has invested in financial-services, retail, and other startups using the innovative model. His family has supported Richner's vision with some investment of capital, though he remains majority owner of Arrandale. Richner notes that his longtime relationships with local media business families, especially next-generation members, have provided an "unfair competitive advantage" for building Arrandale's network and securing investment funds. Though still early in the game, the business model appears highly promising.

The Challenge of Expectations Management

A large challenge related to family investment is management of expectations—around expectations of financial returns and liquidity, along with achieving other family goals through investing, such as providing opportunities for family member employment and goals related to the broader community.

Investing is a highly competitive space. While families have unique differentiators—patient capital, marketplace reputation, years of experience in their fields, and the like—it remains risky to assume that they would drive significantly superior returns, particularly when competing against large, sophisticated investors. In short, there is large potential risk for significant losses.

So what does this suggest? Families should invest where they can play successfully against competition, wherever possible, and put in place structures and processes to protect themselves adequately. For example, many, including Steans, Wilbur-Ellis, and others profiled here, are choosing to invest in smaller, family-owned businesses where they work alongside family operators who may want to stay in the business long term.

Moreover, families that may not wish to achieve the scale required to make larger investments—or that lack the resources to do so—may want to consider the less risky path of *co-investing* with other successful family investors. For example, members of the Pritzker family have raised a fund that will enable other family firms to invest with them without taking on as much risk as solo investing might entail. Similarly, Carlson Private Capital Partners brings other single-family offices into its direct investments.

One way that families can gain investing skill and confidence is by testing and iterating their models. The Schurz family, for example, engaged in smaller-scale investing before creating large liquidity from selling off major media assets; that earned the family's trust in the process, and their subsequent willingness to keep their funds with the family investment operation. Wendy Nelson of the Carlson family notes that their investment model will continue to "evolve" expanding areas of focus over time that leverage the competencies developed over years of operating businesses, the investment teams expertise and experience as well as the reputation and relationships that the Carlson family has established by choosing first to be values-driven with a focus on "business as a force for good".

Families should also consider measuring impact beyond market returns, such as family cohesion and engagement, in line with their purpose and goals. In this way, "success" won't be defined by financial returns alone. As Todd Schurz notes, "We strive to bring more to the investment than just money, such as human, intellectual, and social capital. We also want to receive more than just a financial return on the investment, including learning new insights into consumers and communities."

Best Practices in Family Investing

The earlier material suggests distinct best practices families implement to get the most out of their investing activities and set themselves up for success, in line with their purpose and goals. Here are the main ones, by category.

- *Alignment:* Aim for clear family alignment on investing-related and broader purpose, clearly articulating the broader purpose and consulting with individual family members for their input as well as promoting regular communication around investments.
- *Governance:* Establish a transparent governance structure specifying decision making-authorities for investments of different scale (such as requiring more family involvement for larger-scale investments). Determine where governance of investments will be housed: under the legacy operating company board, in a holding company entity, or with a separate investment company board. Assure coordination across various boards and define responsibility for capital allocation across entities in the family enterprise.
- *Talent and compensation:* Find investment talent with relevant experience and expertise, and compensate them based on market rates—competitive with what they could get elsewhere, including in private equity. Or, leverage the expertise of others by pursuing a co-investment model.

- *Education:* Ensure the broad family understands the rationale for moving to an investing model, the basics of investing, how investments will be selected, who will be involved in governance of the investing arm, and other key areas.
- *Research:* Related to the point about education above, families need to do their homework, to align around the best process for them and understand the risks, returns, and other features of the investing process. Talking to other families is a valuable way of gaining such information and applying it to one's own family.
- *Testing and iteration:* Testing the family investing model and refining it through iteration can help to gain credibility with the family and demonstrate potential returns, as the family's investing approach evolves over time and generation.

A Path to Transgenerational Entrepreneurship

With their long-term commitment to stewardship and desire to perpetuate capital across generations, business families are uniquely suited to pursue entrepreneurship through investment. Moreover, given the rapid change and uncertainty faced across the majority of industries, it is imperative that families seek new paths to achieve cross-generational sustainability. Family investing is a clear route to this end.

That said, moving from allocator to acquirer as a means of transgenerational entrepreneurship is not for the faint of heart. With significant family capital at risk, families must be well-prepared to move into this space before they take the plunge. In-depth family conversations around purpose and expectations set the stage for a range of important decisions around investment thesis, governance, family education and alignment, and how best to iterate, refine, and evolve the family enterprise. Looking to other pioneering families who have already pursued this path can also provide useful insights and advice, as part of a thoughtful, comprehensive approach to advancing the family's causes and capabilities in the investing domain.

And, families must consider their capacity to take on this approach, both as a family and as business professionals. Not surprisingly, the families mentioned in this chapter have third generation and beyond legacies upon which to build their investment foundation. They also have access to significant capital. This is not to suggest that families must be of the size and stature of the role models provided here to successfully pursue an investing approach.

However, families should consider what unique resources they can bring to their investment activities that will differentiate them from other investors in the market. And, they must be willing to invest in outsourced or hired resources to define and execute their investing approach. Finally, they must have a strong ownership group that is willing to invest the time and resources to clearly define their purpose and desired outcomes of pursuing this approach to ensure they are aligned. Families with an entrepreneurial mindset and a willingness to take risk in the pursuit of re-inventing their competitive advantage are ideally suited to evolve their enterprises by espousing a family investing model.

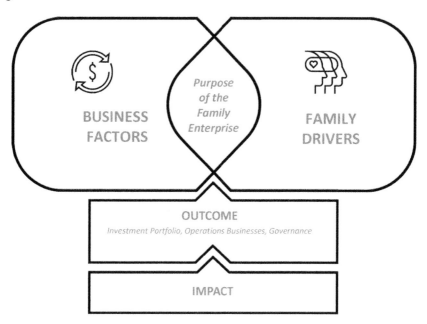

References

Barney, J. (1991, March). Firm Resources and Sustained Competitive Advantage. *Journal of Management, 17*(1), 99–120.

Cavallo. (2020). Retrieved from www.cavallovc.com

Concentric Equity Partners. (2020). Retrieved from www.ficcep.com/introduction/

Freeman, R. E. (1984). *Stakeholder Theory: The State of The Art*. Cambridge University Press.

Habbershon, T., Nordqvist, M., & Zellweger, T. (2010). Transgenerational Entrepreneurship. In M. Nordqvist & T. Zellweger (Eds.), *Transgenerational*

Entrepreneurship: Exploring Growth and Performance in Family Firms Across Generations (pp. 1–38). Cheltenham, UK: Edward Elgar.

Peart. (2019). Retrieved from https://www.forbes.com/sites/nathanpeart/2019/12/11/authenticity-at-work-why-it-matters-for-millennials-and-how-it-can-improve-your-bottom-line/#734238702f75

Rosplock, as cited in Jaffe. (2019). Cite this Article: https://www.forbes.com/sites/dennisjaffe/2019/10/21/how-global-family-offices-respond-to-uncertainty-building-upon-their-roots-as-a-family/#3c4376401e06

Zhou (2017). CITE. Retrieved from https://www.axial.net/forum/family-offices-are-making-more-direct-investments/

23

Because Family Cares: Building Engagement for Family Entrepreneurship Through Sustainability

Marcela Ramírez-Pasillas and Mattias Nordqvist

Introduction

This chapter outlines how entrepreneurial families can build an engagement with entrepreneurship by developing or investing in new sustainable ventures. We connect insights from the family entrepreneurship literature with those from the sustainability literature and suggest three sustainable venturing processes that can help build engagement with entrepreneurship in your business family and, at the same time, stimulate the participation of different generations. Our core message is: *entrepreneurial families can think about sustainability as an opportunity for developing new ventures and also as a way of engaging different generations and branches of a family to build commitment around a purpose, shared values, and principles that stretches beyond the traditional financial goals of the business.*

M. Ramírez-Pasillas (✉)
Center for Family Entrepreneurship and Ownership, Jönköping International Business School, Jönköping, Sweden
e-mail: marcela.ramirez-pasillas@ju.se

M. Nordqvist
Center for Family Entrepreneurship and Ownership, Jönköping International Business School, Jönköping, Sweden

House of Innovation, Stockholm School of Economics, Stockholm, Sweden
e-mail: mattias.nordqvist@hhs.se

© The Author(s), under exclusive license to Springer Nature Switzerland AG 2021   **315**
M. R. Allen, W. B. Gartner (eds.), *Family Entrepreneurship*,
https://doi.org/10.1007/978-3-030-66846-4_23

Increasing awareness about the United Nations Sustainable Development Goals and a stronger commitment for life beyond profit inspire and drive sustainable entrepreneurship in a variety of ways around the world (e.g., Kim, Bansal, & Haugh, 2019). A sustainability agenda results in the formation of new sustainable ventures that work on causes blending environmental issues, human dignity and social justice in a commercially feasible way (Muñoz & Cohen, 2017). Such an agenda advocates the use of alternative forms of hybrid organizations such as for-profit enterprises like B Corps, not-for-profit enterprises like cooperatives, and not-for-profit organizations like foundations (e.g., Muñoz, Cacciotti, & Cohen, 2018). Sustainability influences entrepreneurial behavior, processes, and outcomes, which are currently mostly explored from an individual perspective (Woodfield, Woods, & Shepherd, 2017).

We also know that the emergence of new ventures sponsored and owned by a family has also taken place around the world to build a purpose geared toward sustainability (e.g., Sharma & Sharma, 2019). Examples of these family ventures are certified B Corps such as Cascade Engineering (USA), Solberg Manufacturing (USA) and the cooperative Flor de Doñana (Spain), or the creation of foundations like Fundación Carlos Slim (Mexico), and the Axfoundation (Sweden). During the venturing process, entrepreneurial families strive to balance social, environmental, and economic values, adopt hybrid organizational forms, and seek to maximize benefits for the involved stakeholders (Ramirez-Pasillas & Lundberg, 2019). Such a perspective creates opportunities for discussing how entrepreneurial families create new sustainable ventures as an integral part of their business activities and as a way of building engagement among family members and generations.

When engaging in family ventures, family members and the family business (if one already exists) influence this process in a synergic manner (Bettinelli, Fayolle, & Randerson, 2014; Habbershon, 2006; Nordqvist & Melin, 2010). Specifically, the creation of new ventures by family members is referred to as 'Family Entrepreneurship'. Family entrepreneurship examines how a family and the original family business originate entrepreneurial practices and processes for making a new family venture come true (Ramírez-Pasillas, Lundberg, & Nordqvist, 2020). An entrepreneurial family encourages the development of settings and arenas conducive for entrepreneurship in interaction with the business (Nordqvist & Melin, 2010). Family entrepreneurship can also help maintain a business family afloat over time and also cultivate entrepreneurial behavior, processes, and outcomes among new generations of entrepreneurs through, for example, transgenerational entrepreneurship (Zellweger, Nason, & Nordqvist, 2012).

When encouraging family entrepreneurship, it is important to consider the social, ecological, and economic domains of the family venturing process. Such a direction allows working out various ways of 'how family cares' for life and a sustainable future. In this chapter, we outline how business families can build an engagement with entrepreneurship through sustainability. We organize our chapter into three sections. First, we briefly present family venturing literature. Since there is already an agreement that a new venture formation is a process (McMullen & Dimov, 2013; Shepherd, Souitaris, & Gruber, forthcoming), we discuss the process from the point of view of an entrepreneurial family. Next, we introduce three ways through which entrepreneurial families can engage in new venturing processes connected to sustainability: *igniting family entrepreneurship through sustainability; interplaying between family entrepreneurship and a purpose for sustainability; and interfacing family entrepreneurship and sustainability*. We also present short case illustrations of these processes from three Swedish sustainable ventures where we show these dynamics at play. Making sense of these processes can help in understanding the ways in which sustainability spins the actionability of an entrepreneurial family by facilitating the initiation of a venture, shaping its products or offerings, and building connections to earth systems in a way that the new family venture constitutes a humane equilibrating force between nature and humanity. We conclude our chapter with reflections on the future of family entrepreneurship looking at this field through the lens of sustainability.

Family Venturing

New ventures created by families are a well-recognized phenomenon where a 'family' is a group of individuals who build a sense of belonging and share a common history (Koerner & Fitzpatrick, 2002). The definition of a family differs among cultures, generations, geographical contexts, and times (Aldrich & Cliff, 2003; Brannon, Wiklund, & Haynie, 2013). You might restrict a family to those persons who are a part of your nuclear family, or to those who are a part of your nuclear and extended family, or you may define it broadly to incorporate your blood relatives, or you might include your current life partner. Still, when you seek to start a new venture with your siblings, spouse, cousins, partner, or parents, the founding family team is responsible for driving the new venturing process (e.g., Discua Cruz, Howorth, & Hamilton, 2013). Also, when younger generations wish to jointly materialize their aspirations and interests in a new independent family enterprise, they also participate in the venturing process in a variety of ways (e.g., Ramírez-Pasillas et al., 2020).

The venturing process corresponds to the creation of a new enterprise (Gartner, 1985) where the emerging venture shapes and is shaped by its surrounding context over time (McMullen & Dimov, 2013). The venturing process can be described as a set of activities conducted between a specific starting point and an end point or as a sequence of uncertain and unpredictable activities that occur as the venturing process advances (Sarasvathy, 2001). A venturing process can also be described around major stages like triggering, shaping, or driving processes (Evansluong, Ramírez-Pasillas, & Nguyen Bergström, 2019) or co-creating, organizing, and performing processes (Shepherd, Souitaris, & Gruber, forthcoming).

While family entrepreneurship scholars have not yet fully accounted for the diversity in venturing processes and families, we know that family venturing processes involve family members in decision making, ownership, operations, and goal setting (Kirkwood, 2012; López-Fernández, Serrano-Bedia, & Pérez-Pérez, 2016). A family also provides social, human, and financial capital in the early stages of the venturing process (Anderson, Jack, & Dodd, 2005; Jack, 2005). This means that during the family venturing process, individual entrepreneurial behavior and the family members' processes matter, but so do the collective behavior and processes of the family (Randerson, Bettinelli, Fayolle, & Anderson, 2015). For example, according to Kirkwood (2012) when forming new ventures, women consider their spouses and children and rely more on support from their parents as compared to men who are more independent and bear financial concerns about their spouses and children on their own. Spouses engaging jointly in family venturing have a stronger probability of making their first sale as compared to a team of blood relatives engaging in a family venture (Brannon et al., 2013).

With the above example, we want to show that there is diversity in family aspects which influence a new venturing process. The reason for this is that the family venturing process has its locus in the engagement of individual, family, and the existing family business (in case there is one). Bettinelli et al. (2014) describe such a locus as a nexus between individual-family, family-family business, and individual-family business. Because of this nexus, there is an opportunity to account for how business families develop their engagement with a new venturing process and how sustainability may help spin this engagement, perhaps in particular with the younger generations. We believe that exploring family venturing further is important for a better understanding of how a family can influence the venturing process in a way that embraces family entrepreneurship's alignment with sustainability. We elaborate on this as follows.

Sustainable Venturing and Entrepreneurial Families

In this section, we deepen our ideas regarding how entrepreneurial families can think about sustainability as a way of developing new ventures while building engagement among family members at the same time. Family business literature is increasingly paying closer attention to sustainability (Le Breton-Miller & Miller, 2016; Sharma & Sharma, 2019). We propose that engagement is essential for capturing the opportunities for sustainable venturing that emerge in interactions and connections between individuals, family, business and the earth's biosphere. The climate crisis, social inequalities and human rights, increased migration, poverty and civil conflicts, and lack of access to water and food are posing threats to the survival of humanity and the earth's biosphere. As human activities affect the life and balance of social-ecological systems (Rockström et al., 2009), sustainability provides opportunities for engaging the family in venturing processes that strive for dignity and long-term survival and building a purpose for the business that includes and also goes beyond financial profits. Therefore, we outline three sustainable family venturing processes, which we call *igniting family entrepreneurship through sustainability; interplaying between family entrepreneurship and a purpose for sustainability; and interfacing between family entrepreneurship and sustainability*. We use gerunds rather than nouns for these labels to emphasize that we focus on processes, practices, and activities rather than states and events. This signal movement or individual and collective actions of entrepreneurial families where the actionability focuses on making a new sustainable venture come true. You can look at these processes as strategies or conceptual tools for stimulating the engagement of family members across generations in the entrepreneurial venturing process firmly anchored in sustainability.

Igniting Family Entrepreneurship Through Sustainability

The urgency of working for sustainability has been confirmed by the nine planetary boundaries or biophysical processes that account for the earth's system on which human life depends and which define a safe operating space for humanity (Rockström et al., 2009). In some of these processes, human actions have transgressed or are approaching the safe limits, and this raises the possibility of affecting life (Steffen et al., 2015). Hence, sustainability encompasses the creation of social justice, respect for the earth system, and economic well-being (Robinson, 2004). It also supports the preservation of nature, life support, and community (Shepherd & Patzelt, 2011).

When engaging with sustainability, the family venturing process needs to consider integral and transdisciplinary approaches. This means that only an environmental focus or only a social focus or only an economic focus is insufficient (Robinson, 2004). Thus, *we propose that the process of igniting family entrepreneurship through sustainability comprises of those 'aha' moments of sudden insight, realization, comprehension, or inspiration about sustainability that engage a family to jointly work on social and ecological issues via a new family venture.* The process of igniting can have a profound bearing for you and your family; the *aha* moments change your views of the world and the sustainable world you and your family envision. Through the *aha* moments, a family unexpectedly gets a new and deeper perspective of its responsibility to life and its role in creating ways of operating and sustaining a safe space for humanity.

An interesting example of igniting family entrepreneurship through sustainability is the Swedish family-based start-up Beleco. The venture focuses on 'streaming' furniture 'on-demand,' which means that instead of buying and owning furniture, companies, organizations, and persons can rent their furniture for a limited time. When this time is over, they get new furniture. The furniture that is streamed is owned by the company that manufactures it, and Beleco provides a platform for distributing the furniture through renting. Marie and Sebastian Rudenstam form the founding family team of Beleco in Stockholm, Sweden. This mother and son team started this venture to bring more sustainability to the traditional furniture industry and infuse a higher degree of circularity and consumption of sustainable products, which conventionally have a high environmental footprint. Beleco has attracted significant investments in its venture from investors interested in the business model based on sustainability and the family founders' vision. Their vision shows the igniting moments that led to the creation of Beleco:

> *I started thinking about things such as the food we eat, the extent to which it is sprayed, and what it does to our bodies. I decided to switch to organic food completely, and today both me and my mother Marie are vegans. Beleco's business model is based on our personal commitments and is about so much more than just making money. It's about getting the chance to change the world.* (Sebastian Rudenstam, co-founder, Beleco)

Sebastian's *aha* moment of insight or recognition of the food's impact in a broader humane and planetary context led the Rudenstam family to engage in a venturing process striving to balance a long-term orientation with the urgent need for addressing sustainability concerns:

It is important to have enormous patience and to think long term. It is like a little snowball that slowly rolls and becomes bigger till many people understand that we must change our habits. It is a fact that it will eventually reach all industries. We are careful not to create a bad conscience, but rather we pay attention to the solutions that exist. Beleco is not just about highlighting our habits but about revolutionizing an entire industry. (Marie Rudenstam, co-founder, Beleco)

Interplaying Between Family Entrepreneurship and a Purpose for Sustainability

Ventures can share a broader sense of purpose for creating a common good in society by relating to values (i.e., dignity, solidarity, plurality, subsidiary, reciprocity, and sustainability, Hollensbe, Wookey, Hickey, George, & Nichols, 2014). We believe that a family's values are particularly relevant for examining sustainability in family businesses. Many business families represent values that foster solidarity, cohesion, trust, and loyalty (Muñoz-Bullón, Sanchez-Bueno, & Nordqvist, 2019). Values can influence family members' engagement in venturing as values are created and transmitted through a shared purpose, stories, and symbols (Sorenson, 2014). Some values can help nurture an entrepreneurial orientation (Zellweger et al., 2012) and an entrepreneurial culture (Hall, Melin, & Nordqvist, 2001) that strongly permeates the way a business family engages in sustainable entrepreneurship. A close link between purpose and values means that some family entrepreneurs besides being guided by economic goals, are also guided by non-economic goals. Purpose is also related to a more profound meaning in life generated from the values and multifaceted motivations of a family, that is, 'making a difference', 'sustaining the community', 'helping people in need', and 'restoring nature' (Hollensbe et al., 2014; Ramirez-Pasillas & Lundberg, 2019).

Purpose influences a sustainable venture's development path (Muñoz et al., 2018), and it is important to discuss how you and your family may engage in developing a purpose for sustainability with is interlinked with values and the new venture. We propose that *the process of interplaying between family entrepreneurship and a purpose for sustainability denotes the ongoing interactions between individuals (family members), family, and the original family business (if available) which influence one another in shaping a meaningful shared purpose for the family's engagement in sustainable venturing.*

We know that family members align and agree on views and ideas in the venturing process (Ramírez-Pasillas et al., 2020). Interplaying emphasizes how you and your family can rely on dialogues for aligning, agreeing, and harmonizing a shared purpose for sustainability when engaging in a new venture. As you go back and forth in defining a shared purpose for sustainability, the dialogue continues due to the iterative and interactive nature of the family venturing process. The dialogue allows you to define and better understand how the family's purpose gradually denotes a blended value approach (McMullen & Warnick, 2016) that balances social, environmental, and economic values and results in different hybrid organizations (i.e., B Corps, foundations, cooperatives, partnerships, and social enterprises). Understanding the emerging shared purpose for sustainability is, thus, important since a family venture's non-economic goals can influence its growth intentions and business model.

Let us consider an example of interplaying between family entrepreneurship and a purpose for sustainability. The Swedish family-controlled investment company Gullspång Invest is operated by a father, Christer Brandberg, and his three sons Erik, Magnus, and Gustaf Brandberg in Stockholm, Sweden. In 2015, the family sold its shares in the network camera and video encoder market company Axis Communications, which was acquired by the Japanese multinational Canon. After the sale, the family team decided to create an investment company owned by a foundation, rather than using the released funds for solely enriching individual family members. The new foundation is an example of a hybrid organization that blends social, environmental, and economic causes. The two generations of family members decided to engage in this venture jointly and concluded that their investment company would only finance start-ups and new ventures focused on sustainability as a central part of their business purpose. Accordingly, Gullspång Invest states that today it exclusively *"funds teams of entrepreneurs who seek to transform the fundamental systems of civilization into a more resilient and sustainable state."* Its current holdings include Oatly, Baseload Capital, Färsking, Trine Nick's, Eneo Solutions, and Vilokan.

Inherent to the Gullspång's business model is that it *"optimizes for true value, not exits."* Among other things, this means that it has a much longer investment horizon than traditional private equity companies, as expressed by the second-generation family member Gustaf Brandberg: *"We look at a longer horizon instead of looking at the next fund. The point of departure is that we invest for the next generation, and not for a quick exit."* Gullspång Invest is, hence, described as a passionate, purpose-driven, and for-profit hybrid company that seeks to sponsor entrepreneurs who *"can be a catalyst for positive change on a global scale."* As a concrete example, Gustaf Brandberg explains why he and his family decided to invest in the food start-up Färsking founded by Calle Rosengren and Amanda Larsson:

We saw and still see that Calle and Amanda are two driven people who by launching more healthy products for young people, want to force the food industry to take responsibility for ensuring that the products that they sell to young people are not only good but also make you feel good for a minute, one hour, one year, and ten years after they were consumed. (Gustaf Sandberg, co-founder, Gullspång Invest)

Interfacing Between Family Entrepreneurship and Social-Ecological Systems

Sustainable venturing processes embrace both social and ecological concerns. The reason for this is that a separation of social and ecological concerns has not been helpful. Social concerns refer to the human dimension, including political, cultural, and technological facets and ecological concerns refer to the earth's biosphere (Berkes & Folke, 1998). The earth's biosphere consists of human activities and their interactions with water cycles and biogeochemical cycles, integrating the earth's systems (Folke, Biggs, Norström, Reyers, & Rockström, 2016). Ventures, humans, and society influence and depend on the resources and services of the earth's biosphere (Leach et al., 2012). Social-ecological systems operate in the biosphere and are, therefore, central for sustaining life.

Social-ecological systems are complex and adaptive and are integrated by interactions between human and non-human entities (Schlüter et al., 2019). These interactions generate patterns, structures, and dynamics providing feedback to the systems, influencing interactions, and triggering changes (Levin et al., 2013; Westley et al., 2013). Social-ecological systems underline interactions, processes, and structures of the social-ecological phenomena.

The literature on sustainable entrepreneurship agrees that there is a lack of knowledge about how ventures engage in creating or maintaining social-ecological connections. Investigating how organizations build bridges and synchronize their activities with the natural rhythm of broader ecological systems (Muñoz & Cohen, 2018) can help in a better understanding of how entrepreneurial families engage in sustainable venturing processes. Hence, we propose that *the process of interfacing between family entrepreneurship and social-ecological systems denotes how a family' figures out' how to relate, interact, and feedback social-ecological systems by engaging in sustainable venturing.* Interfacing, in particular, signifies the ways in which individuals and their families figure out things as they enter the (un)known territory of social-ecological systems; it corresponds to a balanced exercise of building an understanding about the earth's biosphere and creating ways of relating, connecting, and interacting with the social-ecological systems by trying-out, experimenting, and learning.

Let us consider the sustainable family venture Marcello's Farm as an example. The spouses Marcel van Sitteren och Inge Schwagermann bought the Farm Ugerupsdal in Kristianstad, Sweden, and transformed it into a farm based on biodynamic agriculture and animal care. Following their "*anthroposophical inspiration*" as expressed by Inge, they worked out how to develop Marcello's Farm as a "*meeting place for biodynamic and organic farming that inspires consumers and professionals in agriculture.*" This entrepreneurial family team drives the farm ecologically and has obtained the Swedish ecological label KRAV. When developing their biodynamic agricultural approach, the spouses recognized that the farm and location had "*several different types of crops, and the surrounding nature needed to have more space to grow and flourish.*" Marcel and Inge focused on finding ways of building a healthy soil and growing healthy products. They are also committed to searching for a careful biological balance and helping in mitigating the impact of climate change. The spouses state, "*We always strive to work according to biodynamic principles, which imply no fertilizers and no chemical pesticides.*" Marcel also describes the interactions and connections needed to sustain life on the farm, "*I really like the change between animal husbandry and plant cultivation. The cows end the cycle on my farm creating a nice atmosphere and balance on the farm.*" Marcel and Inge also share their concerns about figuring out how to sustain life and seeing that every entity and being has a place on earth:

> *Being alive means that we stimulate and cultivate the natural processes of the earth, the landscape, the behavior of animals, etc. Some examples are: We want many worms in the earth. We want many birds on and around the farm. We want the cows to show natural flock behavior. We want the earth to retain its moisture. We believe that our work leads to good and healthy products.*

Marcello's Farm shows how the entrepreneurial family team engages in interfacing processes where the family and the sustainable venture interact with nature and the local community as they 'figure out' how to relate and feedback to the social-ecological systems of their farm and its production. This is central in supporting and developing the social and ecological elements and connections of a sustainable family venture. As a sustainable family venture takes steps to positively, equitable, and ethically influence the earth's biosphere, negative impacts to the Earth system can be faced out.

Conclusion

Let us repeat our core message. As an entrepreneurial family, you can think of sustainability as an opportunity for developing new ventures. You can also think about a sustainable venturing process in a broader sense and as a way of engaging different generations and branches of the family around a shared purpose, shared values, and principles that stretch beyond the conventional financial goals of a business. This means that engaging in sustainability provides an entrepreneurial family a multiplicity of individual, family, and business opportunities for the venturing process. With a sustainable family venturing process, you can foster the commitment of several generations and stimulate family engagement and unity for a shared meaningful purpose.

In this chapter, we presented three processes that entrepreneurial families can use for pursuing and supporting new sustainable ventures that are in line with family values and with a long-term ambition of improving ecological, social, and economic sustainability, shaping the capacity of the biosphere to sustain life on our planet. The three suggested processes—*igniting family entrepreneurship through sustainability; interplaying between family entrepreneurship and a purpose for sustainability; and interfacing between family entrepreneurship with and sustainability*—broaden the spectrum of strategies and conceptual tools that can be addressed by business families, scholars, and consultants. Entrepreneurial families can foster stronger engagement in venturing processes when reconfiguring a broader humane and sustainable purpose and by embracing social-ecological connections in their new sustainable family ventures. We suggest that combinations of family entrepreneurial teams, sustainability concerns, and social-ecological systems influence entrepreneurial processes and outcomes. By outlining the engagement of entrepreneurial families in sustainability, we also broaden our focus on the subtleties that are generated in family venturing processes. We believe that a focus on the apparently small moments, connections, and interactions has the potential to give us interesting new insights about the many families who 'care' about more than profits when they do business.

References

Aldrich, H. E., & Cliff, J. E. (2003). The Pervasive Effects of Family on Entrepreneurship: Toward a Family Embeddedness Perspective. *Journal of Business Venturing, 18*, 573–596.

Anderson, A. R., Jack, S. L., & Dodd, S. D. (2005). The Role of Family Members in Entrepreneurial Networks: Beyond the Boundaries of the Family Firm. *Family Business Review, 18*(2), 135–154.

Beleco. (2020). Retrieved from www.beleco.com.

Berkes, F., & Folke, C. (1998). *Linking Social and Ecological Systems: Management Practices and Social Mechanisms for Building Resilience*. Cambridge, UK: Cambridge University Press.

Bettinelli, C., Fayolle, A., & Randerson, K. (2014). Family Entrepreneurship: A Developing Field. *Foundations and Trends in Entrepreneurship, 10*(3), 161–236.

Brannon, D. L., Wiklund, J., & Haynie, J. M. (2013). The Varying Effects of Family Relationships in Entrepreneurial Teams. *Entrepreneurship Theory and Practice, 37*(1), 107–132.

Bröderna Brandberg och Gullspång Invest jagar nästa techsuccé/The Brandberg Brothers and Gullspång Invest Is Looking for the Next Tech Success (In Swedish). (2020, February 19). Retrieved from https://www.breakit.se/artikel/520/broderna-brandberg-ochgullspang-invest-jagar-nasta-techsucce.

Discua Cruz, A., Howorth, C., & Hamilton, E. (2013). Intrafamily Entrepreneurship: The Formation and Membership of Family Entrepreneurial Teams. *Entrepreneurship Theory and Practice, 37*, 17–46.

Evansluong, Q., Ramírez-Pasillas, M., & Nguyen Bergström, H. (2019). From Breaking-Ice to Breaking-Out: Integration as an Opportunity Creation Process. *International Journal of Entrepreneurial Behavior & Research, 25*(5), 880–899.

Färsking tar in upp till 13 miljoner—öppnar imorgon/Färsking Brings in 13 Millions—Opens Tomorrow (in Sweden). (2020, February 19). Retrieved from https://www.svd.se/bors/news_detail.php?newsid=91ea6c04-a6c9-471e-90fd-fb3b852cf361.

Folke, C., Biggs, R., Norström, A. V., Reyers, B., & Rockström, J. (2016). Social-Ecological Resilience and Biosphere-Based Sustainability Science. *Ecology and Society, 21*(3), 41.

Gartner, W. B. (1985). A Conceptual Framework for Describing the Phenomenon of New Venture Creation. *Academy of Management Review, 10*, 696–706.

Gullspång. (2020). Retrieved from www.gullspong.vs.

Habbershon, T. (2006). The Family as a Distinct Context for Entrepreneurship. In T. G. Habbershon, M. Miniti, M. P. Rice, S. Spinelli, Jr., & A. Zacharakis (Eds.), *Entrepreneurship: The Engine of Growth. Praeger Perspectives on Entrepreneurship* (Vol. III, Chapter 4). Westport, CT: Praeger Publishers.

Hall, A., Melin, L., & Nordqvist, M. (2001). Entrepreneurship as Radical Change in Family Business: Exploring the Role of Cultural Patterns. *Family Business Review, 14*(3), 193–208.

Hollensbe, E., Wookey, C., Hickey, L., George, G., & Nichols, C. V. (2014). From the Editors—Organizations with Purpose. *Academy of Management Journal, 57*(5), 1227–1234.

Jack, S. L. (2005). The Role, Use and Activation of Strong and Weak Network Ties: A Qualitative Analysis. *Journal of Management Studies, 42*(6), 1233–1259.

Kim, A., Bansal, P., & Haugh, H. (2019). No Time Like the Present: How a Present Time Perspective Can Foster Sustainable Development. *Academy of Management Journal, 62*(2), 607–634.

Kirkwood, J. (2012). Family Matters: Exploring the Role of Family in the New Venture Creation Decision. *Journal of Small Business and Entrepreneurship, 25*(2), 141–154.

Koerner, A. F., & Fitzpatrick, M. A. (2002). Toward a Theory of Family Communication. *Communication Theory, 12*(1), 70–91.

Leach, M., Rockström, J., Raskin, P., Scoones, I., Stirling, A. C., Smith, A., et al. (2012). Transforming Innovation for Sustainability. *Ecology and Society, 17*(2), 11.

Le Breton-Miller, I., & Miller, D. (2016). Family Firms and Practices of Sustainability: A Contingency View. *Journal of Family Business Strategy, 7*(1), 26–33.

Levin, S., Xepapadeas, T., Crépin, A. S., Norberg, J., de Zeeuw, A., Folke, C., et al. (2013). Social-Ecological Systems as Complex Adaptive Systems: Modeling and Policy Implications. *Environment and Development Economics, 18*(2), 111–132.

López-Fernández, M. C., Serrano-Bedia, A. M., & Pérez-Pérez, M. (2016). Entrepreneurship and Family Firm Research: A Bibliometric Analysis of an Emerging Field. *Journal of Small Business Management, 54*(2), 622–639.

Marcello's Farm, Ugerupsdal. (2020). Retrieved from www.marcellosfarm.se/.

McMullen, J. S., & Dimov, D. (2013). Time and the Entrepreneurial Journey: The Problems and Promise of Studying Entrepreneurship as a Process. *Journal of Management, 50*(8), 1481–1512.

McMullen, J. S., & Warnick, B. J. (2016). Should We Require Every New Venture to Be a Hybrid Organization? *Journal of Management Studies, 53*(4), 630–662.

Mor och son revolutionerar inredningsbranschen/Mother and Son Revolutionize the Interior Design Industry (In Swedish). (2020). Retrieved from https://www.tre.se/foretag/varfor-3/ha-ett-bra-uppkopplatliv/tre-moter/artikel/beleco/.

Muñoz, P., Cacciotti, G., & Cohen, B. (2018). The Double-Edged Sword of Purpose-Driven Behavior in Sustainable Venturing. *Journal of Business Venturing, 33*(2), 149–178.

Muñoz, P., & Cohen, B. (2017). Towards a Social–Ecological Understanding of Sustainable Venturing. *Journal of Business Venturing Insights, 7*, 1–8.

Muñoz, P., & Cohen, B. (2018). Entrepreneurial Narratives in Sustainable Venturing: Beyond People, Profit and Planet. *Journal of Small Business Management, 56*(1), 154–176.

Muñoz-Bullón, P., Sanchez-Bueno, M. J., & Nordqvist, M. (2019). Growth Intentions in Family-Based New Venture Teams: The Role of the Nascent Entrepreneur's R&D Behavior. *Management Decision, 58*(6), 1190–1209.

Nordqvist, M., & Melin, L. (2010). Entrepreneurial Families and Family Firms. *Entrepreneurship and Regional Development, 22*(3), 211–239.

Ramírez-Pasillas, M., & Lundberg, H. (2019). Corporate Social Venturing: An Agenda for Researching the Social Dimension of Corporate Venturing by Family-Owned Businesses. In J. M. Saiz-Alvarez & J. M. Palma Ruiz (Eds.), *Handbook of Research on Entrepreneurial Leadership and Competitive Strategy in Family Business* (pp. 173–192). Hershey: IGI Global.

Ramírez-Pasillas, M., Lundberg, H., & Nordqvist, M. (2020). Next Generation External Venturing Practices in Family Owned Businesses. *Journal of Management Studies*. https://doi.org/10.1111/joms.12566

Randerson, K., Bettinelli, C., Fayolle, A., & Anderson, A. (2015). Family Entrepreneurship as a Field of Research: Exploring Its Contours and Contents. *Journal of Family Business Strategy, 6*(3), 143–154.

Robinson, J. (2004). Squaring the Circle? Some Thoughts on the Idea of Sustainable Development. *Ecological Economics, 48*(4), 369–384.

Rockström, J., Steffen, W., Noone, K., Persson, Å., Chapin III, F. S., Lambin, E. F., et al. (2009). Planetary Boundaries: Exploring the Safe Operating Space for Humanity. *Ecology and Society, 14*(2), 32.

Sarasvathy, S. D. (2001). Causation and Effectuation: Toward a Theoretical Shift from Economic Inevitability to Entrepreneurial Contingency. *Academy of Management Review, 26*(2), 243–263.

Schlüter, M., Haider, L. J., Lade, S. J., Lindkvist, E., Martin, R., Orach, K., et al. (2019). Capturing Emergent Phenomena in Social-Ecological Systems: An Analytical Framework. *Ecology and Society, 24*(3), 11.

Sharma, S., & Sharma, P. (2019). *Patient Capital: The Role of Family Firms in Sustainable Business.* Cambridge: Cambridge University Press.

Shepherd, D. A., & Patzelt, H. (2011). The New Field of Sustainable Entrepreneurship: Studying Entrepreneurial Action Linking 'What Is to Be Sustained' with 'What Is to Be Developed'. *Entrepreneurship Theory Practice, 35*(1), 137–163.

Shepherd, D. A., Souitaris, V., & Gruber, M. (forthcoming). Creating New Ventures: A Review and Research Agenda. *Journal of Management Studies*. https://doi.org/10.1177/0149206319900537

Sorenson, R. L. (2014). Values in Family Firms. In L. Melin, M. Nordqvist, & P. Sharma (Eds.), *The Sage Handbook of Family Business* (pp. 463–479). London: Sage.

Steffen, W., Richardson, K., Rockström, J., Cornell, S. E., Fetzer, I., Bennett, E. M., et al. (2015). Planetary Boundaries: Guiding Human Development on a Changing Planet. *Science, 347*(6223), 1259855.

Westley, F., Tjörnbo, O., Olsson, P., Folke, C., Crona, B., Schultz, L., et al. (2013). A Theory of Transformative Agency in Linked Social-Ecological Systems. *Ecology and Society, 18*(3), 27.

Woodfield, P., Woods, C., & Shepherd, D. (2017). Sustainable Entrepreneurship: Another Avenue for Family Business Scholarship? *Journal of Family Business Management, 7*(1), 122–132.

Zellweger, T. M., Nason, R. S., & Nordqvist, M. (2012). From Longevity of Firms to Transgenerational Entrepreneurship of Families: Introducing Family Entrepreneurial Orientation. *Family Business Review, 25*(2), 136–155.

24

Social Capital, Entrepreneurship, and Family Businesses

G. Tyge Payne and Nathan T. Hayes

Introduction

The family—defined as a group of individuals that identify as a family (or is recognized as such) due to a shared "biological, genealogical, and/or social history" (Dyer, 2019, p. 15)—serves as the foundation for many business organizations globally. Historically, the relationship between family and business (or at least occupation) has always been present. The family unit is the oldest social unit on record and there are many accounts, over the course of thousands of years, that demonstrate how family and business commonly intersect. Indeed, the biblical narrative in the Book of Genesis describes the deadly conflict of two brothers—Cain and Abel—and ties their quarrel closely to their respective occupations in agriculture and animal husbandry.

While the intersection of family and business has long been the subject of scholarly interest, and there is substantial work that demonstrates how family businesses differ from other forms of organizing, core questions remain underexplored. One of the core questions being asked by family business leaders in today's fast-paced, uncertain, and global environment is: *How do we develop and sustain entrepreneurial thinking and behaviors over time?* While this question is not unique to family businesses, the involvement of family through

G. T. Payne (✉) • N. T. Hayes
Area of Management, Texas Tech University, Lubbock, TX, USA
e-mail: Tyge.payne@ttu.edu; Nathan.hayes@ttu.edu

© The Author(s), under exclusive license to Springer Nature Switzerland AG 2021
M. R. Allen, W. B. Gartner (eds.), *Family Entrepreneurship*,
https://doi.org/10.1007/978-3-030-66846-4_24

331

ownership and control does present important differences that should be considered when addressing entrepreneurial proclivities such as creativity, proactiveness, and innovativeness. In fact, one of the fundamental characteristics of family businesses is their propensity to take a longer-term temporal perspective due to multi-generational intentions (Brigham, Lumpkin, Payne, & Zachary, 2014). Research suggests that long-term orientation varies in its influence on entrepreneurial beliefs and behaviors (Lumpkin, Brigham, & Moss, 2010), but that entrepreneurship is an essential component of a business' long-term viability (Zahra & Covin, 1995). Hence, family businesses may be under even more pressure to engage in entrepreneurial activities than other business forms due to transgenerational expectations for the business.

In this chapter, we address the issue of entrepreneurship—broadly discussed as the process of discovery, assessment, and exploitation of opportunities (Shane & Venkataraman, 2000; Stevenson & Jarillo, 1990)—in family businesses (and business-owning families) through the lens of social capital. Social capital is commonly defined as the "actual and potential resources embedded within, available through, and derived from the network of relationships possessed by individuals or social units" (Nahapiet & Ghoshal, 1998, p. 243). Generally, social capital theory argues that actors (i.e., individuals or social units, including families) can purposely gain access to or create resources (e.g., information, knowledge, trust) through the development or management of relational ties such that their network provides unique competitive advantages (Moran, 2005). Because social relationships between and among actors "drive opportunity discovery, evaluation, and exploitation", social capital has been recognized as a foundational perspective of entrepreneurship (Gedajlovic, Honig, Moore, Payne, & Wright, 2013, p. 455). Indeed, social capital has been studied in relation to creativity, intentions to create a new venture, innovation, growth, venture financing, among many other entrepreneurial outcomes (Gedajlovic et al., 2013). That said, the involvement of the family in a business is an important additional consideration when examining how social capital is linked to entrepreneurship. Family relationships are idiosyncratic, but are typically strong due to shared norms, values, vision, purpose, and goals. Indeed, social capital appears to be inherent in family businesses, providing a unique form of social capital—commonly referred to as family social capital (FSC)—that can provide entrepreneurial and competitive advantages for a firm (Arregle, Hitt, Sirmon, & Very, 2007; Herrero, 2018; Sanchez-Ruiz, Daspit, Holt, & Rutherford, 2019).

In the following sections, we first provide an overview of social capital theory and discuss some key issues that lead to conceptual ambiguity and potentially inhibit its use in practice. Second, we explain how family involvement produces a unique situation that should be considered when social capital and entrepreneurial outcomes are being linked; this naturally involves a multi-level perspective, but generally suggests that the family is a fundamental, yet generally overlooked, level of analysis for understanding longevity through entrepreneurial value creation and discovery. Third, we discuss how social capital theory can be practically applied to a business to establish, develop, and promote entrepreneurial behaviors, beliefs, and values that perpetuate across generations. Overall, we provide insights into how families may become drivers of entrepreneurial activity, thus sustaining the family and the family business(es) over time.

Social Capital: Tenets and Key Issues

While the basic premise underlying social capital theory—that social relation-ships provide potential and actual capital to an actor (i.e., individual, family, or organization)—is relatively easy to understand, there are issues that are much more complex and should be more seriously considered if this theory is to have practical application. Figure 24.1, which builds on Gedajlovic et al.'s (2013) schema of social capital and entrepreneurship, visually demonstrates the basic nature of social capital for a family business, and is utilized to discuss the tenets and key issues surrounding social capital in the paragraphs below.

As one can see, there is a general flow of processes from left to right. First, relationships/networks lead to social capital. Then, social capital—accrued or available resources—leads to entrepreneurial outcomes. This general pattern is consistent across levels—individual, family, and firm—but also flows between the levels. For instance, an individual's social relationships may lead to the accrual of resources and subsequent entrepreneurial activities/outcomes for the family or the firm. Further, any or all of the relationships may be influ-enced by an extensive number of contextual factors (e.g., time, industry, insti-tutions) that can help or hinder these process flows.

This model is incomplete, however, in that it does not demonstrate all pos-sible constructs or relationships. In particular, we do not show the many ante-cedents that lead to the development and maintenance of social relationships. Further, we do not show how entrepreneurship-based outcomes lead to other performance indicators, such as revenue or profitability for the business. Despite limitations, the schematic model is useful because it parsimoniously presents the key topics to be discussed and applied herein.

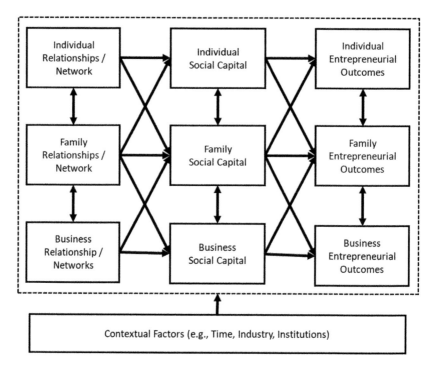

Fig. 24.1 A schematic model of social capital and entrepreneurship involving family members. (Adapted from Gedajlovic et al., 2013)

Social Relationships to Social Capital

Social relationships serve as the conduits for resources and have been recognized as essential components in business and management phenomena for many decades (Payne, Moore, Griffis, & Autry, 2011). Networks represent the complex structures of social relationships between actors (e.g., patterns of relationships, number/strength of ties), which may include individuals or collectives such as families, organizations, or communities. Social capital, on the other hand, represents the resources (e.g., trust, goodwill, information, financial capital) embedded within and derived from the networks of relationships. So, social capital is generally thought of as resulting from social relationships and leading to important outcomes, including entrepreneurial ones (Gedajlovic et al., 2013). Generally speaking, social capital is the linchpin that connects relational ties and networks to activities and outcomes.

While the relationship between social ties/networks and social capital is conceptually straightforward, the reality is much more complex and ambiguous. One key issue lending to the complexity is that it is difficult to fully understand if, how, and in what ways an actor—be it an individual, family, firm, or even a community—holds, controls, and maintains certain resources. This is especially true with regard to intangible resources such as knowledge or information. Who holds knowledge or information? In what cases does the knowledge actually reside in a collective versus an individual? If knowledge or information is freely shared, can it reduce the value of that capital? Such questions emerge when we consider the obscure delineation between human capital and social capital. Consider, for example, scientific knowledge, which may be held by one person, but may flow to others incrementally through interactions over time, eventually passing on some or all of that knowledge. However, if the relationship is broken and the flows stop, a person or business may be placed at a disadvantage relative to competitors due to incomplete knowledge availability. Careful consideration is needed to determine what type of social capital flows from the social relationships, and how these flows can be managed, stored, and protected. For instance, family firms may often have misgivings about employing non-family members into key management positions for fear of losing control of important information or knowledge.

While social relationships can provide access to—and even generate—social capital for family businesses, this is certainly not always the case. In many cases, social relationships can lead to negative flows of resources and may be costly to develop and maintain over time. For instance, some stakeholders may carry more influence and have the ability to exercise power over the focal actor due to their strategic positions within the network. As such, the exchange of ideas, information, and other resources may be one-sided, leading to disadvantages. Unfortunately, conceptualizing a one-way resource flow toward the focal actor is common. In fact, researchers commonly conceptualize and/or measure social capital as a simple aggregation of the number of relationships that a particular actor forms, fosters, and maintains.

While it understandable to consider the accrual of relationships as a proxy for social capital, this is problematic because it does not allow us to analyze and understand the many nuances associated with the types and strengths of relationships. For instance, a salesperson should not just consider the number of clients in a portfolio, but also the size of their accounts (i.e., spending levels) and the how much effort is expended managing the salesperson-client relationship. In other words, more simplistic perspectives do not fully consider the costs and benefits associated with the relationships. Hence, when managing the linkages between social relationships and social capital, one must carefully consider the stability of the relationships, the interaction and exchange between actors, the interdependence of the actors, and the level of closure (i.e., everyone is connected to everyone) in the network (Arregle et al., 2007; Nahapiet & Ghoshal, 1998). These factors not only determine the level of access and type of resources that are available, but can also lead to the creation of new valuable resources such as the development of operation norms, trust, and mutual goals (Ireland, Hitt, & Vaidyanath, 2002).

Linking Social Capital to Entrepreneurial Outcomes

While the development and creation of social capital is important, it is difficult to determine what processes or mechanisms turn stocks of social capital into actions that result in entrepreneurial outcomes. This challenge is perhaps best addressed by first discussing the basic mechanisms that might drive entrepreneurship within a business, commonly referred to as corporate entrepreneurship. Stevenson and Jarrillo-Mossi (1986) in an early paper on fostering entrepreneurship in established businesses, suggested that an organization must create an internal environment that supports: (1) the ability to detect opportunities, (2) the willingness to pursue those opportunities, and (3) the confidence or belief that such efforts might be successful and lead to positive outcomes. Further, the argument suggests that these factors are not independent but, instead, are reinforcing and subsequently more effective over time. For instance, an employee that is encouraged to look for opportunities and pursue them, even if they fail, will be more likely to see future opportunities and be more successful in subsequent tries.

A related and arguably more established construct that builds on these ideas is entrepreneurial orientation (EO). EO refers to the processes, practices, and decision-making styles of firms acting in an entrepreneurial way (Lumpkin & Dess, 1996). Generally, EO consists of five dimensions—autonomy, competitive aggressiveness, innovativeness, proactiveness, and risk taking—and firms vary in their approach to each dimension. Recent research suggests that managers intentionally emphasize different aspects of EO and the ensuing profiles of entrepreneurial activities have implications for outcomes (McKenny, Short, Ketchen, Payne, & Moss, 2018). Further, there is evidence that family involvement directly influences choices of EO emphasis. For instance, Short, Payne, Brigham, Lumpkin, and Broberg (2009) demonstrated that in large publicly-traded family businesses, companies exhibit lower levels of risk taking, proactiveness, and autonomy, relative to their non-family business counterparts. In particular, proactiveness is demonstrated at a substantially lower level in family businesses. All considered, it has come to the forefront in the literature that it is vital that managers create a culture and identity within a business that supports both the willingness and the ability to act entrepreneurially.

Multi-level and Boundary Considerations

Application to multiple levels of analysis (e.g., individuals, groups, organizations) and accounting for temporality (i.e., change over time) tends to complicate matters all the more. Indeed, social capital has been applied at various levels—from the individual to societies, including families—to explain numerous business and management phenomena (Payne et al., 2011). Specifically, Payne et al. (2011) discussed the social capital research through the development of a four-quadrant classification scheme. On one axis, they classified research as focused either on an individual or on a collective, which would include teams, organizations, communities, and families. On the other axis, the research was classified according to the prominent source of social capital, as either derived from internal (i.e., bonding mechanisms) or external (i.e., bridging mechanisms) sources.

For each quadrant, there are unique perspectives that link social relationships to entrepreneurial outcomes. In the Individual/Internal quadrant, the focus is on individuals who derive resources from social collectives (e.g., family or ethnic groups) to facilitate entrepreneurial activity. For example, Kalnins and Chung (2006) examine how immigrant entrepreneurs access resources from their ethnic community. In the Collective/Internal quadrant, internal relationships influence collective entrepreneurial outcomes. Research on family social capital resides primarily in this quadrant because the family—as a collective—can gain or create resources for the family and business, such as knowledge, solidarity, innovation, and trust (e.g., Carr, Cole, Ring, & Blettner, 2011). Within the broader entrepreneurship field, Individual/External quadrant is arguably the most developed because it largely recognizes how individuals utilize external connections to identify, pursue, and exploit opportunities (e.g., Davidsson & Honig, 2003). Finally, the Collective/External quadrant focuses on how external relationships are critical to the development and performance of entrepreneurial ventures. Specifically, research in this quadrant shows the importance of utilizing external relationships to overcome liabilities of newness, such as through gaining access to financial resources (e.g., Fischer & Pollock, 2004).

The key takeaway from this discussion of the four quadrants comes by recognizing that social capital applies to all levels of analysis. Individuals are nested within families, which are nested within businesses, which are nested within industries, and so on. So, while we visually demonstrated these levels in Fig. 24.1, it does not adequately relay the complex nesting of entities that exist in reality.

From a family business perspective, complexity is heightened even further when one considers non-family employees (individually and collectively) and multi-business families where a single family is intimately involved with several business operations. Such situations blur boundaries and complicate relationships. Figure 24.2 attempts to partially display this increased level of complexity by demonstrating two family business scenarios. The first represents a more classic view of family business, where several family members serve as the core team and are fully embedded in the organizations. In this situation, relationships extensively exist between each other, but also exist between family and non-family members both within and outside of the firm's boundaries. The second scenario demonstrates a more complex organization, where a family has ties to two separate businesses. In this case, some family members may not be connected directly, but a central family member (e.g., matriarch) may serve as the bridge between the two sides of the family and businesses. Consider the PP&T law firm, where the controlling partner helped found a separate real estate investment firm, headed by his brother, and a business consulting firm headed by his sister. The three entities are legally and operationally separated but are tied together through the core investments of the lawyer sibling, making for a much more complex family business situation.

In both the traditional and more complex scenarios presented in Fig. 24.2, we see the importance of the family because it—through its members—serves as central node for relationships and the flows of resources. Further, the family, as a social entity, can provide resources that may benefit the business through internal bonding mechanisms and through external bridging mechanism. For instance, consider the value to a buyer and supplier if both businesses were second generation family businesses whose leaders had grown up together in their respective roles. Strong personal relationships with key stakeholders such as with suppliers can produce trust, innovativeness, and even a reduction in the costs of doing business.

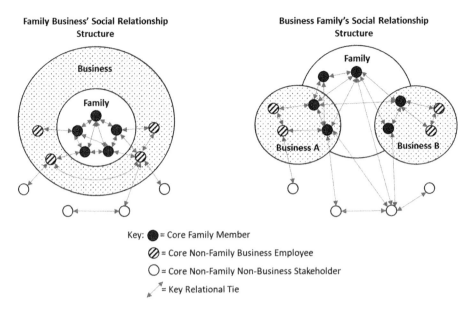

Family Business' Social Relationship
Structure

Business Family's Social Relationship
Structure

Key: ⬤ = Core Family Member
⊘ = Core Non-Family Business Employee
◯ = Core Non-Family Non-Business Stakeholder
↗ = Key Relational Tie

Fig. 24.2 Graphical representation of social relationships structures between family and business(es)

Social Capital Tactics for the Entrepreneurial Family Business

Due to socio-emotional (i.e., non-economic) preferences that often conflict with economic decisions, family businesses often appear to be "Janus-faced", where some preferences support entrepreneurial activities while others do not (Miller, Wright, Le Breton-Miller, & Scholes, 2015, p. 20). This is understandable in that the desires of the family—commonly associated with nepotism, altruism, risk aversion, and appropriation of firm assets—do not always align with the goals of the business, particularly in terms of entrepreneurial behaviors that often require extensive resource endowments. Hence, the challenges involved with promoting entrepreneurship in the family business are very real.

From a social capital perspective, the challenges for family businesses revolve around two broad, yet related questions that are derived from our previous discussion and Figs. 24.1 and 24.2. First, how can family business leaders best utilize social networks to accrue or gain access to key resources needed in the pursuit of opportunity? This involves not only gaining and maintaining relationships, but rather, making tough trade-off decisions about the costs and benefits of the relationships, both existing and potential. Second, how can social capital be transformed into entrepreneurial activities and outcomes? In other words, what mechanisms can facilitate opportunity detection, the willingness to pursue opportunity, and the confidence to move forward, even if failure is possible?

In general, these questions can be addressed by creating an environment that fosters entrepreneurship and embeds it in the culture and identity of the family and the firm. Such an identity and culture are achieved through tactics that build on either bonding or bridging mechanisms to produce an organization-wide entrepreneurial orientation. Bonding creates value in family businesses through "strong, repeated social connections that result in norms of reciprocity yielding trust" (Gedajlovic et al., 2013, p. 458). Bonding emphasizes the collective good that comes as a result of the relationships amongst actors within a network. Studies have shown that smaller (or younger) family businesses rely particularly heavily on bonding as they have not developed extensive external networks (Salvato & Melin, 2008). Bridging, on the other hand, emphasizes the benefits of building external connections outside of the collective's network. Bridging can lead to positive outcomes for a family firm by bringing in new resources from outside of the organization. While the ties generated through bridging are generally weaker than those established via bonding, they produce unique and valuable social capital—particularly information—due to the non-redundant nature of the relationships.

Bonding and bridging mechanisms support the implementation of tactics that may be applied to a family business to develop and maintain an entrepreneurially-driven culture and identity. Some examples of tactics are discussed below; these are separated into internal (i.e., bonding) and external (i.e., bridging) categorizations.

Internal Tactics

Bonding generally results in trust, reciprocity, goal congruence, and related outcomes. Activities that result in increased involvement by family members and/or employees are key. Family members should avoid creating separation, but should instead actively engage in processes both as a member of the family and as a member of the business organization. Attending meetings, engaging in after-hours gatherings, and other bonding activities, allow for relationships to be strengthened. Here are a few specific examples:

- Encouraging employees and family members to bring up new ideas and be creative. An open and constructive environment should allow for the flow and exchange of information and knowledge, which leads to better opportunity recognition. The key to this tactic is in removing the fear of failure that employees or family members may have in bringing up new ideas. Fostering an entrepreneurial environment means adopting an attitude of, "there are no bad ideas".

- Empowering employees to pursue opportunities. Family and non-family members should feel free, and even incentivized, to explore opportunities that go beyond their typical work duties. For instance, some companies offer annual "failure awards" to employees that have tried, but failed at, a new initiative. Employees that feel engaged, valued, and included will be more likely to put in extra effort towards entrepreneurial ideas and strategies.
- Structuring teams to involve both family and non-family members. Creating mechanisms through which communication is improved is key, but particularly when reaching beyond hierarchical levels and work roles in the organization. Also, changing these teams and appointing new tasks to different groups can facilitate new ideas and improve dialogue.
- Organizing social activities outside of the office. Functions such as company picnics, employee appreciation days, or holiday parties can help build cohesiveness and community among employees, both family and non-family.

External Tactics

Bridging social capital generally refers to building relationships between actors with different backgrounds, knowledge, and skills. Thus, family businesses seeking to increase bridging social capital need to enact tactics that facilitate interactions between employees, family members, and external actors.

- Hiring outsiders to key positions within the company to increase information accrual and specialized skills. An example of this type of external tactic comes from A. Duie Pyle, a family-owned transportation and warehousing firm based in West Chester, PA. In 2006, after over 80 years of family leadership, the company decided to hire an outsider to fill the role of CEO. This decision was made because the company wanted to increase entrepreneurial thinking and activity. In 2007, the company also added independent directors to its board in attempts to gain additional perspective and expertise to guide the company's high rate of growth.

- Support travel and engagement with outside entities. This tactic can take the form of encouraging employees to attend trade shows, conferences, or industry presentations. This tactic not only brings in immediate external knowledge and information, but can also foster long-lasting relationships with firms outside of a firm's central network.
- Family businesses can use family ties to increase external networks. A great example of this tactic can be seen in looking at the history of Microsoft. Back when Bill Gates was working out of his garage, his only real network tie was with his mother, Mary Gates, who was on the board of the United Way with a top manager at IBM. Bill encouraged his mother to speak to the IBM executive about the operating system he was developing. The social capital that Mary held with the executive meant that he was willing to listen to the details of her son's projects, which lead to a long and fruitful relationship for both companies.
- Increasing interaction with company stakeholders. Some firms will hold friendly competitions between their suppliers to try and come up with innovative solutions or products. This type of tactic fosters bridging ties and innovations while also building external network ties.

Conclusions

Gedajlovic et al. (2013) suggest that social capital theory should be considered a foundational theory of entrepreneurship. Likewise, social capital has been extensively discussed as central and fundamental component of family businesses (Sanchez-Ruiz et al., 2019). Generally, social capital seems to be essential in understanding how family businesses can develop and sustain entrepreneurship by providing conduits for information, knowledge, financial capital, and other resources. Indeed, it is hard to imagine any entrepreneurial endeavor that is not, in some way, influenced by social relationships. From nascent activities to corporate innovation, entrepreneurship is embedded in a complex array of social relationships which can increase or, perhaps, decrease the chances of success. Hence, both family business scholars and practitioners can benefit from a better understanding of the structures, processes, and outcomes of entrepreneurial networks and social capital.

References

Arregle, J.-L., Hitt, M. A., Sirmon, D. G., & Very, P. (2007). The Development of Organizational Social Capital: Attributes of Family Firms. *Journal of Management Studies, 44*(1), 73–95.

Brigham, K. H., Lumpkin, G. T., Payne, G. T., & Zachary, M. A. (2014). Researching Long-term Orientation: A Validation Study and Recommendations for Future Research. *Family Business Review, 27*(1), 72–88.

Carr, J. C., Cole, M. S., Ring, J. K., & Blettner, D. P. (2011). A Measure of Variations in Internal Social Capital Among Family Firms. *Entrepreneurship Theory and Practice, 35*(6), 1207–1227.

Chirico, F., Ireland, R. D., & Sirmon, D. G. (2011). Franchising and the Family: Creating Unique Sources of Advantage. *Entrepreneurship Theory and Practice, 35*(3), 483–501.

Davidsson, P., & Honig, B. (2003). The Role of Social and Human Capital Among Nascent Entrepreneurs. *Journal of Business Venturing, 18*(3), 301–331.

Dyer, G. (2019). *The Family Edge: How Your Biggest Competitive Advantage in Business Isn't What You've Been Taught—It's Your Family.* Familius LLC.

Fischer, H. M., & Pollock, T. G. (2004). Effects of Social Capital and Power on Surviving Transformational Change: The Case of Initial Public Offerings. *Academy of Management Journal, 47*(4), 463–481.

Gedajlovic, E., Honig, B., Moore, C. B., Payne, G. T., & Wright, M. (2013). Social Capital and Entrepreneurship: A Schema and Research Agenda. *Entrepreneurship Theory and Practice, 37*(3), 455–478.

Herrero, I. (2018). How Familial Is Family Social Capital? Analyzing Bonding Social Capital in Family and Non-family Firms. *Family Business Review, 31*, 441–459.

Ireland, R. D., Hitt, M. A., & Vaidyanath, D. (2002). Alliance Management as a Source of Competitive Advantage. *Journal of Management, 28*(3), 413–446.

Kalnins, A., & Chung, W. (2006). Social Capital, Geography, and Survival: Gujarati Immigrant Entrepreneurs in the U.S. Lodging Industry. *Management Science, 52*(2), 233–247.

Lumpkin, G. T., Brigham, K. H., & Moss, T. W. (2010). Long-term Orientation: Implications for the Entrepreneurial Orientation and Performance of Family Businesses. *Entrepreneurship & Regional Development, 3*(22), 241–264.

Lumpkin, G. T., & Dess, G. G. (1996). Clarifying the Entrepreneurial Orientation Construct and Linking It to Performance. *Academy of Management Review, 21*(1), 135–172.

McKenny, A. F., Short, J. C., Ketchen, D. J., Payne, G. T., & Moss, T. W. (2018). Strategic Entrepreneurial Orientation: Configurations, Performance, and the Effects of Industry and Time. *Strategic Entrepreneurship Journal, 12*(4), 504–521.

Miller, D., Wright, M., Le Breton-Miller, I., & Scholes, L. (2015). Resources and Innovation in Family Businesses: The Janus-Face of Socioemotional Preferences. *California Management Review, 58*(1), 20–40.

Moran, P. (2005). Structural vs. Relational Embeddedness: Social Capital and Managerial Performance. *Strategic Management Journal, 26*, 1129–1151.

Nahapiet, J., & Ghoshal, S. (1998). Social Capital, Intellectual Capital, and the Organizational Advantage. *Academy of Management Review, 23*(2), 242–266.

Nordqvist, M., & Merlin, L. (2010). Entrepreneurial Families and Family Firms. *Entrepreneurship and Regional Development, 22*(3–4), 211–239.

Payne, G. T., Moore, C. B., Griffis, S. E., & Autry, C. W. (2011). Multilevel Challenges and Opportunities in Social Capital Research. *Journal of Management, 37*(2), 491–520.

Salvato, C., & Melin, L. (2008). Creating Value Across Generations in Family-Controlled Businesses: The Role of Family Social Capital. *Family Business Review, 21*(3), 259–276.

Sanchez-Ruiz, P., Daspit, J. J., Holt, D. T., & Rutherford, M. W. (2019). Family Social Capital in the Family Firm: A Taxonomic Classification, Relationships with Outcomes, and Directions for Advancement. *Family Business Review, 32*(2), 131–153.

Shane, S., & Venkataraman, S. (2000). The Promise of Entrepreneurship as a Field of Research. *Academy of Management Review, 25*(1), 217–226.

Short, J. C., Payne, G. T., Brigham, K. H., Lumpkin, G. T., & Broberg, J. C. (2009). Family Firms and Entrepreneurial Orientation in Publicly Traded Firms: A Comparative Analysis of the S&P 500. *Family Business Review, 22*, 9–24.

Stevenson, H. H., & Jarillo, J. C. (1990). A Paradigm of Entrepreneurship: Entrepreneurial Management. *Strategic Management Journal, 11*(5), 17–27.

Stevenson, H. H., & Jarrillo-Mossi, J. C. (1986). Preserving Entrepreneurship as Companies Grow. *The Journal of Business Strategy, 7*(1), 10–23.

Zahra, S. A., & Covin, J. G. (1995). Contextual Influences on the Corporate Entrepreneurship-Performance Relationship: A Longitudinal Analysis. *Journal of Business Venturing, 2*(20), 43–58.

Printed by Printforce, the Netherlands